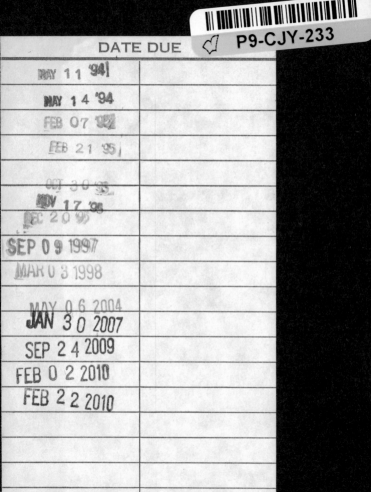

P9-CJY-233

UNSPEAKABLE ACTS

Also by Greggory W. Morris:

The Kids Next Door

UNSPEAKABLE ACTS

The Ordeal of Thomas Waters-Rimmer

Greggory W. Morris and
Thomas J. Waters

William Morrow and Company, Inc.
New York

It is the policy of William Morrow and Company, Inc., and its imprints and affiliates,
recognizing the importance of preserving what has been written, to print the books
we publish on acid-free paper, and we exert our best efforts to that end.

Waters, Thomas J.
    Unspeakable acts : the ordeal of Thomas Waters-Rimmer / by Thomas J. Waters
and Greggory W. Morris.
        p.   cm.
    ISBN 0-688-09483-X
    1. Waters-Rimmer, Thomas. 2. Sexually abused children—United States—
Biography. 3. Foster children—United States—Biography. 4. Child molesting—
United States—Case studies. 5. Foster parents—United States—Case studies.
I. Morris, Greggory W. II. Title.
HQ72.U53W38   1993
362.7'6—dc 20   92-47420
                                                                      CIP

Printed in the United States of America

First Edition

1 2 3 4 5 6 7 8 9 10

BOOK DESIGN BY LISA STOKES

For my mother, my sisters, and their children, and for Tracie and our family.

—THOMAS J. WATERS
August 1993

For kids "toiling under the burden of unspeakable acts and despairing of human understanding," that they do not suffer irrevocable harm.

—GREGGORY W. MORRIS and
THOMAS J. WATERS
August 1993

• Acknowledgments

Shortly before I wrote my first book, I was under the false impression that writers did all the work by themselves. Now, I am a lot wiser. Some writers may produce their works free of help, but I am not one of them. Numerous people made this book possible, and Thomas J. Waters and I would like to thank them. I hope we have not overlooked anyone's contributions.

Sharon Gurfield, who was a promising journalism student at Rutgers, the State University of New Jersey, when I first met her, transcribed tapes, offered invaluable editing suggestions, typed drafts, and was a spiritual adviser, as well. Dr. Sara Elbert, one of my dearest friends, edited all my drafts and offered considerable advice, help, and guidance. Elisa Spungen Bildner and Dr. Hendrika B. Cantwell also helped edit the final draft and provided invaluable information.

Michele Promaulayko, who also was a Rutgers student when I first met her, did much of the library research for me. I also want to thank Dr. Dania Stager-Snow, who read and reread later drafts; Harty Mokros, who read final drafts; and Marsha Bergman, the secretary of the Rutgers Department of Journalism, who gave me substantial logistical support.

Tom also wishes to thank his sisters, Arlene Tabar, Darlene LeMaire, and Patty Waters, for their willingness to be interviewed and for being accessible when we needed information. He also wants to thank his wife, Tracie, and her parents, Paul and Beverly Nadeau.

Others who helped this book come about were: Lynn Burch of Thomas J. Vecchio Co., L.P.A.; Nina Ferrari, Susan Meyers, Claudine Guillemain, Dr. Robert Trelstad, Carl Botan, Gary Skura, Michael Moore, Walter and Velma Morris, John Crist, Mary Ann Moore, Greg A. Moore, Joyce Schwab, Linda Marczi, Robert J. Vecchio, Sammie (a former social worker living in Florida), Thomas J. Waters, Sr., Robert and Pamela Haynes, Tammy Mayle, Dr. Robert Challener, Gordon Evans, and the fall 1992 Rutgers journalism investigative reporting class of Lynn Cosgrove, Jennifer Callegher, Kelly Waldron, Timothy Sullivan, Linda Hatch, Sean Carr, Dina Graygor, Joshua Balling, and Leo Reisberg. We also wish to thank Randy Landenheim-Gil, our senior editor at Morrow when we started this project, and her assistant, Steve Wilson; and Tom Darling, who was there when we finished.

Organizations and professionals who helped make this book possible were: Debra A. Ellis, when she was legal director, the Civil Liberties Union of New Jersey; Sharon Price-Gates, intern, the Civil Liberties Union of New Jersey; Rob Levy, New York Civil Liberties Union; Jane Kirtley, the Reporters Committee for Freedom of the Press, Washington, D.C.; Lorain County Public Library; Lorain County Clerk's Office, Elyria, Ohio; the National Writers Union; Investigative Reporters and Editors at the University of Missouri, Columbia; The New Jersey Press Association, C. Henry Kempe National Center; U.S. Department of Health and Human Services; the *Orlando Sentinel;* the Cuyahoga County Coroner's Office; National Committee for Prevention of Child Abuse, Chicago; Clearinghouse on Child Abuse and Neglect Information, Washington, D.C.; Child Sexual Abuse Resource Center, Huntsville, Alabama; American Bar Association's National Center on Children and the Law.

NOTE TO READERS

People are identified by their real names, except those names marked with an asterisk; some people are identified by their first name and some by their first name and the first initial of their last name. Almost all of the interviews conducted for this book were taped; notes were made of all interviews. The direct quotes are transcribed as people spoke them, except for a few cases. For example, some profanities were edited out of concern that they distracted from the content of the interview; some verbal mannerisms, such as "ah" or "uh-huh," were removed; I also made some minor grammatical corrections.

Some important characters are identified in their relationship to Thomas J. Waters:

Patricia "Patty" Waters, Arlene Tabar, and Darlene "Dee" LeMaire are Tom's older sisters. Arlene and Darlene, twins, are the oldest. Tom is the youngest.

Thomas J. Waters, Sr., Tom's natural father.

Patricia Waters, also known as Patricia O'Reilly, Tom's natural mother.

Linda Semen, Patricia O'Reilly's half sister.

Joyce Schwab, Tom's maternal grandmother.

Brent,* Tom senior's half brother.

Aunt Pearl* and Aunt Joan,* sisters who are Tom's aunts; Tom senior is their brother.

Pam Haynes and Tammy Mayle, Tom's cousins, whose mother is Aunt Joan.

Carl and Jeanne Rimmer, Tom's foster parents, who adopted him.

• Contents

Babies require the certainty that they will be protected in every situation, that their arrivals are desired, that their cries are heard, that the movements of their eyes are responded to and their fears calmed. Babies need assurance that their hunger and thirst will be satisfied, their bodies lovingly cared for and their distresses never ignored.

Is that asking too much?

—Alice Miller
Banished Knowledge

• Introduction

The original idea for this book was to tell a story about what happened to a four-year-old boy after a child protection agency placed him in an unsafe home. Research and interviews, however, revealed a much bigger story, reflecting on serious social issues in the United States, especially the ubiquitous presence of family violence, the pervasiveness of child abuse and neglect, and the "unparalleled state of crisis" of the country's foster care system.

During the period Thomas J. Waters and I worked on this book, approximately 120,000 people were murdered, and 15 percent of those who died were slain by their husbands, wives, fathers, mothers, sons, daughters, and other relatives. Because reported aggravated assaults can be almost fifty times the number of reported homicides, it should be safe to assume, extrapolating from the statistics of the FBI *Uniform Crime Reports* and other studies, that an additional 900,000 people of all ages were either shot, stabbed, bludgeoned, burned, maimed, tortured, or mutilated in multifarious ways by their fathers, mothers, sons, daughters, and other relatives. That figure also includes intended victims who eluded harm.

About 2,500 kids, from a few seconds old to early teens, died from severe violence or neglect in one year, according to a report by the U.S. Advisory Board on Child Abuse and Neglect, which declared child abuse a national emergency in 1990. Dr. Hendrika B. Cantwell, a clinical professor of pediatrics and a consultant on child abuse and neglect, estimated that more than half those deaths occurred because parents left their very young children alone or unsupervised. According to Dr. Cantwell, "This is a national epidemic. Societally, we have said nothing about the appropriate age for kids to be left alone." Other experts surmised that the number of fatalities cited by the U.S. advisory board wasn't higher because of the difficulties in determining a death as a homicide, sudden infant death syndrome, or accidental death. Such determinations often depend on the nature of the investigation. The actual homicides of kids may be as high as 5,000, according to a 1992 estimate by one news magazine.

Because of a lack of national reporting requirements and differences in research methods, there are no solid statistics on the number of children sexually abused each year. Nevertheless, some studies do provide statistics, even though there is a general consensus that the incidence of child sexual abuse may be significantly higher than the numbers cited in those studies. The American Humane Association has estimated that 132,000 children are sexually abused annually. The National Committee for Prevention of Child Abuse released findings in 1991 that child protection agencies compiled 404,100 child sexual abuse reports. That figure accounts for 15 percent of all agency reports about the abuse and neglect of children. The first national study on child sexual abuse found that 27 percent of the women and 16 percent of the men in the sample reported that as kids they were sexually victimized in some form. Two thirds or more of the estimated 3,200 to 4,600 kids abducted by nonfamily members were sexually assaulted, according to the first *National Incidence Study of Missing, Abducted, Runaway and Thrownaway Children*, published in 1990.

The nation's foster care system, which should serve as an alternative for kids denied a healthy home life, is an abysmal failure, according to Gordon Evans, information director of the National Foster Parent Association. Examples of that failure abound. The Minnesota Department of Human Services placed kids with sex offenders, wife beaters, and other violent felons, according to a December 1992 story by the *Star Tribune*. And in four years, according to that newspaper, the department has received more than 500 reports of foster parents abusing their foster children. In Texas, the state's child welfare system was accommodating only 51 percent of the kids whose lives were in peril in their homes, according to Evans. A January 1992 *New York Times* story reported that seven children who had been identified by New York City's child protection agency as victims of abuse or negligence died in 1990. Three of the kids were slain by their foster mothers.

At the start of the 1990s, a rapid reduction in licensed foster homes and an increasing number of children compounded the "unparalleled state of crisis" in foster care, according to a paper co-written by Jake Terpstra of the U.S. Children's Bureau and Emily Jean McFadden of the National Foster Care Resource Center. In 1988, a year after Tom and I started working on his book, there were 280,000 kids in foster care. That increased to 429,000 four years later. By 1994, according to Evans, "It will likely be 550,000 and during this decade 800,000." In October 1991 there were only 125,000 licensed foster families in the country. Services, such as staff and funds, have not kept up with the increasing demands on the system. It is not unusual for a caseworker in a child welfare agency to be assigned one hundred cases; many of the caseworkers need more professionalized training.

According to Terpstra and McFadden, factors causing the crisis include: unemployment, homelessness, and poverty, which destabilize families; a diminished concern for disadvantaged kids; deinstitutionalization, which reduced group care for kids, resulting in those with special needs being put in foster homes ill prepared to help them; alcohol abuse and an increase in drug use—crack-cocaine infants are the fastest-growing population of childen in foster care. An estimated 375,000 "drug exposed" infants are born annually, and 5,000 are born with fetal-alcohol syndrome.

With many homes virtual killing grounds, child abuse and neglect a "national emergency," and foster care in a major crisis, reasonable minds would ponder, what can be done? Ideally, a societal effort mobilized along the lines of a domestic Marshall Plan is needed to eliminate those factors that make domestic life hazardous for millions of kids and their families. A pragmatic first step could begin with a committed federal policy as recommended in both *The Foster Care Blueprint for the Nineties*, developed by the Child Welfare League of America and the National Foster Parent Association, and the 1991 report by the U.S. Advisory Board on Child Abuse and Neglect. Those recommendations, which overlap in some areas, range from improving the quality of deteriorating neighborhoods to developing effective programs for substance-abuse rehabilitation to improving the role of elementary and secondary schools in child protection.

Part I
●
Thomas Waters-Rimmer

1 • "It was, you know, usually oral sex."

*I*n 1987, nine days before Christmas, Thomas Waters-Rimmer, a first-year college student, filed a $5 million lawsuit in U.S. District Court in Cleveland against Lorain County, its commissioners, and its child welfare agency. He accused the three of negligence, holding them responsible for the harm he suffered after the child welfare agency, the Lorain County Children Services Board, removed him from the custody of his abusive father when he was four and placed him in a home where he was sexually abused for twelve years. The focus of the complaint was Children Services but legal protocol required that the county and its commissioners also be named as defendants.

The suit—with its all too familiar allegation of a child protection agency failing to protect a child—sparked major news coverage. A CBS-TV affiliate in Vermont, where Tom lived, first reported the story. The broadcast was carried by a sister station in Cleveland, where the city's major newspaper, the *Plain Dealer,* printed follow-up stories. And the *Chronicle-Telegram* in Elyria where the administrative office of Children Services was located, about thirty miles southwest of Cleveland, also published stories. Tom and one of his lawyers also were featured on a talk show of Cleveland radio station WWWE.

I learned about the lawsuit four months later in April 1988 when a literary agent phoned me in New York City, where I lived, provided some details about the lawsuit, and asked if I would be interested in working with Tom on a book. He called me because of a book I had written about kids who murdered their parents. Several chapters were based on interviews with sons and daughters who, because of the psychological, physical, and sexual violence they had suffered in their homes, killed their mothers and fathers. I believed the slayings were the only means for many of the kids to protect themselves and that the sentences for those imprisoned were exceedingly harsh in light of the sadistic treatment they suffered in their homes.

Those opinions had prompted the agent to contact me. If I could sympathize with murderous kids, he reasoned, then I should certainly be able to sympathize with his client, who had not killed anyone even though he had been cruelly mistreated by his natural father and then savagely abused by his foster father. Tom was seeing a psychologist regularly and attending college full time in Vermont, the agent said. He had not succumbed to the harmful effects of a brutal childhood like the kids I had interviewed. He was leading a normal life. He wanted justice, not revenge. That was his reason for filing the suit. He hoped it would make a difference in the lives of other kids.

Tom, the agent intimated, was on a crusade.

I told the agent I was too busy to take on another project. I was teaching full time in the journalism department at Rutgers, the State University of New Jersey, working part time at the *New York Post* and developing a proposal for a book about kids on death row. But besides having no spare time, I also was skeptical about working with Tom. I had learned from my earlier research that it was very difficult for kids to talk about what they had suffered in their homes even though many of the ones I had interviewed had told me more than they had told their lawyers and their pscyhologists. But I was still unable to persuade them to tell me as much as I wanted to know. I couldn't imagine someone as young as Tom, who had suffered as much as he had, engaging in the kind of indepth interviewing required for a book—a chapter maybe, but not a book.

I thanked the agent for considering me, but told him he should ask someone else. But because he had already been turned down by two other writers, the agent persisted. After several minutes of having him ignore my protests that I already was too busy, I told him to send me more information to help me make a decision.

I'll read the information and then write you a polite rejection, I thought as I hung up my phone.

A few days after the conversation, I received a press package from the agent. I reviewed it a few days later during a lull in my work schedule. The package included a copy of the complaint filed in federal court and copies of the various news stories. Together, they provided a harrowing but not unfamiliar account of what happens every year to millions of kids in and out of foster care. In his interviews, Tom gave candid responses to tough questions. In a voice tinged with pain and outrage, he indicated he would no longer be silenced by guilt and pain. When a reporter from WCAX-TV, Channel 3, in Burlington, inquired in an interview about the extent of the abuse, Tom replied unhesitantly, "Once a week, at least, sometimes more, for twelve years. It was, you know, usually oral sex."

Tom also was asked in other interviews why he had never told anyone what was happening to him, and he replied that he had kept silent out of fear. In the WCAX interview, however, he also said he felt ashamed and "degraded." He compared his silence to that of women who are raped but don't report the crimes. Their reasons for being silent have been well documented: They are held responsible for what happened to them or their complaints are discouraged if not ignored. Tom also said he worried that a disclosure would bring the authorities down on his parents.

His candor about protecting his parents impressed me because I knew lay people are confounded by what experts understand all too well: Kids emotionally, physically, and sexually abused are raised to accommodate their parents' emotional needs and are inexplicably bound to them. Some psychologists use the expression "symbiotic relationship" to describe that destructive bond between abusive parents and their kids. Other specialists refer to it as the "poison pedagogy" because that destructive relationship is passed from one generation to the next. I was impressed again when Tom, who was only eighteen, tried to describe that baffling dynamic of dysfunctional families to a WWWE Cleveland radio talk show host. The radio host was obviously sympathetic to Tom, but expressed disbelief that Tom would neither sue nor file criminal charges against the man who had treated him cruelly for many years. Despite a myriad of news stories about abused kids and the conspiracy of silence that engulfs them, most people, as well as journalists, still find the concept hard to understand. They have a greater appreciation for the intricacies of nuclear power. Tom's attempt to explain that recondite principle started me considering working with him. None of the kids I had interviewed for my first book, or for the proposal I was trying to develop, possessed his insight. Almost all—some growing up on death row, some serving long sentences for killing parents—were not candid about the abuse they had experienced in their young lives. Most blamed themselves for the violence in their homes; they believed, irrationally, that they somehow were responsible for their mistreatment. And it was not unusual for them to idealize their parents. When I inquired if he had been mistreated by his family, one death row inmate who had been repeatedly sodomized by his cousin and another relative before he even

started grade school told me that he had never been mistreated by anyone in his family. That kind of violence, he
insisted, occurred only in black families.

In contrast, Tom seemed so much wiser and more mature
than any of the other kids I had interviewed. He knew who
was at fault. He had survived an extraordinarily brutal childhood and seemed remarkably resilient. It was possible, I
thought, that by working with him I could develop a better
insight into the dynamics of violence committed against children. And I also thought that learning how he had come to
grips with an extraordinarily violent childhood would provide me with valuable lessons for my project about kids on
death row. I also expected that working on a book with Tom
would be easier than any of my other projects. The agent
would do all the legwork finding a publisher. And I had received assurances from one of Tom's lawyers that I would be
provided with all the information I wanted. And because of
Tom's willingness to talk, I would not have to do the kind of
in-depth background research that I was doing for the project
about kids on death row, which was requiring far more interviews than my first book.

Because I was having difficulty developing the project, I
decided no harm could be done if I also worked with Tom.
I had scoffed at the agent's idea that Tom's project could be
done in a year, but I thought the research and the writing
could be completed within two years.

So I phoned Tom in late April and was surprised by his
manner. Despite his articulate responses in his radio and TV
interviews, he spoke hesitantly and with a mild stutter that
suggested not a speech impediment but someone grieving
and in agony. Several times he spoke so quietly, I had to ask
him to repeat himself as we discussed plans to meet. For the
past year, he had been living with his girlfriend and her family
in Underhill, about thirty minutes east of Burlington. I was
to stay with them for a weekend. Our conversation was brief

and strained, and I wondered how he would cope in lengthy interviews and deal with all the questions I wanted to ask.

When we met at the airport in Burlington a few days later, he was as subdued in person as he had been on the phone. He didn't stutter, but he spoke as if he was measuring every syllable. He was handsome, much better looking than he had appeared in his broadcast. Wearing a light-colored sweater, khaki pants, and penny loafers, he looked like a prep school student. But he moved tensely, as if every muscle was under tight control. He showed little expression, and I wondered if I could ever break through his reserve. He had driven to the airport alone to meet me, so I feigned hunger and suggested that we stop somewhere to eat before we drove to Underhill. I wanted some time to assess the situation. He suggested a fast-food restuarant and there we ordered fried chicken and made small talk. Early in the conversation, he said he was shy and did not open up easily to strangers. I thought about the news coverage showing him speaking unhesitantly and with conviction. But by the time we finished eating he had relaxed more, his voice was firmer, and when we left the restaurant he was moving in a confident manner. We drove in silence to Underhill where he lived with his girlfriend, Tracie Nadeau, and her parents, Paul and Beverly, in a luxurious home built by Paul and his brothers at the top of a winding hill. One brother lived on an adjacent property. Paul was a recently retired real estate developer and prominent businessman. Beverly was a homemaker. They were in their early forties and had two older daughters. Tracie, twenty, lived at home while she attended beauty school. Tom called Paul "Dad" and Beverly "Mom." The Nadeaus told me to make myself at home, and they weren't just being polite: There was food in the refrigerator, the microwave was easy to use, and if I didn't like leftovers I could cook. Tom and I eventually went to his room where, except for taking an occasional break or stopping to eat, we spent most of the weekend talking.

Tom was finishing his sophomore year at Johnson State College, a small liberal arts school about forty-five minutes from Underhill. He was on a full scholarship, and worked at a variety of jobs during the regular semesters and summers to pay living expenses. One semester he was the rental agent for several buildings and at the same time held a part-time job. He was planning on a business career, and he and Tracie had talked about marrying after he graduated. He was so serious during the early part of our discussion that I wondered if he ever took time to relax or play. After a while, I told him I had a lot of questions and only a little information, which included news accounts of his lawsuit. Those, I said, were sketchy and probably contained errors, and I said I didn't know much about him or what he expected to accomplish though the agent had told me he wanted to focus on the lawsuit. Tom replied that he wasn't sure what he wanted to accomplish other than to do something that would keep other kids from suffering as he had. But he added that he wasn't so naive as to believe that a book or his lawsuit, even if successful, could change the way Children Services or any foster care agency treated children. But if the suit and an account of what happened to him could make life better for even one child, he would consider that an accomplishment.

I was pleased to hear him express that sentiment. Kids who had been abused and, yet, felt compassion and empathy for others were the ones who, I believed, might overcome their cruel experiences. They were the ones who might heal themselves and be free of the savage effects of family violence. Tom also said he knew that the agent was promoting him as a "hero." He was uncomfortable with that portrayal and didn't want to be described as a hero. He didn't believe he had done anything heroic. What he wanted to do, he said, as he looked me straight in the eye, was to tell the truth. I realized there was more to his words than I could comprehend at the time.

Because we had known each other only a few hours and weren't sure how we should proceed, I suggested that he talk about his life, and told him to begin with the earliest years he could recall and work his way up to the present. At that moment, though we both had the same goal in mind, I was not certain how we would proceed. At the very least we would tell a story about a kid overcoming the vagaries of a cruel fate that allowed him to be born in one abusive home and placed in another. One of his lawyers was quoted in a newspaper account as saying that Tom's lawsuit was a landmark case. But it was much too early that spring to know how his suit would fare in court, or if it would spark benefits for other foster children, let alone do anything directly for Tom himself. However, I believed we had all the elements for us to tell a story with a happy ending.

2 • "He used to burn her with cigarettes."

*T*om's natural mother had died when the family lived in Cleveland, and he was a toddler eighteen months old. But, he told me as we sat in his room in the Nadeaus' home, he could recall one intimate moment spent with her when she was trying to teach him to whistle shortly before her death.

"She was whistling and I wondered what she was doing and I was trying to mimic her. She was sitting on a couch. I was straddling her, facing her, leaning on her chest. I remember I was holding on to her shoulders and I was touching her face, I don't know why, just to feel what she was doing."

He also said, as if anticipating my skepticism, that "some people" had challenged his recollection of that moment. They said he was too young to remember her or many other events from his early childhood. But he insisted in our interview that he had an excellent memory for details and that his three sisters often recalled the same events he did. People who dispute his accounts—even though he could corroborate the information—perturbed him. I didn't doubt his recollection of his mother, though I thought it was possible that someone, such as a sister or other relative, had told him about it. But I also took his comments to mean that his recollections were to be taken seriously if we were to work together. He had made two references to "people" without identifying who they were, and I wondered why he was being vague, but I assumed I would discover that information later.

"Some stories say that she died of an accidental quinine poisoning. She was trying to abort a baby, and she drank quinine, and it gave her a heart attack. And then, just recently, my maternal grandmother told me that my father killed her, you know, told me that he beat her to death. My grandmother told me that he tied my mother to the bed one time and— she had been holding me and I was laying off to the side— and he was whipping her with a belt. I guess he was hitting me, too. My grandmother tells me he used to burn her with cigarettes.

"And I really . . . " he said, pausing slightly. "She died. She's dead. She's in heaven or wherever she's at and that's that. How she died, I guess I'd like to know, really, but it's not of major importance in my life right now."

I suspected that her death was more important to him than he was willing to admit to me, and I thought that I could help him clear up the confusion. I would get a copy of her death certificate or a copy of an autopsy and let the facts speak for themselves. But I doubted that his natural father had beaten his mother to death. Of all the major crimes committed today, homicide is the most difficult to conceal, especially domestic homicides. There are cases of murders going undiscovered for long periods of time, and of coroners, medical examiners, and the police overlooking facts or making mistakes but those are unusual occurrences, even in a country that has more than twenty thousand homicides reported annually. The death of Tom's mother, I believed as he was talking, probably wasn't one of those cases.

Sometime after his mother died, Tom said, his father had packed him and his three sisters into a pickup truck, and they trekked back and forth through Ohio, West Virginia, Florida, and Texas. The truck had been their home, and the kids—

Tom, Arlene and Darlene (twins, who were the oldest), and Patty—slept on a mattress in the back. Tom could not recall the cities or towns they had visited because he'd been too young, but, he said, when they visited Texas they stayed with their father's brother. Tom recalled fondly how he and his sisters had used chicken for bait and fished for crabs in the ocean. He was uncertain about the years and the locations. He or his sisters would occasionally discover a cache of wedding bands his father kept. Women flitted in and out of their lives as easily as he and his family passed through the various towns and cities they encountered on their sojourns. Tom, however, recalled one woman, Rose, because she had been nice to him and his sisters, and another, a baby-sitter, because she had beat them, until one day Tom senior saw the bruises on his kids and beat the baby-sitter. Tom senior believed that he was the only one allowed to beat his kids. As Tom recalled how his natural father had treated him and his sisters, his voice swelled, not so much with anger as with incredulity.

"When he drank he'd get very violent, very violent. He'd start beating us for nothing. He came home from work one day and lined us up like bowling pins and put his fists out and charged at us and just started knocking us around the room."

Thomas Waters, Sr., had kicked and punched them. He had also beat them with brooms and sticks and anything within reach. His rampages, fueled by liquor, had been as regular as the sunrise. At this point in his narrative, Tom paused to point to the scars on his forehead as proof of the ferocity of the assaults. Tom senior, he said, had also made them stay up all night massaging him.

"All four of us would be massaging him, and one would be on one leg, chopping his legs. The other one would be on the other leg, and the two would be up on his torso. And he would fall asleep in front of the TV. The whole room was totally dark except for the TV being on. And if we stopped, he'd kick us. One time I wanted to go to sleep. I was so tired. And I remember laying back and getting this heel in my mouth 'cause I had fallen asleep."

But Tom senior became remorseful as soon as he went on the wagon, and for the kids that meant temporary respites, like cease-fires in a war.

"I remember one time he got all four of us in his room, and he took the belt that he used to beat us with and cut it into little pieces and let each of us burn a piece of that by a candle."

But violence was a way of life for him and his sisters, and Tom senior wasn't the only menace. Tom recalled visits to the home of Aunt Joan,* his father's sister, who was "an incredible alcoholic."

"She hated my sisters, hated 'em, hated girls. Every time they came in, she made them get undressed and she'd strip-search them. And then before we left, she'd strip-search 'em again to make sure that they didn't steal anything. She tied all three of 'em up one time and let me shoot at them with things. She hated them, loved me. She treated me like I was a king. She and her husband would get into incredible fights. He was this big guy, and I remember one time he knocked her teeth out. I remember the police coming. Amongst the family it's a big joke now, 'cause after he beat her up, I was saying stuff like, 'If that goddamned motherfucker comes back here I'm gonna . . . ' I said I was going to pick up a chair and beat him with it. I mean, this was language coming out of a three-year-old's mouth and, you know, I didn't know what I was saying, but I knew it was effective, I guess, to get my point across.

"She and my dad used to fight too like cats and dogs. I remember him getting drunk one time and she grabbed him by the head, by his hair, and dragged him along the floor. He had passed out or something. Another time he passed out with his hands at the edge of the toilet, and Joan came in and pissed on his hands. And I remember one time my father tried to commit suicide or something, and my uncle flipped him into this bathtub and knocked him out so he couldn't commit suicide."

Tom senior's mother also beat Tom and his sisters with a big hairbrush or made them fetch her a switch, which she wielded unmercifully. And the result of all the violence was predictable. As a little boy, Tom's alias could have been Tommy the Terror. He yanked his sisters by the hair and bit them. He butted them in the stomach. He flung lighted matches at them or shot rockets at them anytime he came across his father's arsenal of fireworks. His sisters were equally violent, he said, though he quickly added an explanation.

"We still loved each other. Even at that age we were really close, we were really stuck together. I mean, if one of us was getting hurt or something, the rest of us would be just hysterical, crying. And it wasn't because we were afraid that we were going to get hurt. We were seeing our sibling getting hurt. And that's evident today, because all four of us are really, really close."

By this point in the conversation, I was mesmerized. I was asking only those questions that helped me to identify individuals and locations and dates. I tried not to disrupt his narrative even though he was talking as if nothing could distract him.

Violence was one peril when he lived with his father; neglect was another. Tom senior left them alone for days and the kids fended for themselves. Tom's sister Darlene, "Dee," became their surrogate mother after their mother's death. She was four years old. Tom recalled how she would prop a chair up against a stove so that she could cook for the family. One day she was trying to prepare a frozen pizza but couldn't read the instructions and the frustration made her cry. On days when there was no food in the house, and Tom senior wasn't home, they went to local stores and stole gum, candy, and food small enough to conceal. They had a simple system. The girls stood in front of the counter and talked to the cashier or bought something with a few pennies they had scrounged. Tom—because he was so small—stood behind them and placed things in the small of their back or down the rear of their pants.

About the time Tom was four, he and his family settled in Oberlin, Ohio, after one of their cross-country excursions, and Tom senior was hired as a custodian at Allen Memorial Hospital. One day Tom senior met Cathy Ives, who worked in the cafeteria. They married two weeks later. Cathy, Tom recalled, was kind to him and his sisters but her affection wasn't strong enough to inspire her to protect them. When Tom senior abused the kids, Cathy fled.

"If only one of us was getting a beating, we would run upstairs in the apartment and climb out on this porch, and we would beg her to come back to us. We thought, maybe, we wouldn't get beat as bad if she came back."

Cathy returned only after Tom senior's rage abated. At a dinner celebration at the home of Cathy's mother in November 1973, Tom and Patty met Cathy's sister, Jeanne, and her husband, Carl Rimmer. Jeanne worked as an X-ray technician, and Carl was an air traffic controller for the Federal Aviation Administration in Oberlin. Weeks later in Elyria, during a Christmas party at the Rimmer home, Tom's life took an ironic turn. When Arlene and Darlene were alone with Jeanne in the bathroom, they told her Tom senior was sexually abusing them and that he had started attacking them almost immediately after their mother died.

"I didn't know that he was doing that to them. I knew he was physically abusing all of us. But one time he sent all three of us upstairs, except Darlene. I was playing or something, and I was upstairs and she called me. She said, 'Tommy.' And it was a muffled sound. I was in my room, and I went downstairs, and my father was on top of Darlene on the couch.

And I saw him do it. I must have looked at him for a minute. I mean, if you've ever seen a child's eyes when she's being abused . . . He beat me but I saw him do it."

Carl notified the Oberlin police, who could not arrest Tom senior in Elyria because it was outside their jurisdiction. So, Carl drove an inebriated Tom senior to his home in Oberlin where the police were waiting for him. The kids stayed with Cathy Ives only for a short while and then were placed in the custody of the Lorain County Children Services. Tom wasn't sure why they did not remain with their stepmother but he recalled what happened.

"I remember all four of us going into Children's Services, the people telling us that we're going to go for a ride—Patty and I and Arlene and Darlene—were going to go for a ride. Never told us we were being put in a home. Never told us that Dee and Arlene were being put in a different home. Just drove us out to these people's house. Dropped us off and that was that. We were like, What is going on? Are we staying here overnight or are we staying here forever?"

He and Patty were placed temporarily with an elderly couple who already were caring for other foster kids. He remembered them only by their last name.

"The Greenlesses were really, really gentle people. I feel ashamed because I don't really have much to say about 'em, I guess, because I wasn't traumatized enough to remember anything. They were an older couple, really nice to us. They had a few other kids living with them, foster children. I remember they bought me a Big Wheels. They used to let me ride it around the block. Six months after we went to the Greenlesses, the Rimmers showed up in a blue Nova, a junky blue Nova."

It was a hot summer day and Tom and Patty and the other foster kids living with the Greenlesses were playing in the driveway of the couple's home in Lorain, about six miles north of Oberlin. Some were lying on towels, and others were being doused with water from a lawn sprinkler when Mrs. Greenless brought Tom and Patty inside, helped them dress and kissed them good-bye.

"The Rimmers wanted us because they couldn't have their own children. And because they were family, as Children Services put it, or as close to family or kin as you can get, we were placed with them," Tom explained. For the first few weeks in their new home, he continued, the Rimmers "were really nice. It was the honeymoon stage." The honeymoon ended with Carl screaming and yelling.

"He was hitting Patty for something, and we were sitting at the dinner table and she was crying. I grabbed my butter knife and I was crying and I went at him. He turned and saw me coming and stopped what he was doing. He said, 'You don't like me hitting your sister like that, do you?' And I said, 'No.' I just wanted to stop him. And I just remember crying because I felt so helpless that I couldn't do anything."

When I asked him to describe the first time Carl molested him, Tom tensed and looked away. He remained silent. It was the first question to stymie him, and he was visibly uncomfortable for the first time in the interview. I hadn't anticipated that response. I merely wanted to know about his home life in the early years with the Rimmers. I imagined that after the peace and tranquility at the Greenlesses', it was horrifying, but I wanted to hear about it in his own words. But he couldn't speak. Because I believed that later I could convince him to talk about the early years, I suggested that he start with some other period that he would feel more comfortable discussing. I hadn't expected him to skip the first eight years.

By the time he was in the sixth grade, when the family was living in Grafton, Ohio, about eight miles east of Oberlin, sexual domination had become part of the fabric of family life. Tom was required to submit to Carl on demand. And Tom resisted the only way he could. He fantasized.

"I would be with my friends playing, doing whatever I wanted to do at that time, in my mind. And it would end, I'd get up and I wouldn't even recall what just happened. Literally, like I had not even been there in the first place. I don't remember every instance because it could have happened three or four times a week in some weeks. Sometimes it didn't happen for two weeks, and then it would happen three or four times a day. Like, every Saturday was a given, it was on the agenda: Wake up, Mom leaves, do Dad. And that's what I had to look forward to on Saturday, my dad forcing me to do oral sex. See, on Saturdays, I liked to go down the street and play with my friends. And the only way I could get down there, the only way, was if I did with him what he wanted. So, that's what I would do and totally block it out of my mind. There were times, like when I was in eighth grade—incidents—where I didn't want that incident and maybe three or four times I said, 'I don't want to today.' You know, just where I got so courageous and thought I was a badass or something and said no. It was more because I was so angry at him for doing something that I said no, 'cause I sort of had him in a very nice position, and I knew it too: You either be nice to me or you don't get a blowjob or whatever. And so he would be real nice to me, and then he would say, come on, you know, do it. And, I would, I would do it, but if I said no, whew, you wouldn't believe the tantrum. I mean where I was called everything in the book. I went through hell all day long. He was screaming and yelling at me and getting beat—not beat—he never really beat me like my real father did, but he'd hit me."

There had been occasions when Carl beat him so bad he urinated in his pants. I noticed that Tom, like Eskimos who have one hundred words for snow, had several ways of comparing the violence he experienced with his two fathers.

"So, like I said," Tom continued, "it was like every Saturday it was on the agenda: Wake up, Mom leaves, do Dad, go to Stacy and Beaux's, have fun, come home, eat dinner, and go to bed. I always had to be home, like, by five o'clock. Sometimes, on rare occasions, they'd let me go back out after dinner. Sometimes. That's only if I asked my mom first. Or if I had done a really good job that day with my dad, I could ask him first, and say: 'Can I go down to Stacy and Beaux's again?' "

His friends' parents owned property in a wooded area near Tom's home and the kids canoed in a stream there or rode trail bikes or roamed the area as if it were a magic kingdom.

"And he'd be like, Tom, why do you want to go down there again? You don't like it here? You don't like staying here? Why do you always want to get out of the house? It was about loyalty, I guess. He did not understand why I didn't want to be around the house with them all of the time and why I wanted to get out."

Tom had to pose his requests carefully if he wanted to go outside. It wasn't that he preferred his friends over his parents, he would say, but he merely wanted some extra time to play in the warm weather. When he persuaded them to let him go, he fled the house like an animal uncaged.

"The minute I got out of the house I would take off running. I would quiver when I'd get out of there. I'd get shivers. I would fly down the driveway, running all the way down the street, down this hill, running behind people's yards, through this field. And I'd get those shivers, like something was chasing me, and I'd just book it as fast as I could to Stacy and Beaux's."

Except for the two brothers, he didn't have many friends.

"In seventh and eighth grade, I felt like such a stranger. I felt like an outcast. No one ever asked me to do anything with them because if they had asked me, I'd always have to say no because of my father. Only I wouldn't say, 'No, I can't because of my father.' I would always defend my father. I would always just say, 'No, I can't.' Or I wouldn't even give them an answer. If they'd say, 'Hey, Tom, want to come to the dance?' I'd be like, well, let me see, I'll tell you later. But I would never get back to 'em, never tell 'em. Or if I did, I would say, 'No thanks.' And I'd never say, 'I can't because my father won't let me.' I never said that because I felt that they would look at me as if, well, what the hell, don't you have a good father? What's wrong with you?

"I worried about how people would look at me, and what they thought of me. So, people just generally pulled away from me. I guess they were tired of me saying no. Or I was never around, I was never in the action. I didn't grow up with those kids. A lot of them had grown up together. They had gone to kindergarten together all the way up through seventh, eighth grade. And, you know, I just never really got into a group—because of Carl. That's one of the reasons I hate my father, because he robbed me of my childhood."

Tom was weaned on terror. If he made a simple mistake, Carl fulminated, storming about the house, destroying furniture, threatening, cursing.

"The only way I can show you how he acted is to stand up and do it. And I wouldn't do that. It would scare you. I'm serious. To understand what I faced, you would have to have seen someone at some point in your life so enraged that he was just going to destroy anything in his way."

And if Carl accused him of doing something wrong, Tom bore the burden, even if his father had erred. I asked him if he ever had any good times with Carl, and he paused, his face pained, incredulous. My question probably sounded absurd in the face of everything he had revealed to me, but I had to ask. I had no doubt that Carl could act imperiously or even sadistically. But Tom had said that even Tom senior in rare moments would express remorse or at least indicate that there was a side to him that was human.

What about Carl? What about his human side?

"Right, yeah, he's human. I want to say that Christmases were a good time, but they weren't. I mean they would buy us presents and stuff like that and things would be fine. Everyone would be opening up their presents and all of a sudden, bam"—Tom punched his palm—"he would just go apeshit about something, like the camera wouldn't work right or something would happen and he'd flip out on Christmas Day even. Christmas, he'd freak out. We went on a hayride together. That was fun but I was always scared. I never knew how good of a time I could have with them."

Sometimes they played catch with a football or a baseball. Neighbors believed Carl was a strict but decent father. However, Jeanne and Carl did not have many friends, and they rarely allowed visitors into their home. Carl did not want people to get too close to him or his family. Abusive parents prefer to isolate their families from the surrounding community.

"He put up such a good front for everyone. People pictured him as being very upright, clean-cut. He was the all-American guy. He presented himself well, very literate, intelligent. Nice house. Drove two cars, one a Corvette; had a motorcycle. He was really, really smart in electronics. He could fix his radios, TVs, all this kind of stuff."

Carl was an air traffic controller for several years, and worked at the Federal Aviation Administration's big facility in Oberlin until the pressures of the job, Tom said, frayed his nerves and he had to quit. He collected benefits and attended Baldwin-Wallace College in Berea, Ohio, where he studied accounting. He worked for the Sohio oil company in Cleveland, left and was working as an accountant for another company when he was laid off during cutbacks. Carl returned to school to study to become a technician. He was eventually hired by IBM.

During the interview, Tom showed me a family picture of him, Patty, Carl, and Jeanne having a picnic in their backyard when the family lived in Grafton. It was the kind of picture that one could find in almost any family album. Tom and Patty and Jeanne were smiling; Carl, husky, was holding a glass and glaring at the camera. At the time the picture was shot, Tom said, Carl weighed about two hundred pounds.

After he and Patty had been placed with the Rimmers, they saw Tom senior one more time. It was in court, when Tom senior finally signed the papers surrendering custody of his kids.

"He was wearing a tan corduroy suit with cowboy boots. My father was sitting on a couch across from us. And I was sitting across from Patty. He didn't really say anything. He just kind of asked us a couple of questions. I didn't really see him as my father because he looked different. He just didn't look the same. I guess I had kind of forgotten about him, forgotten his face."

Tom rarely saw Arlene and Darlene, and he expressed anger during the interview that he and his sisters had ended up in foster care because none of the relatives of his natural parents had wanted them. I thought that we should try to learn why.

Sports had become a big part of Tom's life when he was in the seventh grade at Keystone Middle School in Grafton, a small town outside of Elyria. He started on the football and basketball teams and was also on the track team. In basketball, he wasn't much of a shooter—his highest career score was four points. But he could dribble and pass, and on defense he was tough. He was quick and nimble enough to harass taller players as they dribbled. He also was strong enough to jolt them into making mistakes. As Tom modestly described his athletic accomplishments, I understood why he had skipped over the first eight years of his life with the Rimmers. His junior high school years marked the beginning of his renaissance. His athletic prowess nurtured and soothed his battered self-esteem, savaged for years by Carl, and also made him popular, a standout among his peers even if he was not allowed to hang out with them. Tom's successes and popularity made Carl feel proud. He frequently videotaped his son's games. But the popularity also caused problems.

"If I got a phone call from a girl, the shit would hit the fan, bad. He would go crazy on me, I mean, screaming and yelling at me, and make me go to my room. Hit me. I mean, for a girl calling, he hit me."

One night, when he lived in Grafton and was a freshman at Elyria Catholic High School, he was dancing with a girl. It was shortly before eleven o'clock and the last song was being played. Because of the din in the gymnasium they had to yell in each other's ear to be heard. When the song ended and the lights came on, Tom heard a voice that made him cringe.

"My father—get this, the most embarrassing moment in my life—was up in the bleachers. He's screaming, 'Thomas Waters-Rimmer get your goddamn ass over here'—screaming at me, screaming his lungs out. And I was like, Oh, my God. I walked over there. He grabs me from behind the neck, hits me two times in front of everyone, throws me into the car. And when I went to say something, he turned around—smash—right in the face. And all these people are walking up, looking in the car. My dad's honking his horn, screaming at people to move. I was just so embarrassed. I mean, that was so dreadful to me, and in front of the entire school."

I asked him how Jeanne responded to the incident. She gave him an absurd explanation. She told him Carl was jealous because he had attended an all-boys academy from kindergarten to high school, and he'd never had the opportunity to date girls. Jeanne expected Tom to sympathize with Carl. Tom, who believed Jeanne was aware of what Carl was doing to him, knew it was a lame excuse but he could not challenge her any more than he could challenge Carl. His parents demanded not only obedience and respect but subservience.

And it still angered him when we were talking that he had acted submissively even though it was obvious that he'd had no choice. But Carl's violence did not stop Tom from having girlfriends.

"The first time I ever had sex with a girl I was in sixth grade. She was a friend of my sister's that I had met at my cousin's house. It was like she didn't have any interest in me whatsoever. Actually, she was pretty mean to me. She was older, probably sixteen. It was the summer between my sixth and seventh grade. She didn't act like she liked me as a boyfriend. I didn't act like I liked her either. And that turned her on, I guess. And then things just happened. I don't remember how they really happened. So, from there, I just went crazy, I went hog-wild. I had sex with a lot of girls. I don't even know their names—which is not, I mean, in my opinion, now that I am older, is not really anything at all to brag about. I was like, I guess, trying to prove something. Trying to prove, not to somebody else, but to myself that I wasn't gay or a fag. It was especially hard, like in the bathroom, you know how guys talk: Ah, that guy's a fag—look at him. And they make fun of 'em, homosexuals, they make fun of 'em. Kids are cruel, and most people, most people don't like homosexuals. And that gave me a real complex because I felt, like, Yeah, they're looking at me, and they know that I'm a fag 'cause I do this stuff with my father.

"Now, am I a fag? Am I? I was wondering myself. Am I gay 'cause of what I do with my father? I know that what he's doing is wrong, and I know that I wouldn't do it if I had a choice. I knew that. But still, at the same time, performing oral sex on a man when you're a man yourself, I don't know, it's degrading and makes you wonder yourself. And plus, when he would perform oral sex on me, I mean, it would take forever, but I would get off too. I would ejaculate also. And that was really hard to deal with because I was like, If I don't like this, then why can I ejaculate? I must like it. I must be a fag, I must be gay. Then, I had sex with a girl, and then it was like, Wow, I like that a lot better. I like this a lot."

Tom's references to gays—he alternated between the words "gay" and "fag"—revealed his ambivalence about them, and his comments also made me wonder if he wasn't trying to sound out my opinions about gays. If so, I wasn't making it easy for him. I wanted him to reveal himself and not cloak his real feelings to accommodate my attitudes. I can be a little more tolerant of a young person's prejudices because I believe there is always the possibility that he or she will overcome them. I sympathized with Tom. It was obvious that having sex with girls helped to mitigate some of the confusion about his sexual identity, which was being battered by Carl, an apparent pedophile. But if he had asked my opinion, I would have told him that I regarded homophobes with the same loathing that I felt for all the other bigots who are a pox on American society.

Tom's athletic prowess stroked his self-esteem and helped him to win recognition from his peers. But Patty, more than anyone or any endeavor, helped him to cope.

"We were always looking after each other. It was like she and I could be standing there and fighting like crazy, and my mom and dad would come home, and all of a sudden we'd both be defending each other. We would sit there in her room later on at night—my mom and dad would be downstairs watching TV or something like that—and we used to sit there and talk. We were like best friends. We'd sit there and make fun of him about things, and we'd laugh our asses off at him. That was the only way to survive, to make fun of it, to think it was funny. And we'd protect each other. I'm really protective of her, and she's protective of me."

That sliver of protection disintegrated just about the time his social life was showing promise in the seventh grade. He and Jeanne were in the house one day when Patty walked in and announced she was running away. She was twelve years old.

Tom panicked.

"I jumped on her, and I held her down." he said, demonstrating how he gripped her. It was as if he was reliving one of the worst moments of his life. He tensed. I could sense his panic.

"I was sitting on her stomach and I had her wrist pinned to the floor, and she was bawling, saying, 'Tommy, let me go, please, let me go.' My mom's right in the kitchen cutting carrots, cutting these fucking carrots, making a salad, doesn't even care. That was her reaction to everything, just to stand there and do nothing like she did throughout my whole stay there."

Patty begged him to let her go and when he did she walked out the door.

"That crushed me. I mean, I can't even think about it now because my sister running away was the worst experience in my life. I've had a lot of bad experiences but that was the ultimate for me, that was the ultimate blow. I wanted to just go and maul my mother, tear her to pieces and do the same to my father because, I think, it was the first time that I really saw the damage that they had done to her. It was the first time I had really seen the magnitude of it. And I knew right then and there that she had to really be hurt to be able to do that. I mean, really, to be really seriously in trouble inside to just leave like that, that she was just doing that right in front of my mother, that she had the balls to do that, to go, just run away with my mother right there."

He wanted to flee with her but was too afraid.

"I kicked myself for so long afterward. But I was too scared. I didn't know what it would do to my parents, I was worried about what my parents would do without us; I was worried about where I'd sleep and where I'd eat and what I'd eat. I was scared to leave the security I had. I was willing to deal with the abuse just to have that security of a home and a bed to sleep in. That was the control, that was the major control factor that kept me there because I had experiences in my life that I didn't like, I mean, being moved around, being scared of the unknown, and I didn't like that and I didn't want to experience it again."

Carl had often told him how all those fears would be realized if he ever revealed what was happening. After Patty fled, his relationship with Jeanne also grew nasty.

"My mother, after Patty ran away, was very against me. Hated my guts. Resented me, like you would not believe. She would do things, and blame them on me. Tell my father that I did 'em. She just basically resented me because my sister ran away and she no longer had anything. She resented the fact that it seemed that my father and I were so close—what she perceived as being close. And she and my sister were that way. And Patty ran away and she didn't have it anymore. So, she resented me for it—not my father, me.

"There were times I'd like to torture 'em to death," he added. "It's just that I'm not a violent person at all."

Something in the offhand way he expressed himself made me believe that he was giving me a subtle signal. I assumed from our conversations that he was aware of the widely held belief about child abuse: that abused kids grow up to be abusive and violent. (Some research shows that about 60 percent of abused kids become abusive as adults.)

Some people could understand, I told him, why he might be violent if they knew how he had been treated from birth.

"It's understandable, but, yet, that doesn't give me a license to abuse my children or my wife or abuse other people. I know it's wrong, so, therefore, I shouldn't do it. I mean, even though it was done to me that doesn't make it right. That's the way I feel. From the time I was four years old I knew what was happening was wrong. You know, just by him telling me don't ever tell anyone this, we'll both get in a lot of trouble, and you'll get shipped off again, you'll get moved again and I'll go to jail. And everyone will hate you. So, yeah, I mean, that's why I say I'm compassionate. I understand criminals. I can understand why they do what they do. Or I can understand where it's stemming from. I'm not saying it's right. But I'm saying that I have a perspective where I can see."

He understood why some people killed wantonly. In his explanation he used the word "fathers." Murderous kids, he said, acted out the violence perpetrated on them by their fathers, who in turn had been abused by their fathers and so on in an unending chain. But a growing body of research indicates that women can be just as abusive to kids as men though that wasn't true in Tom's life. His natural mother had died when he was eighteen months old, and Jeanne had protected neither him nor Patty, but there was no active abuse there.

As he talked, moved by what muse I didn't know then, I agreed with him that there was a link between the violence a person committed and the violence that person had experienced as a child, though I didn't believe all violence could be attributed solely to abusive childhoods. And we both agreed that someone's abusive childhood did not justify criminal behavior. I also knew that we would have to discuss that issue again when we knew each other better and I could ask him tougher questions.

3 • "Chameleon"

*T*he next morning Tom and I were both anxious to resume the interview. We ate a quick breakfast with Tracie and her parents, and though I enjoyed talking with them, I also found it difficult to focus on what they were saying because I could hardly wait to rush back to Tom's room to resume talking. Tom seemed very upbeat and relaxed and anxious. And the Nadeaus must have understood because no one even blinked an eye when Tom and I gulped down our food and scampered back to his room. He was more casually dressed, in jeans, and the mood was less formal though just as intense. It would have been hard for him not to notice how enthralled I was as he wove his tale. At some point during the interview I planned to tell him about my experiences as a foster father.

After Patty ran away from home, he said, resuming his narrative, he capitulated and did what he had been resisting for years. He agreed to be adopted. He could not deal with the pressure from his parents and the Children Services caseworkers. Despite what he was forced to endure at home, however, he found a niche after he enrolled at Elyria Catholic High School.

"It was just a really nice school. A lot of spirit. Everyone was like brothers and sisters. That was the way they wanted it at the school. We are one, was our motto. We are one. I just felt close there. I felt like I really had a part there. The football team was state champions that year. The JV football team I was on went undefeated."

After the football season ended, he chose not to play basketball because he believed he was too small for the freshman team. He joined the freshman wrestling team. In the early part of the season, however, he questioned that decision. He lost his first match in forty-five seconds. He lost the next four, though not as swiftly as the first. At practice several days before his sixth match, he was reviewing his winless record when something welled up inside of him.

"See, I was getting beat in sports, and in my life I was getting beat. I was always being dominated throughout my life; always being dominated in the wrong ways. And wrestling is the strangest sport because that's what it's all about: You trying to dominate another person. And when I finally put it together, that I was being dominated on the mat just like I was being dominated at home, I decided I was not going to be dominated on the mat."

His coaches allowed him to scrimmage against the varsity wrestlers, who were better than he was, and he quickly learned from them. "I put things together better, different moves, combinations of moves. And I attacked rather than defended. I went out there and controlled the match. I wrestled my match rather than letting the opponent wrestle his."

He won his last seven matches of the season and his victories were beginning to nurture those hidden treasure troves of self-esteem his parents hadn't corrupted when something unexpected happened. IBM offered Carl a job in Vermont. Carl and Jeanne told Tom the new job would allow them to afford a bigger home, better vacations, and luxuries that they had forfeited for several years after Carl had resigned from the FAA. Tom, of course, did not want to go. He suspected that Carl had another reason for moving to Vermont: to get him away from his mainstays of support—his sisters, especially Patty, whom he saw frequently even though Children Services had placed her somewhere else after she ran away. I imagined Carl's concern: If Patty ran away, Tom might also flee. But before the family moved to Vermont that summer, Carl and Jeanne did allow Tom to visit his maternal grandmother, who was living in Florida. Patty also was visiting her that summer. When Tom arrived in Florida, he and his sister spent most of their time with their Aunt Linda, their mother's half sister.

"I was drinking and partying and smoking. I was loving life. Smoking cigarettes, smoking Kools; I was cool, you know. And then I think I loved it so much, that taste of freedom, that something inside me welled up. I just kept telling myself: I'm going to change, it's going to be different. When I go back, it's going to be different."

The decision to tell Carl he would no longer have sex with him was part of a process that started after Tom entered high school.

"I think it was kind of like puberty, only it wasn't puberty. It's something that I grew into, I guess: to stand up to him and say, hey, I don't want this anymore. It's wrong. There was a process of growing up and feeling more in a position to fight my way out, physically, if I had to. It was coming to a head. And in my eyes it was either him or me. Sometimes, I'd wrestle him, you know, when things were cool, when it wasn't this constant abuse. I'm not bragging. He was no match to wrestle with me. I'd flop him on his back within seconds, and I could hold him there, and then he'd get pissed off. And I got satisfaction out of that. Then things started going on in my head: Well, if you can do this just playing around, what if you're mad? 'Cause I know how mad I can get. And I know the potential that's inside me, the anger. I felt that at that time I was prepared to stop him if I needed to, physically stop him. And only until that point was I comfortable—I was never comfortable—but I did get the courage up to tell him that I don't want to anymore."

If he was strong enough to confront Carl, I asked, why didn't he just stay in Florida?

His explanation was simple. The idea of running away never entered his mind. For so long, he had been living in a situation so oppressive and steeped with abject fear, with conditions that required him to think always about what was good for Carl and Jeanne, that I wasn't surprised by his answer.

After a three-week stay in Florida, he returned to Ohio, and then he and Jeanne drove to Vermont, where they met Carl early in August. They were staying in a Howard Johnson's inn in South Burlington until the completion of transactions on a home they were buying in Underhill. The next day, after Jeanne went shopping by herself, Carl let him know he wanted to have sex. He told Tom how much he had missed him and turned off the lights in the room and pulled down the shade. Tom drew a deep breath and told him he didn't want to have sex with him anymore.

"I was real nervous, real scared, I was sweating but after I said it I was like, pshew, what a feeling. I expected him to go apeshit on me right there. I expected him to want to kill me. He didn't. He took it pretty calmly. He cried and wanted me to feel sorry for him. And I did. I felt sorry for him, which is sickening. But I also knew from right there when I chose to say I don't want to anymore, I knew there was going to be a lot of pressure. But what I was so psyched about, I did not let myself go back on it, which normally I would have. And he, I think, realized at that point, too, that it was going to be a fight if he tried physically pushing me back into that situation, back into the molestation, and that maybe he had a question in his mind whether he was going to win or not."

Tom started his sophomore year at Mt. Mansfield Union High School in Jericho, twenty minutes east of Burlington, and it seemed as if every decision he made concerning school was the right one, and almost everything he did made him popular. Because the wrestling season didn't start until later in the fall, and the school didn't have a football team, he searched for something else to do. He didn't want to go home immediately after his classes ended and deal with the escalating tension there. When a school counselor suggested he play soccer, Tom tried out for the freshman team. He had never played soccer until that season, and he was competing with kids who had played in both grade school and summer camp. Two weeks after he tried out he was elected captain and eventually become Mt. Mansfield's best scoring threat. He was excelling in his new sport, just as he had in other sports, and that accomplishment plugged him into Mt. Mansfield's social network. Later that year, he would establish himself as one of the top five wrestlers in the state. In his junior year, he would move up to fourth and captain the team, and by the time he graduated he would be awarded Mt. Mansfield's highest sports award, a white letter.

I was awed that Tom had accomplished so much at school at the same time he was living at home under siege. Carl was criticizing everything he did. When Tom excelled at sports, Carl berated him for being cocky. If Tom performed poorly, his father denounced him as a loser. Carl's tirades were scathing.

"He figured that what he was going to do was pressure me so much that I was going to beg to have him come back and have that same relationship, that I would want to do that to escape the misery I was in."

Tom tried to fight back by intentionally angering Carl at every opportunity. Once, like someone pouring gasoline on a smoldering fire, he told Carl he had a girlfriend and he wanted to invite her over for dinner. Carl exploded. Tom, like a lot of kids locked in heated conflicts with parents, learned that he was no match for Carl, and at night he couldn't sleep because he worried that Carl would enter his room and force him to have sex.

"That's what I thought it would come to. I figured he needed the sex so much because before he had it every time he could, every chance. So, I figured that he could not go without it. I could last indefinitely without it, and I could take all the abuse he dished out to me for the next three years—that's the way I felt."

He was right about not needing the sex, wrong about bearing the pressure. Eventually he arrived at what he believed was his best solution.

"I was going to kill him," he said and described the bayonet that a neighbor gave him as a present. "I thought that that was the only thing I could do, kill either myself or him, and I was too scared to kill myself. I was going literally insane because I could not deal with it anymore. I just wanted him to come in some night so I could kill him. I would tell the police I didn't know who it was. I thought it was a burglar or something like that and I stabbed him, and I didn't know what my father would be doing in my room in the middle of the night and leave it at that. Kill him."

I knew of similar scenarios described by kids who had killed their parents. Their explanations to police or their lawyers were often as unsophisticated and implausible as Tom's. Many of the kids I interviewed could not imagine running away from home, because they didn't know how to survive on their own and could not imagine anyone helping them. So, they remained until the moment arrived when they believed the only way to protect themselves was to kill their tormentors. Many had also considered or attempted suicide.

In November 1984, Tom and his parents returned to Elyria for Thanksgiving to visit family and friends. Patty was there. At dinner at the home of Jeanne's mother, Carl was humiliating Tom in front of everyone.

"He was slamming me in front of the whole family, saying that I was awful and all this stuff, and I just lost it right then and there. I went off by myself, and I was sobbing. I was ready to kill myself. And Patty came back to see what was the matter, and I told her everything."

Later, in December, Patty telephoned Tom at home on his

birthday and told him that she, Arlene, and Darlene were coming to Vermont to rescue him. He knew she wasn't bluffing, and he worried they might cause more problems. So, he told her not to come. A week later, he was eating lunch in the school cafeteria when he noticed his guidance counselor approaching him. As soon as their eyes met, he felt a sudden surge of anxiety. The counselor told him his sister had phoned the school and wanted to talk to him. He worried she was in trouble. But Patty told him she was talking to him from the office of a Children Services social worker in whom she had confided. When the caseworker, Debbie Durrell, got on the line, Tom told her not to interfere. He was suspicious of Children Services because it originally placed him with the Rimmers, and he was afraid that the agency would not follow through on an investigation. He told her he planned to tough it out. But Durrell said she was bound by law to act and told him she planned to follow up the information with or without his consent. That night he was terrified about what he believed Patty had set in motion without realizing that for years he had been moving inexorably in that same direction. But now that something was about to happen, the uncertainty almost paralyzed him. The next day, George Karson, a social worker from Vermont's Department of Social and Rehabilitation Services, and two state troopers showed up at school to talk to him.

Tom repeated what he had told Durrell, that he didn't want anyone to do anything. Karson reiterated what Durrell had said earlier, that once an allegation was made it had to be investigated. But that didn't sway Tom, who didn't trust Karson any more than he had trusted Durrell. Tom told him he was terrified that Carl would hurt him and if anyone contacted his father he would run away. He worried that the Vermont authorities might be deceived by his parents' polished middle-class image and decide not to remove him from the home. He hadn't forgotten how well the Lorain County caseworkers were deceived on their rare visits to his home. Karson said he planned to contact the local district attorney to arrange an emergency detention hearing so that Tom, a juvenile, could be removed from the Rimmers'. In the meantime, Tom would have to live at home and pretend that everything was normal.

Karson also asked Tom several times if Carl had sexually abused him in Vermont and Tom said no. "George Karson was really freaked out about the whole thing. He was like, Are you sure? Are you sure? Why don't you just tell me? He was pressuring to get me to say something did happen and I denied it."

Tom said his parents allowed him an overnight visit with a friend's family. Carl and Jeanne did not know that the visit was part of Karson's plan to get Tom out of the house. When the emergency hearing was arranged, Karson and the police whisked Tom out of school.

"I was freaked, I was just lost. I was praying to God Carl wouldn't show up and that I could go to the home of my friend and I could deal with Carl tomorrow," he said. "But I walked in there. I had a guardian, and an attorney and two state troopers with me. I was not allowed to see my father without the presence of a state trooper or my guardian. And Carl was staring at me with just this weird look on his face."

When he had a brief opportunity to talk to Tom, Carl said three words: "Was it Patty?"

Tom was removed from his home and allowed, under the auspices of Vermont's Department of Social and Rehabilitation Services, to live with a friend and his family. Carl admitted to the authorities that he had sexually abused Tom. Jeanne, the Vermont officials decided, had not known what had been happening for twelve years in her home. Because Tom told the authorities he was sexually abused in Ohio and not Vermont, Carl was not prosecuted as a felon and the affair was handled in Vermont family court. Under a court order, Jeanne and Carl began to see a therapist. So did Tom. For a while, the three of them were seeing the same psychologist.

Tom discovered that his newfound freedom came with its own set of problems. "I was really scared and nervous, like a little puppy. I wanted to run back to my parents, wanted to run home and stay in my own bed, stay in my own house, be secure; know what was going to happen."

He started doing drugs. But he eventually dealt with all his anxieties by imagining he was on "permanent sleep over" with his friend's family. He had learned to cope with painful situations by pretending they didn't exist.

"Things happen, and I don't even think about it," he said as his narrative careened into an area I hadn't expected. "If something made me murder someone, I would murder that person and totally forget about it, totally put it out of my mind. I mean, I could never just go murder someone for the sake of murdering them. But if someone was going to hurt me or kill me or something, and I had to pull the trigger to kill them first, I'd kill 'em. And I'd just put it out of my mind like that."

I was not convinced he could kill as casually as he described. I believed he was indulging in violent, imaginary options as if they were talismans to ward off the aftereffects of the years when he was too helpless to protect himself. Even though he had been removed from the home, he said, he had never completely severed his links with Carl and Jeanne. In the beginning his caseworker supervised all his visits with his parents. Later, Tom consented to unsupervised contacts. Carl and Jeanne were expecting him to move back home at any time, but he balked. He still cared for them but he did not feel secure enough to live with them. Friends and relatives often asked why he continued seeing them.

"People who weren't abused or never have been, never understand," he sighed. "People who've had a normal family never understand why abused children love their parents and why they go back to them, why they can even stand being in the same room with them. People don't understand that. I don't quite understand it. According to my psychologist, and my caseworkers, I was more like their parent than they were mine. My dad would have a problem or something like that, he would unload hours of stuff on me. And I was caught in the middle between them, supporting them both. So, I was forced into this mature situation from the time I was young. I was forced to grow up and support them as a parent."

An abused child is forced to repress his or her emotions to accommodate those of the parents. It is an unhealthy relationship for everyone, but for children the consequences can be catastrophic. The relationship impairs their self-identify. It erodes their self-esteem. Raised only to fulfill their parents' unfulfilled needs and desires, children trapped in such relationships literally don't know who they are. Tom's descriptions were correct, and though it appeared that he understood intellectually what his caseworkers and therapist had told him, it was unclear how much those opinions had helped him to liberate himself from the pernicious effects of the abuse. But his efforts to help himself seemed to me nothing less than heroic.

He recalled the day that Carl, after watching how easily his son could endear himself to different people, called him a "chameleon." Carl was complimenting him. But Tom believed Carl had aptly described a scourge.

"Growing up with him I always had to read his feelings. Like how his mood was, then I would have to make my own mood right then and there. I mean, I never had this stable, straight personality where I was the way I was. Whatever was appropriate for that moment was what I would be. I always knew what he wanted to hear without him having to tell me what he wanted to hear and I'd say it from the time I was seven years old, or even younger, until sixteen. And I got so good at it, I could walk in, look at him and know how I should act. And I found myself doing that with everyone. And that's why I felt that I was popular with people. If I didn't myself believe, then how could I make you believe? You know what I'm saying? And in order for me to lie about something to my father, for example, I had to tell myself inside, You really believe it—even though I didn't. I knew I liked girls but I had to, in myself, say, no, I didn't like girls so that I could be very convincing. You know what I'm saying?"

He was describing the dynamics of denial, of his life within a dysfunctional family, a nightmare in which he had to convince himself that he believed something he knew was untrue in order to avoid being harmed by Carl. Tom persuaded his adoptive father that he wasn't attracted to girls only by masking his real feelings from himself even though, on another level, they were very much alive. That chameleonic quality helped him to avoid immediate suffering, but only at a painful price.

"I just got really good at making people think what I wanted them to think. And that's what I mean about people having this image of me that I don't feel is true, but I don't, at the same time, want to destroy that image. I want to keep that image not because it's a good image or anything like that, but because it's—I just don't want to let anyone down," he said. He confused his real fear of being rejected with the fear of disappointing others. "That was my biggest problem. I never wanted to hurt anyone. Never. And I would hurt myself way before I'd ever hurt anyone else. I mean, even today, I let people walk on me—certain people— and I let it happen because I don't want to rock the boat, and I don't want to lose that relationship. So, it continues until it builds up to a point where I explode. And then the relationship would be over. And I did that to people who were close to me, like Tracie. Did that to her a lot. And sometimes I still do. 'Cause it's hard for me to say at the time that something bugs me. It's hard for me to let you know that, Look, I really don't like that. And the hardest thing is with relationships that are just like friendships. With Tracie, I can bitch at her or whatever, and I can tell her how I feel. I can say, No, I don't like that, because I love her, and I know she loves me. In a friendship, I feel, I guess—this is what my psychologist tells me—I'm nervous that it's not that stable. I'm afraid that the relationship isn't strong enough that if I didn't want to go to McDonald's and told them that they would not want to be my friend anymore. And, so, I'll go along with saying nothing. But, now, I'm getting better."

It was during this period when he was living with a friend and his family and continuing to attend Mt. Mansfield, that he met Tracie. As they were passing in the hallway in school one day, they started staring at each other. They crossed paths several other times, but they never spoke. They only stared. She was a senior, and he didn't believe she would date him, a sophomore. But the urge to meet her helped him to come up with a solution. He told her cousin, a wrestling teammate, to say hi for him, and one day Tracie phoned him, and they made plans to go to a movie. But there was a hitch. He eventually wrote Tracie a letter telling her that he already had a girlfriend and that he couldn't go to the movie.

He felt like a jerk.

And then he phoned Tracie and asked if they could just be friends. She said yes, reluctantly. But his girlfriend later broke up with him. She didn't want to be involved with a guy who was obviously infatuated with someone else. Tom and Tracie then started dating steadily.

"That was three years ago, and we still have the most, you know, in my mind, we have a wonderful relationship. I mean, we want to get married and things like that."

He did not like the restrictions of the foster home where he was living. He had a strict curfew and he believed his friend's mother had become too possessive. Eventually, he lived with the Nadeaus for a while. But he later moved to a group home in Burlington, where he also attended school, and visited Tracie on the weekends. He eventually returned to Mt. Mansfield. After he started college and lived briefly on his own, he again lived with the Nadeaus.

One day when he was in Burlington for a review of his case, and was still seeing his parents, a caseworker told him she had obtained information that Children Services was aware of allegations that Carl had previously abused another child. She urged Tom to sue Children Services and guided him to an attorney who could not pursue the case himself but who put him in touch with Robert Catz, who was a professor of law at Cleveland State University in Cleveland. Catz asked Robert J. Vecchio, a Cleveland lawyer in private practice, to join him on the case. During a telephone conversation, Tom told Jeanne about the pending lawsuit and she cried. He then told his lawyers he would not sue. He changed his mind but balked again when Carl cried after learning of his intentions. The delays almost caused him to forfeit his chance to sue. He filed the lawsuit on December 16, 1989. The statute of limitations elapsed one day later. When his attorneys told him that his case would be stronger if he also filed civil and criminal charges against Carl, Tom refused.

"I have been throughout my life protecting my father. I didn't want to see him in jail. He was Dad, you know. And I didn't want to see him in handcuffs. I didn't want to see him in the blue-type uniform that they use in jail. So, I just didn't want to see it. My parents used to always tell me that I was self-centered. All I ever did was think about myself, not about them, or other people. But that's all I did was think about them: them, them, them, them, them. They've never admitted to me that, they've never come straight out to me and said, Tom, we're sorry about how we used to say all you do is think about yourself. I'd like at least my mom—she was the one mainly saying it to me. And it's been just maybe since, you know, six months ago that I've realized what they've been doing."

He filed his suit when he concluded his parents were manipulating him for their own interests.

"I guess I stopped letting them do that. I wrote my mom a letter. The first step was writing my mom that letter and I pointed out all these inconsistencies in her story that she never knew and how she's never ever wanted to help me deal with what happened," he said. "She's never asked me what happened. She knows I was sexually abused. She doesn't know whether I was sodomized. She doesn't know any of that. She doesn't care. She wrote me a letter back, saying, Oh, woe is me, feel sorry for me. I was just as scared of Dad as you were, and I was abused.

"I don't want to hear that stuff. I was a four-year-old child, I had no control over it. That's the way I feel. She intentionally brought us into that, knowing how he was before."

On a radio talk show shortly after the lawsuit was filed, a caller asked Tom if he thought Jeanne was a victim. He replied that he believed she was, and that she was blinded by her love for Carl. But it was obvious as we talked in his room that he was as angry with her as he was with Carl.

"My mom's a jellyfish. You know, a lot of people will disagree with me, and never until a few months ago did I feel the way I do now. I blame her now as much as I do him because she knew what was going on—I mean, I know all about denial. I know all about your brain taking over and your brain denying it so that you don't have any control over it. I know all about it. But this was not denial. Denial did not come into play here. She had control over it. She did nothing to stop it."

After Tom revealed his plans to sue Children Services, his parents separated and subsequently divorced. Without elaborating, Tom said Carl let it be known that he was gay. Jeanne returned to Ohio. After the news stories about his lawsuit, Jeanne stopped communicating with Tom. He said she was embarrassed because the news accounts contradicted the reasons she had given her family about why he had moved out of the house: She had told them that he became "unruly" and that she and Carl could no longer get along. It was not clear how he was aware of what she said—someone probably told him—but it was obvious he was hurt that she had blamed him for the family breakup.

"I'd really like to thrash her just as much as I'd like to thrash my dad. Only worries about herself," he snapped. Tom sat firmly in his chair and looked straight at me. He was visibly annoyed. "She doesn't care what happened to me. I should just take it, and shut my mouth. She cares only about herself, and what people are going to think of her. She deserves what people think of her, she deserves it, she deserves it. They're not going to respect her. I think she deserves to be laughed at—and so does he.

"He needs an ass-whipping, and I think I'd like to give it to him now. I'd love to do that to him; smack him. He should be put in the same position I was. That would really give him an idea what it was like 'cause I don't think he knows even now. And until you're put in that position, you don't really know how it feels. Thinking about past memories and stuff like this, I'd love for you to turn into him. I would love to kick his ass. But, right now, talking about this, I feel guilty about my feelings."

The anger he expressed as we were sitting in his room at the Nadeaus was not apparent in his news interviews, nor was it present when he talked about his natural father. He had described his brief time with Tom senior as if recalling scenes from a horror movie. Those images awed him but weren't terrifying. Carl was another story. Those experiences resonated as if he was still trapped in a nightmare with him. Tom's exclamations about mauling Carl hardly fazed me because I believed he was only expressing anger. He also sounded as if he was shoring himself up, as if he was still extremely vulnerable and, even in the safety of the Nadeau home, Carl could still wield power over him if he suddenly appeared in the room with us.

"I'd like to kill him. I can picture it. I could maul him

right now. But then on the other hand an hour from now, I'm going to be thinking, Oh, I love him; it's a love-hate relationship; it's bittersweet. If he was in the room right now I wouldn't be able to insult him."

"Kids are so easily taken advantage of," he sighed. "Kids don't understand rights when they're young. And they blame it on themselves like I have. For so long, you blame it on yourself before you blame it on Mom and Dad. Mom and Dad, all-good, all-knowing. Father knows best. It's terrible."

People whom he didn't identify, but who I assumed must have been friends or acquaintances, blamed him for what happened to him and told him he should not have allowed Carl to abuse him.

"I was a four-year-old kid," he said, "I'm not going to say, No, I know my rights, and that's wrong, you don't do that to me. How many four-year-olds do that? I was scared of him. I was afraid that he would stomp me or something if I told anyone. And the harm isn't always visible, and that's obvious with me. I was being harmed from the time I was four until I let on. No one knew it 'cause I didn't let anyone know it. I didn't let them see that side of me that hurt."

An Ohio reporter, in an off-the-record conversation, told him, as others had, that he should have tipped off the authorities when he was older.

"I said, you're so used to it by that point you would take it. You'd shut your mouth and take it," Tom said. "I wondered sometime if I did tell somebody, what he would do. Whether he would actually kill me or not. Drive me out somewhere and kill me. I mean I was worried about stuff like that, so, I never opened my mouth. I felt like, well, I can deal with it. I'm dealing with it fine, and we'll leave it at that. See, the thing is, when something like that's happening, you think, well, I could tell and I would be protected by the law. But, what about the time between when the law gets there and when your father knows that you have told that person?

What's going to happen? You know what's going to happen. You're going to get your ass whipped is what's going to happen. You're going to get hurt.

"People, say, 'Well tell your teacher.' Teachers aren't the movie types—they don't listen to a thing you say. First of all, you never even get the opportunity. What are you going to do? Raise your hand in class, and say, 'Excuse me, but my daddy makes me do this.' No. When do you ever have the opportunity to talk to your teachers? You don't. You just don't do it. You're too scared."

His experiences with teachers whom he couldn't trust, parents who betrayed him, and a child protection agency that didn't protect him were in sharp relief to the images created by the mass media to lull us into tolerating injustices and to persuade us that experiences like his are unfortunate but can't be avoided, or that there isn't much we can do to bring about change.

"You know, I'm wrong right now when I'm saying that you're too scared," he corrected himself. "I don't even recall seriously considering telling anybody. And sometimes when I would think about it, I'd be like, No. The possibility of telling someone, and doing it successfully without getting hurt, seemed too remote. Sometimes I would fantasize about how nice it would be to be out of that situation, fantasize about what it was going to be like when I turned eighteen, and I moved out."

One day, he conceded, he tried to confide in his sister, Patty, but she was experiencing so much abuse herself that she could not recognize his muted plea for help, and he panicked and told her he was only joking.

It was an exhausting two days. Even when we weren't doing a formal interview we talked nonstop. And as I sensed that we were winding down, primarily because we both were drained, I asked a question I had been planning to ask at an appropriate moment. I knew that all of the kids whom I had interviewed about killing their parents had considered suicide and some had tried. He had mentioned at one point that he thought about killing himself but quickly moved on to talk about something else and I sensed that there was more to it than just a mere thought. So, I asked him how serious he was.

"I would think about it more in a sense of getting back at them," he said. "Just writing a letter explaining what happened, what he was doing to me; write a letter and say, I hate you. And this was when I was in seventh or eighth grade. That would be the only motive for killing myself. It wouldn't be to run away from my problem, but it would be my way of doing the most devastating thing I could do to him—just to take away that precious Tom of his, with my own free will. He was hurting me, so I wanted to hurt him. I would never think about suicide if it was for the intention of getting away from something. If anything, suicide would be getting at it. My intention was just to win, to get the final say and win; be dominant, that was the whole thought behind that. But then I said why should I end my life? I should kill him before I kill myself."

I imagined, as he talked, that he or Carl or both could have been killed if Patty hadn't intervened, but I also thought that Tom more than likely would have killed himself. I also thought that his seesawing mentally between murder and suicide ended after he was removed from the Rimmer household, started seeing a therapist and began to decide how he wanted to live. My question about suicide, however, prompted him to start talking about a subject I hadn't expected.

"It's so hard for me to describe how I feel. I mean, it may sound—this may sound warped and morbid. I think that if you went through the same things that my sisters and I went through, then, you'd feel the same. I know you would, anybody would: A lot of kids who get abused, they have feelings about murdering someone and then they go murder people because they are taking out on other people what they could not take out on their parents. And I'm not like that. But I let people know that you mess with someone I love, and I'll kill you."

I wasn't shocked by his words, but I was surprised by the force with which he said them. In a country where more than twenty thousand people are listed annually as homicide victims and many more are maimed and wounded, it is safe to say that murder is on the American mind. People who describe themselves as normal and decent speak figuratively about murdering their adversaries and enemies. At any given time, they may also talk about annihilating girlfriends, boyfriends, wives, husbands, parents, sisters, brothers, sons, and daughters.

"I'm really vengeful; I'm a vengeful person. I've never had to take revenge on anyone, but, I say to myself, if someone hurt my sister, I would kill 'em. That's not a question in my mind; I would find them, and I would kill them. If someone would rape my girlfriend, you wouldn't believe what I'd do to 'em. I would torture them to death; torture them. It may sound morbid for you to think of, for anyone to think about it, but I have thought about what I would do to someone if they ever raped my girlfriend or my sister. I would torture them to death. I would subdue them somehow with a gun in their mouth; or physically, if they weren't very big, handcuff 'em, tie 'em—take 'em somewhere far off in the woods, tie 'em to a tree and take out all my frustrations and anger on them. I'd keep 'em alive as long as I could. I'd pour gasoline on their foot, burn it. I'm not kidding. I would hurt them, bad.

"But other than that," he added, "I'm the most gentle person I know."

We both laughed at that comment.

"It seems like such a natural feeling that I think that everyone should feel that way: If someone kills someone you love, it's a natural feeling to want to kill them. Everyone has that feeling, everyone does. A lot of people won't admit it."

He then launched into a condemnation of the criminal justice system. Using hypothetical tales of heinous crimes and what-if scenarios, he justified mob violence and trial by vigilante. "I believe in Hammurabi's code: An eye for an eye and a tooth for a tooth," he said.

His long and deeply felt concerns about protecting Carl and Jeanne convinced me that he was not vengeful. Even the bayonet under his pillow when he lived with the Rimmers was for self-defense not revenge. But I understood what he felt: his rage at being unable to help himself and his sisters when they lived with Tom senior, and when he and Patty lived with the Rimmers. Compounding his anger was the realization that people either did not understand how he felt when he tried to explain what had happened to him or they criticized him for not doing enough to help himself.

Some of his comments were far more revealing than I believed he realized, especially his constant references to rape. I wondered if he had been forced to do more than engage, unwillingly, in oral sex. Broaching the subject had to wait; from all appearances, he was doing well, but I was feeling some apprehension and told him I wanted to talk to his psychologist. Years earlier I had asked a fifteen-year-old girl, who was the youngest inmate in the maximum security prison for women in Iowa, if I could interview her for my book about kids who killed their parents. My request led her to reflect on what had happened to her, triggering flashbacks that caused her to relive vividly the date and place of her father's death: One morning, he had become convinced that she was pregnant with his child, and had decided to throw her out of his home. But he planned to rape her one more time. He grabbed her. She broke free of him, grabbed one of his guns, and shot him several times. She stabbed him several more times with a knife. The gunsmoke, his dying moans, his blood on her hands, and the reality that she was responsible for his dying drove her into the kitchen, where she grabbed a knife to slit her wrists but stopped. Only her screams reverberating in the prison cell snapped her out of the flashbacks.

I wanted to be careful that the work ahead of us didn't trigger any problems for Tom. Because he agreed so nonchalantly to my request to talk to his psychologist, and because I had already been assured by his agent that he could actively participate in the project, I relaxed. I also told him I wanted to contact everyone he had mentioned during the two days we had talked, and that I had been assured by his lawyers that I would receive copies of his child care records, which he had not seen. After I conducted a few more interviews and reviewed the records, I would know how to suggest an agenda for our project. I told him we would write a first person account of his life, with him narrating it, because the book was initially his idea. We would confer continually with one another as I wrote his narrative and corroborated his memories with other facts and accounts. I imagined that his narrative would begin with his early childhood memories of his natural father, then move on to his life with Carl and Jeanne, and conclude with him now in college and suing Children Services.

If our timing was right, and his lawsuit was resolved by the time the book was completed, we would include that too, although I believed the book would be finished before the lawsuit was settled. I also was planning to use information from interviews with his sisters, members of both his natural and adoptive families and maybe friends if they agreed to talk to me. I expected the project to take no longer than twenty-four months, a schedule that seemed reasonable enough at the time. Tom said his sisters would talk to me, but he wasn't certain about the participation of Jeanne and Carl or his aunts. We both were certain that Tom senior would refuse to be interviewed. I told him I would let him know everything that I learned, and his response surprised me. Speaking as if he hadn't heard me, he demanded that I tell him everything I learned from the interviews and records. I agreed. He repeated his demand to make sure I understood how serious he was, that he wanted to know everything I learned about him or his family. I agreed again. He then told me that there would be times when he would want to know what I was thinking. I joked that there were times when I wasn't sure what I was thinking and that it might be difficult for him to understand my thoughts, especially if I was trying to resolve conflicting information or impressions.

That didn't matter, he said. What did matter was my telling him the truth about my thoughts. He warned me that he would know if I was lying. Others had tried to deceive him, but he had always tripped them up.

Despite my assurances that I wouldn't lie, he refused to budge on his demand that I reveal my thoughts. I agreed to tell him. I hadn't forgotten his earlier descriptions of his difficulty in trusting people, and his latest comments underscored that point.

The moment passed and when I thought the formal interview had ended, we started talking casually about movies. As he was describing one of his favorite types of films I realized he was telling me a parable. He could not recall the title, but the movie he described had features of old Clint Eastwood spaghetti westerns and Bruce Lee karate films and Sylvester Stallone's *Rocky* saga. The hero, slumped ignominiously after a brutal beating, rises triumphantly and sneers, "Ha, ha, ha, you can't hurt me," before vanquishing his foe.

Those words were ringing in my ears as he drove me back to the airport in Burlington. Did he mean he wasn't hurting from what happened to him? I didn't think so. He must have meant that his pain would not hold him back, but I wasn't certain. Another matter was on my mind during that return trip. In the latter part of the interview, he had segued from discussing his painful ambivalence about Carl to explaining why he was talking to me. His comments pricked my conscience: "I mean, just sitting here doing this, I'm not even thinking about the book. The book isn't even in my head. I just had to force myself to think about that. I'm talking to you as a friend; I don't even see that this is going to be put in a book."

I had heard similar comments during other interviews, and I always understood them to be a means for people to rationalize their willingness to tell me intimate details of their lives. And though I knew I would not deliberately betray or misguide them, I also didn't remind them that we were talking for professional reasons. I remained quiet and hoped they would continue talking. That was why I tried to choose my projects and subjects with great care. I didn't want to be hampered by conflicts between my professional demands and concerns about interviewing people who could be hurt or embarrassed by what they said or what I discovered about them. Being impartial means explaining the facts as I perceive them. A friend carefully fits perceptions into the pattern of the friendship. I was slightly uncomfortable with his comments, but I decided to worry about that matter later only if it became a problem.

And something else bothered me.

During the interview, Tom had disclosed some information he hadn't revealed to his psychologist or his lawyers. He was still protecting Carl and uncertain about revealing what were still family secrets. I suggested that we had plenty of time to resolve his concerns.

Tom, of course, would never narrate his story. Circumstances of which neither of us were fully aware would change our plans, and I would have to tell his story for him.

Part II
●
Patty, Darlene, Tom

4 • "You always try to wipe your eyes before they show up."

One day in 1978, when I was a reporter for a newspaper in Rochester, New York, a judge tipped me off that a seventeen-year-old youth was being illegally detained in a juvenile center operated by the State Division for Youth. With the judge's help, I won the youth's release, and when his proposed foster family changed its mind about taking care of him, I convinced DFY to certify me as his foster parent. Within a few weeks, I discovered that Clark* was severely emotionally disturbed. During the six months that he lived with me, I learned a lot about the inner workings of DFY. When the DFY staff concluded he was beyond help, they lost interest and decided to transfer him to another district. They didn't inform me about their decision. Once I discovered their plan, however, I blocked the transfer, and forced them to help me provide for him as best I could. The results were meager. Eventually, I learned that DFY for many years had been bouncing him from foster homes to group homes to detention centers to psychiatric hospitals to foster homes. During one hospital stay, Clark was diagnosed as paranoid schizophrenic; another hospital concluded he was manic-depressive; a third decided he was a sociopath. I was told he had been a patient in other hospitals in the state, but I could not get those records. One former school counselor told me he was a sweet kid but illiterate. Another said he was gifted but belligerent. It seemed as if everyone with whom he came in contact had an opinion, which was usually self-serving. Clark was a casualty of the systemic problems that plague child care services, such as the lack of adequate resources and personnel to help someone like him recognize his problems and gifts, and gain the skills to get on with his life. For severely emotionally disturbed black youths like Clark, prison was inevitable, a DFY administrator told me.

Because I was so personally involved with him, I couldn't treat his life as a news story. Eventually, I reunited Clark with his mother, who was living in Georgia, but a few days after he arrived at her home she threw him out. He was later committed to another psychiatric hospital.

I thought somehow that this experience as a foster father made Tom and me kindred spirits of a sort. He was suing the Lorain County Children Services, and I had once tangled with a child care agency I held responsible for most of my foster son's problems. There were several reasons for my wanting to help Tom tell his story and this was one of the important ones: I thought helping him would be a way for me to make up for the life I couldn't save and the story I couldn't write when I was living in Rochester.

I had been unable to find the right moment during my stay in Underhill to share my own experiences with Tom because I was too engrossed in his spellbinding tale. Over a period of time, however, I decided that it would have been improper to tell him my story. My brief period of frustration paled in comparison to his years of suffering. My former foster son could have rightly swapped stories with Tom about the inequities of foster care agencies, but I wasn't Tom's peer. However, I could empathize with Tom's indictment of Children Services and foster care in general.

Tom and I talked regularly by phone after our meeting

in April 1987. We discussed little about the interview and spoke more about the details for getting the project going. Because we were planning on having him narrate his story, and I believed the project would take only about twenty-four months, I had not stopped researching the issue of kids on death row, though Tom's project was at the top of my list. Meanwhile, he was juggling odd jobs, attending college full time, and working on his lawsuit. The distance between us added to the problems. It seemed that as soon as we resolved one difficulty another one flared up. In addition, there were logistical problems, scheduling conflicts, a rift with Tom's agent, and other matters to contend with. There were moments when we wondered how we would ever get the project moving. That autumn I decided I wanted to interview him and his sisters together in one session because he had told me during our first meeting that they had only recently begun to talk about what had happened to them as children. I thought it might be easier for them to talk if they were interviewed together. Though our plans called for me to do the interviews, I thought having him present when I met his sisters would resolve some of his concerns about what I was doing and how I was proceeding, and that it would be a convenient way to introduce me to his family. I also believed a group interview would speed things up and help us to make up what I perceived to be lost time. I imagined that the meeting would result in spontaneous and dynamic discourse as Tom and his sisters talked to each other for the first time in their lives about what they had experienced. I thought my idea had promise, and Tom liked it.

I learned it was a bad strategy shortly after Tom and I began making plans to meet in Elyria, where his sisters lived. A Rutgers colleague warned me not to do it after I told him that the meeting was to be the first occasion for Tom and his sisters to discuss openly what had happened to them. The colleague, Carl Botan, who taught in the communications department, was a member of the executive committee of the New Jersey Center for the Rehabilitation of Torture Victims. The center helped coordinate treatment in the United States for South American and African people who had been tortured in their own countries. My colleague was not a clinician; he was primarily involved in fund-raising, but in discussions with clinicians who worked for the center he had learned general information about the effects of long-term abuse and torture. I was dealing with "very explosive stuff," he said, and I should not regard the intended meeting as a simple interviewing session with a group of people sitting around casually talking about the worst moments of their lives. He suggested that I have a family therapist present. I eventually told Tom what I had learned from my colleague and suggested that we cancel the Elyria trip. He was surprised but went along with my suggestion. I told him I would do individual interviews with his sisters, with him present if he wanted to be.

After innumerable delays, we decided in the summer of 1989 that I should interview his sister Patty. Tom suggested that I meet her in Underhill because he thought she would be more comfortable talking to me with him there. But arrangements to get her to Vermont failed repeatedly. She refused to fly, nor would she take a bus, and her plans to drive there with a friend fell through several times. After so many false starts, I told Tom I would interview her in Elyria. He could not make the trip because he was working, but she agreed to meet me alone.

Early in July, I flew to the Cleveland Hopkins Airport, rented a car, and made my way to U.S. Interstate 80 heading west. It was a hot, sunny day but after living in New York City, which I considered the concrete metropolis of the United States, I enjoyed the miles and miles of rural Ohio. Farmland accounts for 47 percent of Lorain County, which has its northern border resting on the shores of Lake Erie.

The winters are reportedly gruff with cold, dry weather. Autumns and springs are mild while the summers can be warm and humid. To the casual visitor, Elyria, which is the county seat with a population of over fifty-seven thousand, looks like a sleepy town held prisoner by platoons of shopping malls.

On a hot morning three days after the Fourth of July, Patty and I sat in the backyard of her home on the city's southeast side in a neighborhood of tree-lined cul-de-sacs and large residential houses with trimmed lawns. Some driveways bulged with cars. Others sported mobile homes, campers, and four-wheel-drive vehicles. Patty and her boyfriend, Gregory A. Moore, and their son, Michael, almost two years old, lived in the house, which was owned by Greg's mother, who was a nursing supervisor at the Cleveland Psychiatric Institute. Patty had been recently laid off from her job operating a machine that made lawn and garden tools. Greg, who preferred to be called Buck, was a foreman for Kross Plastics. His two younger brothers, Rich and Rob, seventeen-year-old twins, also lived in the spacious home. Their father, Leonard, had died in an industrial accident on a boat in the shipyard of Lorain, Elyria's sister city.

Patty confirmed that she was nervous about talking to a stranger, saying that she agreed to be interviewed because she believed it would help her brother in some way. Talking about her life and "the really bad stuff" wouldn't bother her too much because, she said, it would be as if she was describing someone else's experiences. Apologizing for not traveling to Vermont, she explained that she suffered from panic attacks and at times couldn't leave the house, let alone the city. Patty was two or three inches shorter than her brother. Her blond hair, which fell past her shoulders, was fashionably curled and teased. She had narrow, light blue eyes, an engaging smile and a beguiling, unpretentious manner as she spoke unhesitatingly, looking me straight in the eye. I was sure most people assumed someone as pretty and composed as she was had to be exaggerating when she told them about her disorder.

During Victorian times panic attacks were called "the vapors" or "the spells." At the time of Patty's interview, three million people in the United States reportedly suffered from the anxiety disorder. In a panic attack, the mind and body join forces, conjuring up periods of sheer terror for victims. Victims often feel severe shame and guilt. Some believe they are going crazy. One out of five sufferers attempts suicide, one study reported. Another study refuted that finding. But one thing was certain about the information in both reports: During an attack, some people believe they're about to die. It wasn't until the mid-1980s that the prevalence of the disorder was discovered. Before that legions had been suffering from a terrifying, debilitating disease that family, friends, doctors, and mental health practitioners could not understand. I suspected that many victims were perceived as crazy or weird or paranoid by families, friends, and neighbors who didn't understand the viciousness of the disorder.

If Tom's case went to trial, Patty, whose full name was Patricia Joyce Waters, was to be a principal witness for him because she lived with him and the Rimmers for about eight years. But I wasn't in Elyria to learn what she planned to say if she was required to take the stand, though, because I wanted her description of life in the Rimmer household, I expected to cover some of that ground. I made the trip because I wanted to corroborate what Tom had told me. I also hoped that my interview with Patty would broaden my knowledge of the Rimmer and the Waters families. I had a simplistic understanding of life in the Rimmer household, but I also wanted to know more about the elements of the day-to-day domestic rituals that made up their family life. Tom had given me an excellent description of his and Patty's lives with the

Rimmers, but Patty, in a discussion that would last more than eight hours, would provide equally compelling information.

According to Patty, even though they were separated by time and distance and circumstance, she, Tom, Jeanne, and Carl felt as if they were still connected by familial ties. Patty, despite Tom's insistence, believed that Jeanne hadn't known that Carl was sexually abusing him. *She* hadn't known, and she was closer to Tom than Jeanne, who, Patty said, tried to be a good mother. Patty revealed more: Jeanne's relatives believed Tom's radio and TV interviews gave unflattering portrayals of Jeanne and that Tom was insensitive and selfish. Patty held that against them.

"A long time ago, my dad made a move on my mom's brother. He made him sleep in this bed with him. So, he [the brother] had an idea that this was going on the whole time. This was way before we got put in their house as foster kids. So, he kind of had an inkling that maybe that would have happened—which angers me because he could have said something to Tommy about it."

Patty and Tom, except for talking about some particular incidents, had never discussed what they had endured in the Rimmer home or how it had affected their lives. Once she had asked him what happened, but when he'd started to reply she changed her mind and told him not to tell her.

"I didn't know that Carl did that to him all the time. I didn't know until later, after I ran away, but now that I look back on it, yeah, it all fits together: Why me and my mom would go to church every Saturday from four-thirty to five-thirty, and then after church we'd go shopping. My dad would freak out if Tommy wanted to go to church with us. He tried to make it so perfect: Well, Mom and the daughter go together and Dad and the son'll stay here together. My mom didn't care if Tommy went along with us. And Carl did show a lot of favoritism toward Tommy because that's what was going on. Tommy said that he lived through hell and he did, very much so. But Tommy got a lot of things, he did a lot of things that I couldn't do, like, he'd get to go down to his friend's house to spend the night at his friend's house because he had the advantage 'cause of what my dad was doing to him. Whereas if I wanted to go spend the night at my girl-friend's house, I'd ask my mom first 'cause my dad would always say no.

"When Tommy was in sports, my dad would always vid-eotape all of his games, and we'd be at every game. For me, never. Never. I played volleyball and softball in the summer, and I was in a baton corps. And I was a flag twirler, and only one time did my dad videotape one of my parades. But besides that, he didn't go to many of my softball games or volleyball games. He would always be there for Tommy. I thought, well, this was his son, dad and son, father and son, that type of thing. I guess maybe my mom was supposed to be part of me, but at the time I didn't think anything of it. But, now, yeah, I got ripped off."

But, because she didn't want me to consider Carl a cruel person, she added quickly: "And I'm not saying it wasn't bad but it wasn't that bad. I still love my father a lot. I think I've totally blocked all the stuff that he did to Tommy right out of my head. I've never really thought about what he did. That's why I don't hate him. My mind won't let me think about it because I love him, and I guess I'd hate to have to lose him as a father because I want a father, and my real dad, he's a waste."

She was struggling with ambivalent feelings about Carl just as Tom was, but her brother at least expressed anger about the way he was treated. Patty didn't show a trace of anger. She was expressing far more understanding for Carl than I thought he deserved and that to me was unreal-istic.

"I'm not as bitter by far as he, Tom, is. And you can see

why. That stuff didn't happen to me. I didn't live that terrible life that he had. In all honesty for my parents—this is in all honesty—it wasn't a bad life for me, not at all. The only time that I really felt that I went through a terrible, terrible time was when I was little. 'Cause, now, like I said, I don't have any problems talking about it. And it just seems like I'm talking about somebody else. My dad, he was an asshole at most times, yes. Like, he'd throw these major temper tantrums. If he did something wrong, something stupid, he blamed it on us—me and Tommy and my mom. He'd yell and scream at us to no end, screaming his head off, punching a hole in the wall. He would just do something stupid, forget something somewhere. That was it. The day was just shot from there on 'cause he would treat us like shit. He'd scream at my mom. She'd cry. She would never say anything to defend herself. Never. She was afraid of him. I mean it wasn't like he was outrageously mean or, you know, beat us all the time."

It was my impression that Patty survived by repressing much of what had happened to her. But as she talked I wondered how long she could continue to treat her experiences as if they had happened to someone else. I was amazed at her matter-of-fact recital. I could detect signs of the harm she suffered when I noticed the inconsistencies in her descriptions of her life in the Rimmer household.

If she wasn't beaten "all the time," did that mean that she was beaten a lot of the time?

"He never hit us, never," she insisted, and in the next breath she conceded, "He threw me down the stairs one time and that was because me and Tommy got in a fight or we did something wrong. But anyway it turned out that it was my fault instead of Tommy's. You have to understand mostly because of what was going on between my dad and Tommy, a lot of things were my fault. Tommy had like the upper hand on me, but a lot of it wasn't too noticeable until now.

"Let's see, my dad might've, yeah, I guess he would slap me once in a while. To me that was nothing compared to what my real dad did. But, yes, I guess if he lost his temper with me he would slap me, never no raw beatings like before. I'd say I'd get spanked as much as every kid did for bad things that I did."

I thought about Tom's differentiating between the beatings he suffered from his two fathers, and I asked Patty for examples of some of those "bad things" she supposedly did that provoked spankings.

One day when she and her family were living on Livermore Street in Elyria, a boy riding past her on a ten-speed bike stopped and offered her some gum. She knew him only slightly, but accepted the offer, and when she got home her parents demanded that she tell them where she got the gum because she wasn't allowed to go to the store and they hadn't given her the money for sweets.

"And I told them this kid rode by and gave me the gum," she said. "And he beat me, Carl gave me a spanking. It hurt like hell. He got this big ol' wooden paddle, and he made me strip down and beat the—beat my butt so bad it was red. It was supposed to be like the family paddle, like a lot of families have."

I didn't know any families with family paddles, but I didn't want to challenge her description of a normal family. And I didn't want to reveal my opinion that she had suffered almost as much as Tom. That wasn't why I was in Elyria. I was there to gather information so that I could write a first-person account of Tom's life as told through his eyes. At the time I was talking to Patty, I considered her interview a footnote for what Tom and I eventually planned to do.

"There's a lot of times that Tommy has said, 'Don't you remember this?,' and I don't remember too much. I don't know why, but I don't remember too much of it. See, I really didn't have too much anger that I would really have to—

well, maybe it was drugs, because I started smoking cigarettes and smoking pot and stuff."

She suddenly became confused: "I wonder why I just got into that because I wasn't raised to be like that, to get into drugs or anything. But I did. I guess that must have been why I would do bad things—just to get attention."

Her parents, when she was thirteen, worried that she was using drugs. They didn't know about her drinking. Whenever Carl and Jeanne left the kids alone in the house, Patty headed for the cupboard where the booze was kept.

"I'd play my records on the stereo and drink and dance and have a good time. It was just time for me to get away from everything. And, yeah, I guess that was my way of escaping because I didn't have very many chances to have any fun. And maybe if they had let me go spend the night over my girlfriend's house and go to the mall shopping and do fun stuff like that, I wouldn't have had to drink just to have a little bit of fun and act crazy."

I wasn't so sure that more overnight stays with her girlfriends or more spending money would have eased her pain, but I asked her what Tommy did when her parents left, and she replied that he "would talk on the phone and eat. Tommy would talk and eat 'cause we weren't allowed to eat when we wanted to, only at breakfast, lunch and dinner time."

When she got sick from drinking too much, Tom would help her to bed and clean up after her. She was about twelve or thirteen when she started smoking cigarettes and then marijuana, like other kids in Keystone Middle School in Grafton. In eighth grade she was caught and suspended.

"From that time on, Carl thought I was a big drug addict. Here I just took a couple of hits off this joint. We got home, and he tore my room apart and made me feel terrible. He grabbed me by the cheeks, and I mean before this time I was scared to death of him just like Tommy was. Oh, God, we were so afraid of him. But after that all I thought was the only thing he can do to me is kill me. And once I'm dead I'm dead. That's all I could think of. Besides that, I wasn't afraid of his discipline and his yelling. And he had me by the cheeks, and he was staring me in the eyes and he was so crazy. I told him right to his face; 'I am not afraid of you anymore.' I was like: You can do to me what you want, but I am not afraid of you."

So, what did Carl do?

"He spit in my face."

I told her I was not trying to turn her against Carl, but I wanted to understand how she could love someone who spit in her face.

"Well, it, uh, I mean, to me he wasn't that bad. He was, but he wasn't. Those were like incidents, but besides that our everyday life wasn't that bad. We went to school every day, and came home, ate dinner, watched *Wheel of Fortune,* and all that stuff. And it was just like a routine. My life was really never unsettled that much there. Like I said, if I had known that stuff was going on with Tommy, then it would've been different. Tommy would have went with me when I ran away."

Once, when they were waiting for the school bus to arrive, Tom did try to tell her about Carl.

"Usually, we were always running late. Tommy would have to rip my curlers out of my head. I mean rip 'em out and help me comb my hair. But this morning we were on time, and we're waiting for the bus to come and Tommy was like, Patty I have to tell you something: 'Do you remember when Carl did that stuff to you that one time? Well he's doing that kind of stuff to me.' I was like, You're kidding me, you're kidding me. And he was like, No, Patty. I said, 'You're joking.' And he said, 'No, I'm not. I'm serious. I'm dead serious.' He was like, Patty, don't tell nobody, don't tell nobody. And I was like, I won't tell anybody.

"And that was it. He got on the bus, and by the end of

the day when I got back on the bus to come home it had totally left my mind. I mean I'm sure I probably thought about it during the day, and maybe even that night before I went to bed, but from what I can remember now, it just totally, totally left me."

Tom's one feeble cry for help had fallen on the ears of a young girl who couldn't help him because of her own severe problems. She and Tom had dealt with the harsh realities of their lives by repressing the unpleasant. And talking with Patty I understood with more clarity that repression was still their way of protecting themselves.

I asked her to describe the day Carl molested her. She was nine years old when it happened.

"One day we were over my grandma's house, my mom's mother, and they were all going to church 'cause my mom and her family are Catholics, strict Catholics," Patty explained, as she lit one of the many cigarettes she would chain-smoke during our discussion. "They don't miss church, they go once a week. My mom does the rosary and everything like that. Everybody said they were going to go to church. And my dad didn't go to church that much. And he was like, well, I'm going to go home."

And Patty decided that she wanted to go home too. Tom went with Jeanne. After she and Carl arrived home, she stretched out on a couch in front of the TV. A short while later Carl came into the room and lay behind her.

"That was kind of funny in the first place, but I didn't think anything of it 'cause I always used to rub his hair, give him massages, rub his back 'cause I used to do that all the time and he would tell me how my husband would be so lucky to have a wife like me. So, I really didn't think too much of it, but it was kind of weird 'cause he was like right up against me, and behind me. And he had me put my hand down his pants and rub him. He said, 'Don't you like that?' And I said, 'No, it's wet.' And, so, he got up. He was kind of smiling, you could tell he was nervous 'cause he didn't know how I would react. But I remembered all that stuff that happened to us when we were little with my real dad. Carl knew I wasn't stupid to what was going on. He went in the bathroom and I don't know what he did. And I just sat there on the couch still watching TV. And he came back and he said, 'Patty, that's going to be our little secret. Don't tell anybody what happened.' And I was like, okay, okay."

I asked her how she felt.

"I felt disgusted. I couldn't believe it. I went from my real dad that did all that terrible stuff to us—terrible stuff—to him, and I trusted him. And this was the first time that anything had ever happened like that with him, and I just could not believe it. And then I told Tommy. He thought I was lying at first: 'You're joking, you're joking,' 'cause we'd always joked with each other. And I was like, No, I'm not joking, this really happened. And we just dropped it, from what I can remember, we dropped it. And like a week after I told him, I was downstairs and I was rubbing Carl's head 'cause, I guess, even after that, it just went back to normal with me and him. I mean I don't think it went back to normal. I didn't trust him after that, but I still rubbed his hair. And he said; 'I thought that was going to be our little secret?' "

She panicked because she believed he was about to hurt her but he was merely warning her not to tell anyone else. Tom, she assumed then, must have confronted Carl.

"That is one thing. Tommy's so brave himself and he'll defend anybody, but I don't know why he didn't do that for himself 'cause when I was weak, he would fight for me. There were a lot of times when I was scared and weak and Tommy would hold my hand all through it. We'd get in trouble for something, and it was time to go home and face the facts or something, and he was like, It'll be okay, and then after we'd get in trouble we'd sneak into each other's room and console each other."

After she was suspended from school for smoking marijuana, her parents discovered more evidence that convinced them she was addicted to drugs, and they considered sending her to a drug rehabilitation center.

"This is no lie, really. I didn't do drugs. They really thought I was into drugs really heavy, and I wasn't at the time. You know how you write notes in school to your friends. Well, I wrote this note to my girlfriend and I was talking about cocaine, and I had never done this in my life, never, but we thought we were so big in school. I wrote this note that I was going to get some cocaine for me and this girl and for a bunch of my friends."

Carl found the note after he brought her home from school and searched her school backpack.

"They freaked. So, my mom, she thought I was like one of those kids in New York City that are in the alleys doing drugs, shooting up drugs. The only time she ever had known about drugs or anything would be on TV, the shows we would watch, *Twenty/Twenty* or something."

But Carl and Jeanne never got the chance to send her to a treatment center. After her first suspension ended she returned to school where she was caught a week later with amphetamines.

"I had speed on me. I think I was selling it. I was selling like three of 'em to some kid. It was no big deal. I was just selling him a couple."

She was suspended again. She went home, gave Jeanne the suspension notice, packed a bag, and announced she was leaving. Jeanne begged her not to go, but Patty was terrified about what Carl would do. When she started to leave Tom stopped her, but she demanded that he let her go.

"I'll never forget that day. He was so sad. And I feel bad because I left him there. I do. I feel really bad. But I was like, Tommy, I'm going. If you want to come, let's go. He did want to, but he was so afraid of what my dad would have done to us. I wasn't afraid. To me there was nothing to be afraid of. The only thing I was afraid of was Carl."

She fled to the home of her cousin, Pam Haynes, who convinced Patty to tell a Children Services caseworker that Carl molested her. Patty didn't tell the caseworker about the physical beatings but it didn't matter. The caseworker believed Patty ran away because she didn't want to live with the Rimmers. There was no investigation as there should have been under Children Services regulations. And no one checked on Tom's safety.

I asked her to tell me how Carl and Jeanne met, and she said they met at a restaurant in Oberlin where Jeanne worked.

"He had a Corvette, and she thought he was, oh, mister fox. He'd come in and order, and she was his waitress. And, he'd come in a couple of times, and they'd talk and then finally he asked her to marry him."

I thought there had to be more but she said that was all her parents ever told her about their courtship. She was unsure why they never had children of their own.

"It was a big risk for Carl and Jeanne to take us in because at that time when they had first met us we were scuzzy kids then. Everybody says that we were scuzzy kids, which I believe we were. They say we were animals. My foster parents' family, like, my uncles and aunts, they were like, you guys were the scuzziest kids we've ever seen.

The relatives remember when Tom Waters senior and Cathy Ives, for the few weeks they were together in December 1973, visited and the kids were left in the car.

"My uncle said that he would sit in his room and listen to us down in the car. We would be fighting and screaming and pulling each other's hair, and we were always dirty."

She talked as if the relatives blamed her and her brother and sisters for being "scuzzy," having little consideration that the kids were victims, and those who witnessed the mistreatment did nothing other than remind Tom and his sisters years later about that helpless period in their lives. I asked her to tell me about her early years with the Rimmers, and she, too, skipped over the first eight years with the Rimmers, and oozed with enthusiasm about that period when she and Tom were attending Keystone School where she was in eighth grade and he was in seventh: "Tommy was in a lot of sports. He was good in a lot of sports. So, we were pretty popular. I was pretty and Tommy was good-looking and a lot of the girls would want to go out with Tommy. So, I think some of 'em would try to talk to me just to get to him."

As she talked, I assumed that some of Tom's buddies talked to him so they could get close to her. When her parents went to work in the morning, and before the school bus arrived, she rushed to change her clothes and put on Tom's blue jeans because they were tight. She also put on her mother's makeup.

"I would wear it real bright 'cause I didn't know how to wear it. My dad would be angry when I got caught. And, see, the big thing was I could start wearing it when I was sixteen and I could go out when I was sixteen, but you know how you always wanted to do stuff before you were allowed to? So, yeah, I'd wear Tommy's clothes, wear his jeans and some of his shirts. Even if he was going to wear it that day, he would sacrifice it for me."

When their parents allowed them to play away from home, they usually visited Tom's friends, Stacy and Beaux, whose parents owned land covered with trees and trails.

"Tommy tried to get away from the house as much as he could, but he included me in everything. It was nice. Even though I was a girl, he would include me in everything. All the sports. If I wanted to play, he would let me play even if the other boys objected."

After she fled to her cousin's house, Children Services placed her with new foster parents. When Arlene and Dee ran away from their foster home, Patty joined them. At first, the three eluded the authorities by staying with friends for a while. Later, they camped out in a tent and bought food and other items with two hundred dollars in savings from a bank account the Rimmers had opened for Patty. It was summer and they were having a ball. After four raucous, joyous weeks on the lam, they were caught and incarcerated in the Green Acres Children's Home operated by Lorain County Children Services.

"I was classified as a bad kid—and worse. That's what I could never understand. See, when you're in that institution they treat you like you're a bad kid. Your father might have had sex with you and molested you and beat you, but now you're in that institution because you ran away. You ran away, so you're a bad kid. You're unruly. They treat you like shit 'cause they think it's your fault."

Dee adjusted to the new environment, but Arlene and Patty chafed under the restrictions and escaped, fleeing again to Pam's house. They couldn't stay with Pam indefinitely, and they didn't want to return to Green Acres. The police were looking for them and they weren't sure what to do next. Pam suggested as a last resort that they contact Tom senior in Florida. Patty, who liked the idea of going to Florida, hadn't seen her father in about eleven years.

"And the only thing I could remember of him was all bad, everything was bad. Even now, his real family doesn't want to believe that that stuff happened. Joan, his sister, she knows that he beat us and stuff, but as far as the sex and stuff like that, they don't believe it at all. They feel that we made it up."

Just as she and Tom have never fully discussed what happened to them when they lived with the Rimmers, Patty and her brother and sisters have not talked at length about their lives with their natural father.

"I don't really remember if he attacked me. A lot of bad things did happen to me that I can't remember that my sisters and Tommy remember. But I can remember times when he beat the hell out of them, that I can remember. See, we help each other. Tommy'll remember some things that me and Arlene and Dee don't, and Arlene and Dee'll remember things that me and Tommy don't. But at the same time we never really talked about what really happened."

She remembered little about her mother. Once on a dock in a city she couldn't recall—I would later suspect it was Cleveland—her mother gave her an ice-cream cone. Patty couldn't be certain if that incident actually happened or if someone told her about that day. She did, however, recall what her sisters were forced to endure.

"I myself found out because when he would have sex with them he'd lock me and Tommy in our room so we wouldn't know what was going on. And he would take 'em downstairs on the couch and do this stuff to 'em, and you could hear 'em screaming, you could hear all these noises, and I was so young I didn't know what they were doing, but I would hear it all the time. And one day he was done with Darlene, and she was taking a bath, and she wanted me to get her some bubbles for the bathtub. And I guess the door wasn't locked, so I opened up the door, and I couldn't tell where she was calling me from—the bathroom, downstairs or what? And I walked downstairs and seen my dad on the couch laying there with my sister on top of him. And he beat the hell out of me after he got done with her because I went down there and saw what he was doing."

She recalled, as Tom did, that Tom senior made them stay up all night to massage him, and he punched, kicked, and beat them if they fell asleep. One day he beat her bloody because she couldn't find the right channel on the TV. On another occasion Tom was beaten severely after Patty let a pet bird out of its cage. She blamed Tom to escape Tom senior's wrath. She and her sisters and brother covered for each other when they could but each also lied and informed on one another, fruitlessly trying to escape Tom senior's brutality.

Patty also recalled the family brawls between Tom senior and Aunt Joan.

"Him and his sister would get in drag-out fights, rip each other's hair out, punch each other, knock each other's teeth out. My aunt is just as much a man as my dad is—a fighter, a man, an animal—just as much as he is."

Patty talked about the countless days on the road when they roamed with their father to places she couldn't remember, and when Tom senior left them alone in the car they survived on the can of sardines and crackers he left them. When Tom senior and Cathy Ives lived together in Oberlin and Tom senior started abusing his four kids, Cathy left the house.

Despite all they suffered as children, Patty and Arlene fled to Florida. They wanted to learn for themselves if Tom senior was as bad as they recalled or, as some of his relatives had insisted, he really loved them and was too overwhelmed by their mother's death to take care of them properly. Their foster parents were shocked and hurt by their decision. But Pam helped them contact Tom senior and he sent them money for airline tickets. Arlene delayed going, so Patty flew alone. Confused, she didn't exit the plane when it landed in Orlando and ended up in Miami. The airlines made arrangements to fly her back to Orlando where Tom senior had been waiting for her.

"And, finally, I met up with him. He told me he had been drinking. He told me he'd quit drinking, but that day he drank because he was so nervous because something supposedly happened to me—that mixup at the airport."

She eventually thought he was cool.

"I looked up to him kind of, because I was fourteen or fifteen, and he was all for drinking and going out and partying and I was like, okay, I can handle this. He didn't make any advances toward me. We drank all the time, whiskey. When a kid does something that you know you're not supposed to do, it's exciting. He owns some land and stuff—he had his own business. He's an electrician. When he works, he makes really good money, really good money. But he works like two weeks out of the month. Two weeks he'll work straight and not drink 'cause he says he's quitting drinking. And then for a month he'll drink."

Arlene eventually arrived. She and Patty didn't get along with Brent,* Tom senior's brother, or Brent's girlfriend. Brent owned the house where they lived. "The house was a filthy hole. My dad's room was really clean, because he was clean, but the rest of the house was a filthy hole. My dad had sliding glass doors in his room, so we could leave and go in and out through his room, which we kept locked all the time. And it was disgusting."

The house was infested with palmetto bugs. The son of Brent's girlfriend was kept in a locked room that reeked of human feces and urine.

"He would rub his poop all over the walls and stuff. We'd take him away, and take care of him because he was abused so badly."

When Brent and his girlfriend stripped naked and stretched out on the floor, Patty and Arlene left immediately.

"They would literally try to do this stuff right in front of my face."

She and Arlene enrolled in the local school. Tom senior insisted that school had little to offer and suggested that they learn a trade. They worked with him during the summer. Though they didn't like the South or the derogatory descriptions of themselves as "Yankees," they planned to stay. It didn't work out, of course. Tom senior was drunk almost every day. And once he took Arlene with him and was gone for two days.

"I guess they went out to where his property is, this land

he owns, and just drank and stuff. He told her he wanted to
have sex with her and—this is how crazy he is—he wanted
her to be the clone of my mother. He talks about how he
sees my mother and they dance on top of roofs, and angels
fly around her head. And when we lived there, he would sit
on the couch drunk as a skunk, and we'd walk past him or
something, he'd say, 'Stop, turn around.' We'd turn around
and walk back. He'd go, 'Now, I want you to walk back through
here like your mother.' And we'd walk, and he'd say, 'No, no,
she doesn't walk like that.' And he'd get up as drunk as he
was and try to show us how she would walk and how he
wanted us to walk. He wanted us to be just like her 'cause
even to this day, he really grieves that my mom died.

"They don't even know how my mom died," she continued, causing me to believe that "they" referred to family
members or relatives.

"You know, they said it was something to do with her
heart, but they don't know if my dad killed her or what. They
don't know what happened at all. He's really hooked on her
death."

He wasn't the only one, I thought, as Patty said she and
Arlene somehow came in contact with the Florida Department of Health and Rehabilitative Services. The sisters were
planning to live with their father. HRS contacted Lorain
County Children Services and an HRS caseworker visited the
house. But the girls were never able to move in. Tom senior
decided that he didn't want them, and they ended up in a
confrontation later with Brent.

"It was in the morning and he wanted to know why we
didn't go to school today. And he said; 'Well, if your stuff is
not packed and out of the house in fifteen minutes, your stuff
is going to be burned and I'm going to shoot you guys.' And
he had this gun, pointing it at us, so we packed what we could
and left. I don't know where my dad was."

An HRS employee put them on a plane back to Ohio. At

a stopover in Orlando they considered running away again to gain what Patty described as "a real life of sitting down in the evening and watching TV and having a good dinner and going to bed, having our own bed. We were sick of living on the streets and in disgusting houses. So, we were like, let's just go back."

And so they returned to Green Acres. Darlene graduated and Arlene left about eighteen months later. Patty stayed. The summer before her senior year in high school her maternal grandmother and her husband invited her to Florida. Patty enrolled in school and got her first job. She later lived with her aunt. Tom joined her for two weeks before he moved to Vermont with Jeanne and Carl. When he left, Patty remained.

"I was going to finish school and live down there because I really liked it, and I was having a really good time. And my aunt wanted to adopt me. My caseworker at the group home in Ohio was like, go ahead and stay, have a good time. But I missed my sisters. They were my whole family. I would have missed them too much 'cause our family's really close, us four: me and Tommy and Arlene and Dee. We're really close, more than most families are. I couldn't have lived without them."

It was difficult to understand why she couldn't have lived in Florida and visited them or have them visit her, but even though I didn't follow her reasoning, I accepted her explanation. One day, about three months after she returned to Green Acres, her heart started beating rapidly, and she started shaking. She had trouble breathing. On a sudden urge, she rushed outside and then discovered that the outdoors terrified her even more. She dashed back inside, where she looked in a mirror and couldn't recognize her own reflection. And those feelings have plagued her "twenty-four hours a day, every minute of the day" since the onslaught of the panic attacks.

Therapy and medication can help, and people who have

the disorder but who have overcome its effects advise that sufferers should not give up if the initial attempts to find help are unsuccessful.

"My caseworker took me to a psychiatrist, and he wasn't helping me. I mean he knew what I had but he was telling me that I'd have them for the rest of my life, that they'd get worse before they got better. And so I told her I didn't want to see him anymore, that I would just handle it on my own. Now, I won't go in an airplane. I won't ride in an elevator. It's anything that I don't have control of. If I can't control it, I'll get panic attacks. Like, being in an airplane, I'm not afraid of it crashing. It's just the fear of once I get in the plane, and I'm in there for twenty minutes, and it starts taking off in the air, I'd want to get out. I can't control getting out. In twelfth grade I quit school because of it. We'd be in the classroom and I had so much fear when the door closed. I couldn't breathe. I'd just be sitting there, and all of a sudden I'd want to go home. So, I quit school. Of all the people I thought wouldn't graduate from school, it surely wasn't me."

She talked to me in a calm voice. She was not whining or asking for sympathy. I believed what she was saying even though my senses couldn't corroborate what I was hearing. Patty looked the picture of health.

"I sit down and watch TV and watch these movies where these ladies are flying here and there every day in their business suits, and lawyers and all that, and it really excites me, it really does. I want to live like that. Patty wants to live like that. But there's the other side of me that's so afraid of everything that it prohibits me to want to do all that stuff. I have no self-confidence anymore, and these feelings, it's like they overtake me to the point where I feel like I don't have any control over myself. They have control of me. Even like right now all I do is sit around the house every day. I feel like I'm a nobody."

She blamed Carl.

"Like I told you, every time he did something wrong, he hit me in the head. He never let me be my own person. If I was happy about something he'd say, 'Stop acting so cute.' Or if I combed my hair, they," she said, referring to Jeanne and Carl, "made fun of me: You got to always be so cute. They didn't let me grow up myself, and find things out myself. I just kind of went along with what they wanted, and what they wanted me to be. I wasn't what I wanted to be. If I hadn't had those feelings, I would've stayed in the group home until I graduated, and then gone out on my own. I wanted to have my own apartment. I still do, you know, 'cause me and Greg just got back together a couple of months ago. We had split up for a while. I was on my own for a while, and then I just ended up coming back. I don't know why."

It was after she started experiencing anxiety attacks that Carl and Jeanne and Tom returned to Ohio for Thanksgiving, and when she was alone briefly with Tom at the home of Jeanne's parents, Tom told her what Carl was doing to him.

"And he started bawling, crying: 'Patty I'm going crazy, I can't handle this, I'm going to kill him,' " Patty recalled, explaining that she tried to soothe him until it was time for him to leave with Jeanne and Carl. "So, Tommy, he was like, Something'll work out. You always try to wipe your eyes before they show up, And, he did, and he was like, Well, maybe something'll happen."

After Tom returned to Vermont he sent her a letter.

"He said he killed my dad. And I believed every word of it. I'm reading it and reading it: Oh, my God. I was crying: He killed my dad, he killed my dad."

But she discovered on the other side of the letter that Tom had written: "Ha, ha. It was a joke. But next time it won't be."

"So, I told my caseworker," she continued. "This was Debbie Durrell. Anyway, I was really cautious about this because I loved my mom and I loved my dad, and I loved Tommy. And I was like, How do I go about this? And I thought about it day in, day out. And one day I just walked into her office and told her everything."

When Durrell told Patty she planned to notify the authorities, "I freaked out. I was like, Are you serious? I'm shaking 'cause just to think about the look on my dad's face. I was like, Oh, God, no. I was scared for Tommy. He was afraid of what my dad would do, just the final blowout of my dad. It finally coming out is the biggest fear you have. Tommy was protecting him for so long, you know. Plus, he was scared and sad because he knew that, I mean, he loved my dad, and he knew that something bad was going to happen to him, and he was just gonna get taken away. It's just that initial fear of what's gonna happen, and looking in my dad's face, feeling that you betrayed him. About a week later, he called me. He thanked me. He said, 'You saved my life.' But Tommy's pretty brave himself, and I don't know why he didn't run away or beat my dad up or just tell my dad, Don't touch me again. He doesn't put up with any shit from anybody to touch me or Arlene or Dee. But when it comes to himself, I guess, maybe it's the same for everybody: They have so much strength for everybody else but not for themselves.

"I got a letter from Carl too, after this all happened. He said, 'I wouldn't ever have had the bravery to turn myself in.' He thanked me for doing what I did. He was like, I can get the help that I need because of you, for doing this for me. He said that he didn't hate me, that he still loved me and he hoped that I could consider him my father. And that letter crushed me. He came here a couple a years ago for Christmas after this all came out. He was like, You know, Patty, I never noticed how pretty you are and what a nice person you are.

"And I was thinking to myself: You mean you never noticed me the whole time that we lived together? And he was like, I hate to say it but, no, I never really paid too much attention to you; I never noticed how much you had to offer. Now, I do, but not then."

*   *   *

This summer she was spending a lot of time with Darlene, her oldest sister, who was married and had two kids.

"And one night we started talking about the past—we just call it The Past" Patty said. "And I asked her, 'What really did happen?' Because I never really asked her and Arlene what really happened. Because I try not to think about it, and when I do ask 'em and I do realize in my mind what really happened it just blows my mind to think that I went down to Florida and stayed with him. After all the bad things that he did to us, to think that me and Arlene ran away and went down there and stayed with him just blew my mind two weeks ago. 'Cause Dee told me like, how he made her do these things to him. And I couldn't believe it. I wanted to go down there and kill him. We just stopped talking about it as soon as I told her I wanted to go kill him.

"My sister Darlene is depressed almost all the time. She's always depressed. And I think it's affected her the most because like I said she took care of us and stuff when my dad would leave us at home for days by ourselves. She was like a mother to us. So, even to this day, she's still the one, if you have a problem, you go talk to her. Me and Arlene are closer as far as sisters go, but if you're in trouble, you go talk to Darlene."

"Even though all this stuff has happened," Patty said, "I don't know if I would want my life to be different because I feel I'm a good person now, and I'm pretty satisfied with the person I am now, besides those attacks, panic attacks. But if I could give those up I wouldn't give up anything else as far as what's happened."

She and Arlene and Darlene recently attended a family reunion of her father's folks. "I went there just to see what they're like and how they act, and try to picture myself with 'em, as if I had lived with my dad all of my life. No thanks. I'm happy with how I am now; so are my sisters. We left there, and we were like, Thank God we didn't stay with them."

Patty regularly watched the Oprah Winfrey and Phil Donahue shows and viewed with mild displeasure the guests who describe the sundry tragedies that affected their lives.

"Their life is over because this stuff has happened to them. And me, I'm fine and I just kind of can't understand how stuff like this can wreck people's lives," she said. "I guess I can say from experience it hasn't wrecked my life, and I'm not any less of a— As a matter of fact, I think I'm more of a person since this happened to me. I've asked myself if I could change what happened, would I? The only part I would change is just the beatings and stuff, but as far as the way we got put into homes, no, I wouldn't change that. Because I would rather live with Jeanne and Carl than my real father the rest of my life. He was a hillbilly, and me and my sisters and Tommy, we would have just ended up being hillbillies. Carl did show Tommy a bad life, and me in some respects, but he always gave us a good education and good clothing and a nice house. Whereas, my real dad and mother, they would have never been able to give us what these foster homes could have given us."

She preferred Carl over Tom senior, and I thought Scylla over Charybdis, electrocution instead of lethal injection, crack rather than heroin. She groped for a ray of light in a stygian nightmare, and I didn't know what to say. I sat there and hoped that she didn't ask me for my opinion.

As our conversation wound to a close, she surprised me when she said Tom and Carl were still in touch with each other. Patty wasn't specific about how they communicated. Also, Patty, like her brother, talked a great deal about the Waters family but little about the Rimmers. Neither one could recall the name of Carl's mother and father. Though Patty talked briefly about Jeanne's brother and his wife and Cathy Ives, she would not or could not talk about Jeanne's parents. It was as if her and Tom's minds went blank when asked the simplest information on Jeanne and Carl. I was concerned that I had asked them the wrong questions or I had not phrased the questions properly or followed them up with other questions. Maybe, I thought, I was expecting too much too fast. I couldn't be sure. I also was beginning to sense that I was missing the significance of certain facts. But I couldn't imagine doing anything more than asking more questions.

5 • "And there was blood everywhere."

*T*om and I talked so much on the phone that it was hard to believe that we had seen each other only once in eighteen months. The jokes and wisecracks during our conversations sometimes blurred my impressions of the hideous twelve years he was forced to live. Shortly after my interview with Patty, I told him in general terms what we had discussed and that prompted him to reveal a little more about his life with Carl and Jeanne. He said Patty probably was beaten as much as he was and that it wasn't a matter of recalling which beatings were the most severe because they all were. Carl's beatings, he said, weren't as vicious as Tom senior's. Patty didn't bleed and there were few telltale signs of bruises that had to be concealed. But the assaults were still severe. I couldn't get him to be more specific than that, and I wondered again if I had asked enough questions or posed the right ones about their treatment by Tom senior and Carl. However, I learned in that phone call that Tom constantly worried about her and that concern hadn't been evident when he and I first talked. He recalled that she had been very smart in school until one day in seventh or eighth grade she decided she was "stupid" and unattractive and that no one liked her. She started hanging out with other kids who were alienated from the mainstream and considered the school misfits. She tried drugs. She was expelled from school. And eventually she ran away. Now, just leaving the house was a major effort for her, and he felt guilty that he hadn't been able to help her as much as he wanted when they had lived with the Rimmers and that he wasn't able to help her as much as he wanted now that they were free. On the one hand, he wished she would just get her act together, and on the other hand he knew the obstacles she faced and he worried that she might not be able to overcome them.

It also became apparent during that phone call that I would not get much more information from him or Patty about Carl and Jeanne and their families. I told him Patty said he was still in touch with Carl, and he conceded he had been in touch with him though not in recent months. He was still vague about their contacts. I assumed I would eventually learn what I needed to know, so I didn't try to question him more. He had not hesitated to tell me about his strong ambivalent feelings about his parents, but I wondered if those feelings were as seismic as Patty's.

I was still awaiting the copies of the child care records that the Ohio and Vermont agencies were supposed to release to Tom's lawyers. And until I got them I had planned to focus my attention on the Waters family. Tom and his sisters did not know much about their mother and I wondered why. Neither one ever mentioned their mother's name during the hours we talked, and I wondered if that was for the same reasons that they did not discuss other matters with me: Tom and Patty were struggling with enormous emotional burdens and did not talk about unresolved matters that caused them severe guilt or shame or confusion. I believed we would put to rest the rumors of his mother's death when we got a copy of her death certificate. What was important was for me to develop a better understanding of the past to make more sense of the present. And that was why I wanted to talk to Dee.

Dee was considered the oldest twin, I assumed, because

she was born first. She was also considered the wisest, and she was willing to talk. The twins were about four and a half when their mother died, and they were the ones who finally exposed what their father was doing to them. I hoped that Dee could give me enough information to start forming a more defined picture of the Waters family. I wanted that information before contacting their aunts and Tom senior, though I was certain no one would talk.

Tom and I made arrangements for me to meet Dee in the second week of August 1989 at a summer house he and two roommates were renting in Johnson, Vermont. By having us there, Tom could visit with his sister without spending funds that he needed for school, and he could also support her during the interview. Tom, the youngest of the family, behaved like a protective big brother.

I would have preferred interviewing Dee alone. I wanted to corroborate independently what each family member told me. I knew from experience that honest people sometimes fabricated or exaggerated what they thought I wanted to know while withholding information they believed unimportant.

Dee arrived in Burlington by bus in the second week in August with her two sons, Kyle, four, and Daniel, almost two. It was an exhausting, eighteen-hour journey, and her sons kept her busy most of the trip. Kyle and Daniel were at those ages when everything captivated them and everything had to be investigated. Dee, who was just experiencing the early symptoms of a stomach virus, was casually dressed in jeans and a blouse. She had blond, stringy hair and light blue eyes. She was pale but still attractive, and her pregnancy with her third child did not yet show. She exuded a stoic air, which softened when Tom was present. She looked as young as he was, yet, it was obvious by her demeanor that she was the oldest. And around her, he was transformed again, cracking jokes openly, his every gesture meant to reassure her.

We stopped off at the Nadeaus to have a meal before heading to Johnson. Tracie and her parents had developed graciousness into an art form. Everyone ate and laughed and joked, and I decided to postpone formally interviewing Tracie and her parents. They appeared to be such a stable influence in Tom's life that I was unconcerned about arranging interviews. The Nadeaus would be there for me; their hospitality was reassuring.

When Dee and I started talking, the journalist in me took over and we slipped into a serious interview. She didn't need her brother's support. Like Patty, she was ready to talk because her brother had said I could be trusted. But there were too many people around, and I didn't have a notebook or recorder with me, and even though I wanted to continue because the conversation was flowing, we decided to hold off until the next day in Johnson, where she and I sat at the kitchen table and talked. As we did, I noticed that Tom began to drift farther away from us and in a few minutes had disappeared. Like Patty, Dee would be talking about matters that she had never discussed with him or anyone else for that matter. And Tom did not want to hear them.

Darlene LeMaire—Dee to her brothers and sisters—was twenty-four. Michael, her husband, worked as a furnace operator at a copper and bronze foundry in Elyria. They owned a home. Despite a virus and considerable fatigue, she wanted to talk and expressed admiration for her baby brother, who called her first, she said, and not only for advice. In all likelihood, if his case went to trial, his sisters could be affected by the litigation. Publicity about the lawsuit was at the whim and caprice of the news organizations, and his sisters might have to hear intimate details about their lives exposed by the media. Tom had worried about them before he filed his lawsuit, but he shouldn't have been concerned. His sisters were eager to support him.

"There's nothing we wouldn't do for each other. I think it's because of everything we've been through and all. There was times when we didn't grow up like a regular family does. So, it seems like we're sort of making up for the time we didn't get to spend with each other. We really didn't get to know each other until we were older, basically, and I think that's what made us a lot closer."

After Children Services put them in separate homes, they saw each other infrequently. They probably felt closer because they grew up without parental support during the most impressionable and vulnerable years of their lives. They were betrayed by their father and by relatives who witnessed what was happening and did nothing and scorned them as well. They drew support from each other. And Dee was the one principally burdened with filling the void caused by their mother's death and their father's narcissistic ways. She recalled more about her mother than Tom and Patty, and her recollections were more like lurid chronicles of gothic nightmares.

"One time he was drunk. He was trying to mess with us, the girls. And she got in front of us and they were fighting, and he was hitting her and then he just grabbed her and knocked her down on the floor and raped her right in front of us. That was one of the most traumatic times I remember, when he did that."

She couldn't recall the police ever being there or her mother trying to leave.

"Mostly I just remember how mean he was to her. I don't ever remember him being very nice to her. I don't remember that, but then, I don't know, I mostly remember the mean times."

Unlike Patty and Tom, Dee said she remembered the day her mother died. The kids were in their bedroom, and under her brother's crib was "a big hole" that allowed her and her sisters to peer into their parents' room.

"I don't know if they were fighting or what. I can't remember. They were watching something on the TV and she was drinking something. We had our light on and everything, and we were in there messing around. She was drinking—yeah—and just fell over, and my dad was trying to give her CPR. And then we were locked in our room, and my dad, he was just completely freaked out."

After their mother's death, their maternal grandmother, Joyce Schwab, convinced the authorities to take them away from their father. Dee couldn't remember how that was accomplished, only that it was short-lived.

"My dad got us back 'cause I don't know if my grandmother could prove what she was saying or not. She had a lot of hatred towards him, and I don't know what else she was telling the authorities. I don't know if it could be proven that he was abusing us or whatever or if they just thought it was that she was just out to get him. And then when we were returned that's like basically when it started really, you know, where he'd really, really hurt us. 'Cause before, he'd have her to hurt and not us."

She couldn't recall the first time he sexually abused her, but one attack was not much different from another.

"You'd be upstairs or something, and he'd be calling you, and you didn't want to go. And you knew he was drunk. And you knew that if all four of you weren't down there that you were in deep trouble. I mean, if he called all four of you, you were fine 'cause all you had to do was stay there and rub his feet and his back all night. But if he just called one of you, you were in trouble and you knew it and you didn't want to go. He'd try to penetrate. He couldn't. I don't remember him penetrating. And he'd make us give him head, stuff like that. I don't ever remember him calling Patty's name or calling her down there. I don't know if he did. Now, one time she thought he did. I don't know if she wants to remember or not."

Violence was a way of life, and she recalled, better than Tom and Patty, just how violent they were to each other.

"I remember one time we were all in the car, and Arlene

made me mad. And I picked up a big ol' pipe wrench, and I said, 'I'm going to throw this at you.' And she begged and begged me not to throw it at her. And, finally, I said, 'Okay, I won't.' And when she didn't think I was going to throw it at her, I did. Hit her right in the face and there was blood everywhere."

Her baby brother, she said, was a diminutive pyromaniac who chased them around the house with firecrackers and matches and was just as violent as she and her sisters were, with a slight exception.

"He got away with a lot more than any of us did, especially with our aunts. That was 'cause he was the baby and he was the boy. Aunt Joan, Tommy was her baby. And she used to strip-search us when we came in and came out of her house 'cause she was afraid we'd steal something. And Tommy never had to do that, really."

Dee recalled the battles between her father and his sister, Aunt Joan, as well as the occasions when she was forcefully conscripted as a gladiator in the Waters version of Saturday night at the fights.

"Me and my cousin, Tammy, we'd have to fight and they would like put bets on who would win. If you lost, you went home and got beat for losing."

There was the time Tom senior stomped Patty for selecting the wrong TV channel. She was covered with blood. But Dee could also recall his periods of sobriety. He took them to fast-food restaurants or to a carnival and sometimes he even cooked for them.

"I remember one time he felt bad because he forgot our birthday, and he bought us some earrings and a little necklace. But the earrings were pierced earrings, and we didn't have pierced ears. But we still thought it was neat that he did that."

They rarely attended school, and when they did the experiences were unpleasant.

"The kids would call us white trash because we were

filthy. Our hair was disgusting. We had ticks in our hair at times, ticks on our body—and I mean we were filthy. We didn't have nice clothes, not even halfway decent clothes. And the kids would make fun of us. White kids, black kids, didn't matter, didn't matter. My dad didn't want us to go to school because, you know, there were times when he tried to conceal that he had beaten us. Like, one time one side of my face was all bruised up. And I don't know what his girl-friend's name was then, and I can't remember her face or anything, but they had sat there and literally put makeup over my face, trying to conceal the bruises on my face. It didn't work very well, but they tried."

She and Arlene have never discussed what happened to them.

"We both knew it was something that didn't have to be said. It wasn't something that we talked about," she said about the years they lived with Tom senior. "We just knew it was going on, and we've never really talked about it, to be honest, never. Yeah, we've talked about certain beatings and stuff like that, but as far as the molestation, no, we haven't really talked about it."

Their father's family partly discouraged them.

"My dad's sisters and them basically called us lying little bitches when my dad was arrested. I don't remember who said it specifically 'cause I was just so, I was afraid, I was very afraid. But they didn't believe us. And I'm sure I have a chip on my shoulder about that. When I saw my Aunt Pearl the last time, she asked how Tommy was doing, and I told her he was doing pretty good.

"And she's like, Well, what's happened to Carl? She's very upset that he wasn't arrested, you know, that nothing hap-pened to him while Tom senior had to go to jail. I mean that's the most that's ever really been said about the whole ordeal. It's, Your dad had to go to jail, why didn't he?

"For a while, it was hard to deal with, to talk about. Arlene, now, she just doesn't really want to talk about it, and really, I haven't. I mean, Mike, my husband, knows that that happened, but we've never even talked about it in detail or nothing. We've talked about some of the beatings and stuff, but not much more than that. Some people, like Mike, he thinks that my dad just went over the edge because he's seen my dad when he was sober. And my dad's not a stupid man. He's not an ignorant man, and he's not a rude man when he's sober. But Mike thinks that it, my mom's death, just pushed him over the edge. But he was the same way before then."

She recalled the day the Rimmers changed their lives. Cathy Ives and Tom senior took the kids to a party to celebrate their wedding. Cathy and Tom senior also were planning to leave for Texas a few days later. But at the party, Arlene and Darlene, who were about eight and a half years old, noticed their father getting very drunk, and they knew what that meant for them when they returned home. So, Arlene, who ended up in an upstairs room with Jeanne, told her their father was sexually abusing them, and the kids never returned home with him.

Police officers and social workers talked to them. Dee recalled how two Oberlin cops, one whose name was Henry C. Marsico, brought them a puppy, a Christmas tree, and "little things that we wanted." When Cathy Ives said she could not take care of the kids, Lorain County Children Services took custody of them. Arlene and Darlene were separated from Tom and Patty and placed in a foster home where the boys in the family regularly made advances on them. The twins were eventually removed and placed with Jakob and Franziska Hafner, a German-American couple in their sixties. Jakob was retired and Franziska was the homemaker. The twins saw Tom and Patty on rare occasions.

The first Christmas at the Hafners' boggled Dee's mind.

"It was unbelievable. It was a dream. Our eyes probably stuck out of our heads for weeks afterwards because we couldn't believe that people lived like this. And even when we first went there they were so nice. I mean, they were feeding us, stuffing our faces full of food and buying us stuff, clothes and clothes, because we didn't have very much. They went overboard. They got so much of an allotment of money for clothes, but they were always buying us more than what they got. They weren't like some people are who just buy you clothes based on how much money they get from the state. They were never like that at all, never. We probably couldn't've asked for any better foster parents than we got. They didn't treat us like we were foster kids like most people would."

Tender loving care, a stable home life, and clean clothes helped them to fit in at school. Arlene got good grades; Darlene got A's and learned that reading evoked a transcendent state that swept her to other worlds and times and away from her despair. Despite all the love and affection the Hafners showered on her, Darlene thought regularly of killing herself.

"When things bother me I get real depressed and, for a long time, I just didn't know how to pull myself out of it. And then there came a point when I was like, You know, you can't keep replaying history. You've just got to make the best of your life as it is now. You got to quit feeling sorry for yourself."

Life was uneventful for Darlene and Arlene until they reached their teens and wanted to keep up with their friends, who seemed to have more freedom. The sisters weren't allowed to date until they were sixteen and only on Saturdays when they had to be home by 11:00 P.M. And even though Dee rarely dated, the rule seemed restrictive. She and Arlene also couldn't wear makeup. They weren't allowed to have visitors during the week and they couldn't leave home once they returned from school. The Hafners, she and Arlene decided, were too strict. So they ran away. Patty joined them. They were on the lam for two weeks until the police caught them and they were placed in Green Acres. In the beginning, Dee adjusted quickly and excelled at the institution, where privileges and freedoms were tied to a point system. But children incarcerated at the institution were stigmatized, and the staff was harsh: "I liked some of the people who worked there. I'm not saying all of them were bad. But if you got caught talking to a boy, you were a slut, a whore. And they were not supposed to call you that kind of stuff, but they did."

Patty and Arlene rebelled and ran away. Darlene was supposed to flee with them but she hesitated, and they left her. She was depressed until they returned. When she left Green Acres she moved in with the Hafners' former foster daughter and her husband for a while until she found a roommate and an apartment. They convinced her not to join the army and to attend college. She worked as a telephone solicitor and a baby-sitter, and enrolled in evening classes. But at eighteen she was shy and uncomfortable around the students, many of whom were in their late twenties and early thirties and raising families, and, predictably, she also wanted less regimen in her life. Dee wanted to live what she imagined was the life of an ordinary eighteen-year-old—going to bars and parties, searching for fun and excitement. So, she dropped out of school. She was planning to return when she met Michael LeMaire, whom she found dashing. They got engaged. And one day she discovered she was pregnant.

"He wanted to get married when I was pregnant, and I didn't want to. I didn't want Kyle to think we got married just because of him."

Friends suggested that she get an abortion, but Dee, though she didn't oppose abortions, refused. One day, when they were living together, Michael went to work and discovered that the restaurant he managed had closed without warning. That's when the problems started.

"We'd get in big, massive blowout fights. And it was mostly money, not having any, not having any food. And all the pressure was put on him because I was very sick when I was pregnant with Kyle, too, very sick, the whole nine months. We had no insurance. And it put a lot of pressure on him, a lot of pressure. And he did hit me. He never hit me with his fist, but he hit me. And he would grab me by my throat. I'm not trying to justify anything. It's been a very long time since he's hit me.

"Mike, he has an attitude. He thinks he's always right. And I'm stubborn, and I hate to back down. And I'm like a dog with a bone. Once I get my teeth on it, I'm not gonna let go, especially if I know I'm right. And he got in my face one day, and I said, 'Go ahead, go ahead and hit me.' I said, 'It'll be the last time you'd see me or your kids.' And we haven't had any problems since then. I think it scared him. And I told him I can't live like that. I can't live my life being afraid of him because he was never like that when I first met him, for the longest time he wasn't like that. He knows I love him, but he knows the kids will always come first. He knows how important they are to me, which I don't know if that's right or wrong. And I know in his eyes that I would probably come before them, and he knows that they would come before he would. I probably don't show my emotions as much as I should, which is harder on him. I probably show my kids more love than I show him."

They married in 1986 and managed to pull through. The Hafners' daughter and her husband helped, and Mike worked at a Sohio station where the manager allowed him to work as many hours as he could. Mike worked eighty-hour weeks— sometimes longer—and got several raises. And then he landed his present job at the foundry. Kyle was born July 20, 1985, and he eventually helped her to mend her relationship with her foster parents, who found Kyle irresistible. Her foster mother was accommodating, but it took a while before Dee and her foster father could communicate.

"He was just so completely hurt that we had done that

(run away from home). That was one thing they demanded, trust. And it took a long time to rebuild that relationship between us and him. When I had Kyle, our friendship started all over again because he loved kids and that's how we started communicating 'cause he loved Kyle to pieces."

Jakob died in October 1989.

I asked her about the first time she saw Tom senior after Children Services took permanent custody of her and her sisters and brother. She was seventeen.

"Ahhh, it was very stressful. I was supernervous about going there, but it was something that I had to do. Everything that I remember of him, he was just like a complete giant to me. He was larger than life when I was kid, so dominating, and then when I saw him I thought, God, I can't believe this. He's not a very big man at all. In fact, I think I'm taller than he is, and he's very skinny. He acted like nothing had happened either. He was like, I know you hate me more than any of 'em do. He always said I was the loner, the one that, you know, always went off and played by myself. He was like the most pitiful person I'd ever seen. He's never gonna change or apologize and I've pretty much resolved myself to knowing that he's not. And even if he did, I don't think I'd want him in my life. Too much has happened to say, Hey, how you doing, Dad? Or even to have a friendship with him, I don't think it would be feasible.

"And I don't want him to make any kind of impression on my children. I don't mind him seeing 'em once in a couple of years or something, but I don't want him to have any part of my children's life. I don't want him to be Grandpop because he's not. But I think Kyle and Daniel have the right to know their real family, hereditywise, and just for their own interests, because I know for the longest time I've had a lot of questions. And even when I was pregnant with Kyle, I had, you know, problems with a medical history and stuff that I didn't know about, and I had to go through these tests 'cause I hadn't the faintest idea. So, I want them to know who their family is if they can call them that. They'll know that they have these people that they're related to, but I don't think there'll ever be that kind of contact as this-is-my-cousin, this-is-my-aunt type deal. I don't think it could ever happen. They know their aunts and their uncles are Patty, Tommy, and Arlene and my foster family. That's their aunts and their uncles and their grandma. And that's probably how it'll always be, and I don't ever want it to change 'cause to me they're my family. They're the ones that gave me the emotional support I needed. They're the ones that taught me how to ride my first bike, picked me up when I fell down, bandaged my knee, bought me clothes. They're the ones that gave me my moral beliefs."

Dee spoke about the family reunion she had attended with Arlene months earlier.

"I just didn't feel like I belonged there, none of us did. And they just act like you've been there all your life and nothing had happened. And I've got, maybe, I have a chip on my shoulder, too, I don't know. But they just act like nothing had ever happened. Everything was just peachy keen."

Dee worried, as her brother and sisters did, that they could be heirs to a cruel legacy.

"When I get very angry with my kids, I won't hit 'em. I'll stick 'em in the corner; I'll walk away. If I'm very angry with 'em, I won't even touch 'em. There's times when I wanted to hurt them, you know, I've wanted to. And I see it, and I know it's there and that's another reason why I can't forget my past because I'm so afraid that if I do I would just, you know, I know I have those capabilities of hurting them. Because there's times when I wanted to hurt them. I mean, seriously wanted to hurt them. But I haven't. And I've never hit them where it's left a mark on them, a bruise or anything. And I'm sure it's there in all of us. But, Patty, see, I don't think she hardly ever ever touches Michael. She's very patient, very. I'm more impatient with my children than she is with Michael.

And I don't know how Arlene will be as a parent. She's good with my kids, but it's always different when it's somebody else's and not your own."

Darlene also said she drank very little. The history of alcohol addiction in the Waters family hangs over her head like the blade of a guillotine.

Near the end of the interview, Dee recalled a day in West Virginia when one of her elderly male relatives "pulled me back behind a shed one time. I remember that 'cause it scared the hell out of me, 'cause it was bad enough that my dad was doing this to us." She believed it was her grandfather but she wasn't certain. She also told me that Tom senior had two sons, Michael and David, and that he was married to their mother and living with them when he met her mother. Dee was not clear about the details, but the two older sons would occasionally baby-sit for them when her mother and Tom senior were not at home. She did not know if they or their mother were ever abused. She believed Tom senior and their mother divorced when her mother was pregnant with them. David and Michael, she said, don't associate with their father's family. Tom returned by the time the formal part of the interview ended, and shortly after he walked in, Dee reached into her wallet and pulled out a copy of her mother's death certificate. Because of the rumors surrounding her death, Dee said, she had gotten a copy of the certificate from the Ohio Department of Health in Cleveland. According to the information, her mother, Patricia Waters, twenty-two, died at her home, 1920 Holmden Avenue, Cleveland, because of an acute interstitial myocarditis, etiology undetermined. At that time in Tom's apartment, our best understanding was that she died because of an inflammation of muscular tissue surrounding the heart and the cause of the inflammation was undetermined. There was no foul play. There was other information on the certificate, but at the time it went unnoticed. I felt we could put one major rumor to rest.

* * *

Dee and I talked over a two-day period, and it wasn't easy. We took several breaks. Sometimes she wanted to tend to Kyle and Daniel. At other times, she had to excuse herself when she became nauseated because of the virus. There were other occasions when we both decided we needed a break, and it was interesting how we moved to the far ends of the house, as if we were trying to get as far away from each other as we could. We ignored one another until the interview started again and then we acted like two confederates discussing a great adventure. But after the interviewing sessions formally ended, we both relaxed and over the following days we were fairly comfortable in each other's company. It was during this period that Tom took me with him on several trips to different brooks and streams to fish. He gave me some quick instructions about baiting and casting and then became so quiet and self-absorbed it was as if he was alone. Then, suddenly, he would decide to abandon a fishing site, and we would race to his truck and dash off to another pool of water. One day I caught a fish in a stream behind the house that he and his roommates rented. It was my first. Tom reacted as if I had won a lottery. He jocularly slapped me on my back and then ran off to stalk his own quarry.

It was during that second visit in Vermont that I got another idea about the project. Tom had said when we first met that he not only wanted to reveal what happened to him and how he was overcoming it, but he wanted to do something that would help other kids so that they might not have to experience what he had in foster care. However, after talking to Dee, I realized I might be able to help him help himself and his sisters in a way he hadn't anticipated. I told him I was expecting the release of confidential child care records, which I was hoping would be a gold mine of information. His lawyers had promised to give me copies of the records. I believed I could help him learn why no relatives or family members of his natural parents wanted, according to him, to take custody of him and his sisters. I could help him get to the bottom of all the rumors and reveal the truth and expose all the lies and deceit that he and his sisters had had to endure when they were growing up, and we could fill in the gaps of missing information about his family.

When Dee and I had talked, I noticed that even though she knew without a doubt what her father had done to her and Arlene, she still expressed doubt as to how responsible he was for his actions. She still was no match for the rumors in the Waters family that she and Arlene had fabricated their sexual abuse and that their father really loved them but suffered severely at the untimely death of his wife and couldn't overcome his alcohol problem. She was willing to concede that maybe his drinking problem influenced his behavior. I thought the drinking might be a factor but it was a poor excuse for what she and her sisters and Tom suffered at the hands of Tom senior. I believed I could develop a far better explanation because of the lawsuit, which was encouraging him and his sisters to talk more about what really happened to them.

Tom was developing a list of people who he thought might be willing to meet with me. The list included some cousins and some people who had told his lawyers that they were willing to be witnesses for Tom's lawsuit. I planned to focus on the Waters family members because Tom wanted to know more about them.

In early September, I called Jeanne Rimmer. I hoped she would consent to an interview because Tom had said so much about her, and I believed she at least needed to know what he had told me before the information became public knowledge. Patty had provided me with a little more insight about Jeanne, but I wanted Jeanne to talk about herself. But Jeanne said she wanted time to consider my request, and later she wrote to say that she was under too much stress to meet with me. She might consider meeting when "the turmoil of this

ordeal" ended, she wrote. I assumed she was talking about
Tom's lawsuit. I considered her letter a polite brush-off because she knew that Tom's lawsuit could be in court for years.
I also knew I would be persistent in contacting her, and I
thought I had plenty of time.

I sent Carl a letter at his home in Kingston, in upstate
New York, where he owned a condo and worked for IBM. I
needed to know how he would respond to a letter before I
phoned him or appeared on his doorstep. I normally disliked
appearing unannounced at the home of people with sound
reasons for not talking to me. I did it regularly as a newspaper
reporter but I always tried to do it with finesse. I thought I
did not have to be too concerned if Carl and Jeanne were
initally unwilling to talk to me, because I had plenty of time
and I would eventually wear them down or convince them
to talk.

Because I so wanted to believe that time was on my side
and that the project was under control, I was ignoring signs
that indicated otherwise. I finally took notice when Tom, in
one of our frequent telephone conversations, told me he had
been subpoenaed by a Lorain County grand jury investigating
Carl.

Bad timing, I groaned.

I couldn't imagine Carl talking to me as he was being
dogged by a grand jury. I was upset. Tom was upset. He said
Patty was upset. Six weeks after I had left Underhill, I had to
return. Tom was anxious to talk, about what I wasn't really
sure, but I had another reason for returning so soon. During
one of our many phone chats, Tom mentioned casually that
he had not been honest with his psychologist. And when he
added that he hadn't been honest for three years, I imagined
it was something that he had to resolve in therapy as many
other patients had done with their psychologists. At the time
I was primarily concerned with logistics—whom I should
interview and how I would find him or her and if people

would talk and what I would do if they wouldn't. Tom's relationship with his psychologist was not a paramount interest for me at the time. I would talk to his psychologist later. Because Tom was working on his college degree and making plans for the future with Tracie, I didn't anticipate any problems. But after hearing him say several times that he had told his psychologist only what he thought he wanted to hear and that he was not telling him everything that he could, I realized that there was a good possibility he was also withholding information from me as well.

6 • "The nice-guy tantrum"

*E*arly in November, Tom picked me up at the airport in Burlington. It was our third face-to-face meeting and I recalled our first airport meeting and my doubts that the project would get off the ground. During my second trip, his outspoken, sometimes outrageous humor surprised me. It was in Dee's presence that I noticed his mercurial nature, that different people brought out qualities I previously hadn't recognized. Around the Nadeaus, he appeared somewhat reserved and moved through their home like a dutiful son. He called them "Mom" and "Dad." With Dee, he was by turns boyish and mannish, both big brother and little brother. And with me he had been deferential and angry and sad and compassionate and humorous. I had not been around him and Tracie enough to notice their chemistry, though on my visits Tracie always appeared to be hovering on the periphery.

On my third visit to Vermont, Tom was exuberant and drove with reckless glee. Racing through the side streets of Burlington to get to Route 15, which would take us to Underhill, he cruised over white and yellow lines in wild abandon. We barreled through traffic signs. Sometimes he took his eyes off the road. At other moments he took his hands off the wheel. There were moments when it appeared he had his eyes off the road and hands off the wheel as he fidgeted with a cup of coffee or reached for something that always appeared to be just out of his grasp. And he was doing all this and chattering nonstop. It was almost comic, but I was beginning to doubt we would make it to Underhill alive. We whizzed through a third stop sign, and I was just about to growl when he admitted apologetically that maybe he had cruised through one sign too many. He slowed down, and for the rest of the trip, his pickup truck meandered only occasionally here and there over a white or yellow line.

I wasn't sure why he was so exuberant and bristling with energy. He was casually dressed in jeans and a shirt, and could have been one of my Rutgers students speeding to a class or to a bar. I was subdued. I had the impression that something was up and that I might be in for a surprise. About thirty minutes later in Underhill, Paul and Beverly Nadeau greeted me as if I were a visiting dignitary and again gave me free run of their home. Tracie spent more time with Tom and me the first day, but eventually she drifted off and Tom I went to his room to discuss current events. When I tried to initiate a formal interview, he stiffened, and I was surprised. Thinking I was pushing him too fast, I turned off the tape recorder and stopped taking notes.

Tom, of course, did not appear before the grand jury. He had learned about the criminal investigation in late September when Patty called and told him that a friend of Dee's, who was in the jury room, heard that Tom, his sisters, Jeanne, and Carl were to be subpoenaed. The friend was dismissed because he acknowledged that he knew some of the witnesses to be called, but he told Dee, who told Patty, who told Tom. When a Vermont state trooper showed up at the Nadeau home with a subpoena, Tom was surprised but not startled. He knew he would not appear before the grand jury. One reason involved the scheduled date of his appearance. He would not have had time to make arrangements to skip classes and his job in order to get to Elyria. He didn't have to tell me the second reason. He wasn't participating in any criminal investigation of Carl. He wouldn't allow strangers to force him to do something that even his lawyers couldn't convince him to do, regardless of the effect on his suit. The promise of big money wouldn't make Tom surrender Carl to the law. And during a casual discussion about his resentment of people critical of that decision and suspicious of his motives, we slipped into a formal interview.

"I do have a lot of mixed emotions and feelings for him," he said about Carl. "Prosecuting him would cause more damage for me, to have to go through a trial, to have to sit there in front of him and persecute him. He's trying to get help. I can be compassionate towards that. I'm not saying by my not prosecuting him what he did was right. That's not what I'm saying by any means. What he did was wrong. I know it was wrong. The DA is the one who has to have him indicted. The final responsibility isn't with me."

I assumed "people" referred to relatives or friends but whom he specifically meant he again was not saying. I knew he was not referring to Patty and Darlene. Patty was as protective of Carl as he was, and Darlene impressed me as a big sister who respected her brother's sentiments too much to say something that might hurt him. I didn't suspect Tracie or her parents because they had supported him for so long that they too knew how sensitive he was about Carl. When I first met Tom, he had speculated aloud about killing Carl, but now he expressed compassion for him. Carl was responsible for Tom's suffering but Tom believed there were mitigating circumstances that people either overlooked or did not understand. Tom believed Children Services was more responsible for what had happened to him than Carl, that Carl was driven by emotional problems over which he had little control.

"He wasn't able to make rational decisions while raising me. He had impaired mental ability in terms of relationships and the boundaries of relationships. Those boundaries to relationships for him were blurred and distorted. He had distorted visions. But sometimes there's accomplices to crimes and the accomplice in this case—who is more responsible than he is for the crime—is Children Services. They were able to make rational decisions. They had the resources to stop the crime. They stood and watched the crime being committed. They might as well have turned Carl Rimmer into a caseworker."

I believed that Tom was trying to rationalize Carl's actions. I, however, didn't feel sorry for Carl. But because I respected Tom, I did not say anything harsh about Carl, who deserved the heat, even though I also believed that the Lorain County Prosecutor's Office was acting not in the interests of justice, but to strengthen the county's defense in Tom's lawsuit. Too much time, almost six years, had passed since that day Patty and Debbie Durrell rescued Tom. The county's intent was obvious. I also thought that by launching a grand jury investigation, the county was in fact admitting that Children Services had acted negligently. It was possible that the investigation could strengthen Tom's suit. I also believed Tom would suffer if Carl was indicted.

One matter that caught me off guard was his announcement that he wanted to participate directly in the interviews. He suggested that we visit Elyria during the Thanksgiving holiday and start interviewing the relatives and witnesses whom I had been planning to meet by myself. There were two exceptions. He did not want to be present when I interviewed Jeanne and Carl. Whenever he and Jeanne and Carl came together, they could not stop playing their roles: Carl the father, Jeanne the mother, Tom the obedient son. For that reason and because of the obvious problem of his intense ambivalence toward his parents, he did not want to be present if I interviewed them. He had strong reasons for his new decision, and his wishes had to be respected. But he then raised so many reasons why he would be uncomfortable in many of the interviews that I thought for a moment he didn't want to participate. For example, he recalled his sister Arlene's wedding in October 1988, and a family reunion held earlier. At both events, people whom he didn't know told him how happy they were to see him and that they were impressed he was enrolled in college and doing well. They treated him like a favorite son. When I told him that we should contact them, he demurred. He was wary. They had talked to him as if they hadn't known what he and his sisters had endured when they were young and that made him suspicious. He also told me that he couldn't recall their names and didn't know their telephone numbers and addresses. And he was concerned about how it would appear, assuming we had somehow managed to locate them, if he suddenly showed up on their front porch with a writer at his side asking them about intimate family details. He had purposefully avoided keeping in touch with them, he admitted, and now out of the blue he was going to ask them numerous questions. He was also reluctant about meeting Tom senior face-to-face. I wanted to send his father a letter asking for an interview. Tom was afraid that Tom senior might refuse. I suggested that we could just show up on his doorstep if we could locate it, and Tom didn't like that suggestion either. It was too confrontational. He had brutal memories of his father, plus, he would be embarrassed seeing him. When he had met Tom senior for the first time in more than ten years during that same family reunion, Tom snubbed him, even though Tom senior was acting friendly. Tom worried how it would look if we showed up to ask him to talk to us, but I didn't believe there was any reason for concern. I couldn't imagine Tom senior agreeing to an interview. But he had been mentioned in all the interviews that I had done so far, and we were ethically bound to get his side of events. We both knew that if Tom senior abused his kids, it was more than likely that he had been abused as a kid, and that if he was an alcoholic, the malaise probably ran in the family. We wanted to know what was and was not a family legacy. Eventually, after listening to Tom express his concerns and equivocations, I suggested that he should decide to attend only those interviews where he would feel comfortable, and the rest I would do alone. I wasn't going to ask him to do anything that would make him uncomfortable. At least, that's what I thought at the time.

On the third day of the trip, Tom and I drove to Burlington to the local office of the Department of Social and Rehabilitation Services. Tom had signed a release for the agency to give his lawyers copies of his records, but despite several follow-up requests by him and his lawyers, the records had not been released. Just the day before, a caseworker told Tom during a phone conversation that he could pick up the records whenever he wanted to and then she called back five minutes later to tell him to wait a month. Tom believed SRS was delaying release of the records because of his lawsuit against Children Services. He reasoned that one foster care agency did not want to assist in a lawsuit against a sister agency. He had planned the trip ostensibly to obtain the records, which he was entitled to have under state law, or to at least confirm his suspicions. It was an innocuous scheme, but he also had another reason, of which I wasn't immediately aware.

We went inside the building and Tom asked for the caseworker. When he was told she was out for the day, he asked if he could get a copy of his records and when he was told no, he asked to speak to a supervisor who refused to give Tom copies of his records, explaining that it would tie up the copy machine. The man told Tom to follow the instructions of his caseworker and come back next month. We listened politely to the explanation. We didn't believe him. And we didn't like his tone. Tom told him that he didn't believe him or SRS and that even though his relationship with them had been very positive, he believed they were deliberately with-holding the records. Not at all, the supervisor said. It was a matter of bad timing. He promised Tom he could pick up the records in November. The agency would eventually turn over the records several months later but only because of a federal court order.

When we left the building Tom told me that a year earlier he would have been unable to tell the SRS supervisor that he didn't trust him, nor would he have been able to demand an explanation for the delay, and, after hearing it, verbally express his dissatisfaction. Tom said he had reached a watershed in his life because he could express dissatisfaction with some-one he hardly knew. But he also firmly believed that a year earlier he probably would have left the office with the rec-ords. He had learned, growing up in the Rimmer home, to be so manipulative that he could convince people to do things he wanted them to do or to believe what he said. He joked that he could have pushed the right buttons and the super-visor would have begged us to take the records.

He had told me before about his ability to charm people. I felt there was some truth to what he said, though I believed he overestimated his persuasive powers. He confided that trying to be honest about his feelings caused him consider-able anxiety, that striving to be genuine and to know what he felt and to say aloud how he felt created new dilemmas for him. He preferred the old ways because he knew they brought results, but he wanted to be healthy and had decided to give them up.

As we drove off, he suddenly decided to take me to Rock Point, the SRS residential home for youths where he had stayed briefly after he was removed from the Rimmers' home. He said he wanted to know if any of the staff remembered him. He also wanted to introduce me to them. I thought it was a good idea because I could meet people, other than his sisters, who knew him. On the way, he also casually mentioned that he still was not being as open with his psychologist as he should have been.

How much?

He didn't say. But that comment and what happened at Rock Point next were related.

As soon as Tom entered the building, which is located on Burlington's northern end, and word circulated that he was there, staff members rushed to see him and asked us to stay for lunch. They were excited. They treated him like visiting royalty and were effusive in their praise. If they had been a chorus, their chant would have been: Tom is a wonderful person, Tom is a wonderful person. After lunch, when Tom went off to visit someone, I was alone with the headmaster. I asked him to describe what kind of a resident Tom had been. He said that Tom was a wonderful person. I told him that Tom wasn't sure whether people really liked him for who he really was or because he was able to project a nice image. The headmaster looked at me oddly. He could only vouch for what he knew about Tom when he was there, he said: Tom was a wonderful person with a bright future; he should go far in life.

Back in Underhill later that evening, Tom and I were rapping about the princely treatment various people accorded him. He talked specifically about relatives and staff members at Rock Point and in general about schoolteachers and counselors and relatives. He was so relaxed and laid back that I changed my pace, moving into a formal interview. He again stiffened and, without missing a beat, started speaking guardedly. I continued with the interview. He said that although he was treated well by his relatives, he hadn't forgotten that his sisters were not treated with much respect. Women in the Waters family, he added, were often treated as second-class citizens. He pointed out, as an example, how his aunts doted on Tom senior. When the three of them were together, Aunt Pearl and Aunt Joan competed for his attention, and each jockeyed to be the first to have him light her cigarette. Before I had started taking down his comments, he had spoken frankly about the shabby treatment of his sisters and women in the Waters family, but he was now measuring his words, and trying to anticipate what I would ask. And I was miffed that I couldn't get him to repeat what he had previously enunciated so well. So, I asked him, instead, to elaborate about his stay at Rock Point. I wanted evidence of his finesse at manipulating people.

Tom was placed in Rock Point after he decided that he didn't like being in foster homes and wanted to try a group home setting. Within weeks, he acquired the special privileges that took some residents several months to get. "I was allowed to see Tracie when I wanted to. Granted, she could only come down, being so far from Burlington, once a week. And then I would go to her home on the weekends. There were kids on level four and level five who couldn't do anything without someone breathing down their neck. The higher the number, the worse off you were. Level four wasn't allowed to do much of anything. I did good in school, of course. The teachers there loved me, 'cause I was the all-American boy. I treated them with respect. The staff almost put me on level one. In the whole history of school, there was only one person who ever got put on level one."

On level one a resident could come and go as he or she pleased, but Tom was content with level two. I didn't understand why he believed there was something wrong with doing what people expected or wanted in order to get what he wanted. If he could convince them to do more for him, I suggested, that didn't mean he had a meretricious personality or that he was Jekyll and Hyde—unless, of course, I was missing the point of what he was saying. He never spoke of ulterior motives. He hadn't hurt anyone. He didn't exploit anyone. His payoff—more freedom, more privileges—did not come at the expense of someone else. So, he was playing the game. Better than that, it sounded as if he was beating the system. He admitted he enjoyed beating the system, but at the same time he didn't like being a phony. And when he lived at Rock Point, he said, he pretended to be more friendly and more of the all-American boy than he really was.

I countered: He was in a system that awarded the residents certain privileges in return for certain behavior. Why did he believe he was being manipulative if everyone—him and the staff—got what they wanted?

Because, he said, he wasn't sincere.

"A lot of kids throw temper tantrums to get what they want. I didn't. I didn't usually throw temper tantrums. I threw the nice-guy tantrum, but I'm shedding that. I'm molting and I'm not so good at manipulating people because I'm unlearning everything that I had learned from Carl. Like I was telling you today. We were down there talking to that supervisor. Man, a couple of years ago, I could have just looked at him and put him on his knees, whether through force of my look or whatever. But I didn't."

As long as he was talking, I decided it was time to try to fill in some holes and ask some follow-up questions. Patty had told me, when I had interviewed her, that Carl had tried to fondle a kid who spent the night at their home in Grafton. I asked Tom if he remembered the occasion.

"Yeah, he did. He would play it off like he was wrestling with 'em and whatnot and he would grab 'em."

"In the crotch?" I asked.

"Yeah, oh yeah."

"Did your friends ever complain?" I wanted to know.

"Only once did one of my friends ever say anything to me. But they didn't need to, because I would see it going on. Carl would be pretending like he was tickling 'em or wrestling with 'em. Everything was fine until he'd grab 'em."

The kids protested but not strenuously.

"They didn't really have the nerve to say stop what you're doing, bud, don't touch me there anymore. None of my friends really had the balls to do that. And then one time, it was at my adoption party, a friend said; 'Hey, Tommy, you know your dad's grabbing me in the balls?' He was laughing about it. That just ripped me apart inside. And I just played it off. And he also did it to a kid up here. Okay?"

Tom said the kid told him how Carl invited him and another youth to play tennis and that later he invited them back to his home, where he made a pass. The kid called Carl a "fag."

"And I said, 'Fuck off, man.' He goes, 'Your dad's fucked up.' And I just about broke the kid's arm that day in practice. I sent him to the hospital during wrestling practice. Granted, see, I shouldn't have been mad at him for telling me, but it was the way he told me and his not considering the possibility that maybe other kids would hear and that I didn't want other people to hear some other kid say that."

Tom made it appear as if it was an accident. He and the youth were on the mat, wrestling during practice.

"I wasn't really getting bad with him. He was trying stuff, and everything he tried I was stopping 'cause I was a better wrestler than he was. And I was putting him in a couple of painful positions, and he started getting cocky and pissed. And you could feel it. You can sense in a guy when you're wrestling with him. You can sense and feel when he's getting mad. And that got me mad. He was getting mad, I was getting mad. He posted his arm, and I went, wham."

He demonstrated how he executed the illegal blow that injured the kid, whose arm was in a sling for a few weeks.

"I didn't like him for what he said to me that one time. He should have known better. If I can hurt him in wrestling practice and not get in any trouble for it, hey," Tom said, signaling an end to the anecdote by quietly singing the words, "You better watch out, you better not cry," to the tune of "Santa Claus Is Coming to Town."

Patty had talked about a party to celebrate Tom's adoption, and I asked him who attended. Tom said Carl's half brother Lew and his wife from Erie, Pennsylvania, were there. Carl's mother, whom Tom called his grandmother, was there too. Tom couldn't remember her name. But he remembered that he didn't like Lew.

"Now, I once liked my uncle Lew. Man, I had so much respect for him. I had so much respect for that guy 'cause he was cool. He was so cool. He's young; very, very muscular build; good-looking."

But the more time Tom spent with Lew, the more he noticed his cruelty. Once they were playing a pickup basketball game, and when Tom was about to block his shot, Lew elbowed him in the face.

"He'd be like, All right, come on T-bird, let's play. And get all real kind of whack aggressive, kind of psychotic. He used to call me T-bird. He was a monster. He had me fooled just like my dad had everyone else fooled. He had everyone in the world fooled by putting that big ol' facade on. He comes off as the nicest guy in the world, but he's mean. He's crazy, crazy. I just totally lost respect for him; absolutely lost respect for him."

Lew was a developer, and that was about all Tom would say. He resisted the rest of my inquiries about Carl's family, but he suggested that one day we should visit Erie and meet them.

"I'll take you over there. We'll drive back to Ohio sometime, and we'll stop by and we'll talk to all those dudes. Okay? My dad blames everything on his mother. She put him in a boarding school when he was like four and whatnot. And she had several, I guess, husbands." Carl, he said, had other half brothers. I would never meet any of them because Tom and I would never go to Erie.

At one point during our conversation, we got around to Tom's temper. "I have different variations of freakouts. I freak out where I scream and punch things. And I have freakouts where I just kind of yell and raise my voice and goddamn swear. And then I have freakouts where I yell very loudly, and maybe punch things. I have freakouts where I punch things and I'm mad and, oooohhhhh, you better get out of my way. And then I have had three times these freakouts where I just screamed as loud as I possibly could."

Tracie, who had joined us by this time, said he wasn't boasting. She had been an eyewitness to his explosive temper. After SRS removed Tom from the Rimmers' home, she and Tom dated regularly. Tom usually lost his temper after visiting Carl. One time, after a visit, he ripped the gearshift out of her car in an explosive rage, and ordered her to take him for a drive. She was shaken, but he later broke down and cried. And on another occasion—after another visit—Tom came to her house and punched a hole through a wooden door. She said she had begun to wonder what kind of guy she was involved with, but she decided to stick by him because he needed her and she loved him.

I was wrapping up the formal part of our interview when I decided to test one of my impressions. I told Tom we might have to indicate at the end of the book that some information "could not be revealed because you wanted to save certain people some anguish." I wanted him to tell me that I was wrong, that he was not withholding a great deal of information. I wanted reassurance. I didn't get it. He thought my suggestion was a good idea, and I realized then how important the trip to Ohio would be. There were facts I needed to know, and I would have to get the information from someone else. And what happened later that evening supported my concern. He, Tracie, and I were talking when the conversation got around to the summer, when I had interviewed Dee.

Did I notice what was happening in the house?

I said I noticed nothing unusual, other than the fact that all of us had taken turns suffering the symptoms of a virus, which we assumed we got from Dee. I was the last to get it.

Tom and Tracie stared at me with mild disbelief.

Had I noticed, I was asked, how Tom and his roommates went downstairs a lot?

I hadn't.

There were more questions about what I had noticed, and each time I confessed ignorance. Tom eventually got to the point. That summer he had experimented with cocaine, found it irresistible, and then panicked because he feared he had become addicted to it. He and his roommates had been making frequent trips to the basement so that they could snort their coke in secrecy. For a while he was terrified that he couldn't beat it. And that was one reason he had moved back in with the Nadeaus. He needed a safe house, a stable, drug-free environment. He had only recently informed his psychologist about the problem and was just beginning to believe that he could beat the addictive grip of the drug. He described himself as someone with an addictive, obsessive personality. He believed he could get hooked on anything: drugs, sex, alcohol. He believed he had to be careful about everything he did because he could never be certain what would become an obsession. He was trying to become more temperate in his life. He didn't want to experience more problems.

I felt foolish. Right before my eyes, things had been happening, just as I had worried, and just as I had also worried, I hadn't been able to recognize them. I wondered what else was going on. I had been concerned about his reticence, but now it appeared that he would not be able to talk as much as I had been led to believe. There was a great deal of information he could not or would not provide. I feared the effects of his abuse were not about to allow him to deal with my journalistic timetable, no matter how much he said he wanted to comply. In four days together, we had done only about two hours of formal interviewing, far short of the kind of in-depth discussions necessary to write a book narrated by him. When I left Vermont, I hoped our scheduled fact-finding trip to Ohio over the Thanksgiving vacation would be more fruitful.

Part III
●
Ohio

7 • "Make a big fuss."

On the Saturday before Thanksgiving, Tom and I rendezvoused at the airport in Newark, New Jersey. He flew in from Burlington and I bussed in from New York City. Together we caught a plane, and late in the afternoon we arrived at the Cleveland Hopkins Airport, where we rented a car and drove to Avon, about fifteen minutes from Elyria. Tom had made plans for us to stay with his sister Arlene and her husband, Kurt Tabar. Tom also had scheduled interviews with his cousin, Pam Haynes, who was to help us with a history of the Waters family; Robert Vecchio, one of his lawyers; and a former neighbor of the Rimmers who was providing Vecchio information for Tom's lawsuit. We were also hoping to meet with one of Tom's aunts and, if we had time, to squeeze in other interviews, perhaps with Cathy Ives or maybe even Jeanne Rimmer. Carl, whom we believed was in Saugerties, New York, was actually in town, but we wouldn't learn that until after we left.

Tom was excited about the trip, and not solely because of the project. There were two additional reasons. It was the first time in a year he would see all his sisters together, and he was about to become an uncle again. Arlene, Patty, and Darlene were all pregnant. Arlene was expecting her first child in December; Patty was expecting her second in March, and Dee was expecting her third the same month. But the trip was also causing Tom anxiety. His plans to stay with Arlene had re-ignited a long-standing sibling rivalry. When he visited Elyria, he explained as we drove to Avon, he had to avoid causing dissension among his sisters. It was understood that he might feel closer to Patty because of the years they spent together in the Rimmer household—they were former POWs who had survived an extraordinary experience. But he did not want this special bond with Patty to make Arlene and Dee jealous. So he always tried to compensate. And because he had stayed with Arlene on a previous visit, he would have to execute a bit of shuttle diplomacy this time to keep everyone happy.

As soon as we arrived at the Tabars', he called Patty and Dee to tell them he would see them on Sunday. We settled in for a leisurely Saturday with Arlene and Kurt, who lived in a home with big bay windows on a narrow road that stretched for a few miles. Across from the Tabars' home and extending the length of the road was an undeveloped field of tangled growth and brush. On their side of the road was a line of one-story homes with manicured lawns in front and back. The Tabars had set up a sleeping area for Tom and me in an upstairs alcove they used for their TV room. I was living in Manhattan then, and I told them that a similar home in New York would be considered a palace. Throughout our stay, the Tabars treated us royally.

Arlene, I was surprised to learn, did not look exactly like Dee. Fraternal twins, they had similar features that clearly identified them as sisters, but Arlene had dark hair and deeper blue eyes and her voice was a tad raspier than Dee's. Until a few weeks before we arrived, Arlene had worked part time at the service station her husband managed, and also at a second job in Elyria. She had dropped the second job because she was nearing her due date. While Arlene prepared a sump-

tuous steak dinner, Tom, Kurt, and I downed beer, talked about plans for the trip, and watched television.

The next day I learned that Sunday was an occasion for a Sabbatarian observation as solemn as any church ritual. Tom and the Tabars were all acolytes of the Cleveland Browns—and so were the LeMaires and Patty and her boyfriend. Again, I settled in front of the TV with Tom, Arlene, and Kurt. We were joined by Kurt's father and a friend. Together, we were all one with the fans in the Cleveland stadium, and I waited for an epic battle to unfold on the TV screen.

The Browns were playing the Kansas City Chiefs in what was billed as a grudge match between Cleveland and its former coach, Marty Schottenheimer, the Chiefs' head coach. In the first quarter, the Browns stymied the Chiefs' Christian Okoye, the league-leading rusher, and knocked the Chiefs' starting quarterback out of commission, but there was no epic confrontation. It was a sparring match, and both sides made mistakes. The first quarter was scoreless. Spirits in the Tabar home were more tempered at the start of the second, which turned out to be as nondescript as the first. A fumble fouled a Browns scoring opportunity, but, with less than a minute remaining, the Browns intercepted a pass that helped them to score a forty-yard field goal. They led 3–0 at the end of the half.

As the two teams rushed off the field, Tom and I said good-bye and raced to our rented car. The end of the first half signaled the next stage of Tom's shuttle diplomacy, which required him to watch the second half at Dee's home. Tom was anxious to see his sisters, but he also didn't want to miss the opening play of the next half. We arrived with time to spare. Dee, exuberant about seeing her brother, gave him a big hug. Michael LeMaire, tall and lanky, with a scruffy beard, greeted Tom in a jocular manner. I settled into a comfortable chair as if I had been a regular Sunday visitor.

Dee was in better shape than she had been when I had

talked to her in Vermont, and on this occasion she was playing NFL hostess to all the visitors who wandered in and out in a neighborly way. The LeMaires' modest one-story home on Elyria's west side was packed. While Michael and some neighbors lamented the Browns' poor offense, Kyle and Danny played with friends. When the game resumed, all attention focused on the TV. Tom and Michael bantered, addressing the TV as well as each other. In the third quarter, after a Browns player muffed a handoff—prompting groans and cries of exasperation in the room—the Chiefs recovered three yards from the goal line and went in for their only touchdown. The Browns later scored on a one-yard plunge, and that caused some sighs of relief, but there was no gridiron joy in the LeMaires' living room.

During the fourth quarter, Patty arrived and expressed her unhappiness that her brother was not staying with her and Buck. Tom left his spot near the TV to smooth things over. Dee would later pull me aside to explain that she and her sisters did not see Tom as much as they wanted, and when he came to town they all liked to "make a big fuss" over him.

The Chiefs scored a field goal in the fourth quarter and the Browns, angling for what the fans in the room said was field goal position, fumbled at the 39 yard line. They ended in a 10–10 tie. The overtime play was not much different from the action during regulation time. The Browns fumbled on their first possession and the Chiefs' field goal kicker— the second best field goal kicker in NFL history—missed from 45 yards out but got a second chance because of an offside penalty and missed from 39 yards. I thought the tie was better than a loss, but the fans in the LeMaire living room did not agree.

Later, Arlene and Kurt showed up, Dee turned on the stereo, and the evening became a pleasant one that was part homecoming celebration and part family reunion.

The next day Tom and I were in an upbeat mood when we drove to downtown Cleveland to meet with his attorney, Robert Vecchio. It was an opportunity for Tom to check on the disposition of his case and to introduce me to the lawyer whose firm was Vecchio and Schulz. Robert Catz, Tom's other attorney, had reduced his role in the suit because he had been involved in defending Alcee Hastings, a federal judge in Florida fighting congressional efforts to impeach him. Hastings had been acquitted of bribery and conspiracy charges in a trial, but Congress was more sanguinary. Hastings was impeached in October. I had talked to Catz several times on the phone, and though I knew of the impeachment proceedings, I was surprised he was not as involved in Tom's case as I had been led to believe. Catz had assured me of his and Vecchio's cooperation in the case, and though they still consulted, Vecchio was doing almost all the legal work. I wanted to know how much information he intended to provide about the strategy for Tom's suit. Although he was to supply me with more depositions and records, I was in the dark about the legal maneuverings as well as the strengths and weaknesses of the case. In the Elyria newspaper, the *Chronicle-Telegram*, Vecchio was quoted as saying that Tom's suit could be a landmark case in Ohio because there appeared to be no record of a negligence suit being filed by someone who had been under the care of a child care agency.

For the first forty minutes, after we shook hands, Vecchio and I made no eye contact. He looked directly at Tom and talked exclusively to him. He was, I concluded after several minutes, deliberately ignoring me. I jotted down notes as he and Tom talked. I thought Tom's inquiries reflected a good working understanding of the litigation, and in Vecchio's presence he exuded a maturity and confidence I hadn't previously witnessed. And Vecchio didn't patronize him.

One of the attorneys originally representing Lorain County, Vecchio said, had been replaced by a new law firm.

There could be at least five attorneys working to defend the county. Vecchio expected that serious negotiations for a settlement probably would occur near the start of the trial. But no trial date had been scheduled, and both sides were still preparing their cases. Vecchio himself was still looking for witnesses. Although Children Services was under a court order to turn over all its records regarding Tom, Vecchio wondered aloud if all pertinent materials had been given him. For example, newspaper, TV, and radio accounts of the lawsuit had reported that a woman had contacted Children Services after she learned that Carl had become a foster father and described how he had sexually abused her young son. That information should have been written up in a report, which should have been included in the records turned over to Vecchio. But there was no such report in the material turned over to Vecchio because of the court order.

Vecchio also talked to Tom about potential settlements. It was the first time, I learned later, that he mentioned a settlement sum to Tom. Although the lawsuit asked for $5 million, Vecchio discussed the possibility of a settlement figure of about $500,000, and Tom became visibly subdued. Vecchio also mentioned various payment plans. If both sides reached a settlement, Tom would not get a lump sum payment. He could get a chunk up front and the rest would be paid over a period of time. Tom became even more quiet, and it was obvious that he was hearing news he had not anticipated. Then came my big surprise. During their conversation, Vecchio admitted he was not happy about Tom working on a book before the case had been settled and speculated that Tom had possibly made admissions to me that could be potentially damaging to his case. Tom was surprised. He had been led to believe he was doing the right thing, and now he learned he was engaging in an exercise that could hurt his suit.

I asked Vecchio, in that irritating way of asking someone

to repeat what had been clearly enunciated, if he was really opposed to Tom doing the book.

Catz thought it was a good idea. He didn't.

I wondered how much Vecchio's comments would compromise my working relationship with Tom. I was already concerned that Tom was withholding information from me, and there in Vecchio's office he had heard an excellent reason not to confide at all. Tom said he wanted to continue with the book, but his comment lacked zeal. I sympathized with him; I would have been worried if I were in his position. And I personally did not like the added burden of worrying about how my plans could jeopardize his $5 million lawsuit. When Vecchio and I did finally establish eye contact, he complained of reporters who were inaccurate or who reported stories in a misleading fashion. He cited examples. I listened patiently. I nodded in agreement on some points. I had been a working journalist for more than ten years and had been teaching journalism for three, so his comments weren't unfamiliar. I was stirred to argue my point that he didn't have to worry about me, but I changed my mind.

I was uncertain how I wanted to proceed. I was angry. I wanted to assess the damage to my working relationship with Tom and consider my options, but I knew whatever I decided I would have the last word. Tom and I had a signed agreement that gave me the right to a final edit of the manuscript. If Tom had not signed the agreement, I would not have worked with him. I had wanted protection in the event that his lawyers' version of the facts differed from mine. Despite the popular myth spread by the media that good lawyers want the truth and bad lawyers fabricate lies, all lawyers seek facts and manipulate them in the best interests of their clients.

I could have told Vecchio of my firsthand impression of lawyers. In my research on kids who killed their parents and kids on death row, I had come across lawyers whose unethical and unprofessional and sloppy behavior resulted in their clients getting harsher sentences than they deserved. I had been in touch with lawyers who should have been brought up on charges or at least reprimanded but weren't because their clients, who were much younger than Tom, were too naive to know their rights. I also knew of other attorneys whose behaviors, if not unethical or unprofessional, were repugnant. In a study of fourteen juveniles on death row, a team of clinical experts disclosed that lawyers representing some of the condemned inmates withheld information that their clients had been physically and sexually abused by parents and relatives because they did not want to embarrass the inmates' families. That information should have been introduced as mitigating evidence at the youths' trials.

But I understood Vecchio's concern. He was litigating a $5 million lawsuit, and his client was confiding details to a stranger, who was planning to publish them in a book, that he, the principal attorney, was not privy to. But there were other details that I thought were more pressing at the time, and I didn't want Vecchio's worries interfering with my plans. If he wanted to know what Tom was telling me, he would have to ask Tom; I wasn't planning to provide him with any information. Nevertheless, he and I agreed to some limited terms. He wanted to know everyone Tom and I interviewed. That was all right with me, but I wasn't planning to volunteer information. Vecchio would have to ask Tom or ask me about specific people. I told him I was planning to contact some of the principal defendants in the suit, such as Tom's case-workers and social workers and their supervisors. I also wanted to contact the attorneys representing the county. I didn't expect any of them to talk, but I at least wanted to contact them. Vecchio wasn't pleased with the idea but asked that we not approach the defendants until the summer. That seemed a reasonable request and I agreed. It was obvious we were to have an adversarial relationship, but we were both willing to go through the motions of being polite.

Near the end of the visit Vecchio turned over more records and depositions. Tom and I told him we planned to interview Tom's cousin, Pam Haynes, that evening. Vecchio told us she was friendly and indicated that she might be helpful. His comments sounded encouraging, but Tom and I left his office a little less upbeat than when we had entered.

8 • The demon "was a deathly alcoholic."

Tom and I drove to the home of Pamela Haynes and her husband, David, who lived on Elyria's east side. They were just putting their son and daughter to bed when we arrived, and after they kissed them good night, the four of us sat in the kitchen, where Tom and I explained what we wanted to do. Tom had told me before we arrived that he expected Pam to be a good source of information, and that she would not withhold details or deceive him, as some relatives had in the past. He had sound reasons for that belief. When Patty ran away from the Rimmers, she fled to Pam. When Patty and Arlene ran away from Green Acres, Pam helped them flee to Florida despite the legal risks she faced in assisting juvenile runaways to elude the law. Vecchio had contacted Pam, and she had agreed to cooperate with his investigation. Because her mother, Aunt Joan, was Tom senior's elder sister, and because Pam was about nine years old when Tom's mother died, we believed Pam could provide history that Tom and his sisters did not know, fill in the gaps in their accounts, guide us to other relatives who would also talk, and help us get to the root of the rumors about his mother's death.

The evening started amicably with everyone sitting around the kitchen table as Pam recalled that after Tom's

mother died, he, his father, and his three sisters had moved
into the apartment that she, her half sister, Tammy, and her
mother called home. Pam was uncertain why Tom senior,
who had still owned a house in Cleveland, moved into her
home. The oldest of the six kids, Pam became the designated
baby-sitter when Joan and Tom went to work; the kids called
her "Pam-o."

Pam couldn't recall how long the two families lived together. When conflicts erupted, Tom senior and his kids slept
in his van. Pam also recalled how Tom senior would suddenly
bundle his kids into his van and drive to Florida or Texas or
some other destination. She wasn't sure what inspired him to
leave. In Texas he stayed with his brother, Brent. During the
nonviolent moments, the girls played house and Tom, wearing
diapers, stomped around the apartment in cowboy boots,
squashing bugs. One day he smashed a six-legged critter and
his father told him that real men picked up the dead varmints
by hand and discarded them. Tom, who did not want to
disappoint his father, shuddered at the suggestion and devised
a plan that was less mannish but just as effective. He gave
Pam-o a piece of paper and asked her to get rid of the bugs.

Everyone laughed.

It was the only hearty laugh of the evening.

We asked Pam for the phone numbers of her mother and
sister, and she responded that she no longer associated with
her mother. It wasn't clear if she had the number and didn't
want to give it to us or she didn't have the number to give.
It wasn't a major setback. I believed we would get the number
from someone else, but I considered her odd response a cue
to pay more attention. Pam said she would ask Tammy for
permission to give us her number, but she said her sister
might be reluctant to talk to us. There were rumors that Tom
filed his lawsuit only because of the money, and not for some
noble cause, and for that reason, Pam implied, Tammy was
offended. Tom looked surprised but remained quiet. I won-

dered if her comment reflected some element of family intrigue. I could have told her—but I didn't—that money was not the purpose of the lawsuit and that, in all the months I knew Tom and in all my discreet and direct inquiries about his motives, we had only once discussed the issue of money. His responses were all the same: He wanted to make a statement, he wanted to help other kids.

Pam, responding to other questions, began to narrate Waters folklore. She said Tom senior and his sisters were born and raised in West Virginia and that the woman Tom and his sisters knew only as Grandma Waters, their paternal grandmother, was born Iva Beatrice Pauley. She married John Workman and had five kids by him. After Workman died, Pam said, Iva married Thomas James Waters, moved her kids into his home, and then had five kids by him: Aunt Joan, Aunt Pearl, Tom senior, Aunt May,* and Aunt Gail.* Tom learned for the first time that Brent and Tom senior were half brothers. Pam said Tom's father was Thomas James Waters II and her information implied that Tom, before he was adopted by the Rimmers, was Thomas James Waters III.

I asked her how she acquired her information, and she replied that her mother was one source and people whom she could not recall provided her with other bits of information. As she was growing up, she said, she picked up things from overhearing the conversations of adults. She suggested that Aunt Pearl would tell us more. Pam also told us she had been corresponding with a writer in West Virginia who was working on a family pedigree, and she showed us a stapled, soft-covered manuscript, *My Family Connections, Volume 1, The Pauleys.* The writer was Ruth Williams Cornell. Pam said she had been providing the writer with information for a second volume that was to include information about Tom and his sisters, but Pam had been unable to keep up the correspondence. She did not know the status of the second volume. Pam also said some names in Volume 1 were inacccurate. At one point Pam told Tom that a man named Guy French was Iva's father and, by implication, that he was Tom's great-grandfather. And Tom, after looking through the book, said that French married a woman named Jane Mullens. She, Tom concluded, was his great-grandmother.

As the four of us took turns examining the book, Pam told Tom that his aunts opposed his adoption because they did not "want to lose" a male Waters, even though Tom senior had two sons by another marriage. Tom responded that he was planning to change his name back to Thomas James Waters. That surprised me. He had never mentioned that decision to me, but Pam appeared engrossed in her recollection of the crisis created by the adoption and apparently did not hear him. She continued her criticism, telling him that she and Aunt Pearl had planned to rendezvous with Tom senior at the courthouse, where they were to oppose the adoption, but Tom senior, who had been released from prison, never appeared. Pam added that she recalled telling Tom outside the courtroom not to go through with the adoption. She sounded as if she believed Tom wanted to be adopted. He could have told her that he opposed the ceremony even as he told a judge he agreed to it. But he didn't. He was tiring of explaining his actions. He was constantly reminded that relatives and friends could not comprehend what he had endured or understand why he couldn't provide them with simplistic explanations that might have satisfied their curiosity.

The four of us had started bantering about the book when I asked Pam what she recalled of Tom senior. I had already interviewed his children, and I was merely hoping to recheck some facts in a roundabout way.

"Uncle Tommy was my best uncle. He was my favorite uncle. Until Tom's mother died, my uncle was the greatest. He was the apple of my eye," Pam responded merrily.

I was surprised. Tom bore physical scars, each a reminder

of his four years of life with the apple of her eye. And the best that Tom senior's daughters could say about him was that sometimes when he wasn't drunk he didn't beat them, or that when he was on the wagon occasionally he cooked for them, or for a birthday someone once got a trinket for her ear instead of a foot in the face. But I was willing to consider the possibility that alcohol and his wife's death fueled Tom senior's rages and that he had been a decent, compassionate person before his madness took over. I, however, wanted proof. I hadn't forgotten how Dee described her mother fighting to protect her daughters from him before she died. But Tom and I didn't interrupt Pam. We were there to learn, not to argue.

"Uncle Tommy would come and I'd run to him just like a father. Tom's mother died of"—she paused briefly before adding—"I would appreciate one thing before I go any further."

I cringed. I was concerned that she was about to say she wanted to talk off the record. And I was relieved when she said she wanted us to promise not to reveal to Aunt Pearl or Aunt Joan, two people we wanted to interview, that she had talked to us. She worried she would be harassed by relatives for revealing family secrets. Once the information was published, she said, she didn't care that they knew. Tom and I agreed to her request, but Pam did not impress me as someone who could be easily harassed. She was plainspoken and an ingratiating hostess who made sure that my coffee cup stayed filled and that Tom did not run out of Coke, but there was an unmistakable tone of authority about her. She was taller than Tom and a good size wider. But, then, I realized, we were talking about family matters, and I knew formidable men and women who were still intimidated by their folks.

Pam's comments about Tom's mother, information she said she got from her mother, were blunt. "She came to my mother and she told my mother that she was pregnant and she knew that it was not Tom senior's baby. Now it could've been Tom senior's baby, but she thought, no, it wasn't Tom senior's baby because she was messing around with her boss. And she wanted an abortion. Back then, abortion was illegal. And the only way that abortions could happen was if they happen in back alleys. My mother got a hold of the person about the abortion and they gave this medicine to my mother and my mother gave it to Pat. And she was too far along to have an abortion by syringe, so they administered a quinine pill to kill the fetus, but what happened, it killed her."

Pam told us, without providing details, that Tom senior "thought that he killed her, but he did not kill her. She was pregnant. And it wasn't his baby."

I again asked Pam how she got her information.

"This was what I was told by my mother, by conversations and everything," she said. "What happened was Pat told Tom this night, the night that she died: 'I am pregnant and it is not your child.' Well, what does a man do and what did Tom do? He turned around and he smacked her. And then he got up to change the TV station and when he turned around she was blue and he thought he had killed her. But he didn't. He thought the initial smack killed her, but that wasn't what killed her. The abortion effect killed her. She had a heart attack caused by this. On the death certificate, it should probably read heart attack, and she was pregnant with a fetus. I don't know exactly if it would say on the death certificate that they found this drug in her body, but I know about my mother talking about it."

Pam continued. After Tom senior left the hospital where his wife was pronounced dead, he returned to Joan's house and tried to kill himself. He cut his wrists. He was taken to a hospital and released. Later—she wasn't clear how much time had passed—he tried to kill himself again by stepping in front of a speeding truck, but his two sons by his earlier marriage, David and Michael, restrained him. Tom senior wanted to die because he believed he had caused his wife's death, but Pam insisted that he was not responsible, that the quinine caused complications that killed Patricia Waters.

Thoughts flashed through my mind.

Dee's copy of the death certificate noted that Patricia Waters died of natural causes. It contained no information about a drug contributing to her death. An autopsy would have been performed if there were allegations of a suspicious death, but according to the Children Services records Tom's lawyers sent me, no autopsy was performed. Tom and I would have to learn why one was not performed. I had not known that Tom's mother had been pregnant with a fifth child nor had I known of the allegations that Tom senior was not the father. I didn't know if Tom was learning this information for the first time or if he had decided not to tell me, but I wished he wasn't there at the table. It appeared that we had turned a corner in our quest for information and that we might have to wade through rumors and various other apocrypha. What we were to learn would have to be sorted and corroborated before we could distinguish fact from fiction, and there were no guarantees that we could. That time-consuming process could be painful for someone who knew little about his mother or his family and who might have to sift through all manner of deceptions before arriving at the truth, which could be just as distressing as the fabrications. Truth is no protection against pain.

I asked Pam when Tom senior started drinking heavily, because she seemed so certain that the violence started after his wife's death.

"A little party here, a little party there just to drink and this and that but I never seen my uncle violent; I never seen my uncle drinking, you know, this way or that way; never seen him until after she died. Then he just didn't care, he didn't care about his appearance; he didn't care about his children's appearance; he did not care, he just wanted to die.

The man went to prison for the rape of his children and he
didn't care. He did not fight it at all. He said, 'I don't know
if I raped those girls or not because when I'm drunk I don't
know what I'm doing. I could have.' There was not sufficient
evidence to put him behind bars, but he would not fight it.

"All they found on Arlene was this mark that big on her
vagina," said Pam, using a finger and thumb to indicate an
inch, "and the doctor even said she could have scratched
herself or anything like that. That's the only thing they found.
They never could find anything and, you know, if a man would
sexually abuse a little girl, you know, that there would be
blood and everything. There was no evidence whatsoever.
He was shanghaied, is what I'm saying. I'm not saying that he
did not abuse those girls. I'm not saying that. He could have
sexually abused them by oral sex. Okay? But what the authorities went on was sex-sex. They didn't go by anything
else."

Pam was correct on some accounts and wrong on others,
according to records I received from Tom's lawyers. She was
right that there was no conclusive evidence of rape but wrong
about him being convicted of rape. He had pled guilty in a
plea-bargain arrangement to carnal knowledge of his daughters, a minor felony. And her comments about him being
"shanghaied" reflected not the impartial findings of an investigation but the biased sentiments of relatives. According to
the records, relatives interviewed by the police believed he
was innocent. The naysayers who denounced Dee and Arlene
as "lying little bitches" and the court that tapped him with
a light sentence could not have considered the years of beatings and neglect and emotional terror that were to leave an
indelible mark on his kids. Tom senior spent five years in jail,
but the kids' suffering had continued long after Tom senior
was released on parole. I thought he got a light sentence.

I also couldn't understand Pam's sentiments. When she
said Tom's mother was "messing around" with her boss, I

couldn't determine if she was speaking plainly about infidelity as something that occurred or expressing scorn for something she considered immoral, or both. She also seemed to be implying that Tom senior shouldn't have gone to jail or that he received a stiffer sentence than he deserved. I wasn't sure if she was dispassionately but forcefully parroting what she was told or expressing what she believed. I knew that if I was having difficulty understanding her sentiments, Tom, who had originally suggested interviewing her because he believed she was an ally, was probably having more problems. And just when I was about to conclude that she shared the sentiments of the naysayers, she segued almost immediately into a description of Tom senior as "the uncle that I learned to hate."

Pam explained that after Tom senior was taken into custody, she and Iva gave statements to the police that Arlene and Darlene, as much as a year before their father was arrested, had told them he was sexually abusing them. According to the records, Pam told the police that she told her mother's boyfriend, and he supposedly made an anonymous call to the Oberlin police, but there was no record of such a call. It wasn't clear what Iva did after the kids revealed the violence. Even though Iva gave the police a statement about what the kids said, she expressed disbelief that her son sexually abused his daughters. But Pam and Iva eventually earned the enmity of relatives who learned of their incriminating statements to the police.

"The day my grandmother was laid out in a casket at the funeral home, I was downstairs smoking a cigarette," Pam said, "and Tom senior told me, 'I didn't get my chance to stick the knife in her, but I will live to see the day that I can stick the knife in you.' So, I don't associate with a lot of my family. I am scared in a lot of ways."

She reiterated her fear that she would be harassed if we prematurely disclosed her as a source of information. She had been labeled a traitor for revealing family secrets in the past. For example, she said, her relatives became upset when she informed Tom senior's two sons, Michael and Dave, about their father's arrest and incarceration. The relatives had told them he was traveling around the country. Pam's disclosure brought reprisals in the form of harsh phone calls, causing her periods of painful anxiety. She bit her nails until they bled; and she stopped eating, becoming too weak and sick to work. The situation also triggered crying jags and flashbacks.

Flashbacks to what? I asked.

Her mother, she said, terrified her more than Tom senior. "She's a demon person. You understand what I'm saying? She can be happy-go-lucky right now, and then," Pam said, snapping her finger, "just turn on you like that. You don't know what's going to flare up. She can think of what Tommy did, oh, maybe, breaking something of hers when he was four years old and just go right after him right now and beat the hell out of him."

The demon, she said, was "a deathly alcoholic."

She recalled a day when she was seven and her mother took her and Tammy, who was about eighteen months old, to the Harvard-Denison Bridge, where Aunt Joan had planned for them to die as a family. Her mother told her to jump, that she would toss Tammy, and then she would follow them down. No one died because her mother's boyfriend spotted them on the bridge and interrupted the plan. That episode ended without bloodshed. Others didn't.

"She had beaten me and beaten me and beaten me and done everything she possibly could to me—sexually abused me, mentally abused me in every way that she could possibly—to where I didn't care anymore. I didn't care if I went to school, I didn't care about nothing," Pam said, as her voice weakened and tears formed in her reddened eyes.

In her early teens, Pam frequently ran away from home. She also guzzled alcohol and abused drugs, flying high on some narcotics and crashing on others. She also flirted with suicide. One day when her mother attacked Tammy, Pam summoned enough will to punch her out. Aunt Joan called the police, who arrived to find Pam uninjured and Joan with a black eye. I thought Pam was about to say she was taken into custody but it was unclear what happened after the police arrived—whether Pam was arrested or removed from the house—because facts, events, and allegations poured out of her in a confusing medley. She talked about her sister Tammy being locked in a room while a hallway was being set afire; of a semiautomatic gun being pulled on her grandmother; about beatings she took to shield her sister and cousins from harm; of a stepfather raping his stepdaughter and the child born of that incestuous union.

Pam was skipping helter-skelter through what I believed were the most painful and confusing episodes of her life. Tom sat almost motionless at the table. David, who had hardly uttered a word that evening, had quietly moved to a nearby couch where he thumbed through the Cornell manual. Except for my occasional questions, Pam was the only one talking.

By her own account, relatives, teachers, and neighbors denied the family violence, and she stayed in trouble at school, at home, in the streets. She eventually was placed in the custody of the Cuyahoga County foster care system and ended up living with her grandmother. When her mother persuaded the authorities to return her home, Pam convinced the authorities that if they removed her from her grandmother's custody, she would kill herself.

That threat they believed, she said.

Pam linked her brief comments about her experiences in foster care in Cuyahoga County with her cousins being taken into custody by Lorain County Children Services. She was blunt about Tom and Patty being placed with the Rimmers and Arlene and Darlene being put with another family.

"See, Jeannie and Carl didn't want the two other girls. They just wanted a boy and girl who were young enough to where they could raise them the way they wanted to raise them. The two older girls had already had knowledge; they had already been corrupted. They didn't want nothing to do with them. Tommy and Patty hadn't been touched. That's the reason why the Rimmers wanted them."

The family—Iva, Aunt Joan, Aunt Pearl, Tom senior—did not want the kids in foster homes, Pam said. Some Children Services records corroborated Pam's accounts. Iva tried to get custody, but Children Services decided that she was too old. And Aunts Pearl and Joan had expressed an interest, but Children Services ruled against them as well—Aunt Joan because the agency didn't believe she could provide a stable home life and Aunt Pearl because she was too close to Aunt Joan.

I knew her comments about Arlene and Darlene being "corrupted" sliced through Tom like a sharp blade. I assumed she was repeating gossip discussed among Tom senior's relatives. I also believed it was significant for Tom to learn that Tom senior's relatives tried to keep him and his sisters out of foster care, though I couldn't fail to recognize the bitter irony that he and his sisters would have lived in jeopardy if they had been placed with Tom senior's relatives. Just as Pam finished her comments, Tom bolted from the table in anger. He joined David on the couch, where together they perused the Cornell manual. Pam and I continued, as if we hadn't noticed how upset Tom was. I didn't want to stop her from talking.

I questioned her again about Tom senior, and Pam insisted again that he was not violent or a heavy drinker until after his wife died. I asked her what she knew about his father, and she said her mother had described him as an alcoholic and that he beat all the kids and sexually abused his daughters.

What about Iva? I asked.

He had beaten her too, and the violence frequently drove her from home. Pam didn't know if she stayed with friends or relatives, but when she fled she sometimes took her youngest daughters, May and Gail, with her. One day she and the two kids left permanently and ended up in Ohio. The other kids followed when they were old enough to leave or run away from home. But they never forgave her for leaving them with their father. Pam said Joan was the first to leave and that at some point, Joan and the other Waters kids ended up living in a house on West Forty-seventh Street in Cleveland. Pam offered little information about that period. She was not sure how old her mother and the others were when they arrived, nor could she provide a time frame. Marriages and other circumstances caused people to move, but Pam was not sure of any details, not even how family members arrived in Lorain County. She did say, however, that Joan's hatred for her mother continued until Iva died in 1980. "The day my grandmother died she was the most hurt person there at the wake," Pam said. Iva's husband also died in Ohio in 1978, but Pam didn't know where.

When I asked about Brent, Tom senior's half brother, Pam insisted he did not like being around the family because of their heavy drinking. Brent drank occasionally. If he got drunk, he got sick. And she insisted that he was not violent like Tom senior. Then I told her what Patty had told me about her confrontation with his gun in Florida.

"Oh, yeah. You know why? I'll tell you what his violence was. He wants things done his way. He was like my grandmother. Brent was exactly like my grandmother was, very strong-headed. And when he came in and if the house wasn't clean, you're gonna get a butt-whipping. And he didn't beat you. He spanked you. I know, I got many a spanking. That man never hurt me except to give me a spanking. My uncle Brent was a very good man. Now, what he did with those girls down there was to put 'em in line. I can tell you some of the things that the girls put me through when they came to stay with me."

Patty and Arlene, when they were still living in Green Acres, were allowed weekend furloughs with Pam. They were required to be in by 10:00 P.M. Pam, trying to be flexible, set a midnight curfew; however, the girls, being typical teenagers, frequently violated it, and if Arlene had been drinking, she would grow cantankerous. She once accused Pam of being insincere, saying that the only reason she wanted them to visit was so that they could baby-sit or help with household chores. Pam and Arlene argued a lot. One day they clashed after Arlene soiled her couch.

"From that day forward, Arlene and I have not been close. From that day forward, the kids and I, we haven't communicated too much," Pam said.

An unexpected event, in December 1987, put them back in touch. On that day, Pam had been watching the evening news on Cleveland's Channel 8 as she was eating dinner. She had no sooner taken a bite of food than she saw Tom on the screen. He was discussing his lawsuit. Pam said she became upset that she had never been told of his plan to sue and that she had had to learn about it as a viewer and not as the privileged member of an extended family. She was upset, but not enough to stop her from agreeing to help Vecchio.

As Tom sat on the couch, Pam inquired circumspectly if he had sued Lorain County just to get money, as the rumors intimated. She also wanted to know why he hadn't sued Carl or filed charges against him. She listened intently as I briefly explained Tom's rationales. My explanations evoked something from her I hadn't expected. Empathy. She understood Tom's ambivalence about his adoptive father.

Her mother raised her to hate but Iva taught her to love, and by living with Iva and believing in God, Pam found meaning in her life. She lived with Iva until it became obvious that she was about to die of cancer and Iva's suffering compelled her to move into her own apartment. But on the weekends she stayed with Iva. A few months before Iva died, Pam met David. Their early years together were marked by struggles. Public assistance, food stamps, and odd jobs provided a little sustenance, and when those became inadequate she and her husband relied on venison from his hunting trips. Life became so harsh at one point that an employee at the county welfare office told Pam, when she was pregnant with her first child, that she was too far along to have an abortion but she should consider putting her baby up for adoption. They didn't and pulled through. After the birth of their second child, they were able to buy a home, she said, without offering any details.

I asked Pam again about Tom senior's drinking. I told her that even though she said Tom senior didn't become violent until after his wife died, Darlene recalled him beating her mother before her death.

"Oh, yeah," Pam replied. "He would hit her because she was known as a wharf rat."

A wharf rat is someone who frequents wharves, but I knew Pam's usage implied something else and I wished again that Tom wasn't present as I asked her to explain what she meant.

"A whore," Pam replied.

I didn't know if she was talking about prostitution or promiscuity.

"She was a wharf rat in Cleveland?" I asked.

"In Cleveland. And she would not hide it. She would tell Tom senior that to make him jealous: Ha, ha, ha—I went to bed with this one, or ha, ha, I went to bed with that one. And he was hurt so he'd hit her."

I asked her how she knew Patricia was a "wharf rat" who mocked Tom senior with her alleged affairs.

"This was just the conversations that was going on during the family and stuff."

"And you would hear them?" I asked, suspicious that she was implying that she knew more than she could have.

"Yeah. I'd be over there and he would tie her up to the bed; he would tie her hands to the bed, and her legs to the bed and lock her in the room so she wouldn't go nowhere while he went to work as a chemist. Like, I'd go over and spend the night when my mother worked and he'd take me and my sister home that morning, but before he left, he would tie her to the bed. And she'd pee in the bed all day."

Pam segued to another topic as Tom returned to the table.

"See, it was told many a time, so many times to the family that he did not—that he was not Tom senior's son, that he was Brent's son," she said, suddenly indicating she was referring to Tom.

Tom, incredulous, replied, "That I was Brent's son?"

"Yeah, it was told," she said as she gave Tom a hug and touched his knee.

Pam believed that Tom's mother was unfaithful and that her unborn child was not Tom senior's. And now she was telling us that Tom was not Tom senior's child. Did she really believe that too? If I had just walked into the room I would have believed Pam's hug was an expression of affection. But I had been sitting in her kitchen for three hours, and she was not expressing affection. I could not make sense of what I was witnessing. Tom looked helpless. And Pam eventually explained the reasoning in the Waters family: Tom as a baby didn't have much of a butt, and Brent as an adult didn't have much of a butt; Patricia "messed around." Those three elements had convinced family members that Brent and Tom's mother had an affair and that Tom was the result. Pam, as she had several times during the evening, refused to identify her sources.

I asked Pam how Tom senior and his wife had met.

"Uncle Tommy had a boat, and he would take the boat down and dock it and his mother would be down there all the time looking for rides on a boat from any guy, and then that's how they met," she said. "That's how the word 'wharf rat' came about."

"Was he aware of her reputation? Didn't he care? Or did he just fall in love with her and it didn't matter?" I asked.

"She was a beautiful woman, and that's what he fell in love with, and he fell in love with something that his wife— he was married at the time—could not give him," Pam replied. "The wife that he had would not go on the boat with him, would not do the fun things that he wanted to do. Pat would. Pat would go out on the boat. Pat would do that and everything. Pat was a good woman, but, see, everybody has skeletons in their closets. When I said that my uncle was a kind person before, what I meant was he never showed his violence, but he did it behind closed doors. You know what I'm saying?"

I nodded yes but I was perplexed and irritated.

"So, he was violent before she died," I said.

"After she died, he just got really worse," Pam said.

9 • "What we remember is what we remember."

*T*he next morning a cloudless sky and brilliant sunlight made me imagine it was pleasantly warm outside. I was experiencing the visceral joy of a summer day on a frigid morning in late November, and I felt schizoid. I have wondered ever since growing up in Chicago, where winter days can be dazzlingly bright and brutally cold, if anyone else has ever been tormented by that hoax of perception and feeling. Just once I wanted to overpower that reality with the force of my imagination, and force frigid cold to fade away as soon as I walk outside.

I was recalling that wish—to make a bad day better—as I stared out the front bay window of the Tabars' home in the late morning and reflected on the meetings with Vecchio and Pam. I had tossed and turned all night, and when I awoke I felt as if I had spent the previous day walking into ambushes. I assumed Tom felt worse. He must have been smarting from his lawyer's caveats about confiding in me and from Pam's comments that *the family* considered his mother a whore. We had driven back to the Tabars' home in virtual silence, and we went to bed almost as soon as we arrived, even though I knew we should have rehashed Pam's interview as soon as we walked through the door. But I had not been able to engage Tom in conversation on the car trip back and we were both tired. I decided to wait until the morning to learn how he felt and how much he wanted to discuss.

I was also upset that I had allowed Pam's blunt statements to affect my assessment of her. It was important for me to remain impartial as I helped Tom search for the truth about his family and his mother, but I had gotten angry and, worse, had expressed it. Without taking the time I needed to reflect, I had joined Tom in a postmortem denunciation of her as soon as we got into our car outside her home. Tom, however, was entitled to his anger. He had heard harsh descriptions of his sisters and the mother he could hardly remember, and he could not defend them. Pam's information, as spurious as some of it appeared and as harsh as all of it sounded, was too valuable for us to risk offending her. Tom also had to listen to her question his motives for filing the lawsuit—as if it would have been unfair or unthinkable of him to seek revenge or money for what he had suffered.

I was considering going to Cleveland to get a copy of Patricia Waters's death certificate to try to learn why no autopsy had been performed. Dee had a copy of the information, but I was hesitant about asking her to let me see it again. I didn't want anyone to know what I was doing until I sorted through the information I obtained. I didn't want Tom caught off guard by any more bad information.

About noon, Tom and I were in the living room where we were discussing plans for another interview that evening. I was trying to think of a way to open up the conversation about the previous night when Arlene joined us, and he gave her a watered-down version of the meeting with Pam. Tom chose his words carefully because he didn't want to hurt his sister's feelings, but Arlene recoiled as if she had been poked in a wound that hadn't healed.

"So, she doesn't think he did anything to us," Arlene said with resignation about Pam and Tom senior. "The whole family doesn't think he did anything."

Tom reacted as if he too had been poked but he was more concerned about Arlene.

"Arlene, don't get upset about this stuff that she's saying because you know like I do that if we weren't being abused, number one, he wouldn't have gone to jail," Tom said. "Number two, what we remember is what we remember. That stuff really happened. Regardless of what his damn family says. That's number two. Number three, we got taken away from him obviously because he wasn't a good father. They had to have found him doing something wrong in order to throw him in jail."

As they talked, I recalled what Dee had told me months earlier, and though I believed her, I had not appreciated its significance until Tom and Arlene started talking about *the family.* Tom senior's kids still bore the burdens of guilt and shame dumped irresponsibly on them by *the family,* which, I learned from Tom and Arlene's heated discussion, referred to Aunt Pearl or Aunt Joan, individually and collectively. It could also include Tom senior under certain circumstances. *The family* always insisted that Tom senior was a good father and that Tom and his sisters were too young to remember accurately their lives with him, or it argued that they lacked the insight to understand the grief that affected his behavior. Tom senior, and by implication other family members, were blameless for what happened to the Waters kids, who for years had tried to reconcile vivid memories of their childhoods with *the family's* insistence that their memories were wrong. *The family's* arguments became less persuasive as Tom and his sisters got older, but their caustic opinions were effective at blunting criticism of Tom senior.

As Tom talked to Arlene and began to repeat what Pam had said, he spontaneously opened up. I joined in the conversation and the three of us talked for about thirty minutes. When the discussion wound down, and Tom and Arlene went into the kitchen, I overheard her asking him why I hadn't interviewed her. Patty, Dee, and Tom had told me that she did not like talking about the past, and so I hadn't asked her, but it became apparent that she had changed her mind. Thus, I interviewed her while Tom stayed in the kitchen. He remained at a distance but did not leave as he had when I interviewed Dee. Arlene told me that Dee was considered the oldest because she was born first. I told her that Grandma Waters's first name was Iva, and Arlene repeated what Dee and Tom had said about their paternal grandmother being cruel to them. Arlene, like Dee, was not upset when she died. I told her about Pam's reverence for Iva, and she remarked that Tammy, Pam's sister, also revered Iva. Why Iva's largess was not extended to Tom and his sisters, I thought, would probably remain a mystery. After a few more cursory questions, I asked Arlene to talk about her mother. Much of what she recalled I had already learned from Dee, but Arlene put her own spin on that history and added information that I had not known. Neither Dee nor Patty had told me about the guns Tom senior kept in the house. Arlene speculated that the weapons played a significant role in her mother's life: "That's probably why she was petrified of him, too. He had a whole case of just guns, shotguns; he used to collect them. She probably thought he was gonna shoot her."

Arlene grew up in Dee's shadow: "Even though we were the same age, she was all overpowering over me, too. She was probably more mature. She matured faster than me. Of course, she always got to go to school more. My dad would always keep me at home."

I had been told that Tom and Patty were too young to attend school when the four kids lived with their father and that Tom senior occasionally allowed the two oldest to go to school, but Arlene insisted that Dee was allowed to attend school more often than she was and that she was more often forced to take care of Tom senior. She also described the kids' horrific visits to Aunt Joan, again insisting she suffered more than they did. Tom, she recalled, was the favorite, and I heard him chuckling in the background as Arlene, in a fawning voice, described how their aunts doted on him. She also recalled the Christmas party where she, with Darlene egging her on, told Jeanne Rimmer that Tom senior used them for sex.

"We didn't want him to really get in trouble, we just wanted it to quit, to stop and we were afraid that he was gonna probably beat us too because he always said: 'If you ever tell I'll kill you, I will kill you.' We wanted our dad to be with us, 'cause, I don't know, you always have this, Your dad can beat the hell out of you and you would still love him."

She did not like her first foster home. The foster parents put pepper on her thumb to keep her from sucking on it, and Arlene was very sensitive to criticism from them even though she regarded the adults and their kids as a clan of aliens. Their son, who was in his early teens, frequently tried to fondle her and Dee. Children Services eventually placed them with the Hafners after Arlene started throwing temper tantrums.

"Dee told Oma [Franziska] right away, the first night: 'Oh, I love you, I want to stay here.' I had a real bad attitude, I mean, just towards life in general. I was just like, Let's stick together, us four. I didn't trust anybody. I didn't want to have nothing to do with anybody because I didn't trust 'em. I mean, Oma was a nice lady and everything, but I wasn't real secure with them at first."

But the Hafners lavished her with enough love to help her overcome her fear of them. At Westwood Junior High School on Adelbert Street in Elyria, she and Dee went their separate ways.

"She was into school and doing homework and hanging around people in the theater. Dee would dress up every day and wear dresses and fix her hair different."

Arlene preferred blue jeans and a denim jacket and she did not like hanging out with "the Goody Two-Shoes." She was more comfortable with the school outcasts, the group of kids who brazenly used drugs and drank booze. One day her best friend's boyfriend accused her of being a coward because she wouldn't smoke marijuana. She smoked a joint to convince the others that she was not afraid. Later, she had to convince them she was not afraid of LSD. Other challenges followed. She met each one head-on like a real trooper. Because she was so good at deception, she concealed her drinking and drug abuse from the Hafners.

What about the teachers?

"The teachers did not care then. I'd be right in school tripping, just tripping, totally tripping. They wouldn't catch on. I never got busted. And I mean, me and a whole group of girls would be on it. It wasn't like I was the only one. I'd bum quarters all day in school until the break—you get a break at eleven or twelve to go outside and smoke a cigarette—and that's where you bought your drugs. Right outside."

She talked about the summer she and her sisters ran away from their foster homes and described how she and Patty eventually made their way to Florida, where they stayed with Tom senior. Initially it was fun because they could drink as much as they wanted. But the living arrangement began to falter. Tom senior started drinking heavily. One time Arlene and Patty had to sign Tom senior into a "detox" unit. His heavy drinking caused him to recall their mother. And he also started propositioning her and Patty. One time he took her with him in a van; they were gone for two nights. He told her he wanted to have sex with her.

"And I don't know why I wasn't afraid of him. Maybe, because I was older and I thought that I could defend myself better or whatever. So he said, 'Well, if you don't do it, I'm gonna go off and you're not gonna see me no more; and I'm gonna go out and kill myself.' And I cried, I was just like, I'm sorry you're so sick that you have to do that, but if you have to kill yourself, fine, because there is no way that I'm gonna sleep with you. I cried and bawled, I didn't understand why he was doing this to me."

She said he denied sexually abusing her and Dee when they were kids, but then started asking her "to do it one more time" for him.

Arlene was explaining how she and Patty eventually returned to Ohio when Patty walked in and sat down. It was about 2:30 P.M. Tom, who had stayed at a safe distance, eventually joined us. But Arlene and I were the only two talking. Arlene, continuing with her account, said she and Patty were returned to Green Acres. She eventually moved into a group home and then later, when she was eighteen, into her own apartment. She worked at a restaurant near Kurt's service station. One day they met in a bar. He asked her out; she refused. Later, she relented. That had been five years ago. They married in 1988, and she was expecting their first child at any time.

What happened to the drug and alcohol problem? I asked.

"Kurt was the one who got me out of it. He's the one who changed me. He, really, really, really helped me," she said. "I really don't drink anymore. I mean, holidays I'll have a couple of drinks, but not like, Let's go get a bottle and get trashed, because for a long time he wouldn't buy any alcohol. He quit drinking himself just so it wouldn't be around me."

He also persuaded her to stop smoking pot: "He thought that I was like addicted to it and I had to show him that I could quit without needing it, which I don't smoke it now. But I'll have to see after the baby. I know he's not gonna allow it, and maybe I won't want to do it but then who knows? Who knows?"

After I finished interviewing Arlene, Tom and I recapitulated for Patty what Pam had told us. That triggered an intense discussion about the day their mother died. I hadn't planned on a group interview with Tom and his sisters because I had been warned of the potentially dangerous consequences if they started collectively reliving traumatic episodes from their childhoods. But the group discussion happened spontaneously when Patty revealed that their maternal grandmother, Joyce Schwab, told her that her mother died after drinking from a can of Coca-Cola poisoned by Tom senior. Patty's comment started everyone talking at once. Tom and Arlene and Patty tried to recall what they had been told and compare that information with what they were now hearing from each other. I told Patty that Pam said her mother died of a complication caused by her taking quinine to abort her fifth child. Patty became upset that her mother would want an abortion, but I told her the information hadn't been verified yet. Under my questioning—because I wanted to know their sources of information—Patty and Arlene tried to recall which grandparent, aunt, or uncle told them about their mother's death. I could see, judging from Tom's reactions, that he was learning some information for the first time. Arlene insisted that Joyce Schwab demanded an autopsy, and I told them that according to Children Services records no autopsy was done. Arlene insisted that one had been conducted.

I asked them who was in the house the day their mother died.

"Us kids," Patty said.

"Us kids and my dad and mom," Arlene said. "My dad called the neighbors—I remember exactly. My dad called the neighbors. He wanted somebody to watch us four kids so he could go to the hospital."

I asked Arlene if she recalled that happening or if someone told her about that day. I was hoping that another adult besides their mother and father had been in the house. I couldn't be certain how much Arlene actually recalled; she had been only about five years old at the time.

"I remember this," Arlene insisted. "So, that lady, I remember her going, Oh, you poor children; oh, you've lost your mother."

"And all I remember," Patty added about the day, "is people telling me that they lifted up her arm, and it dropped; they lifted up her arm and it dropped; they lifted up her arm and it dropped; and Dad was freaking out. He was saying, 'I can still hear her heartbeat, I can still hear her heartbeat.' And they're like, 'Sorry, sir, but she's dead.'"

I told them I wanted to take another look at Dee's copy of her mother's death certificate and then go to Cleveland to inquire why there was no autopsy. I couldn't imagine one not being performed on a woman who was physically abused by her husband over a period of time and then died suddenly of a heart attack. Tom asked his sisters if they remembered the name of the hospital where his mother was taken. He was planning to phone and ask for any records about her death. They didn't. I thought that too much time had passed for us to get any information over the telephone, and I told him that I thought that autopsies had to be performed in a morgue by a medical examiner or coroner. Tom insisted that we contact Dee so that we could take another look at her copy of her mother's death certificate. Patty phoned, but Dee was too upset to talk. Her son, Daniel, had a mysterious swelling on his neck and she was waiting for an important phone call and didn't want us tying up the line.

It was about 3:30 P.M. and I felt it was safe to say that Tom and I would have to go to Cleveland and get our own copy and then make an inquiry about the autopsy. But I really didn't want Tom along. I wanted to check any available information before he saw it. I thought it was too late for us to go.

Tom didn't see it that way.

"I want to do that now," he said. "This is all driving me nuts."

I told him the city offices probably closed at 4:00 P.M. and that we wouldn't make it through rush hour. He still wanted to try.

I told him I didn't know how to get to city hall. He said he did. I gave up and we raced for the car. This time I was the one driving like a madman.

The copy of the death certificate indicated that an autopsy had been performed. We had overlooked that information when Dee showed us her copy in August. We then raced to the Cuyahoga County Coroner's Office, which we discovered was on the campus of Case Western Reserve University. We arrived a few minutes before closing. The autopsy report, signed by S. R. Gerber, contained six pages. The cause of death, of course, was listed as acute interstitial myocarditis, etiology undetermined. We glossed over the technical and anatomic descriptions that we didn't understand and focused on the information that made sense to us. Patricia Waters died when she was six and a half months pregnant. Her upper teeth were missing. Information listed under the heading "Marks and Wounds" revealed the following: recent contusions on her head and left knee; a tiny scratch on her left jaw; healing contusions on her right wrist and right leg; and scars on her chest, abdomen, left breast, and extremities. Under the heading "External Evidence of Injury," information, numbered 1 to 14, indicated scars and discolorations, ranging in size from three eighths of an inch to four and three-fourths inches. The wounds were on her breasts, chest, areas of her abdomen, wrists, ankles, legs, and jaw. A chemistry lab report indicated nothing unusual. We tried to compare the scars on her body with the information we had learned about her mistreatment when she was living with Tom senior. The contusions on her right wrist and right leg could have resulted from her being tied to the bed. We were at a loss about her missing upper teeth. Could he have beaten her so badly that he knocked out the upper ones and missed the lower ones?

It was sobering information, and it didn't help us to understand any better why her death was ruled natural.

We both realized that we were not being scientific, and we knew some of our assumptions were possibly inaccurate, but we believed we had corroborated what we had been told. Tom insisted that we talk to S. R. Gerber, but I wanted some time to study the autopsy report and consult with another expert before I started asking questions. But Tom was insistent, and he went to a desk and asked if he could speak to Gerber. We were told he had died a few years earlier. As soon as I noticed Tom's disappointment, I saw my opening and convinced him to leave. We could have asked to talk to the present coroner, or asked to talk to someone else and explain our mission, but I didn't want to do that then. When we got into the car, I told Tom I planned to consult with a forensic specialist.

We returned just in time to visit Candy,* one of Tom's former girlfriends, and her mother, a former neighbor of the Rimmers who was providing Vecchio valuable information for Tom's lawsuit.

10 • "Victims of circumstances"

Candy was Tom's sweetheart when he was in the sixth and seventh grades at Keystone Middle School in Grafton. She was a year older and a grade ahead of him.

"At the time, Tommy was Mr. Popularity and Mr. Jock and it was kind of like he was the top kid in the school. All the girls wanted to be Tommy Waters's girlfriend," Candy recalled effusively as her mother, Tom, and I sat with her at a dining table in her mother's home in Wellington.

Carl, of course, did not know that Candy and Tom were going steady, and Candy did not understand why Tom concealed their relationship from his father, but she never made it an issue. Carl was aware, however, that Candy and Patty were inseparable friends, but that didn't cause him much concern—at least not in the beginning. Patty frequently spent the night at Candy's home, and the girls attended the same seventh- and eighth-grade classes, twirled batons in local parades, and, on summer weekends, roller-skated. They also got into mischief, sometimes in school, sometimes outside. One day they sneaked up on the house of a man whom they considered the neighborhood grouch and strewed ribbons of tissue paper about his garden.

"We were always trying to put something over on somebody, but we never did anything bad," Candy explained.

They were pranksters but not malicious, Candy's mother, Laura,* told me, in the event that I considered her daughter and her friends to be bad kids. She conceded, however, that they "made me a little nervous, sometimes. I mean, I never knew what they were up to. They seemed to be restless, but they enjoyed each other's company tremendously. They were always laughing but you never knew what about."

Candy and Tom smirked at the recollection, hinting of secrets shared and a camaraderie that would be revealed that night only in the sudden flicker of a smile or the quick exchange of a glance. They were trying to be discreet and it was obvious to me that it was taking some effort. Tom and I were there to interview Candy's mother, who had agreed to assist Tom in his lawsuit even though she had only met him a few times when he lived in the neighborhood. She was obviously uncomfortable about the interview and spoke guardedly. Laura was born in Lorain and had "probably" lived in Elyria twenty-four years before moving ten years ago to Wellington, an upscale neighborhood of lavish homes and affluent residents who were virtual strangers to one another.

"The people here don't neighbor a whole lot," Laura said. "Since I've lived here I've probably seen this neighbor lady across the street maybe a half a dozen times up close to talk to her. You just never see her except mowing the lawn in the summertime, and at the time when we lived out here I was probably the only wife that was staying at home because the ladies on both sides of me, you know, they worked. So, they were gone all day. And people just didn't neighbor out here."

Laura declined to give her age. She was married and told me I could describe her as a housewife. She had a younger son who was in the fifth grade. We did not talk about her husband or what he did for a living. Her cautious manner allowed her daughter to seize the moment. Candy was living in her own apartment, raising a son and wrestling with the aftermath of a difficult divorce. She was studying to be a surgical nurse. Candy obviously still had a crush on Tom, and his presence inspired her. She grabbed the center of attention by recalling events that occurred over a nine-month period about eight years before. Some episodes from that period were of special concern to Vecchio and had caused him to contact Laura. But that night Candy emphasized her role in the events, and her candor encouraged Laura to add details and share perceptions. Together, the mother and daughter gave shape and substance to a Grand Guignol drama eight years earlier.

"It's like things that you do sometime come back and smack you in the face," Laura would say later.

It started like this.

One day in the summer of 1980, Laura and a friend, Carol, were sitting at the picnic table on the lawn of Laura's home when Carl drove into the driveway to drop Candy off at her home. Jeanne and Patty were inside the car. Carol recognized the driver and passengers and grabbed Laura's arm.

"And she goes," Laura recalled, " 'Laura, do you know who Candy's with?' And I said, 'Yeah, she's with the Rimmers.' And she said, 'Do you remember Cathy Waters?' "

Carol reminded Laura that they had worked with Cathy at a company that made medical equipment. There was more. Carol, Cathy, and Cathy's sister, Jeanne Rimmer, had been childhood friends in Oberlin. Carol reminded Laura that Cathy was married to Tom Waters, Sr., when he was arrested on charges of sexually abusing his two older daughters. Laura was stunned when Carol explained that her friendship with Jeanne ended when a mutual friend of theirs, Gwenda Adams,* accused Carl of molesting her son.

Carol and Gwenda ended their friendship with Jeanne, Laura said, because Jeanne defended Carl when they confronted him about molesting Gwenda's son. Laura could not recall details of the allegation, but the knowledge of the contretemps created a conflict for her. She worried about her daughter being around Carl, but she also didn't want to mis-judge him for what she was willing to believe could have been a one-time mistake. She resolved her dilemma by with-holding harsh judgment of him, but warning her daughter to be careful. She also asked Candy not to tell Patty.

Candy agreed. But the next day she told Patty.

Patty was incredulous and accused her friend of lying. Then Patty, because she wanted to know the truth, confronted Jeanne and asked her if she knew Carol and Gwenda.

"My mother's jaw dropped to the floor," Tom recalled.

Jeanne told Carl, who, Tom added, "went absolutely nuts. I mean, he went into a frenzy."

Carl vehemently denied he did anything and railed against Laura and Candy. Jeanne called Laura and told her that Candy and Patty could no longer be friends. Nevertheless, the brou-haha quieted down, and Candy and Patty were allowed to see each other, though not as much as they wanted.

One day in October of that same year Candy and Patty and two friends, Marie* and Gertrude,* were spending the night at Marie's home. "It was the night before my birthday," Candy recalled. "I remember Marie had this beanbag chair in her bedroom, and she went over to this beanbag chair and unzipped it and pulled out a little box of rubbers, and she said, 'My dad bought these for me.' She said, 'And he told me to hide them in my room. It's getting to a point, Candy, when he comes home, I'm hiding and he's coming looking for me.' "

That same night Marie's father accosted Patty when she was alone briefly in another part of the house. The next day Candy told her mother. Laura called Children Services, which investigated the complaint. Marie's father eventually left the home, and her mother surprised Laura by thanking her for doing what she wouldn't do herself.

That resolution to an unhappy affair apparently prompted Patty to tell Candy that Carl had molested her. Candy told her mom. Laura didn't call Children Services. Instead, she went to the school to talk to a counselor. She wanted custody of Tom and Patty, and she wanted to do it without fanfare. She recalled the publicity when they were removed from their natural home, and she believed they had been embarrassed by the controversy sparked by Carol's disclosures the previous summer. So, she reasoned, seeking help at school would alleviate the embarrassment that Patty and Tom might experience.

"Since I lived in the same school district, and Candy was such close friends with Tom and Patty, I thought, well, I'm not working, I'm staying home," Laura explained. "And, you know, I have a big home here. There's no reason why they can't live here with me. And, so, I thought, well, maybe, if I explain this to this guidance counselor at school, that she might give me a little bit of an edge—help me out."

Laura didn't want to adopt them, but she was willing to raise them. She told the counselor what Patty had revealed to Candy, and the school counselor's response was that Carl was unemployed at the time, and that child molestation was not uncommon in households where the father was unemployed.

"I didn't know why she said that," Laura recalled. "I didn't feel very satisfied when I left, but I hoped that I was wrong, that she would do something. She said that she would get back with me, and for me not to talk to Patty and Candy about what we had discussed. I had told her that Candy had confided in me and that I wanted her to know what was going on. I figured if anybody could help, you know, the school had to be of some help."

The counselor phoned several days later and demanded to know if Laura had discussed the situation again with either Patty or Candy. Laura hadn't.

"And I didn't feel very good when we got off the phone, and somehow, I just had the feeling that nothing, nothing was happening at all," Laura said. "So, I pondered over this, and

I felt really shaky inside. I just was really upset because, you know, here's all this going on and I know all this and I felt like my hands were tied, that this wasn't right."

What had apparently piqued the counselor's ire was a visit from Gertrude who had been with Patty, Candy, and Marie the night Marie pulled out the condoms. Sometime after Patty had confided in Candy, Gertrude told Candy that her father had been sexually abusing her for years and, aware of the Children Services rescue of Marie, told the guidance counselor. The counselor didn't believe her and called Patty and Candy into her office.

They were told, Candy recalled, that "we was liars and to quit saying these things and that we were all starting to make up stories. She told us, 'You guys are spreading lies; you guys just want to all be included in this and that's why you're making up the lies.' And that's just how she told us, and Patty came out of the office and she's like, Have they pulled you in yet? I said no. She said: 'They're calling us all liars. They said we're making stories up just to stick together.' "

Sometime in January or February of 1981, Laura called Children Services and reported that Carl had molested his daughter.

"The woman who answered the phone," Laura said, "was shocked to hear what I had to say. And I was very upset on the phone. She knew I was upset, but she just kept saying, 'What is your name? Who are you?' I didn't want to give out my name because I had a feeling that I was stirring up a hornet's nest over there at the Rimmers', anyway. And I just lived right in the same neighborhood, so he didn't have to have much of a reason to come over here and bang on my door—which I wouldn't have put it past him. So, I just, I said, you know, I've given you all the information you need. I've given names, an address and circumstances and some information about what I knew was going on, and I told her, all she had to do was check it out. And when I hung up I was just shaking like a leaf because I just was—weak. I knew I did the right thing, but I was frustrated. I really was because it seems like you tell these people something and they question you like you're not being truthful or something. I just get this feeling that they don't believe anything you tell 'em."

Laura was saying that she could understand why the woman would be reluctant to check out an anonymous tip when Tom, who had been sitting relaxed at the table, became incensed.

"That's not true at all," he said, and then explained what he had learned from Vecchio's investigation of his case. According to the policy of Children Services at that time, all allegations were supposed to be reported to the sheriff's department.

"Even if they don't give a name?" Laura asked.

"Any allegation," Tom replied. "Any allegation. You don't need to give your name."

The reason for his anger was obvious. If Children Services had followed policy, Tom's sentence in hell could have been reduced. And it was while he was talking that I recalled something he had said the first time we met. He had expressed scorn at suggestions that he could have told his teachers what was happening to him. At first I had thought that he was speaking hypothetically as someone who could imagine no solution to end his suffering, and so found reasons to criticize the most plausible suggestions. But at Laura's home I learned that his scorn stemmed from experience. Patty, Candy, and Gertrude had not approached a teacher but they had talked to a school counselor and she had scolded them for telling lies.

Laura said that the aftershocks of the whole affair, from Carol's revelations to Children Services' failure to act on her complaint about Carl, created problems for her family. Candy, who had been so active and carefree, stayed home and brooded, and she stopped confiding in her mother. She took the situation so seriously that Laura took Candy to a therapist.

"Candy was very vindictive that I took her to a psychologist," Laura said, "but I tried to explain to her that I needed to go, and I needed to feel that she was all right, but, somehow, at the time she felt like she was going because she had a problem, and that's not what it was all about. So, it kind of reflected on us, too; even though we weren't the victims, you know, we were still involved in all this."

As Laura spoke, Candy sat motionless and stared straight ahead with a wry smile on her face. That was one of the few moments in the night when she didn't have much to offer, other than to say that she ended up in a hospital with a respiratory infection. I imagined that the episode was still a sensitive issue with them and that Laura was addressing her daughter as much as she was talking to Tom and me.

Throughout the evening, Laura found reasons to protest what I was recording. When Tom mentioned Patty's problems with alcohol, he also recalled that she and Candy had been drunk together on some occasions, and Laura immediately asked me to turn off the recorder. I didn't. Tom and Candy, after about two hours, had started playing off each other and recalling past incidents about which she was just learning—such as the day Carl discovered several kids smoking and drinking beer in his home. Tom and Candy laughed uproariously, describing a wild chase around the house. Laura didn't think it was funny—I did.

"First thing they're going to think," Laura said, "is all the kids are bad. And these weren't bad kids, ornery, yes, but these weren't bad kids. I really didn't believe these were bad kids. There's no way. They were all victims of circumstances."

I told her I didn't believe they had been bad kids, but she insisted that I write something upbeat and optimistic about them to let people know that they were all doing constructive things with their lives. Tell them, she said, that Tom is going to college and that Candy is studying to be a nurse. Marie had been helped by Laura's intervention, but there wasn't much to say about Gertrude because no one in the room could recall what happened to her after the school counselor denounced her.

Laura also wondered why Carl never sought revenge against her, and that inquiry revealed her fear that he might still do something.

"Mom's biggest fear," Candy said, "was always, she was like, Carl's gonna do something, Carl's gonna do something. She was always fearing Carl was gonna blow up about the whole thing, and that's why she was trying her best to resolve the situation but not give her name out because she was scared to death of Carl."

"Well," Laura said, "I thought he'd drive by here sometime and, maybe, you know, shoot through my window or something. I just didn't trust him."

Their responses prompted Tom to talk. He started off by telling her that Carl would be too ashamed to come to Ohio, where he might be recognized. "And I know him well enough to know that he can be the biggest jerk in the world, but he would never go to the extreme to hunt someone down to hurt them. He's a very impulsive person. He won't sit down and contemplate how he is gonna get you back. He's not like that. He would not drive from New York to here to hurt anyone because that whole ride he would sit and have to think about what he was gonna do, and he's not at all a conspiring person. He was never the type of person—since I was a four-year-old child living with him—to sit me down and say, What you did was wrong, and I don't ever want to see you do it again. He didn't think things through. No, it was just grab me by the head of my hair and pound on me for a few minutes, and then afterwards tell me how sorry he was.

It was just everything he did was impulse, impulse, impulse.

"All Carl ever lived for," Tom continued, "was his reputation. I mean he acted according to the people who were
around him, and he acted the way he thought he should. And
there were times when he lost control and showed his true
side. Even around you, Candy, he acted the way he thought
would be a good way to act. And every situation he tried to
act the way he thought the situation required of him. That's
why he rarely, rarely ever went out in public. I mean, to do
social things, you know, like he went roller skating with us
one time, you know, one time. And even then he had a fit
about something."

Late in the evening, after responding to numerous questions,
Laura decided she wanted some answers. She asked Tom if
he had told anyone what was happening to him when he lived
in the neighborhood.

No one, other than trying once to tell Patty, he said.

"Is it true that you didn't want to talk about this in high
school, though, because of the embarrassment of it all?" she
asked.

"Yeah, and just the fear of it getting out," he said, giving
a simplistic explanation that did not reveal the labyrinthine
confusion of emotion and ambivalence that gripped him when
he lived with the Rimmers.

Laura said Vecchio told her that someone other than her
called Children Services about Carl, and Tom said he knew
of three or four other anonymous calls but she was the only
caller whom they were able to locate. Tom had a strong case
even though it would have been stronger if Laura had mentioned his name along with Patty, or if the other people who
called Children Services to complain about Carl could be
identified. Vecchio couldn't be certain that Children Services
had turned over all the records, as it was required to do in
accordance with a court order. Tom was reassuring, though

Children Services would probably argue that it had not been notified that he had been abused. And there were other problems: All the damage inflicted on him was inside, where no one—especially jurors—could see it. On the newscast first announcing the lawsuit, he looked just fine.

"Now, if I were a person who would go on rampages and beat the hell out of people all the time, then it would make my case so much stronger," he said. "But people can look at me now and say, Yeah, but he's normal. People look at me now and they say, Are you serious? That really happened to you? I don't believe you. I can't believe that."

Laura pressed on, "Well, then, what side effects do you live with right now?"

"I'd rather not go into that," Tom said.

"He doesn't want to get into that," I added quickly.

Then, when Laura responded apologetically, Tom changed his mind.

"It's things that most people don't see about me," he said. "I do freak out. I throw bureaus across rooms and smash cars. I put my fists through dashbaords and rip shifters out of cars when I'm mad. And I put holes through doors and walls and absolutely freak out on people just like Carl did. I don't trust people, either. That's a big problem. I mean, I cannot carry on normal relationships with people. I start getting close to people, five months down the road, I'm like, Sorry, I'll see you later. Not in so many words, but I'll start doing stuff to them that will make them leave and make them not want to talk to me anymore. That's the way I've been my whole life."

As he talked, I recalled one time in Vermont when we pulled into a service station to get gas. It was less than five minutes before 5:00 P.M. I overheard the attendant gripe to Tom about him driving in just as he was about to close up. Tom got gas and we left, and as he drove he fumed until, after about a mile, he announced his intention to return to confront the attendant. If he had been screaming or gesturing wildly or cursing, I would have figured that I was witnessing a foolish young man's bravado and blustery swaggering. But he was pensive and talked slowly and deliberately, and I knew I was witnessing smoldering rage. I convinced him to let it pass, but I wondered what would have happened if I hadn't been there.

Laura told Tom she believed he would eventually overcome his problems, but Candy challenged her. She told her mother that some people can't change no matter how hard they try.

"See, I haven't even hit the tip of the iceberg," Tom resumed. "I've been seeing this guy for four years, going on four years, a psychologist. And I have just started three months ago being honest with him. I mean I lied to this guy for years. I had him so fooled it was incredible. During the whole time I was growing up Carl portrayed an image to everyone. Patty portrayed an image to everyone. I portrayed an image to everyone, as did Jeanne. Behind those images, everything was absolutely different. I lied to everyone. I mean, I grew up manipulating people. I manipulated Carl. Okay? I manipulated him and I started manipulating everyone else, and I grew up having to portray an image to everyone about the way I was. So, I moved out and was taken out of the home and until this day, I still have trouble not portraying an image to people. Everyone portrays an image, but to me— I had never realized it—but it was an obsession. It was something that I had to do because it was the only way I knew. I mean I didn't even know that I was doing it. I didn't know I was portraying images until my psychologist told me so. But I'm just starting to learn who I really am, and what I really do like to do, what I really do like about life and what I don't like about life. I'm starting to be honest with people when they step on my foot. I tell them that I don't like it. Everyone's different, though. Some people, they go out and they murder. They beat people. They rob, steal. They commit crimes. Other people, they keep it all to themselves, and they sit there and say wait 'til they have kids—and they do it to their kids."

That prompted Laura to tell him that she lived in a foster home when she was young. "I know some of the scars some of those kids have on their hearts, and I think I grew up thinking hostile thoughts toward people. It took me a long time to also realize that there's a lot of good people out there. There is. But there is an awful lot of bad ones, too. It seems like the bad ones sometimes, you know, they get more attention. But don't think the whole world is terrible."

"Do you think that you tried a lot harder in life because you knew you had two strikes against you and a lot of people probably thought you would fail because of how you were treated?" she asked Tom.

"I really can't answer that," Tom replied. "I have no idea. That's something that I'll have to discover with my psychologist. What I do think is in terms of doing good in school, and things like that, most of that was always to please Carl. I had to do good in school or I'd get my butt kicked. Now, I don't know whether I still do good in school because I want to do good in school or whether I'm still just caught in that mode where I have to do good in school or I'll get my butt kicked. I don't know."

He added, "I know in sports, though, that I did good because I was mad. I was mad."

We all started laughing hard at his gleeful description of his reason for playing sports.

"And I'd go out on the football field and I would just crush kids because I was mad. Honestly."

Laura said that young boys who play football are taught to be intimidating, but Tom told her, "I didn't need any intimidation. I was a no-pain kid. I didn't feel it. I mean, I could just smash someone as hard as I wanted to and I would not feel it. I just went out to destroy people and, you know, it was just fun. I think that's why I kept my head together a lot 'cause I could go out and pound on people."

I asked Laura if she would get involved again if the same situation arose.

"If I had to do it over again, I wouldn't be so nice. I really wouldn't. I wouldn't keep all this to myself. I would let everyone and his parents know exactly what I thought of them; and I would've gone to Children Services sooner and gave 'em my name. I'm sorry now I was such a coward and I feel bad about it. That's exactly how I feel."

Tom and I insisted that she wasn't a coward, that she had tried her best. She had done more for him than his teachers, more than the other neighbors who had suspected that he was being abused but did nothing. She had done more than any of the people who had witnessed Carl's raging tantrums in public. She had tried to help. That was more than his adoptive mother had done.

11 • "If I take the risk, then I'll die."

We were in a buoyant mood when we drove back to the Tabars. We had conducted a long interview with a woman who not only was sympathetic but angry that she hadn't done more to help Tom eight years ago. And I noticed how he had swelled with pride when her daughter recalled Tom's popularity at Keystone. No one that night had implied that he was suing Children Services for pecuniary reasons or told him that his mother was a whore or that his plans to tell his story could damage his case. The evening went smoothly, but, as we drove from Laura's home, I wondered if Tom understood the implications of her questions near the end of the interview. Her inquiries were discreet, but it was clear she suspected that despite his accomplishments, which were significant, he was suffering more than he was willing to admit. He, however, was upbeat, and I was happy that he had talked without hesitation. His extemporaneous comments were based on some enigmatic formula that I didn't quite understand, though I recognized some aspects of it. For him to express his feelings, he had to be in the company of people who he knew respected him, and he had to perceive any questions as nonintrusive. I would continue to try for the kind of detailed, direct question-and-answer sessions I preferred, but I didn't expect those to be very successful. I also was no longer reluctant to have him participate in the interviews, though there still were no guarantees that what lay ahead of us would be as easy or productive as the night with Laura and Candy.

When we arrived at the Tabars', we learned that Aunt Pearl had called while we were gone and that Arlene had inadvertently mentioned our meeting with Pam. That caused us some concern. We had promised Pam we would not tell anyone she had talked to us. It was too late for us to call Aunt Pearl that night, but Tom contacted her the next morning. He exchanged some banter with her for a few minutes and then, as Arlene and I listened, they argued. I was impressed, and Arlene watched in amazement as Tom jawboned with the matriarch of the Waters family. Tom spoke confidently. His voice rose and fell throughout the conversation. Sometimes he laughed, as if they were sharing an inside joke. At other times he politely admonished her, and there were occasions when he recoiled, as if she was reprimanding him. She opposed what he was doing and argued that I was in search of sensational material to write. Tom denied it. She accused him of exposing the family's "dirty linen," and when he denied that, she accused him of writing the book for revenge. He argued that he had been misled and deceived about his natural family and that he was on a mission to learn the truth. He told her about the conflicting accounts of his mother's death, and when asked who misinformed him, he told her that he could not recall the sources of the allegations. But now, he continued, he had a copy of her autopsy report, which said that she died of natural causes. He used that as an example of how his mission could help him find the truth. Aunt Pearl wasn't buying it.

"I'm not trying to pressure you by any means; if you don't want to do it, you don't want to do it," he told her.

They resumed arguing.

Aunt Pearl told him that he couldn't remember as much as he thought and he assured her that he could. Their conversation got around to the day that Aunt Joan attacked Jeanne Rimmer, who had brought Tom and Patty to Aunt Pearl's house to celebrate Tom's graduation from eighth grade.

"Aunt Pearl, I remember that like it happened yesterday," Tom assured her.

But Tom learned for the first time that his mother and father weren't married. Aunt Pearl said that they had talked about it, but never got around to doing it.

After about thirty minutes Tom and Aunt Pearl agreed to some conditions. He could visit and ask questions but I was not to accompany him. Her doctor had told her that an interview would cause her too much stress. She also told him he couldn't bring a tape recorder. I told him to take a recorder and leave it in his car. After his meeting with her he should tape his recollections and impressions while they were still fresh in his mind. I also gave him a quick course on interviewing, which involves more than just asking questions. Good interviewers are also good listeners. I told him we needed as much family history as possible about her childhood in West Virginia and to save the difficult questions for the end of the interview. I also told him to tell Aunt Pearl that we knew that he had an aunt in Georgia and that he wanted to contact her. Tom had discussed some details about his mother's autopsy with Aunt Pearl, but he had left out other key ones about the description of her body. At some point in the interview, when he felt comfortable, he should confront her about the bruises on his mother's body.

Tom was anxious when he left for her home. He and his sisters regarded Aunt Pearl with respect and suspicion. She lived in a nice home, her husband had been a local politician and her two adult kids seemed to be living normal lives. Tom and his sisters had never spoken of Aunt Pearl being cruel to them, but her brother had treated Tom and his sisters abominably, and she had always acted as if their experiences with him had never happened.

As Tom left the Tabars' home, I admired his pluck. Tonight he was wearing two hats: one as a favorite nephew, the other as an investigative reporter. It would be an unpleasant and confusing task, and I did not envy him.

After more than three hours talking with his aunt, Tom got into his car and turned on the recorder. His voice was edged with resignation and fatigue: *"It was pretty weird actually. I got to talk to her about a lot of stuff she said she didn't want to talk about, not a whole lot. But, according to her, her parents never abused her, ever, nor anyone in the family. In fact, she could only remember two times that she ever got whipped by her dad. She never really said anything about her mom. She was pretty much an emotional basket case while talking about all this stuff. I can understand that. I tried to be as gentle about everything as I could. I got into areas about my mother with her. She loved my mother very much, according to her. According to her, my mother was very sweet. Again, she liked her very much, loved her.*

"She told me the story about my mother dying. She and her husband, Jake,* were over at my mom and dad's. She was over at the house the night my mother died. My mother, according to her, was extremely sick with the flu or some sort of viral infection. And Aunt Pearl offered to take her and us children over to her house and take care of her so that she could get better. My mother refused because she said that she didn't know how my father would approve of it. Aunt Pearl said that my father and my mother, according to my father, on the night that my mother died they had an argument. They were arguing, she just collapsed. She was drinking a pop. She dropped her pop. My dad thought she was goofing around. He picked her up, tried to put her up

and she fell back. Tried to sit her up again, she fell back. And she went limp. He ran out to get help, got help and then was trying to administer artificial resuscitation.

"There's a lot of things here, so, I hope I don't forget anything. Maybe this might be an aside: My Aunt Joan told my Aunt Pearl that—probably because of guilt, who knows—told my Aunt Pearl that my mother was trying to have an abortion because she was six and a half months pregnant and that she was trying to have an abortion and that my Aunt Joan had these pills that would cause her to abort. Well, she gave these pills to my mother, like I said, and she doesn't know for sure if my mother was taking them or not, but still feels very guilty and feels that those pills, if she was taking them, might have been the cause of her death.

"As far as Tom senior beating my mother or tying her up to the bed, the only thing that Aunt Pearl knows was to try and keep her home by taking the keys to the car. The situation was that they had two cars and that he took the keys to both cars. But he also had a motorcycle, and he didn't even think to take the keys to the motorcycle because she had never driven one and, so, he thought that there would be no way that she would take this motorcycle. But she did because she really wanted to and she took the motorcycle.

"That just goes to show how brave my mother was, according to my Aunt Pearl, and how stubborn she was, and to what extent she would go to do what she wanted to do, according to my Aunt Pearl. When she found out that my mother had died, she smashed a big huge window because she was so upset. She threw something through the window; she had to be sedated at a hospital just so that she could go to the hospital to be with my father."

On the tape, Tom said Aunt Pearl became "really defensive" when he asked her if she had been abused as a child.

She told him her father had hit her only twice. The first time occurred on a day when he had just finished working a double shift in a coal mine and she was annoying him because she was wearing her mother's shoes and jumping for a towel hanging over a door. He asked her to stop. When she continued, he hit her a few times with a switch. The second time he spanked her, her brothers and sisters because they were smoking, spitting, and cursing. They were spitting into the creek and saying "shit." He took each one inside and spanked him or her with kindling wood. Tom said he also asked her if she was sexually abused when she was young, and Pearl denied it and asked him how he got that impression. Tom didn't tell her that Pam was his source. He told his aunt that he'd heard that Grandma Waters would leave home and take two kids with her. Pat replied that her parents fought like other couples, and sometimes Iva did leave, taking the two youngest kids, Aunt Pearl and Aunt May. Tom persisted in questioning her about whether she was abused. He didn't accuse her of lying but told her what he believed: *"You can see why I would believe it because Aunt Joan's so ornery; she's so mean. She likes to fight and beat up on people. And, also, my father doing the things he did. I said why is this, and her answer was that Aunt Joan has had a temper that she was born with. She has a temper that she was born with and she probably always will have it. And my father, she basically said, she didn't know that any of that stuff was going on."*

Tom and Aunt Pearl also talked about the day Aunt Joan attacked Jeanne Rimmer. They were both at a celebration for Tom's graduation from eighth grade. Aunt Joan had been drinking and doing "shooters," as Pearl called them. Tom believed "shooters" were shots of straight liquor.

"There's a lot of stuff that I just can't remember. It was a good conversation. It's hard to remember everything because I heard a lot of stuff."

At one point, he inadvertently revealed that he had talked with Pam, and agreed with Aunt Pearl that Pam had an ax to grind with the family.

"And I just simply said yes, my co-author and I felt that way also.

"I don't know, this is really hard. She said that my father was a very hard worker. He was working to support two families. She said that he did not jump into the bottle, as she put it, until after my mother died. They drank but they only drank socially. I questioned her about what Pam had said to me as far as my mother being a "wharf rat" and a whore and whatnot. She said that Pam was absolutely ridiculous in saying that.

Aunt Pearl told Tom that his mother and father first met at a pier in Cleveland. Tom senior had a boat and one day he took her for a ride. She did not know at first that he was married. Aunt Pearl also accused Joyce Schwab, Tom's maternal grandmother, of not doing enough to help her daughter when she was alive and living with Tom senior. Aunt Pearl recalled an occasion when Joyce visited her daughter on Holmden Avenue. Tom's parents were upstairs cleaning a room to rent, and the house was a mess. Tom's mother, who was expected to do all the household chores, didn't have enough time to clean the downstairs because she had to help prepare the upstairs room, work at her job as a waitress, and take care of four kids. And Joyce commented, according to Tom's account from Aunt Pearl: "You would think that he could help her with some of this stuff." Aunt Pearl said she didn't say anything, but she told Tom she should have criticized Joyce and should have told her to help them if she was so concerned.

"Perhaps my grandmother is feeling a lot of guilt because she didn't help my mother out very much; she didn't help out with the kids, she didn't help out with anything. Pearl said that Joyce could have brought over a casserole

or done something to make things easier. Pearl also said that Joyce was more concerned with Linda, her youngest daughter. Pearl also said again that Tom senior did not start drinking heavily until after Tom's mother died and that Tom senior was an extremely nice man and that everyone who knew him loved him."

Pearl also told him that Tom senior poisoned himself one day when he was trying to siphon some chemicals and suffered severe stomach and chest problems, which developed into chronic ailments.

"Maybe that is truth to her because that's what he told her. To me it seems it could be that he was in the hospital trying to detox himself or something—I don't know. Right now, I'm pretty confused as to what the whole truth is. Again, I say Aunt Pearl was very shook up the whole time. On a few occasions she started to cry."

On the tape Tom said that Aunt Pearl also told him she tried to get custody of him and his sisters and that Children Services had deceived her and awarded custody to the Rimmers. She was told that it was in the best interest of the kids if they were placed in a home that would provide them with the least contact with Aunt Joan and Tom senior. And when she learned that Tom and Patty were placed with the Rimmers she became very resentful. Tom asked her if she would be willing to testify in court about that matter and she agreed.

"I don't know my Aunt Pearl that well, but she was shaking like a leaf. She had very bad shakes. Her voice quivered, and the whole subject upset her. She told me that she refused to be interviewed today because of the fact that she talked to her doctor—I take it that it was a psychologist. She told me that she had previously had a nervous breakdown and whatnot. She had talked to her doctor and another person for advice—she did not mention the name of the other person—but that they both suggested that she do not do it. Her doctor said that she shouldn't do it and that

it could lay her out again, lay her out flat—I take it meaning
a nervous breakdown. It looked pretty apparent to me that
she was pretty close to having a nervous breakdown today.
    "I do feel good about the talk we had today. There's a
lot of stuff I got from her that's in my own head. It's good
for me and my own head, but hopefully that there are other
things to be remembered, other important parts to be re-
membered, other important aspects of the conversation to
be remembered or to be recorded here during this recording.
I'll remember them later after I get some food in my belly
and I'll later record them, hopefully."

When Tom returned to the Tabars' home, he appeared a bit
melancholy, and I regretted that I hadn't been with him when
he met Aunt Pearl. I told him I wanted to debrief him while
the meeting was still fresh in his mind. I needed to know the
questions he had not asked and the areas he hadn't covered.
I asked him about her childhood in West Virgina, and he
replied that she hadn't said much about the early years of her
life, only that she and her brothers and sisters lived on a big
farm and read a lot and that they weren't "just a bunch of
hillbillies." During the meeting Aunt Pearl had asked him if
he had any desire to establish contact with Tom senior. He
told her that he neither loved nor hated his father, that he
didn't feel anything for him, that he wasn't interested in the
father-son relationship that she was intimating. Tom was honest, but I wished he hadn't made those comments, and if I
had been present I would have tried to keep her from knowing the truth. I wanted to contact Tom senior even though I
suspected he would not agree to an interview. I assumed that
Aunt Pearl would contact him, and it was hard for me to
imagine him consenting to an interview if he knew his son
was indifferent to him, that we only wanted to talk to him
because we wanted to ask questions about the death of Tom's
mother.

I asked Tom what caused Aunt Pearl to cry, and he replied that he upset her with questions about his mother, him, his sisters, and her upbringing.

"Those were some tough times, Tommy," he quoted her as saying.

Tom said he asked her if she thought his father should have gone to prison for abusing his sisters, and he quoted her as saying, "I think that if he really did what the girls said he did, and if what he did was true, yeah, he should have gone to prison."

Tom didn't believe she really felt that way. And she again accused him of trying to expose his relatives to shame. They argued heatedly at one point when she yelled that he was forcing her to relive a painful past.

"I have a right to know," he said he told her. "It was my family, it's my past, I have a right to know these things. You have the luxury of knowing your roots and where you came from and what your grandma or grandpa were all about. Whether that was all good or bad, you still have the luxury of knowing. I don't."

He also told her that he was more loyal to the Waters family than the Rimmers.

"I want to change my name back to Waters because that's my name, and I want to carry the name out," he recalled telling her. "I want to keep it going. I want my son to be Thomas James Waters the third, and his son to be the fourth and go on with the name."

Tom, of course, didn't believe her when she told him that her father didn't abuse her. She wasn't lying, he told me. In that same manner that his sister Patty denied that Carl mistreated her, Aunt Pearl denied that she had been mistreated by her father. That comparison caused Tom to segue to an issue that gnawed at him unmercifully.

"When Vecchio first talked to her," he said about Patty, "she couldn't really remember Carl ever really beating on

her, and to me that was absolutely crazy. I could spout off a
hundred times when he pounded her, times that if I recalled
them, she would remember. She got beat up more than I did.
I think she did because my dad favored me. I'm not saying
he wouldn't beat on me. For every fifty times he beat on me,
he probably beat on Patty seventy-five times, and it was over
dumber things, like—I'll never forgive him for beating on
her for that gum; I'll never forgive him; I'll never forgive him
for it."

He had told me about the "gum" incident when we first
met. I had considered it just one of the countless cruel experiences he and Patty suffered in the Rimmer household,
but as he recalled it, I realized it was one of the worst. He
was playing football when he and his friends heard loud an-
guished screams coming from his house. At first he shrugged
it off, and told his friends his family was just playing. But the
screams got louder, and he left his friends and rushed inside.

"There's my mom standing in Patty's bedroom. My dad's
on top of her, Patty, beating the fuck out of her. I mean, like,
you wouldn't believe; freaking out on her, just slamming her,
beating her."

Helpless, he could only watch.

"And she never remembered that; she didn't remember
it. I had to remind her of it."

Patty didn't sue Children Services because she worried
about hurting Carl and Jeanne, Tom said. He blamed the Rimmers, especially Carl, for Patty's panic attacks and her poor
self-esteem.

"If you knew Patty back when she was in sixth, seventh
grade, man, that girl was something else. She got straight A's;
the smartest. I mean, she was like the smartest girl in her
class. Candy was straight A's. They were both the most popular girls in the school. Patty was incredibly popular. All the
girls liked her, they all tried to hang out with her."

But Carl, Tom said in a voice pulsing with anger, regularly

criticized her as being stupid, and Patty caved in from his relentless invective. "She started believing what he was saying and then she just started saying, 'I'm not accepted; those girls don't like me 'cause I'm not pretty like they are. I'm not as smart as they are. I am stupid.' "

He watched helplessly as she began to yield, like a willow in a savage storm, to Carl's enervating methods. She befriended "the losers" of Keystone Middle School in Grafton because she believed she was a loser. Tom conceded that her friends, too, probably had severe family problems that made them outcasts, but he was more concerned about Patty.

"A couple of years ago she was having what she would call these incredible feelings. She wouldn't leave the house for two weeks. She'd stay inside, scared to go anywhere; hiding in a corner somewhere. She can't go out of state. She can't go too far from home. She'll eat at McDonald's—you listen to this: And she'll examine her food. Okay? And she'll start just picking little pieces and flicking, putting them aside. And I'm like, Why do you do that, Patty? And she says, 'I look at that piece and something just gets in my head, like it's poisonous, and I better take it off or else I'll die. I'll say, 'Why don't you tell yourself it's not poisonous and eat it and take the risk?' And she says, 'I can't, if I take the risk, then I'll die.' "

People suffering from panic disorders can appear bizarre. I was about to tell Tom that when he surprised me by admitting that he too suffered from such attacks, which almost paralyzed him but weren't as severe as Patty's attacks. Unlike her, he made himself attend classes and hold a job. But like her—he didn't have to tell me—he concealed the pain so that no one would know.

12 • "A lot of me is bummed out."

On Thanksgiving Day, we drove back to the Cleveland airport. Tom was returning to Vermont and I was flying to Chicago to visit my parents. We both needed a rest. He needed it most. His spirits had soared and plunged with each innuendo and allegation, as if he were on an extraordinary expedition that required him to swim in a turbulent sea of tsunamic waves. He was too smart to ignore Vecchio's warning and too committed to stop what had been started. His discussion with Aunt Pearl had left him feeling somber and confused, and he hadn't ignored her caveat about the consequences of unlocking the doors of the Waters's family closet. He was still angry at Pam for calling his mother a "wharf rat," but I assumed he understood that she was probably parroting the family line. However, Pam's comments, like so many others he had heard on the trip, stung, and the few pleasant hours with Laura and Candy and his three sisters and their families were not antidotes for his pain. And too much had occurred during our stay in Lorain County for him to have had time to reflect on everything he had learned.

The trip, nonetheless, had been revelatory for me, not just for what I had learned, but also in how the scope of the project was expanding. Because of all the unanswered questions about Tom's family, it was obvious our task was about to become more demanding.

We, of course, were going to Florida. We had some information about his father's family but not much about his mother's folks, and we needed to know more about his mother. Our plans tentatively required Tom to set up interviews with Joyce Schwab, his maternal grandmother, and her daughter, Linda. They lived in Palm Bay, Florida, about ninety miles from Orlando. Based on what he had said about them, I wasn't expecting any extraordinary angst for him, but, then, he hadn't expected a grueling meeting with Pam. There was no way of knowing what to expect. We would also have to try to locate Tom senior, and just the thought of hunting for him was enough to make us both anxious.

At the airport, I suggested again that he reconsider his role in the face-to-face talks. It wasn't necessary, I said, for him to participate in every interview. I, of course, wanted him along. Tom was the catalyst. People talked more, and he talked more, and the information flowed. Moreover, it was easier keeping him abreast of what I was doing when he was with me, and that, in turn, helped us to learn to trust each other. He did not have to worry about me withholding information, and I had better insight into how he was feeling and what he was thinking. But I knew he was carrying a heavy burden, and he had to decide how much he could handle.

I was pleased that his plane left first. I didn't want him sitting alone in the airport, comparing himself with all the travelers who were rushing home to Thanksgiving meals.

I was feeling more protective of Tom, and wondered if I was reliving my previous role as a foster parent, trying to get it "right" this time. Certainly Tom and I were developing what some would consider an unusual relationship: an abused white youth struggling for his identity with a black journalist as his advocate. A few days later we talked on the phone and he said he wanted to go to Florida. He talked as if he had found an elixir that had restored his spirits. And that, unfortunately, set him up for the next wave of bad news. When I returned to New York from Chicago a few days later, Tom phoned and said Carl had been arrested and extradited to Elyria, where he was being held in the Lorain County jail. Carl had been incarcerated on November 11; he had written to Jeanne, who called Patty, who contacted her brother. Tom felt guilty.

"He spent two years working to get degrees and advance himself and now, boom, he's gone." Tom sighed. "I didn't think he would get an indictment. I thought it was a show. Now, it's really real. Half of me feels he committed a crime so he should do the time. A person like that deserves to go to jail. I feel I shouldn't be feeling sorry for him. He's a grown man. But on the other hand, a lot of me is bummed out."

But a few days later, I called to check up on Tom and he was in better spirits. Patty had phoned to tell him that Carl had been released on bail and was back in Kingston and that he hadn't yet been dismissed by IBM. Tom also told me he received a letter from the office of Lorain County Prosecutor Gregory White; he became strangely subdued when I asked questions about it, so I asked for a copy. A few days later, I received a package. The letter from White's office gave the date of Carl's pretrial hearing, December 8. In the form letter with Tom's name and address at the top, one sentence read: "Your attendance at this hearing is not required; however you may attend if you so desire." Another read, "Please feel free to contact this office if you have any questions concerning this case."

I stopped snorting with amusement when I read the second page, and began to understand Tom's reticence on the phone. The underlined, three-word title of the second page read: *"Victim Impact Statement."* It inquired about "Monetary Loss," "Physical Injury Suffered," "Amount of Medical Bills," "Change in Personal Welfare," "Psychological Impact

on Victim and/or Family Members," and "Other Information."
Also with the package was an enclosure from the state's attorney's office.

"In the aftermath of violent crime often come pain, financial loss, and court proceedings that may seem impersonal
and confusing," read the first sentence on the first page of
the *Information for Crime Victims* pamphlet. "Fortunately,
you are now involved with law enforcement officials who
recognize that this difficult time is when you most need advice about your rights as a victim of violent crime. In the
weeks ahead you will be asked to assist as the charges against
the perpetrator proceed through court. You may also find
yourself in need of medical care and counseling services.
Later, you may want to obtain compensation in order to pay
your bills."

I wondered if the people responsible for sending the package knew about the lawsuit. I tried to imagine Tom's initial
reaction. The letter, statement, and pamphlet probably were
the result of an impersonal bureaucratic reflex, though it was
tempting to regard them as material for an absurdist drama.
But it also was possible that the letter, statement, and pamphlet were part of a ploy. After all, White's office was working
hand in hand with big Cleveland law firms defending the
county from Tom's lawsuit, and his office was not by any
means interested in what was best for Tom—no matter what
the pamphlet indicated. I considered calling Tom to suggest
that he fill out the impact statement and request $5 million.
But I also worried that it wasn't a good idea, that Vecchio
would object to tampering, that maybe in an attempt at satire
I might create problems. Instead of contacting Tom, I did the
next best thing. I phoned Carl. Though I suspected his attorney had warned him not to talk to anyone, I contacted
Carl on the day of the pretrial hearing. He was not required
to be present. And he, of course, told me I would have to
talk to his attorney. In the brief minutes on the phone, how-

ever, Carl moaned about his predicament. He complained that he had been led to believe that after admitting that he had abused Tom and agreeing to get therapy, as ordered by the Vermont family court, he had done everything required of him and was free to get on with his life. I wished him luck and told him I planned to keep in touch with him.

A few days later I phoned his attorney, Jack Bradley, who had an office in Lorain, the sister city of Elyria. Bradley said Carl had been indicted for rape. I was surprised. Tom had told me and others that the sexual violence committed against him involved only oral sex. Regardless of Tom's reasons for his limited disclosures, he was facing another dilemma and I wondered how he would deal with it and how I would raise the matter with him. Bradley also said he believed Carl was being used as a "scapegoat" because the county wanted to strengthen its position for Tom's civil suit. He said one of White's investigators on the case, Henry Marsico, had gotten Carl to make statements during a phone conversation. Bradley said he would try to have the statements suppressed and try to show that Carl "was tricked into this by this guy," but he wasn't certain he would succeed.

"The prosecutor knew about this in 1984. He should have prosecuted it then," said Bradley, who expected a trial date set for March or April. "Hopefully," he said, "he won't have to go to trial."

If there was no trial, that implied that Bradley somehow would manage to have the case thrown out of court or that Carl would agree to a plea bargain.

I recognized Marsico's name. He was one of the Oberlin police officers who had arrested Tom senior in 1974. Shortly after the arrest, Marsico and another police officer bought Tom and his sisters a pet dog and a Christmas tree. Dee told me she would never forget their kindness. I wondered why an Oberlin cop would be working on an investigation that wasn't in his jurisdiction, so, I called the Oberlin Police Department and learned that Marsico had recently resigned and was working as an investigator for the Lorain County Prosecutor's Office. That was interesting, I thought. Marsico was involved in Tom senior's arrest and now he had helped nail Carl. Was this just an ironic turn of events or careful planning on the part of the Lorain County Prosecutor?

Later in the month, I called Tom to make sure he received his plane tickets for our January 2 trip to Florida. He had. He also had received a birthday card from Carl. On one side, Carl scribbled a note about wanting to talk to Tom about all his problems—Carl's problems, not Tom's. Carl also wrote, "Why?" concerning Tom's reasons for his lawsuit and plans to write a book. I surmised that Carl believed that Tom had deliberately set out to get him arrested. Tom hadn't. Tom also had another bit of news: Arlene had a baby boy, Christopher, a little over six pounds. A few days later, I sent a copy of the report of the autopsy on Tom's mother to a county medical examiner's office that had agreed to help me understand the medical terminology in it. I was expecting a response by the time Tom and I returned from Florida.

Part IV
●
Florida

13 • A "cotton-pickin' redhead"

*J*oyce Schwab was working an evening shift at a Sears, Roebuck department store on May 18, 1970, when a Holmden Avenue resident phoned just about quitting time and told her that her daughter Patricia was dead.

She dropped the phone and ran to her car.

"I went down U.S. Seventy-one doing a hundred miles an hour. I got on West Twenty-fifth Street, Scranton Road, came down Scranton Road, laying on my horn. I come through the red lights—there were two of 'em—and I came around that corner on Holmden Avenue on two wheels, a hundred miles an hour, coming around a corner. And I pulled in front of that house, brakes squealing."

Her daughter's body was on the floor in the bedroom and covered with a sheet.

"And he," she said about Tom senior, "was walking around moaning, 'Oh, my Patty; oh, my darling, Patty.' I said, 'What the hell you crying for—you killed her, you son of a bitch.' And I took the sheet off. A policeman said, 'What are you doing that for?' I said, 'I want that bastard to look at her.' "

The neighbors had heard them arguing that day, Joyce said. Her daughter's body bore bruises. The Cuyahoga County Coroner's Office ruled the cause of death an interstitial myocarditis. Joyce, referring to the myocarditis, said she was told that a "heart attack" plus stress caused her daughter's death. She, however, believed Tom senior had killed her.

How?

Joyce said he worked as a chemist for a Cleveland company and that he had kept "little bottles" of chemicals in the basement of the Holmden Avenue home, "and then all of a sudden the things disappeared after she died." For Joyce, that was proof.

Poison.

The authorities had either not considered the possibility of a poisoning or hadn't detected it. That, in her eyes, was more plausible than the findings of the coroner, who ruled a natural death for her daughter, whose body bore bruises and contusions; who had been beaten and bound when she was pregnant with her fifth child; who had told her mother that her breasts and vagina had been burned with cigarettes; who had said she was forced to submit to sex on demand when Tom senior was drunk; who had died the day of a physical confrontation with her husband.

Poison.

Joyce ackowledged that her opinion would not stand up to the findings of the autopsy in the eyes of the law, but she saw Tom senior's hand in her daughter's death even if the coroner hadn't. And she indicated she wouldn't be upset if Tom and I, sitting in the kitchen of her home three days after the start of the new year, did not accept her hypothesis. Nothing, not even time, had withered her resolve. After twenty years of living in resignation with the ghost of what she considered a hideous injustice, Joyce was a little blasé at Tom's recounting of what Aunt Pearl had told him about the quinine that Aunt Joan supposedly gave his mother.

"You can't prove anything," she said.

Tom explained that we were consulting with a forensic specialist to sort through the confusion and allegations surrounding the death.

Joyce was not impressed.

She told us to do what we thought was best. She was a veteran of a great war fought almost twenty years earlier and she had lost. Several times Patricia, with eyes blackened or jaw swollen, fled with her kids to the safety of Joyce's home. And each time Tom senior beckoned, she returned to their Holmden Avenue home despite her mother's warnings. Twice, Joyce took her daughter to the authorities, but when it came time to sign the complaint, the young woman refused. Patricia, she said, was "deathly" afraid of Tom senior. When Joyce learned of her daughter's false upper teeth, she assumed Tom senior had knocked out her natural ones, even though Patricia told her she lost them in a car accident. For several years before the day she saw Patricia under a sheet on the floor of 1920 Holmden Avenue, Joyce had worried that Tom senior would kill her. And for more than two years after her daughter's death, she was swept by the swells of deep depression and manic highs. Screaming jags that struck without warning shook her as if they would never end. Just when she believed that she, too, would not survive, she was prescribed lithium. The black-and-green pills of the antidepressant helped her to cope.

"I couldn't live without 'em," Joyce said. "I was a bitch to live with. Then I thought to myself, after taking 'em for over two years, I said to myself, What the hell is this? What am I taking that for? But they kept feeding them to me, you know, kept giving 'em to me. So, I just broke myself away from them. I said, No, this isn't for me. I can't bring her back."

Tom and I had traveled to Florida to gather more information about his mother's death, and also to learn more about Patricia and her family. He was following in the footsteps of Arlene and Patty, who had fled Lorain County years earlier and come to Florida to learn for themselves the truth about their family. But their youth and naïveté worked against them, and they were roundly criticized by people who didn't understand their reasons or were insensitive to their quest. And there were some people, of course, who didn't want them to learn the truth. That, plus so much other turmoil in their lives, convinced them that it was better to forget the past and get on with their lives by doing what they believed were the socially acceptable things young women their age did. But Tom would not be hampered by age or naïveté, and he had more support than they had. The trip also held a special significance for him. He was returning to the place where he had gathered the courage to stand up to Carl.

Before he arrived, Tom had cautioned me about doing an extended interview with his grandmother. He was concerned that the questioning would wear her down, and he told me he would end the discussion at the first sign of fatigue. When Joyce and her daughter, Linda Semen, met us at the airport in Melbourne, about thirty minutes from Palm Bay, I guessed that Joyce was a spry woman in her early sixties. She walked crisply with her back straight, and she kept up a constant chatter in a gravelly voice. I quickly learned she was seventy-three and more than spry. I imagined that if I had asked her to describe herself, Joyce, a former captain in the U.S. Marine Corps Reserves, would have told me she was a lean, mean fighting machine. Tom's maternal grandmother was irascible and irreverent and pugnacious: "I'll be seventy-four this year, the twenty-fourth of September, seventy-four, and I'm thankful for every day the dear Lord gives me. I might be ornery as hell, but I'm thankful as hell." When she imagined aloud several scenarios with her killing Tom senior with a gun, I assumed she was exaggerating, but I also believed she had a gun and would not hesitate to use it. She had a sardonic sense of humor and an acerbic wit, and I could imagine that on a given day she could, if she wanted, insult every member of every race, color, creed, religion, or national origin.

Or political persuasion.

"Carter was no goddamn good—he let all the goddamn Cubans in here after that damn Castro let all his trash out of the jails," she said tartly. "Reagan was full of shit—the actor becoming a President." Roosevelt was running for his fourth term the last time she voted, she snorted with satisfaction.

One of the few persons above reproach that day was her grandson, and he basked in her warmth as if she was the Florida sun. Joyce, her husband, Fred, and Linda, thirty-four, had moved to Palm Bay some time after they buried Pat. Joyce did not like the city where she had lived for more than twenty years, but she loved her home. It was a marvelous haven, with large rooms and a den and carpeted floors. She officially retired from her last job as a waitress when she was sixty-seven.

"I got tired of the bullshit the people were handing out being a waitress," she explained. "I damn near let one guy wear his breakfast. Yeah. Howard Johnson's in Hero Beach. It wasn't my fault the way the cook was sending out the potatoes. And he says to me, he says, 'I don't like these potatoes.' I says, 'Fine, I'll take 'em back.' So, I took the whole thing back, and she gave him a new plate. I brought the new one back. And he said, 'This is the stuff that I had just returned.' I said, 'I can't say that it's true, but I saw her give you a new meal.' He said, 'Well, I don't like these potatoes.' Three times I took 'em back. And the next time I says, 'Look, I don't cook this damn thing, the cook does. You want to have something to say to her, you go ahead and say something to her.' So, my boss came, and he started hollering. I said, 'Look, you can take this job and shove it.' And I walked out. I said that son of a bitch should be glad he's not eating that breakfast on his head."

Fred worked as a security guard. His thirty-three-year-old son by another marriage drove a truck and lived farther south. Linda, who owned a home, worked at Harris Company, which built semiconductors. She was the single parent of her four-year-old daughter, Brittany. Her husband, Bernie, died in 1988 in a car accident.

Tom and I stayed at a Holiday Inn in Melbourne, about twenty minutes away. He had set up the trip so we could interview Joyce first and Linda later. We also planned to look for Tom senior, who we believed was living in Ocala, several hours north. Our plans called for us to be in Florida about a week.

Joyce, Fred, Tom, and I sat in the kitchen as Tom conducted the interview for the first hour. It was the first time he had asked questions without hesitation. He didn't have to survey the surroundings; he didn't have to be cautious. He was in a safe house with the matriarch of unconditional love. After another thirty minutes of discussion that focused on Tom senior's brutal treatment of Patricia, Fred left for work, and Tom, Joyce, and I explored the past even deeper.

Joyce's parents were born in Czechoslovakia and married after they moved to Cleveland. They came to the United States "because the streets were paved with gold," she said, responding mischievously to my question. Her father worked as a carpenter, and her parents had eleven children. The first five died, and another daughter and two more sons were born before Joyce and her twin sister, Clara, were born in 1916. Joyce said she could not recall much about why or how her first five sisters and brothers died. She and a younger brother living in Ohio were the only ones still alive when we interviewed her.

When she was young and living on Irving Street in Cleveland, she was a "cotton-pickin' redhead" who spoke fluent "Slovak," but as she got older and associated with people who communicated only in English, she became less fluent in her native language. She gave us a glowing description of her neighborhood and described her early years in broad strokes.

"It was a wonderful neighborhood, a wonderful neighborhood. Everybody knew everybody. I had a lot of friends in that neighborhood, a lot of friends."

On Sundays, she attended Holy Trinity Chruch, which was

Lutheran. "You didn't dare miss a Sunday, whether it was a snowstorm up to your rear end or not you had to go," she said.

Her father and grandmother raised her. Her mother "hated my guts" from the time she was born, and they were virtually estranged when Joyce was a teen.

Why?

"Well, I shouldn't even say anything, dear soul resting. I'm sorry, Mom, but it's the truth. Why my mother disliked me I'll never know," she said. "I was like my father. I'm like my father all the way around. Of course my twin sister was like my mother. In fact, my oldest sister was like my mother."

Joyce was in her late twenties when the man she had planned to marry was killed at Anzio during World War II. In her grief she joined the U.S. Marines and, after six weeks of basic training, was assigned to a base at East Ninth Street, Cleveland. She worked in an office for a military medical staff. She enlisted as an ingenue from Irving Street and emerged ten years later as "one solid rock of muscle" who did not flinch at the ribald pranks of her male comrades, who had delighted themselves by unsettling her when she first arrived at the base. When her enlistment was up, she joined the reserves. She also married Edward O'Reilly.

"I got pregnant on my wedding night. Nine months later came Patty; exactly nine months later," she said. "I got married January twenty-fifth. October twenty-fifth came Patty—exactly. My mother's counting the days, counting the days, and I told her, I says, 'Hey, Mom. I did not have to get married.' It was just my time you know, and I just got pregnant. And she wanted me to get rid of the child, and my doctor—oh, what the heck was his name? Roberto. Doctor Roberto, yeah. He said to me, he said, 'Joyce, you can jump off the Terminal Tower, and you'd never get rid of that child.' That's how I carried 'em, I carried 'em good."

A year after Patricia was born, Joyce and Edward divorced.

"I wasn't gonna put up with his horseshit," Joyce said, without blinking an eye. "He used to work on the railroad as a switchman, and his superiors would keep calling him at home: 'Is Irish there?' I'd say, 'Well, he went to work.' And they'd say, 'Well, he's not here.' So, I'd go on West Twenty-fifth Street and he was at Carl's bar drinking with this pig he was shacking up with, Ruth."

Ed was an alcoholic, Joyce said, and he died of cirrhosis of the liver. She was contemptuous of him but the two of them, she conceded, produced a "beautiful baby" named Patricia Joyce O'Reilly, half Irish and half Slav.

"When my dad lived on Holmden Avenue," she reminisced, "he used to take her in a stroller; take her all over the neighborhood. My dad was well liked. Not my mother, but my dad was well liked. Everybody used to talk, you know, 'What a beautiful baby.' I'd put a hat on her, and he'd have the umbrella and make sure she didn't get sunstroke. He'd always carry an umbrella, always when he took her somewhere. And she was a very good baby. I nursed her 'til she was fourteen months old. And then when I weaned her, oh, she screamed bloody murder. She bit me, and I wasn't going to nurse her anymore. Of course I was like a Guernsey cow. I'd be nursing her on this one, this one would be leaking. I could've fed fifteen kids at one time, but for, oh, six or seven months, I had problems with her."

What kind?

"She wanted my breast, and I wouldn't give it to her. I put her on the bottle. My mother: 'Why don't you feed her?' I says, 'I am not gonna feed her no more. She's not gonna be biting me'—fourteen months, shooo. I nursed Linda until she was a year old, also. But they were two different kinds. I didn't have any problems breaking Linda like I did Patty."

After she divorced Edward, she lived with her parents until she married Frank Kurtz and moved to a home on Schiller Avenue. Linda, her second girl, was born; Patricia, who was in grade school at the time, stayed with her grand-parents in the house at 1920 Holmden.

"My mother and dad both asked me if I'd leave the kid there, and I says, yeah, but I'll take care of her, you know. I paid for her clothes and everything. I saw her every day," Joyce said.

Patricia learned early to hate school and began cutting classes.

"She got mixed up with the wrong crowd there for a while. She wasn't a bad girl or anything but she was a follower in other words. She was hellbound for what everybody else wanted to do," Joyce said. "I damned near killed her one night. My mother called, she can't find Patty; Patty's not home. This was eleven o'clock. So, I went walking on Twenty-fifth and Thirty-second and all the streets with neighbors and the people she knew looking for her. And in the meantime she'd come home while I was going up and down the streets look-ing for her. I grabbed her by the neck and I start choking her. I says, 'You goddamn punk. Where do you get this idea of scaring the shit out of your grandmother? Eleven o'clock, you had no goddamn business being out this late. Your curfew was nine o'clock.' I start choking her, you know, wringing her; I really had her by the throat. If my mother wouldn't have gotten me off her, I think I would have choked her."

Patricia, thirteen at the time of that confrontation, did not have her mother's temperament. She was easygoing, not feisty.

"If she had been she wouldn't've put up with Tom Waters. She never would've put up with him," Joyce said.

Patricia was attending James Ford Rhodes High School when she dropped out. She met Tom senior at the East Ninth Street pier when she was about fifteen, but Joyce said she wasn't sure of the circumstances. Tom senior owned a speed-boat and he took Patty on rides with him. Joyce considered Tom senior a braggart. By this time, Joyce's father had died, and Patricia lived alone with her grandmother. She eventually started seeing Tom senior regularly.

Now, Tom and I were sitting in Joyce's kitchen with Pam Haynes's comments on our minds. We wanted to get to the root of the rumors about Patricia's alleged promiscuity, but we didn't want to upset Joyce or put her on the defensive, making her feel that she had to defend her daughter's honor. I wanted the truth and so did Tom, even if it would hurt him. I asked about her boyfriends instead of lovers.

"She was going with a nice Navy boy; he was in the Navy, but a nice kid, really nice kid. But of course he was on a boat, he was never around. He lived in Pennsylvania, I think. Yeah. But every time he came into town he'd see her and he'd be buying her stuff. He'd always bring her something. Never, never came to visit her without leaving her something. Then she met that joker. How? Where? I don't know."

I knew more information was needed. Tom and I would learn later from another source that Patricia might have dated the young seaman on a few occasions, but neither he nor Tom senior was her first lover.

One day, Joyce continued, she and Fred and Linda and Tom senior were at a New Year's Eve dance on the lakeshore when Fred noticed that Patricia looked a little heavier. When they were alone, Joyce asked if she was pregnant, and Patricia "hemmed and hawed, hemmed and hawed" and denied it, Joyce said. Patricia later admitted she was pregnant and when Joyce asked her what she planned to do about it, she replied, "I'm going to have it." Patricia later told her that she and Tom senior were planning to marry. Joyce told us she did not know then that he was married and had two sons. And she did not know until Tom himself told her that day in her Palm Bay home that his mother and father had never married.

Joyce's accounts lacked some details. Although it was obvious that she had despised Tom senior and objected to her daughter's relationship with him, it wasn't clear what she had done to try to discourage her underage daughter from seeing him. It also wasn't clear when Patricia and Tom senior started living in the house at 1920 Holmden. Joyce told Tom and me that her mother would have never allowed Tom senior to stay in the house while she was alive. But then, at another point in the interview, Joyce recalled that her mother had told her Patricia and Tom senior had married during a trip to West Virginia. What was clear, however, was that after Joyce's mother died, Patricia asked if she and Tom senior could buy the house and Joyce consented. Joyce agreed because it was an opportunity to keep the house in the family. She and Fred helped Tom senior and Patricia to get a second mortgage on the house.

One of the papers Joyce turned over to Tom and me was a notice from the housing office of the city of Cleveland. Tom saw the name of Tom senior's first wife on the paper and asked why she was listed as one of the owners. Joyce told him Patricia couldn't sign the deed because she was a minor.

"So," Tom said, "my father lived in this home, 1920 Holmden, when he was married?"

"Right," said Joyce, who added that she never would have lent her daughter and Tom the money if she had known Tom senior was already married. "I didn't know a damn thing about it till it came on this thing here," Joyce said about the housing notice in Tom's hands. "I didn't have the deed to the house."

The name of Tom senior's wife on the housing notice raised some questions Joyce couldn't answer. She was certain she never lived in the house, and Tom and I assumed by that time she was estranged from Tom senior. But we couldn't figure why she would sign her name to a deed to make it easier for her husband to live with another woman.

Joyce told us she could never get a straight answer from Tom senior about the deed. When she and Fred sold their home in Brunswick the bank took $10,500 from the sale to pay back the loan on the Holmden Avenue house, which had become a source of misery for its inhabitants. Its condition and Patricia's life seemed inextricably linked. After five years both were in a state of despair; one died and the other continued to decline until it was condemned. Joyce shared anecdotes typifying her daughter's life over that period. One winter day—Joyce could not recall the exact date—Patricia called Joyce at her home in Brunswick, located about twelve miles south of downtown Cleveland, where she lived with Fred and Linda. Patricia told her mother she and her four kids had been thrown out of the house. Tom was about a year old. Joyce and Fred drove to Cleveland to pick up her daughter and grandkids and then went to the Holmden Avenue house to confront Tom senior.

"And I kept ringing the doorbell. He wouldn't open that door," Joyce recalled. "I was gonna call the police, but Patty kept begging, 'Don't, please don't, Mother. Please don't, Mother.' She was deathly afraid of the guy."

Joyce, on that day, just like on other occasions, took Patricia and her kids home, and they stayed in the basement, where she and Fred had set up a kitchen, bedroom, and recreation area. But Patricia usually stayed only a day or two. One summer after she and the kids had sought sanctuary in her mother's home, Tom senior, Joyce said, drove back and forth in front of the house in Brunswick. He was screaming for Patricia to come home. She did. On other occasions, "he'd be on the phone, calling all hours until she would say, 'Mom, I'd better go back,' and I'd say, 'I think you're nuts.' I told her one time, I said, 'One of these days he's going to kill you.'"

Joyce could not recall when she first noticed her daughter's bruises, or the order in which she recognized them. One time it was a broken wrist. On another occasion, on a hot summer day when Patricia was nursing Tom, Joyce asked her why she was wearing long sleeves.

"And I told her, I said, 'Patty, what are you doing?' And that's when she told me he tied her to the bed, eagle-spread [*sic*]. And every time she opened up her mouth, he burned her with the cigarette. She had rope marks on her wrists, on her ankles, and she showed me her busts. And she said he burned her in the vagina, on the buttocks. That's why I took her to the prosecutor, and she was scared, she was scared to sign the thing. Twice. I gave up after that. I couldn't do anything without her signature. I said, 'Well, you're just wasting my time. You're not gonna do anything about it. All you do is talk. If you don't do anything about it, I can't. You can, I can't, even if he's just your common-law husband.' She says, 'He's my husband.' I said, well, whatever. Even the prosecutor said, 'Mrs. Kurtz, you can't do anything'—because I was Kurtz at that time. I said, 'I know it—what am I gonna do? She's wasting my time, coming from Brunswick all the way down to the jailhouse on Kane Avenue in Cleveland. Like I said, she was deathly scared of him—deathly, deathly afraid of him. Yet, she kept going back for more—which I'll never understand. You never hit me and expect me to come back and ask for more. Uh uh."

During this time, Joyce said, Tom and his sisters regularly looked like "ragamuffins." They wore dirty clothes with holes. The four were always filthy and it seemed that the only times they were clean occurred when Patricia brought them to Joyce's home. Joyce also spoke of spending money for pants and sweaters and shirts and shoes, but the kids never got the clothes.

"You've always been giving," Tom told her. "You used to give us stuff, I mean, big-time. I mean, just for no reason, send us clothes. Grandma, do you remember that green suit you gave me?"

She did.

"My dad took it and sold it," Tom told her.

Joyce described a pair of red velvet pants and a vest and a white shirt and red tie she bought Tom for a Christmas present.

"Snazzy, snazzy stuff," Tom said.

"They never put it on him," Joyce replied.

Tom reminded her of a "big jar of coins" that she gave him and his sisters. The coins, Joyce said, were collectors' coins. Tom told her that his dad took the coins. Joyce said she was told that the coins were put in a safe deposit box. That tidy sum, Tom told her, was spent on whiskey.

As Joyce described her grandchildren's plight, Tom pointed to some of the scars on his forehead.

"You see those marks on my face there?" Tom asked Joyce. "That's from impetigo, from being terribly dirty."

Shortly after her daughter's death, Joyce contacted the county welfare department and told child care authorities that the police suspected that Tom senior killed her daughter. The authorities awarded Joyce temporary custody of the kids. According to court papers Joyce gave us as we sat in her kitchen, she was ordered to appear before Juvenile Court Judge Angelo J. Gagliardo on May 22, 1970. When the authorities learned of the coroner's report, the kids were returned to Tom senior.

Joyce was not deterred. When she, Fred, and Linda moved to Florida, she still tried to get custody of the kids. She filed complaints and attended several hearings, but each time she showed up in court Tom senior didn't appear. He left town, taking the kids on one of his expeditions to West Virginia or Florida or Texas. Those trips, which Tom, his sisters, and Pam had believed were just sudden bouts of Tom senior's wanderlust, were actually his means of eluding a courtroom confrontation.

I asked Joyce why a warrant wasn't issued for him and she replied, "They couldn't. For some reason or another, I don't think I pressed the issue that much."

One year she showed up in court twice but Tom senior never appeared. She also drove up to Cleveland "a couple of times" and "a couple of times" she flew, but the trips began to wear her out.

"Every time we went up, I'd pull Linda out of school, so she could help me drive because that's a long haul driving," she said.

She could never get him into court so she tried negotiating with him. She wanted the kids just for the summer. He agreed. One summer, she and Linda drove up from Florida and when they arrived at the Holmden Avenue house, Tom senior told her he had changed his mind. He might have done it to spite her but it was also possible that he suspected that once Joyce got the children he would have to fight her to get them back—and he would be unable to intimidate her as he had her daughter.

After that last unsuccessful trip, Joyce felt defeated and stopped trying to get custody of the kids, though she tried to stay in touch. In 1973, Iva B. Waters, Tom senior's mother, called her with the news that Tom senior had been arrested on charges of sexually abusing Arlene and Dee. Joyce told us she wanted custody of all the kids, but it wasn't clear why she didn't get them.

On trips to the Cleveland area to see relatives or friends, she would visit her four grandchildren when they were living with their foster parents.

"They couldn't have found foster parents that were better than that," she said about the Hafners, who raised Arlene and Darlene.

She also visited Arlene and Dee when they were incarcerated in Green Acres. And it was during that part of the discussion that she complained ever so delicately about them and Patty.

When Patty and Arlene ran away from Green Acres and fled to Florida, their decision to stay with their father angered Joyce. She didn't understand their reasons for wanting to live with a man who had treated them very cruelly as kids and who she believed killed their mother. A few years later, when Patty returned for a visit, Joyce gave her money and bought her clothes, but Patty wanted to spend most of her time with some friends she had met working at a Taco Bell in Palm Bay. Joyce was so offended by what she considered Patty's lack of consideration that when Patty decided to return to Ohio, Joyce gave her a chilly farewell and refused to kiss her good-bye. Tom's sisters, Joyce lamented, had lost track of her and she did not understand why.

Tom was eloquent in their defense.

"We are so traumatized—the girls especially—are so trau-matized from everything," he said, explaining that he and his sisters didn't know whom to trust and that they couldn't always explain to people's satisfaction their behavior, which at times could appear eccentric to those who didn't under-stand the trauma they had experienced.

"We've heard so many different stories, so many different lies. We don't know what the hell is the truth," Tom contin-ued. "We never really got to know you. We never got to know our Aunt Linda. That's the number one reason why Patty and Arlene came down here to Florida to live with my dad, be-cause they didn't know him. Okay? They were older, they figured, oooh, we can defend ourselves against him. So, they came down here. The curiosity got to 'em. And now they're grown and they just say screw it. They don't want to have anything to do with any of the Waters. My Aunt Pearl says the same thing to me. I went over there—she's like, Why don't those girls ever talk? Why don't they ever come over? Like I say, they don't want anything to do with anyone— whether they've been good to 'em or bad to 'em. It's because of how mixed up we've gotten that we don't know what relationships are all about."

"They've got kids of their own now," Joyce responded. "They'll learn. They'll learn—in a hurry."

"But," Tom replied, "I fear for them because I think that, that with their kids the same thing might happen. Because they don't know what it's like to have a relationship with another adult. They have no clue. We don't have roots. I'm here looking for my roots. I want to piece things together. I'm not excusing the things that my sisters did, but I'm saying for them we don't understand what a family was all about. It's inconceivable to them and to me to know what it is to feel for a relative. I mean, we say, oh, that's our grandma and that's our aunt, but it's inconceivable to us what the realistic feeling should be.

"Like, Jeanne and Carl, I grew up with them," he said, describing how he once called their parents his grandparents. "And I said, ahhh, that's my grandma, that's my grandpa and this is the way I should feel for them. And I cried at my grandfather's wake because I was supposed to. I cried when we found out he was dead—only because I was supposed to cry, I was really supposed to feel something for him but I don't. I don't feel anything for those people. And I don't know why. Maybe that makes me a bad person."

"No," Joyce responded.

"I don't have feelings for him, I mean, if someone called up and said, look, your Grandma Ives died," Tom continued, talking about Jeanne's mother, "I would probably be hurt the most if she died because I have the most feelings for her. But I honestly do not think I would lose sleep over it. But blood with me is different. My blood is my blood, and I have feelings for them just because they are in my blood. I mean, if anything ever happened to one of my sisters, I would be absolutely crushed."

Joyce and Fred were divorced for a while but remarried after they realized life was better together. Joyce admitted, though, that she occasionally growled at him. She also relished being the grandmother who could not resist her youngest grand-daughter's every request. But in spite of her anecdotes about peace with Fred and joyful moments with Brittany, there was an unmistakable tone of melancholy in her voice. Several times during the three hours of the interview, she recalled the calamities of a six-week period in 1988. Shortly after she returned from Arlene's wedding in October, her oldest sister died in Ohio. On the day she returned from the funeral, Fred, who picked her up at the airport, told her that her son-in-law, Bernie, Linda's husband, had been killed in a car accident. A few weeks after his funeral, Joyce's twin sister died. Joyce wasn't complaining to Tom and me. She certainly wasn't asking for pity. But she talked about those episodes of unexpected death like a child awed by the enormity of events over which she had no power. She was not afraid of death but overwhelmed that it could cause her so much pain without harming a hair on her head. It was impossible for us to ignore her sadness and Tom tried to soothe her. When Joyce said her father lived to be eighty-seven, her mother eighty-nine, and her grandmother ninety-seven, Tom remarked how their longevity boded well for her. Joyce conceded his point but talked about her Palm Bay neighbors who had died and how she planned to bequeath almost everything she had to Linda. Tom and his sisters, she added, were included in her will. Tom sighed. During a moment of silence, he wished aloud that life could have been different for his family and relatives.

"Well, if Patty would've moved down there with the kids, it would've been fine, you know, with you kids," Joyce told him.

"Yeah. Everything would've been different," Tom replied. "See, I get sometimes enraged, I don't know what I want to do. I don't know whether I want to kick Carl's ass. I don't know if I want to kick Tom senior's ass. Sometimes, I just think I should kick everyone's ass."

"That's being belligerent," Joyce advised him.

Tom continued, expressing pity for Tom senior's addiction and anger for the harm Tom senior had caused. "He deserves to have his ass kicked; he deserves for me to beat his head in, and he deserves for me to beat him silly for what he did to my sisters and my mother."

Joyce warned him that violence could lead to jail. Tom joked about eluding the law if he decided to pummel Tom senior. Joyce, speaking like a sage, told him about William Bryan Cruse.

"Cruse?" Tom asked.

Our conversation drifted inexplicably to violence, as if we were three old war-horses recalling theaters of battle. Late in April 1987, Cruse used a high-powered rifle to kill six people and wound dozens of others in a shopping center not far from Joyce's home. He was on Florida's death row.

Joyce brought up Ted Bundy. Tom said he was a psychopath. I speculated about whether he had been abused as a kid. Tom recalled my descriptions of confrontations with obnoxious yuppies and thugs on New York City subways. I mentioned the time when I worried about his wanting to pummel an obnoxious service station attendant during one of my visits to Vermont. Tom talked about one of his idols, Mike Tyson, and how the heavyweight champion could "disrupt" an opponent's medulla oblongata with savage blows.

"Tyson can do it from anywhere because he's got so much power that he can disrupt your brain stem," Tom said, vividly describing how Tyson devastated opponents.

Joyce and I broke out in laughter at Tom's descriptions and that prompted Tom to laugh as loud as we were.

14 • "Body to the Morgue by Car 203"

*T*he day after we interviewed Joyce, I located the former Florida Health and Rehabilitative Services caseworker who was assigned to work with Arlene and Patty after they ran away from Ohio and came to Ocala. We talked by phone. Her first name was Sammie, and she was no longer working for the agency but she recalled her encounter with Arlene and Patty.

"They were adorable, they were real characters," she said, adding that "they were extremely angry with me" for putting them on a plane back to Ohio.

"I remember it was a very bad situation," she said about their plans for living with Tom senior. After Lorain County Children Services contacted her agency, she was sent to the house in Ocala where Tom senior lived with his half brother Brent, Brent's girlfriend, and her son. Sammie described her assignment as dealing with "an illegal placement from another state." Before foster kids can be sent to a parent in another state, she explained, a home study must be done in advance. No home study had been done because the girls had run away from Ohio, but Children Services wanted the placement done.

"There was something very bad about the situation there

and we didn't want them in the house," Sammie repeated without elaborating.

"An intake was done about the young boy who was living there," she also said without elaborating. I assumed she was referring to the son of Brent's girlfriend. Sammie told me I would have to get approval from HRS if I wanted more information from her.

That same day Tom called Dee. We had asked her before we left for Florida to contact Aunt Pearl and, without tipping her off, try to obtain Tom senior's address. We believed he was living in Ocala. But Dee had been too distracted by a family emergency to be concerned about obtaining an address for us. For several weeks, she and her husband had been fretting over a swelling in the neck of her youngest son, Daniel. She told Tom when he called that she had just learned that the swelling had been caused by an infection and Daniel was being treated with medication. There were no other complications. She apologized for not getting the number, but her family came first. So that evening I dialed directory assistance and learned of a "Thomas J. Waters" residing on Fifth Avenue in Williston, a small town about thirty miles northwest of Ocala. I told Tom. Acting on an impulse, he dialed the number, and, after a few seconds, signaled me that someone answered the phone. Tom was talking to Fern, his father's wife. She told Tom that his father usually arrived home from work about 5:00 P.M. Tom hung up without identifying himself.

We started out the next morning. It was January 5, and we wanted to arrive in Williston by about 3:00 P.M., to give us plenty of time to stake out Tom senior's home. We drove west from Melbourne and then north to the Florida Turnpike, which we took north to U.S. Interstate 75. Driving north to Ocala, we picked up Route 27 to Williston. We had planned a four-hour drive. During the early part of the trip, we made idle chatter and listened to the country music stations and amused ourselves by trying to spot an alligator in every marshy field or puddle of water we drove past. After an hour, however, we drifted into silence. We were both tense, but I knew that Tom was under more pressure. When we had met at the bar of a lounge in Newark Airport before boarding our plane to Melbourne, he admitted he was nervous because he didn't know what to expect from the trip. He had been drinking beer before I arrived, and, though not drunk, he expressed concern that he was drinking to relax. The specter of alcoholism haunted him and his sisters, and he worried that by trying to ease his nervousness he might be indulging in destructive folly.

When Linda and Joyce met us at the airport in Melbourne, and the four of us drove to Linda's house in Palm Bay, I again noticed how uncomfortable he was. Shortly after telling everyone how happy he was to be there, he said, as if making an announcement, "Well, it's time to go." Several minutes later he repeated himself. I ignored him because I wanted to stay longer and get acquainted. He repeated himself again, and at one point he looked as if he was pacing his aunt's home, and, after about forty-five minutes—and much sooner than I wanted—we excused ourselves and left. I was probably the only one who knew how anxious he was.

There were other sources of anxiety for him besides the interviews. He and Tracie were constantly bickering. They should go their separate ways, he would explain to me at one point, and then in another moment he admitted he couldn't live without her. She and her parents had been his main source of support, and he owed them so much for helping him overcome major obstacles as he worked his way through college. But his sense of debt to them did not help him get along with Tracie any better, and they quarreled regularly. She wanted him to call her every day of the trip, and let her know everything that he did. Her constant checking on him angered him, yet I noticed that he almost always made sure he called her. But I understood his dilemma. He had explained it to me when we first met. He had a problem with intimacy. He didn't want anyone to get too close to him, and he made life difficult for anyone who tried. Yet, at the same time, he wanted friends and relationships, even as he regarded such ventures with trepidation. And there were probably other concerns weighing on him that he had not discussed with me.

Except for the sound of the car engine and passing vehicles, it was a quiet trip, which lulled us into an eerie quietude that ended when we left the interstate and headed northwest on Route 27 to Williston. I could feel the tension in the car increasing. We both sat straight up in our seats, fidgeting as if we were airplane passengers bracing for a rough landing. The last time Tom met his father face-to-face, they were at a family reunion. Tom, who hadn't spoken to him in twelve years, had snubbed his father. Now, he was about to show up on his front porch with a stranger, and the two of us wanted him to talk about *the family* and Patricia O'Reilly's death twenty years ago.

About fifteen minutes outside Williston, I suggested a plan of action. When we located his father, we would knock on his door and stand close enough to it so that he couldn't shut it in our faces. We would try to convince Tom senior to talk to us. If he got violent or went for a gun, I would pounce on him. Tom, who was to hold the keys to our rented car, would dash to start the motor and be ready to speed away when I came running. On the other hand, if Tom senior invited us inside, we should make certain we kept him boxed in between us. If he got violent inside his home, I would tackle him while Tom, with the key, dashed to the car. I, of course, was playing big brother. Tom was a former high school football, soccer, and wrestling star who had enjoyed punishing opponents. He was lean, solid, and in excellent health—with a punch, I imagined, to match his temper. But I wanted to assume responsibility in the event that something happened.

If Tom senior was merely bellicose about being interviewed, we would leave once we were certain there was no way to reason with him. My what-if scenarios probably added to Tom's anxiety, but I wanted to be honest with him and at the same time be certain we were prepared for any contingency. My impressions of Tom senior were based on descriptions of him as a violent alcoholic. I had heard nothing that had suggested he had reformed.

We arrived in Williston at about 3:00 P.M. and because it was so small—it had a population of slightly more than twenty-two hundred—we decided to drive around until we came across Fifth Avenue. A few minutes after arriving we discovered that I had driven out of town. On our second pass, I drove more carefully, but we couldn't locate Fifth Avenue, and I again inadvertently drove out of town. After almost ninety minutes of futile searching, we surrendered the element of surprise. We drove back to a small store, which had a public phone, and Tom dialed Tom senior's residence to get directions. He was on the phone for a minute or so and when he got back in the car, he told me he had talked to Fern. She and Tom senior weren't living on Fifth Avenue in Williston, and she had given him directions for another thirty-minute ride that would take us to Williston Highlands, which was not on the map we had been using. Tom senior wasn't home, but Fern knew we were coming, and we sped off, hoping to arrive at their home before Tom senior did. We drove on paved roads that took us to poorly paved roads that led to unpaved roads that ran through an undeveloped area of tall trees and wild growth. We saw no houses and passed no cars. We knew that we were getting close to their home because of a few landmarks that Fern had identified for us to use as guideposts. When we came to the last one—three utility poles that together reminded us of the Crucifixion—we knew that we were close. A few minutes later we came to a clearing with a trailer home that seemed worn by age, and just outside the trailer door a woman and man stood talking. Tom immediately recognized his father and Fern.

We both took a deep breath. I swung the car around and backed into their unpaved driveway as a barking dog approached. Tom laughed. He thought I had maneuvered the car to keep the passenger side of the vehicle between me and the dog. I wanted the car in position for a quick getaway, but I never got the chance to tell Tom. Just as I stopped the car, he hopped out without waiting for me to give him the key. The dog wagged its tail as Tom petted him. And Tom, smiling broadly, walked up to Fern and Tom senior and gave them a warm greeting. As I walked up behind Tom, with my eyes fixed on Tom senior, the images in my mind clashed with the images before me. I should have remembered Dee's description of her father when she met him for the first time in twelve years at the same family reunion where Tom had last seen him. The great ogre he wasn't. He was thinner than I had imagined, and looked as if he weighed less than the jeans and work shirt he wore. He appeared frozen where he stood, like a deer mesmerized by the lights of a car bearing down on it. When we shook hands, I felt as if I were wiggling the limb of a dead man or the hand of a man who believed his past had just caught up with him. We learned later that Fern was just telling him that we had called. After a few awkward moments, he invited us inside. It was about 5:00 P.M.

Tom and I sat on a small couch. Fern sat on a chair facing us. Tom senior sat on another small couch. He was closer to his son. The couches were comfortable but worn. It wasn't as bright inside, and the home seemed cramped even for two people. A TV and a VCR next to me appeared to be relics, but I assumed they worked because of what I had been told about Tom senior's finesse as an electrician. A small air conditioner kept the heat at bay. I saw no guns.

I was tense, and I assumed that everyone else was equally

uncomfortable. But Tom, Fern, and I smiled. Quiet and subdued, Tom senior was clean-shaven and wore thick glasses.
He had light brown hair, and his white skin appeared as if it
had been broiled by the sun. Inside his home he appeared
less timid than he had been outdoors. People who ordinarily
might be hostile, I had learned from experience, will try to
be cordial if they invite me into their homes. So, I assumed
Tom senior was at least willing to listen.

We started with small talk, and Tom pulled out of his
pocket an old faded business card for T. J. Electric, a company
that Tom senior and his brother Brent had been operating
when Arlene and Patty ran away to Florida. Tom senior said
the company went out of business after his business relationship with his brother soured. Tom senior said he preferred being an employee because there were fewer
headaches for him. He was currently working as an electrician
and did contract work. He was responsible, he said, for the
wiring in numerous hotels, motels, banks, and shopping centers in Ocala, where he did most of his jobs. Fern worked
odd jobs, but Tom senior said he was trying to get her hired
by his company.

Fern and Tom senior, who had remarried a week before
Tom and I arrived, were planning to build a home on the
crest of a hill about one hundred yards away from the trailer
where they had been living since June 1989. After a few
minutes, it became apparent to everyone that it was time to
get down to business. Tom and I, with Tom doing much of
the talking, gave Tom senior a broad description of what we
were doing, and informed him that we had interviewed people who had said a great deal about him. We were in Williston
to hear his side. That struck a nerve.

"I don't care how anybody wants to stare down their nose
at me or how they want to feel or how my children want to
feel about it or anything," he said. "I did my best, under the
circumstances."

He was talking about his treatment of Tom and his sisters when they were young, but we hadn't even started that line of questioning. He continued nevertheless, telling us that he had explained that same opinion to his sister, Aunt Pearl, who, he said, a sly smile forming on his face, was supposed to arrive the next day to convince him not to talk to us.

"But you don't tell anybody I said so, and don't you tell anybody that if they go to looking for her she's supposed to be here," he said. "She doesn't want anybody to know. Evidently she maybe heard you're coming down here, and she wants to come down here to be here so that you—you know."

"I won't say anything," Tom told him.

It was obvious there was no reason for us to tell anyone what Aunt Pearl was planning. I thought Tom senior was being coy, but then, of course, Tom and I were playing coy ourselves. We might have startled him by driving up as he was talking to Fern, Tom senior hinted, but his sister had warned him that we were coming and had probably told him what Tom had discussed with her over the Thanksgiving vacation.

"The way I look at it," he continued, "I've had my problems and downfalls and I've been off alcohol now for quite a while. What I'm saying is, I have my couple beers and that's it."

"That's great," Tom responded.

"And I'm trying to get things going for me," Tom senior said about putting his life in order. And then he surprised me and, I assumed, Tom: "I don't mind anything that you want to know. What I'm saying is, I don't want no problems from Joan or Pearl or any of my brothers and sisters or anything like that. I don't want to hear their problems."

It should have been obvious, but I didn't know what he meant about "their problems" until later.

"See," Tom told his father, "I wanted to tell Aunt Pearl this, and I couldn't, but this is no joke: We all had it rough."

"Right," Tom senior agreed.

"You had it the way you had it, and I had it the way I had it, and everyone does things different," Tom said.

"But it's time to change things," Tom senior replied.

"It is, it is," Tom said excitedly, "and that's what I'm trying to do. Okay? That's what I'm trying to do. You know, my name is Waters-Rimmer. I'm having that changed back to Waters. Because when I have a son, I want my son to be named Waters. I want him to know that he is a Waters. I want to carry on my family name. That's what I was born with. I don't have the knowledge of what my roots are. Everyone wants to know where they're from, what their parents were like. And I didn't get to know that because when I was a little kid—something I can barely remember—I got taken away from my family. But I'm trying to find this stuff out for me. It all got taken away from me, but it's something I've got to know for me."

His mission, beside discovering the truth about his family, was to expose the negligent and slipshod operations of Lorain County Children Services. His explanation, which was sincere even though we both knew that we also wanted Tom senior to account for his treatment of Tom and his sisters and their mother, struck another chord. Tom senior responded about his treatment by the criminal justice system in 1973. He said it had abused him: There was no evidence that he had sexually molested his daughters.

"No one ever directly came out and said, or as a witness, said that I did what they were accusing me of. No evidence ever came out," he insisted.

He admitted to drinking heavily and awaking to discover himself fondling his daughters.

"That happened approximately two or three times, that I remember, waking up—they were in the bed," he said. "And I'm not saying I was falling over them, but I do remember a couple of times I did have one of the girls cuddled up and I was fondling her. Now, as far as anything else, what I might have did when I was in a blackout I don't have any idea about."

He had agreed to plead guilty to lesser charges, he said, because he was "scared to death" after he was told by his lawyer that his mother, Iva, "was one of the witnesses against me and the other one was Pam." He also expressed anger that he was held in the county jail for eight months because he was too poor to make bail and that no one in his family would help him raise the money. He denied that "anything" happened to Tom and Patty other than him spanking them for wetting the bed. But Arlene and Dee, he insisted, got into bed with him.

"Now, what they might remember about it, you'd have to get from them, as to what happened when I was drinking or I was high or stoned 'cause I stayed stoned for days," he said.

I had asked Arlene and Darlene what they remembered. Arlene said she was raped and that he forced her to perform oral sex. Darlene said he tried to rape her and failed because he was impotent, but he forced her to perform oral sex. That—along with the beatings and the neglect and the hunger and the squalor and the terror—went on for three years. And I did not assume that they had told me everything. Adults subjected as kids to the kind of terror they experienced can forget some episodes or refuse to speak about the ones that cause them the most shame or guilt. Tom senior, I assumed as I sat in his trailer, hadn't anticipated that I would interview them or he didn't care if I did. Tom, his son sitting next to him, had recalled being beaten after seeing his father on top of Darlene, and I had also interviewed Patty and Arlene about their trip to Florida where, according to them, he wanted Arlene to have sex with him. Those accounts, of course, were never introduced into court, but they were as informative and telling as the information I got from court records.

According to copies of the records of the Oberlin police department and the Lorain County Court of Common Pleas, Tom senior was arrested in Oberlin in December 1973, on two counts of rape. Cathy Waters, Jeanne Rimmer's sister and Tom senior's wife at the time of his arrest, signed the original criminal complaint alleging that he "did rape and ravish" his two daughters. He was indicted on the same charges, and was held on $100,000 bail bond. Medical examinations of his daughters were inconclusive as to whether they were raped. To Tom senior that probably meant there was no evidence of any sexual abuse, and that lack of corroborating medical evidence also might have added to the difficulty of getting a rape conviction. It also was a different era, and I doubted that Darlene, Arlene, Patty, and Tom would have been allowed to testify because they were so young. According to the records, which focused only on the allegations of sexual abuse, the girls told police that they also were forced to engage in oral sex. The written accounts were more graphic than the stories they told me. The girls told the police that he threatened to beat them if they didn't do what he wanted or if they ever told anyone. And there was more: Tom senior's mother, Iva, signed a statement that in July 1972, "the children told me that their father was getting drunk and making them have sex relations with him. They had told me many times before, but I just couldn't believe it was real." Pam Haynes, who was a juvenile when Tom senior was arrested, signed a similar state-ment. The only ones, according to the records, disputing the sexual abuse were Tom senior and his sisters, Joan and Pearl. Tom senior pleaded guilty to reduced charges of two counts of attempted carnal knowledge of his daughters. He was sen-tenced to one to ten years. He served five.

We were giving Tom senior a chance to tell his side of the story, and it was too early for us to know how we should respond to what he said. I also didn't know how Tom was feeling, though I was pleased that at this point he was not trying to compel his father to account for his actions. That might have caused Tom senior to stop talking. Tom was asking straightforward questions but not in an accusatory fashion.

Because Tom senior blamed alcoholism for his problems,

I asked him why he drank so much. The death of Tom's mother had driven him to drink, he replied, and he became addicted before he realized he had a problem. Then, after giving me what he apparently believed was a satisfactory reply, he directed his next comment to his son. He said that Tom was "a prime candidate" to become addicted to alcohol "because of the psychological damage that was done to him as a child. He's set up. All it takes is for something to cut his legs out from under a few times like I had and he'll turn to alcohol."

Was he referring to Tom's traumatic early years with him or his twelve years of trauma with the Rimmers? Was Tom senior, the prototypical failure as a father, merely ruminating philosophically about the problems his son faced or was he using subterfuge to express a wish that his son would fail as miserably as he had? I was suspicious and uncertain of Tom senior's motives, but Tom tried to explain, earnestly, that he knew the risks of addiction because of the problems with alcohol of his maternal and paternal families. He did not say anything about his suffering at the hands of his fathers.

Tom senior was relentless on this point, saying that his father was a "stone alcoholic," which increased the risks for Tom and his sisters. Tom responded that he believed he had a personality that could cause him to become addicted "to anything" and that he and his sisters were cautious about what they did. When Tom senior kept insisting that Arlene and Patty would succumb to alcoholism as he had, Tom, who could become irate at uncomplimentary remarks about his sisters, changed the line of questioning. He asked his father about his, Tom's, nationality.

"You're a mongrel," Tom senior replied. "A mongrel like me."

His deadpan reply surprised us, and we laughed when we realized he was joking.

"My mom," Tom said, trying again, "was Irish and Slavic. So, what are you?"

"We have German, Irish, English, and—God, I don't know

how much—Indian, even," Tom senior said. "My grandma was half Indian and French."

His grandparents, he said, were Jim and Victoria Waters, who moved to West Virginia from Kentucky.

"Tell me about what it was like for you when you were growing up, when you were a young kid. What was your dad like?" Tom asked. "When you were young, and growing up, Aunt Pearl was saying that you guys lived on a big farm. She says that your dad never, never once hit you guys."

"Ha!" Tom senior scoffed.

Tom told him that Aunt Pearl recalled one incident of them being spanked after they were caught spitting and swearing and smoking. Tom senior laughed derisively, and his son, asking most of the questions, elicited the following information. Tom senior was raised in Boone County, West Virginia. When he was about three years old, his father bought a farm and eighty-seven acres of land near the town of Wharton, which was about thirty miles south of Charleston. A mountain and huge rocks took up much of the property. A "couple of strips of land" were used for small-scale farming. The farm had a creek. He described his father as "one of the hardest-working men you ever seen, and he worked that farm and worked in the coal mines. He also cut timber on the weekends for extra income." There were ten children on the farm, five by his mother's first marriage to John Workman, who died and left her a widow, and five by Tom senior's father. Eight were still alive. Jane and Luther Workman were dead, he said.

When Tom senior was about eight, his family lost the farm because of a bizarre accident. His father "was coming home in a snowstorm back then and there was this big winding S curve like in the land and he ran into a dry cleaning plant," Tom senior recalled.

The plant owners sued, and his father, representing himself in court because he couldn't afford a lawyer, lost the lawsuit and was required to sell the farm to pay for the damages.

"That's what it is, is money talks and bullshit walks, and that's really the truth," Tom senior said, then directed a question at Tom.

"Wasn't you molested?" he asked Tom, though Tom senior knew the answer.

"Yeah," Tom replied softly.

"Is he in jail?"

Tom shook his head.

"Why?"

"I don't know," Tom replied even more softly.

"Money. If I had had the money, I wouldn't've been in jail," Tom senior reasoned aloud.

"No," Tom said meekly, his voice a whisper.

"First thing is," Tom senior said about what would have happened if he had been richer, "is the way they took you children and stuff. That would've never had happen."

Tom senior had a point. If he had been rich and influential, he could have had the best lawyers represent him and improve his chances of getting away scot-free. Rich and influential people always have better opportunities for eluding their criminal culpabilities. Tom senior had been a cruel father, and yet the best he could do years later was gripe about being poor and try to manipulate his son, whose own firsthand experience with poverty and powerlessness made him vulnerable to Tom senior's specious entreaty. As he listened, Tom's emotions were in conflict and he wasn't going to have time to sort through his confusion as we talked to his father.

I asked Tom senior to explain why Children Services took his children from him. I hoped he would say something that would reveal his unworthiness of his son's sympathy. Tom senior responded by telling us that the Rimmers had invited him to a Christmas party because of his marriage to Jeanne's sister, Cathy, who, he said, was "retarded." He told us he had married her because he needed a baby-stitter for his kids. His wife, he said, attended a special school, and from his description, I concluded she might have had some kind of a learning disability. But Tom senior insisted she was "retarded." They had met at Allen Memorial Hospital, where she worked in the cafeteria; he was a maintenance person and electrician. He had recently moved to Oberlin after roaming the country for about two years, "drinking and moving and this and that and just taking hundred-dollar-a-week jobs" to survive. I didn't mention that his children had already told me about the treks. Tom senior made it a point to say, smugly, that he also was collecting rent off two apartments in the house at 1920 Holmden as well as social security benefits because of Patricia O'Reilly's death. He had briefly tried living in Houston with his brother, Brent, but for reasons he wouldn't discuss, they didn't get along. He had moved back to Oberlin because "the board of education and some social workers" in Cleveland or Oberlin, he wasn't sure which, "threatened to take the kids away if I didn't settle down." He said he was accused of enrolling his kids in four different schools in one year. I believed he was referring to Joyce Schwab's repeated attempts to get custody of the children and the pressure that was coming from family court in Cleveland, but I didn't interrupt him.

Tom tried to tell him that he and Patty were too young to be in school during that period and that Arlene and Darlene, who were of age, rarely attended school, but Tom senior ignored him and continued with his account.

"You were in school, but they said that by me taking you in and out of school—see, four times in a year—they said by the time you kids had made friends or really got to know your teachers, I was jerking you out of school and taking and putting you in another," Tom senior explained. "And that wasn't to your best interest because you couldn't really get settled down, and you were kind of insecure."

Kind of insecure?

The experience of roaming from place to place and never knowing when he would eat and where he would sleep had so deeply affected Tom that he had been too terrified to run away from the Rimmers.

So, Tom senior continued, once he returned to Oberlin, he was spending as much as sixty dollars a week for baby-sitters.

"And, so, I sat down with some devious plan," he explained. "I mean, I took this broad because, simple reason is, trying to raise four children and work is damn difficult. And she couldn't cook or nothing like that. She was just a nervous wreck, somebody who should have been in the loony bin, really. I said to myself, they got this broad trained, and she was. I used to sit there and mess with her. I tried to keep her from doing something they had specifically trained her to do. She went to a special school and they trained her that the minute she gets through eating—she had these little dinners that she'd cooked in the oven—the minute she gets through eating that, you know, she'd get up and she'd do her dishes, like, wipe off the stove or clean her knives and forks and all this and that. And I used to try to keep her from doing it when we ate."

His description provoked laughter, not because of what he did to her but because of the malicious glee he exuded as he recalled his harassment. "I used to try to make her sit there and watch some TV or something. Boy, I'm telling you, it was just like somebody broke out in a cold sweat. Sweat went to falling off her and she'd keep trying to move toward that kitchen, you know, to make a move to do the dishes.

"I just wanted me a baby-sitter, someone to try to take the load off. I didn't just jump into this like. I had this discussion with her family and this and that. I went over to visit her apartment a couple of times. Place was spotless. And to me, I said, well this is all right. She'll watch the kids and this and that and keep the house good and clean. All I have to do is cook and no more baby-sitter."

But his plan failed when he was arrested two weeks after their marriage. "Because what she did was, she supposedly seen me fondling one of the children. She went and told her mother."

Maybe Cathy did see him fondling one of his daughters or doing worse, and maybe she did tell her mother what she saw, but he was arrested because Arlene and Darlene, after futilely telling Pam and Iva how they were being treated, told the Rimmers and Carl called the police. Except for the fact that he had attended a Christmas party with the Rimmers, the rest of Tom senior's information was inaccurate: He had been invited to a Christmas party where, he said, he had only two drinks. According to the police records, and the testimony of Tom and his sisters, he was drunk. He said the police were waiting for him at the party, but he was arrested after Carl drove him from the party in Elyria to his home on College Street in Oberlin.

When Tom senior had finished his version of his arrest, I asked him to talk about what happened after his family was forced to sell the farm. The family moved to Wharton, which he described as a coal mining camp "more or less," with houses built by a mining company for its workers.

"They'd just built a new junior high school, and the school was fairly good but, really, it was just a bunch of rednecks," he said.

His father hated working in the mines and frequently told Tom senior he wanted him to become a pro baseball player.

"I hated it with a passion," Tom senior said about baseball. "I listened to it for hours and hours and hours and hours on the radio. I got my ass stomped on and I don't know how many damn times for closing the door just a little too hard. I mean, he didn't want to hear click. He'd be sitting right there listening to this here old battery radio to a ball game.

And, boy, if he heard that door click or something else that he missed a word here or there, you'd get the hell stomped out of you."

Normally, his father was not violent when he was sober, but after the family lost the farm, Tom senior said, the man started drinking heavily.

"I was raised up like this," Tom senior said. "My dad apologized just about every Monday. That was after the drunk beatings or this or that or something that went on.

His father, he said, would either not recall what he had done or would apologize. "See, he would be drinking, he was in blackout. He wouldn't remember it. I understand it now because I had blackouts, my God, it must a be a thousand, two thousand times now. That, maybe, possibly he was telling the truth. He did not remember."

It seemed he was using the description of his father to rationalize his treatment of his kids; he was intimating that he was not responsible for his actions because of the so-called blackouts. I refused to believe that over a period of three years he unconsciously tortured his children. I was willing to believe his drinking lowered his inhibitions so that he could do what he would not do sober.

"I hated my mom," he continued, "for the simple reason that she started those goddamn arguments and fights. 'Cause he would come home in a really jolly good mood, and she would start it. She knew what the result was going to be. And with him drunk, and plenty more to drink, hell, it, the violence, would go on for three and four days sometimes. And no food was fixed, nothing. He would line all of us up against the wall and make you stand there. If you started sinking down, he'd grabbed you by the head and go beating your head into that wall."

I noticed how Tom stirred at Tom senior's description of his father making all the children line up against the wall. Tom was about to remind Tom senior of the times when he had made him and his sisters stand up all night, and if one of them tired or fell asleep, he kicked or punched them. But Tom senior brooked no interruption. It appeared obvious to me that he knew what his son wanted to say. Tom, however, was not trying to incriminate him; he was merely seeking acknowledgment that it had happened.

"Then it got so," Tom senior said about Iva, "she'd get him arrested every once in a while. And he'd fight the law, too; didn't make any difference. My daddy, when he was drinking, he'd fight a circle saw. It didn't matter. He was in jail practically every week or every other week. He was the meanest son of a bitch you ever seen walking up that hollow. And the only time I've ever seen him cry—cry like a baby and beg and beg and beg—was when he was behind bars. He'd fight like a son of a bitch 'til they got him there, but after they got him behind bars, he was just like a sheep. But he would give you the last nickel from his pocket, you know, when he was sober. Always was ashamed of what he done, every time. I never believed him 'cause I didn't know anything about blackouts or nothing like that. But since, like I say, since he died, I know the terrible hard work that he did, the pressure and strain he was under. I know my mom ran around on him and men would come in the mines and tell him that.

"And I know my mother did run around 'cause I went with her a few times to the men's houses and stuff," he continued. "And I know they sent me out to play—I know what went on. And I'll even go farther. I've seen her ass up in the air, naked, with a man on top.

"I don't have any hatred or malice for either one of 'em," he continued. "Fact, I love 'em more, because, you know, I found out one thing: They're human. They're only a product of what preceded them."

"Right," Tom said. "I firmly believe in that. You don't know any different because you're a product of what you've learned."

This portrait of the Waters family was taken shortly before Tom senior was arrested and Tom and his sisters were placed in foster care. *From left:* Arlene, Darlene, Patty, Tom, and Tom senior.

Patty Waters when she was about seventeen

Patricia O'Reilly, the mother of Tom, Darlene, Arlene, and Patty. This portrait was taken when she was still in grade school (year unknown).

Tom Waters senior and Patricia O'Reilly with Arlene and Darlene in the living room of their home on Holmden Avenue in Cleveland

Tom when he was in kindergarten

Patricia O'Reilly and her sister, Linda Semen, with a department store Santa in Cleveland in 1958

Tom when he played football for the Elyria Catholic High School junior varsity football team. At the time, his last name was Waters-Rimmer because he had been adopted by Carl and Jeanne Rimmer.

Tom (year unknown)

Joyce Schwab with her daughter Patricia O'Reilly and her daughter Linda Semen in 1960

From left sitting on couch: Kurt Tabar (Arlene's husband), Tom, Buck (Patty's boyfriend), and Michael LeMaire (Darlene's husband). *From left in back:* Arlene, Tracie Nadeau (Tom's girlfriend), Patty, and Darlene.

Tom, eighteen, during commencement ceremonies at Mt. Mansfield High School in Mt. Mansfield, Vermont

Arlene, Patty, Tom, and Darlene in Underhill, Vermont, shortly before Tom and Tracie wed

Tom and Gregg Morris at St. Thomas Church in Underhill Center, Vermont, shortly before Tom married Tracie Nadeau

Tracie and Tom Waters

Patricia O'Reilly and an unidentified friend in Tom senior's boat in Cleveland (year unknown)

Tom, twenty-three, in Florida, after a day of fishing on the ocean

From left: Arlene, Patty, Tom, Darlene, and Michael LeMaire (Darlene's husband) in Elyria

Tom when he was still living with Carl and Jeanne Rimmer in Ohio (date unknown)

Tracie Nadeau and Tom when Tom was attending
high school in Vermont

Darlene and
Arlene on the
floor in their
family's
Holmden
Avenue home
in Cleveland

Arlene, Tom, Patty, and Darlene on the campus of
Johnson State College in Johnson, Vermont, the day
Tom graduated

"If you know it, then you should know what to watch for, right?" Tom senior asked Tom rhetorically.

"Right," Tom replied.

"You had a hell of a lot. You should know if you get a good swift kick in the butt, you should take counseling and stuff now," Tom senior said.

"I do," Tom said.

"Not to reach and grab one of these or this or that or start tokin' or shootin' or doing this or doing that," he said, referring, I believed, to marijuana, heroin, and cocaine. "They've got a saying here in Florida. If you don't like the weather just stick around fifteen minutes, it'll change, and it will. It's the same for life.

"But if you can imagine me and your mother bought that place, you know," Tom senior said, seguing to another topic.

"Nineteen-twenty," but Tom did not get the opportunity to finish saying "Holmden Avenue" because his father brought up another topic.

"I mean, I left one hell of a good woman before your mother," Tom senior said. "I'm gonna have to hurt your feelings, Tommy, because I caught your mother many times, you know, messin' around. But you have to know about your mother's upbringing, why she would've done something like that, and why she was so loose with sex, and the reason, probably I picked her out, is she stood out so much is because she was identical to my mother. I was always wanting my mother to love me, but she was always leaving me."

In a matter of a few seconds, Tom senior had moved swiftly from expressing his hatred for his mother and father to expressing forgiveness for their human foibles to telling his son that knowledge of the family pathology should be enough for Tom "to know what to watch for" and be prepared to get counseling. Tom senior had sermonized like a preacher, and his son had responded like an acolyte. During that swift interchange the two appeared to be harmonizing. But redemption and counseling were not the only subjects on Tom senior's mind. During an hour of questioning, Tom and I had not tried to rebuke or accuse him. We had indicated that we were very interested in his childhood, and the result of this was that Tom senior was responding—consciously or unconsciously—to our nonconfrontational manner by slowly relaxing his caution and telling us what was really on his mind. Now it had appeared that the time had arrived and this was one of the moments Tom and I had been anticipating. I was expecting Tom senior to unleash a slew of scurrilous anecdotes about Patricia O'Reilly's alleged promiscuity, and I worried that the rest of the evening would be more agonizing for Tom than the worst moments he had experienced that November evening at Pam's home. I also worried that we might not ever be able to discern the truth, that we would be left with Tom senior's version of circumstances and events, and that his son would have to bear the scars for the rest of his life. But Tom senior, who had opened the door wider to what was on his mind, was not about to let us all the way inside yet. Instead, he digressed.

Iva would leave home for as long as six months and when she returned she would give her kids presents.

"This is what you get for me leaving a whole year and you being nasty and ragged and underfed and everything else," Tom senior said, satirizing his mother. "We wasn't really raised by our parents. We were visited occasionally to catch the latest flak."

Tom and I howled with laughter. The tension in the room plus Tom senior's sardonic wit and insouciant manner made the absurd and the profane appear as funny as hell. I visualized a Norman Rockwell *Saturday Evening Post* cover of Iva, a coal miner's wife, giving toys and trinkets to a bunch of "nasty and ragged and underfed" kids with outstretched hands.

When I managed to stop laughing, I asked him who raised him if his parents didn't.

"I really couldn't say," he said. "Every time I'd become attached to someone in a foster home or a neighbor or a this or that, they were always shifting you off to someone else."

He digressed again.

"You know, up until a few years ago, or a couple of years ago, the most hated words I hated to hear was, 'I love you.' That's the goddamn biggest lie that was ever born. When somebody said that, I started pulling away, and especially if they put their arm around you and said, 'I love you,' " he cooed sarcastically. "And the other one was, 'I'm sorry.' Those words I hate, and I wish they would take them out of the goddamn English what-you-call-it-there. Because how can you explain to some asshole that he fucked up?

"I mean he was doing things to fuck up," Tom senior said, and I realized he was talking about his father. "Then he'd turn around after you're hurt or something, or after he's done something to you, or affected your life tragically, and say, 'I'm sorry.' You know what it makes you think or feel like? It is too bad we fought on the wrong side. It's too bad Hitler did not win because we wouldn't had to put up with all these ignoramuses. We wouldn't've."

I assumed that Tom senior was saying he had not apologized for his treatment of Tom and his sisters because he had learned during his childhood the meaninglessness of apologies. And I didn't want to change the topic, but I wanted to know what he meant by "ignoramuses" and why he thought Hitler had a solution. I didn't know much about Tom senior at that point in the interview. Maybe, I thought, he was a member of a white supremacist group or perhaps he just shared their sympathies.

"He would have eliminated that, he would've eliminated that," he replied, without clarifying what would have been eliminated. I assumed he knew that the groups targeted for elimination by Nazi and neo-Nazi groups were Jews, people of color, and gays, not belligerent white males who abused their kids. Tom senior moved on again to talk about the "young people" whom he had met at various construction gigs and how they weren't serious about life. I wasn't sure what that had to do with Hitler or if Tom senior was just saying whatever crossed his mind.

"But what I'm saying, I've seen all kinds of tragedies happen out of stupidity," he continued, without answering my question.

"If I ever do something to you I will not say I'm sorry," he said, speaking rhetorically. "That don't get it. It really don't. Saying I'm sorry just don't get it."

To someone else I might have suggested that one doesn't have to say the words, that it was possible to apologize through deeds. But I didn't believe he was interested in suggestions, and as I was thinking about his reasoning, he had started talking about the agony he experienced after Patricia O'Reilly died.

"I was going insane after your mom died," he told Tom. "You go deeper and deeper and deeper and deeper, and the first thing, you lose all perspective of really what reality is. You know, insanity, believe me, it's easy to get into."

He mentioned that his sister, Aunt Pearl, was an example of the kind of paranoia he experienced. "She don't trust anybody. And then you add alcohol to that and she can be potentially dangerous."

Tom expressed disbelief that Aunt Pearl was addicted to alcohol.

"Oh, Pearl drinked for years, man," Tom senior said. "Pearl has drinked for years and years and years and years. I've seen fits she pulled. She's broke up the freakin' kitchen walls and all in her home, and I had to repair it before [her husband] came home. Her and my sister Joan get into it, and I'll tell you how bad they are: If the two of 'em are right here, and I happen to light one's cigarette, the other one'll get mad. They'll get into a big hell of a fight. 'Cause, really, they'll say I'm their only brother, yet they don't like me the way I am."

I asked him again about his being in foster homes. I wanted to know what kind of foster care system operated in Boone County way back then. I wanted to know if he had encountered a negligent and bungling agency, as his son had. He replied that he didn't know if he had been placed into a formal foster care system or agency, but what he resented most was that once he felt comfortable in a place, his parents would appear and take him away.

"They didn't have to go to court, they didn't have to do nothing. They just come there to pick you up," he said.

I asked him how many different placements he had experienced. I was trying to establish a time frame.

"About three or four I know of, that I can remember that were supported by the state," he said. "The others were, like, with neighbors, relatives."

Sometimes one of his half brothers or half sisters—who were all older than any of the Waters children—took care of them when Iva left. "Sometimes it was my grandpa, grandma; just various people, whoever was around that could take us. Sometimes, my mom. One time she took my sisters Joan and Pearl. I think she took all the kids at different times when she would leave, except me. Sometimes she left, she didn't take none of us. But most of the time she'd take maybe a couple. Now, the reason she took only the older children or something was because I think she had a use for 'em or something.

"They always used us kids in some way, always: either for money, working to make money. Ever since I was seven, eight years old where I was pushing a lawn mower or something they'd take the money when you got home. Or anytime you was working for anything, they were always taking money."

He recalled how he had learned to charge ice cream to his father's account at a local store. His father didn't know and Tom senior's recollection made us laugh.

"Yeah, there was a great big fight," he said. "My daddy tore the hell out of the place where he said other people were charging all this stuff on his bill. He didn't know we did it. Well, the girls didn't do it. They were scared to do it; they were scared."

He wasn't as terrified as they were.

"After you take so damn many whippings," he said, explaining why he dared to do something that could enrage his father, "you ain't afraid of one after a while. Don't hurt."

Those comments struck a responsive chord in Tom.

"You cry only 'cause . . . ," said Tom, who didn't finish the sentence.

"Maybe he won't kill you," said Tom senior.

The four of us erupted in laughter. Everyone knew Tom senior was not joking about the fear of death. Father and son laughed because they had survived, because they shared a common knowledge that came from the firsthand experience of terrifying fear. I laughed because I sensed what they shared. My awareness was derived from interviews with kids who had been abused so much that they lived under the belief that death was imminent. It was in the way Fern laughed spontaneously that I knew she was a survivor, too. It was an insane moment of gallows humor. More would follow.

"I remember when I was little with the Rimmers," Tom said, as he was still laughing. "I wouldn't cry 'cause it didn't hurt. But when I figured it was time to stop, then I'd start crying. Then Carl made this big paddle. He drilled holes in it and that sucker hurt. I'd start crying before he even hit me with it."

"They whipped us at school with switches," Tom senior said, "but after we got in that junior high, they usually had a board with holes. They used to whip the hell out of us in school and everything, and we got it twice as bad when we got home for getting a whipping. Everything in West Virginia was whipping at that time. I mean, they did not spare the rod."

I recalled how Tom described his whippings at his school

in Grafton. I thought he was about to mention it to his father, but he had something else on his mind.

"So, you're Thomas Waters. I'm Thomas Waters and your father was Thomas Waters," Tom said.

"No," Tom senior replied. "You see, my grandpa was James John Waters. Okay? Or James Thomas—I forget how it was. They aimed to name my dad after him, but Grandma put it down on the birth certificate wrong. She put it down as Thomas James Waters."

Tom senior's father wanted to name Tom senior Thomas James Waters, but his mother wrote James Thomas Waters on the birth certificate.

"I've always went by Thomas James Waters because my dad would never let me go by anything else," Tom senior told Tom. "I told her [Patricia O'Reilly] that I only go by Thomas James because it's been that way ever since I was a kid, in school and everything else because he [his father] wouldn't let me go by anything else."

When Tom was born, Tom senior wanted him named James Thomas Waters, which is Tom senior's real name, but Patricia wrote Thomas James Waters on the birth certificate. Patricia, I thought after I sorted through the confusing explanation, probably had been as confounded as I was about who was who.

"But your mom was raised the very same way, you know that," Tom senior said in another segue. Patricia O'Reilly lived with her grandmother because she was neglected by her mother, Joyce Schwab, Tom senior said. And because her grandmother was too old to keep up with her, Patricia roamed the streets.

Joyce, Tom senior said, traveled around the country when she was in the Marines. "She never did take responsibility for the girl, she never ever paid her any attention. Her grandma raised her. Her grandmother spoke nothing but Polish and very, very little English."

He was wrong, of course. Joyce and her mother and daughter spoke Slovak. I thought it was significant that he had had four kids by Patricia O'Reilly and still didn't know that she spoke Slovak and that her family came from Czechoslovakia.

"See, she was in the street having sex at the age twelve," Tom senior said.

Twenty minutes had passed since he had first broached the subject of Patricia's alleged promiscuity. Girls as young as twelve may have sex under certain conditions, such as incest or curiosity or parental negligence, but his expression that she was having sex in the street implied she was immoral. I asked him how he knew.

"I know she was," he said. "When me and her got together she was only fifteen, actually."

I might have believed him if he had said she had told him about her pre-adolescent affairs, but he didn't use those words. He knew without telling us how he knew. I decided his answer was about as accurate as his description of Patricia O'Reilly speaking Polish. But it was information that would have to be checked and I wasn't sure then how we would do it.

I asked him if she seemed older than she was.

"Oh, yeah. She was big-busted and everything. I mean, she had her hair dyed platinum."

He claimed that Joyce had Patricia get her dates with young men and he explained how he knew.

"I had a real nice outboard. I mean, one of the—might as well say the nicest-looking boat on Lake Erie at that time. And, she [Joyce] would have Pat go out and pick up a couple of guys that's got boats there at the Ninth Street pier. She'd bed one, Pat'd bed the other.

"I really suspect that your mom was pregnant," he said, then added, "if Arlene and Darlene would consent to a blood test, you'd probably find out that one belongs to me, one belongs to a Dennis Leaper."

Straight from the front pages of supermarket tabloids, I thought about his comments, which surprised me and startled Tom.

"What do you mean?" Tom asked.

" 'Cause haven't you ever heard of that where a woman that would bear twins like that has been double-seeded?" Tom senior responded.

Tom tried to explain that because Arlene and Darlene were fraternal and not monozygotic twins didn't mean they had different fathers. Tom senior ignored him.

"Well, there was quite a few fights, you know, and a few times I had to escort her into the house with a gun," he said.

It was time to seize the moment, but I knew I had to be discreet. I wanted to know what he meant by "fights." Was he talking about arguments or fisticuffs? I wanted to know how many times he threatened her with a gun. I wanted to know the occasions and the kinds of weapons, but Tom was still trying to get his father to see the fallacy in his reasoning about Darlene and Arlene and would not let me interrupt.

"See, I don't understand how one could be conceived and then another be conceived after that," Tom said in a manner far more soothing than he felt. He understood, but he wanted his father to see the fallacy in his reasoning.

"Oh, yeah, women have had 'em even a month or so after they had the first one," Tom senior insisted. "I mean, twins run in that family.

"The reason I said this—I've set down and I figured it out, figured it out," Tom senior chuckled. "Your mom was acting so crazy about being this and that, and she had came to Florida on a vacation. And she came right back. She had only left me one time. She came right back, came over to my house and would not leave me alone, all this and that, and kept it up. She was pregnant then."

I didn't understand him. I had noticed, after almost an hour of talking, that he spoke in a certain manner when he couldn't recall or explain specific facts or didn't want to admit that he didn't know as much as he pretended or was ashamed to admit something. He would lapse into jargon with inexplicable or cryptic expressions that were supposed to make it sound as if he knew what he was talking about and that we should understand his reasoning. However, all I understood was that he believed Patricia was pregnant and anxious and that he was responsible for one of the twin sisters.

"See, when your mom died I didn't know she was pregnant," Tom senior said. "And the coroner told me she was six months pregnant. I kept telling them that I heard a heartbeat. And they [police officers] pulled me off of her, and took me to another room. And they was only interested in if I'd killed her. They would not check her for that heartbeat. The child that she was carrying, it was her heart still beating. You could hear it. The coroner told me that the child died in the morgue. It pumped every bit of oxygen out of her system that it could and it suffocated. It was a little girl. The city of Cleveland is actually responsible for killing the child because he [the coroner] said if they had took it right then on the spot, the child would have lived."

Everyone but him, according to Tom senior, was responsible for Patricia's sad life and untimely death, as well as the death of her unborn child. Joyce was responsible, according to him, because she didn't raise her daughter right, and the city of Cleveland was responsible because no one performed an emergency cesarean to save the unborn baby girl.

I asked him why the police at the scene suspected he had killed Patricia.

" 'Cause her mom was sitting there ranting and raving that I killed her," he said. "We [he and Patricia] had been fighting all the day. See, I had just got out of the hospital a few days before that. We had this five acres in the country, and I wanted to go out there for the weekend."

But for reasons Tom senior couldn't make clear they were short of money and he held Patricia responsible.

"So, we had been in an argument and I canceled out all the credit cards, and I would not let her pick up my check and I canceled bank accounts so that no checks, no money could be drawn out. So, she told me we didn't have any money," he said.

I didn't understand what he meant by fighting. Did he mean arguing? It also wasn't clear why he had canceled the credit cards and bank accounts when he needed money. I decided to be patient.

"So, anyhow, you know, she was a Pepsi hog. There must've been ten dollars worth of Pepsi bottles on the stairway in the house. So, we took all those Pepsi bottles up there and cashed them in for the money," he said. "We had enough for food and gasoline to go out to the lake where I had that land. So, we went out there for the weekend."

They came home Sunday evening, and he asked her to go to a gas station at the corner to cash a check. He planned to call the bank on Monday "to open the bank account and tell 'em it's okay." In other words, it was a good check.

"So, while she's gone, I mean, she's like every woman, she just took off with the car keys, cigarettes and this and that," he said. "I'm looking around for a light to light a cigarette, and I open up her handbag to see if there were some matches inside, and here's this wad of money. It's two hundred dollars, it's a hundred sixty dollars. I said to myself why the hell did we go through this here Pepsi thing and everything to get money to go out to the lake? She's telling us we're broke, and she's setting there with a hundred sixty dollars in her purse. So, when she come back, the fight started. Her mom lent her two hundred dollars to have an abortion 'cause she told me in the hospital she was going to have an abortion. That's why I shut the credit cards down."

Patricia O'Reilly died that evening, May 18, 1970.

Tom senior's account was confusing. He had said earlier that he did not know that she was pregnant until the coroner told him, but now he said that she had told him that she wanted to have an abortion. Also, if she was planning to leave him, and did have money in her purse as he insisted, maybe she planned to use it for the trip. But I was speculating and became concerned I would not be able to corroborate information as much as I would like.

"Anyhow, the fight started," he said.

I still wondered what he meant by "fight." I couldn't imagine Patricia O'Reilly physically fighting or even putting up much of an argument. She was six months pregnant and, Aunt Pearl had told Tom, so sick that Aunt Pearl had offered to take care of her and the kids at her home.

"But anyhow, we argued this and that," Tom senior continued. "She told me that she was leaving with her mother and Fred Schwab. They had bought a place here in Florida, and they were leaving in the next couple of days. It was true, she was really going with you kids. And she says that all she's gonna do [he was referring to Joyce] is to take him down there and get him to invest all the money 'cause he inherited money from his mother and father. Joyce was going to get him to invest all this money and soon as he did, she was gonna divorce him and take half of it and come back to Ohio. And she did exactly that—without Pat because Pat died."

Joyce and Fred did divorce, but Joyce stayed in Florida. They remarried. Joyce had told us they had moved to Florida because of Fred's health. But for Tom senior the divorce was proof that Joyce was only interested in Fred's money. He ignored the reality that she did not return to Ohio and that she and Fred remarried. But what really interested me was that Patricia O'Reilly died the week she was planning to take the kids and leave. I could have asked Tom senior what he was prepared to do to keep her from leaving, but I was thinking about other things.

According to Joyce, whenever Patricia fled to her mom's home in Brunswick, Tom senior either called repeatedly on the phone or drove around in front of the house and heckled them until she returned. I also couldn't understand why Patricia, who was running away from an abusive man, would tell him her mother—her intended rescuer—was about to pull a scam on her husband. It might have been conjecture dressed to look like fact, or maybe Patricia had said something. It was becoming very complicated.

"Your mom done everything she could to satisfy her mom, to try to get that love she wanted," Tom senior told his son. "She went out and got boyfriends and she bedded one while Joyce bedded one, younger guys and this and that just to try to get that approval."

Tom senior then turned to a discussion of Fred and Joyce and how much money he believed they were making. I didn't see the connection between his discussion of Patricia and his interpretation of the financial situation of Fred and Joyce. I thought he was rambling. But then I hadn't understood the connection earlier between my question about Children Services removing his kids and his scathing description of Cathy Waters. But it would all make sense later.

"I think Fred was making eighty-five dollars a week. He had that nice home and everything in Brunswick up there. And he had two nice new, brand-new cars and everything else," Tom senior said. "Would you believe me and your mom, at that time, 1969, would have to borrow the money, and we were bringing in eighteen hundred dollars a month?"

He worked as a chemist for a corporation that produced chrome and Patricia was working, he said, at the Top of the Town and Captain Frank's restaurants. I couldn't determine what period he was discussing. I knew Patricia was not working when she died.

"She would bring home some night, a hundred dollars in tips," he said. "That was the most biggest places in Cleveland, you know, that would tip you. I know it's true because she catered to parties and this and that. We used to have a company party every month that salaried people'd go to for one of these here pep talks. And the girls who'd take care of it, our table, I've seen him [a boss] write on those tabs, anywhere from a fifty- to a hundred-dollar tip. And the party would only be for about three hours, setting around eating some steaks and having some cocktails. So, what I'm saying is my wife worked at the same thing. Sometimes she'd exceeded my salary, and I was making anywhere from—sometimes four or five, six hundred dollars every two weeks. That was good money back in '69."

When Tom senior told us he "knew" something that was not what someone had told him or what he himself had witnessed or experienced firsthand, I became very suspicious. I believed he was telling us what he had surmised. So, when he said "I know it's true" that Pat was making hundred-dollar tips, I didn't believe he knew it as fact—but that he arrived at that conclusion after witnessing what his bosses were tipping the waitresses at the company dinners. But, again, I didn't realize at the time the significance of what he was saying about her tips, only that he sometimes passed off suppositions or allegations as facts.

What also interested me was how a man who had completed only tenth grade in high school was able to work as a chemist. I was thinking about asking him when Tom asked.

Tom senior said he was working for the chrome company when an executive forced into retirement started training him about the various chemical procedures for plating chromium.

"They let him work two or three years past his retirement, you know. All this time he's training me, and plus they sent me to I don't know how many schools," Tom senior said. "I was just in one school after another after that. I was working and going to school, and trying to work part time to make extra money."

He started talking nonchalantly about a basic "analytical procedure" and purification procedures and "plating baths" and "stripping solutions." I was impressed, though I didn't understand him, and I thought Tom was impressed too. His father lacked a formal education but he was very smart.

After working at the company awhile, Tom senior traveled around the country on business trips. He also said he had developed several new procedures that were patentable. But when Patricia died, he went to pieces.

Shortly after her death, one of his colleagues "had made some slur remarks about Pat," Tom senior said. "See, is, my sister Joan and them would've had some conversations with him. And, see, me and your mom wasn't married. I regret that. I've always regretted that 'cause she asked me many times, and we always kept saying after we get this worked out where we really have a good honeymoon or this and that, we'll do it. Well, it never did get to that point. And I had tried to commit suicide. He [the colleague] said, 'You know, hell, if I went home this evening and found my wife dead in the kitchen, it wouldn't bother me.' He says, 'You can't go all to pieces, 'cause some bitch died.' After the episode that took place in the office that day, I just handed in my keys. And for a couple of weeks, or three weeks, they called and begged me to come back to work, and I wouldn't go back to work. But I did go over there and get my lab books and stuff, and left for Texas, and I let everything go. I didn't try to sell nothing, didn't try to do nothing, just left."

According to him, the company tried to get him to return and when he refused, it tried to have him arrested for allegedly stealing papers that belonged to them.

"They followed me for years. They followed me into Texas. I don't know how many invitations I had to come back," Tom senior said. "They always used to contact Joan, trying to get me to come back. I knew that the only reason they wanted me back was to find out what I knew. I caused them great pain because what I did come up with it and everything, I kept it in my head. Some of it was in those books."

Tom senior said he rented the Holmden Avenue house

and left for Texas and Tom learned it was a house just outside Houston, Texas, where he had set the floor on fire when he was young.

"It's a wonder you guys don't remember your mom so much more because it was nothing but torment every day when I come home," Tom senior complained, as he again switched topics. The baby-sitters he hired either abused Tom and his sisters or kept prying into the private matters of the Waters family.

"They'd be asking you kids all kinds of questions," Tom senior said. "And then when I got home, I got a double dose of it from every one of you kids, you know, about Mommy, about this, about that. I couldn't forget the woman because I was reminded of her every day. I had a question-answer session, and half of it got to be nothing but bullshit because by the time I got home I'd get into booze then, and you guys would be sitting around asking me questions. It was nothing but a fairy tale bullshit thing."

It was a telling comment. He had lost a wife and felt as if the weight of the world were crushing him, and his kids had lost their mother and he considered that "bullshit."

We had been talking for about two hours when Tom senior told us how women in his Holmden Avenue neighborhood pursued him after Patricia O'Reilly died, but he said he was not interested in having sex with them. Then he started talking again about his agony over her death. It was about 7:00 P.M., and I was anticipating another round of self-pity when Tom expressed sympathy for his father and then started questioning him about his mother's death again.

"When we were growing up we heard all kinds of different stories," Tom said, "and you said earlier that Grandma said that you killed my mom."

"She said that the very first night," Tom senior replied. "She always said that."

"Why'd she said that?" Tom asked. "She said that you poisoned her or something."

"Well, why didn't the coroner find that out?" Tom senior replied sarcastically. He was about to say something else, but Tom did not allow him to talk, asking him how he felt about the allegations. Tom senior became angry. He had been telling us about his agony, and his son wanted him to respond to allegations that he had killed his mother.

"Being in prison from the time you were born, all of a sudden knowing what freedom is, knowing what love is. I never ever loved anybody in my life 'til I met her. When [his wife] did something wrong, didn't bother me," he said. "I wouldn't pay no more attention to anything she did wrong than a dog barking out there in the yard. When your mom did something wrong, my God, you'd thought the ceiling was coming down. It mattered; I loved her. Didn't want her making mistakes, didn't want her to do this or do that and so on and so forth. But the point is, if you can imagine what it was like to have someone like that die on you?

"See, after the argument," he continued, "we had sex, kind of made up, all this here stuff. She died about a half hour later or something like that on the bed, watching television. And then on top of it, for the law to take your kids away, they took you kids for six, eight weeks. That's why I left Ohio for Texas 'cause your grandma was constantly filing some kind of goddamn charges on me. It was just lawyer's fees after lawyer fees just eating up everything I could make. And I didn't have to give her visitation rights 'cause the court said I didn't after what she did."

Joyce had convinced the social service authorities to give her the kids by claiming that Tom senior was under suspicion for murdering her daughter.

Tom senior appeared upset that we did not appreciate his agony. For almost an hour he had been telling us about his anguish. But we were trying to reconcile his descriptions of what he called love with what we had been told about his treatment of Patricia O'Reilly and what he had told us about brandishing guns. And too often, as far as I was concerned, he gave incredible responses to our questions. For example, Aunt Pearl told Tom in November that Patricia was six months pregnant and so sick that Aunt Pearl had offered to take her into her home. So, why would Patricia want sex? Did she have a choice? He also never directly answered our questions about allegations that he had poisoned Patricia. He sarcastically asked us why the coroner's office hadn't found poison. We could have told him that we were checking with a forensic specialist but we didn't. When he felt more comfortable that we sympathized with his plight and weren't critical of him— we weren't anxious to alienate him—he resumed telling us about his great loss and that no one among his relatives seemed to care.

Then he digressed again and described how Aunt Pearl and Aunt Joan continued to deny that they were sexually abused by their father. Tom and I simultaneously asked him to explain.

"He tried it even with me several times when he was drunk," Tom senior replied about his father. "My mom forced me into sleeping with him 'cause she wouldn't sleep with him. And that went on for months and months. I don't know how many years as a child, seemed like forever. And he was always trying to sexually harass me in the bed and stuff and like. He needed companionship, my mother didn't supply it, and all the time when she'd take off or be gone or something, he was drunk. He'd get in there, even naked, just napped and he'd call the girls and so on and so forth."

What he told us next was both confusing and revelatory, but I didn't know if what he said showed a dark secret about his family in West Virginia when he was growing up or if it was indicative of their understanding of themselves.

"They," he said, without identifying to whom he was referring, "said that May,* my niece, May, that belonged to my sister Jane, that he [his father] was the father. But Jane was not his daughter in any way. She was his daughter by his marriage to my mother. Jane's father was Gary Black,* I know Gary Black well and Jane looked like him. My brother Brent, and Raymond,* belonged to a guy named Rick Cole.* I've seen him too. They looked just like him, you know, except Brent, he favors my mom. He's short, looks like her and his hands are like her and everything else."

I was mentally translating what Tom senior had just said while he and Tom resumed talking about Aunt Pearl and Aunt Joan denying how they had been mistreated. *The family* believed that Tom senior's father raped and impregnated his stepdaughter Jane. However, Tom senior had intimated to us that although Jane was raped and became pregnant, it was not a case of incest, in his opinion, because Jane was not a Waters. Jane also was not a daughter of John Workman, Iva's first husband. According to Tom senior, Jane was born as a result of Iva being involved with Gary Black and Jane's surname was Workman for reasons he could not clearly explain.

Tom senior concluded that Jane's father was Black because he perceived a resemblance between them. And that was not all. Tom senior had said Brent and Raymond "belonged to Rick Cole," the implication being that his mother had been involved with Cole and that Brent and Raymond were the result. This wasn't the first time I had heard such a disclosure. Pam, when Tom and I interviewed her, had offended Tom by relating family rumors that he was Brent's son. The implication, we believed at the time, was that Patricia O'Reilly was a slattern whose promiscuity had no boundaries. But Pam had also told us about Jane, so more was involved than Patricia O'Reilly's alleged infidelity. It was as if Tom senior's family was trapped in a vicious whodunit game of who sired whom. And Tom senior played the game zealously. He insisted that one of his daughters was not his. I wasn't certain what all this meant, other than that there was great uncertainty within *the family* about where the bloodlines began and ended, and that women more often than men were blamed for the confusion.

As I was about to try to get Tom senior to clarify this matter, Tom zeroed in on something else that had been bothering him since I had first met him in 1989. In the nonaccusatory manner he had used all evening, Tom asked his father if he actually tied his mother with rope to keep her from running away. He also wanted to know if he had beaten her as she held him when he was a baby.

"I'll straighten your mind out about that real quick," Tom senior said, smiling like a fox. "I did slap her a few times in my life. Once, I did tie her up. It was to keep her from going someplace because there was a serious argument going on about something and she would always run. Instead of tell the truth, she would run, go stay at your grandma's. And she'd come on back then after a week or so. One time I was determined to get to the bottom of things. I tied her up."

He said he didn't hog-tie her.

"All she was, she had her arm tied to this arm of a chair"— he demonstrated—"an arm tied to this other arm of the chair—not with ropes or anything. It was like a bailing twine. Anyhow, she pulled at those so hard, that it burnt the skin because it wasn't a very big thing, it burnt the skin while I was out of the room. I didn't know she was doing it or I would have cut her aloose. And it didn't do any good 'cause she told me so damn many different tales, and I found that none of them were true. There might have been one of 'em that was true, one story that she told. But, God, she had me about ready to kill a guy one time. Guy didn't even know it. She took me to his house, and he didn't even know her, literally. By that time I had about twenty-eight guns: rifles, the shotguns, this or that. I took a gun out, I had a P-thirty-eight [a World War II German semiautomatic pistol]. I put it right to that guy, you know. I was gonna blow his head off.

Guy didn't even know her. She had never really been to that residence. She just took me to a house."

He laughed. We laughed—as a reflex, not in support. But I knew it appeared as if we were all good old boys bonded together by our maleness. I believed Tom senior about Patricia O'Reilly's deceit. I was aware of similar accounts. Women accused of infidelity and threatened with a gun or knife or a beating took their husbands, lovers, or boyfriends to any male convenient by time or place and hoped that the confrontation satisfied the bloodlust without ending in bloodshed.

When we stopped laughing, I asked him about the man who he believed was the father of one of the twins, the person whom he had called earlier in the evening "Dennis Leaper." Tom senior described him as a boyfriend and school-mate of Patricia's. He talked about how Joyce Schwab threatened to turn him in to the authorities because her daughter was underage and then, after more than a half hour, finally got around to explaining the connection between the tips Patricia O'Reilly was supposed to be making as a waitress and what Joyce and Fred earned when they lived in Brunswick.

"Like I say, Fred was making eighty-five dollars a week, and you can imagine how much Joyce was making at Sears, and to own all they owned," he said, speaking more to Tom than me. "What your momma was doing was taking our money, though, and giving it to her, trying to find approval from her. What she was doing was, she was giving it to Joyce and them. That's how they was paying all these bills, two car payments, house payment, and everything else."

I told Tom senior that Joyce and Fred apparently seemed to have been doing well on their own, and he explained his reasoning.

"They had car payments, house payments, Sears, this, that, charges, and everything else," he said. "There's no way they could've paid it on their salary. If you just stop and think,

Brunswick, pretty rich neighborhood, you know, to have a house out there and they had two brand-new cars, two car payments, furniture payments—I know they completely bought all brand-new furniture when they moved into that house in Brunswick. They had Sears charges, every kind of bills you could think of. There's no way they could've paid that on maybe a hundred, well a hundred and eighty dollars at the most. I know he made eighty-five dollars a week. That was his bring-home pay. He was nothing but a grease monkey [a mechanic]. His bring-home pay was eighty-five dollars a week. And hers—how much could you work as a floor salesman at Sears at that time? I'm talking back now '66, '67. I bet she wasn't bringing home more than same as him, eighty dollars a week, if she was bringing that much. How in the hell could they've been paying all them bills? There's no way they could've covered 'em."

I thought of a few ways. Joyce and Fred worked extra jobs. That wasn't unusual. My father worked two full-time jobs for more than twenty years, and Tom, as he worked his way through college, had worked double jobs because he needed the money. Or Joyce and Fred, who had helped Tom senior and Patricia O'Reilly with the ten thousand dollars to buy the house on Holmden Avenue, had inherited some money. Or Joyce and Fred worked extra jobs and also drew upon inheritances. The possibilities were limited only by someone's imagination or paranoia. Tom senior also had left out some information. Aunt Pearl had told Tom that Tom senior had struggled financially because he was still supporting his first wife and his two other sons when Patricia O'Reilly was alive. But not once during the first two hours did Tom senior mention that information, nor did he mention that Joyce and Fred were the ones who had helped him and Patricia buy the house on Holmden Avenue. The real issue, I believed, was Tom senior's imagination. He didn't know. He speculated. And it was easy to recognize that Patricia had paid dearly for it.

"I know Pat was giving a lot of money to 'em 'cause, hell," Tom senior continued, "we was struggling. Like I told you, man, we was making the money. It was nothing for your mom to make a thousand dollars a month. She was waitressing some of the biggest nightclubs there in Cleveland."

Joyce had told us that Patricia had worked at two nice restaurants, but she worked as a waitress primarily at diners. Joyce also said Patricia stopped working because Tom senior accused her of having affairs with her bosses. Tom senior conceded, however, that Patricia "did her sharing" and that "she didn't work so much all the time."

Tom again asked his father how he believed his mother died. When Tom senior said it was a heart attack, Tom asked if it was "something that ran in her family." I wasn't sure why he asked the question. I knew he and his sisters often wished they knew more about their family's medical history. But it was clear that he hadn't gotten a satisfactory answer about his mother's death.

"She had had so many pressures so close together," Tom senior said, as I thought about the bailing twine, the P-38 and the twenty-seven other guns, his accounts of slapping her, Darlene's and Arlene's accounts of rape and mayhem. "I had total loss when she died," he said.

"And the coroner called me down there several times to ask me," he continued. "He said that, you know, your wife hasn't been poisoned."

He had finally responded to Tom's inquiry of a few minutes ago about the poisoning, but it was an odd response.

"She hasn't been stabbed or anything else," Tom senior recalled being told. "He says, 'We cannot find out what your wife died of. He said could you go over exactly what you guys were doing.' And the story I told him—later on in years I started having these dreams—was totally different. It did not even happen the way that I told him. Finally he came up: He said that your mom died from a pin-size infection in her heart, 'caused her heart to flutter. He said, what it did was, it reversed the current in your wife's heart. And it stopped and it didn't restart. That's all. It just stopped for a second and didn't restart."

What he described was almost consistent with an interstitial myocarditis, according to my preliminary research.

"And she had told me that day," Tom senior said, "or the day before, that she wasn't feeling too good or stuff like that. And she had like a small cold or a flu or something like that."

He continued, telling us that during the next four to six weeks he had found evidence of pills and medicine that his sister Joan had supplied to Patricia so she could abort her baby. He also claimed he discovered the name of the doctor she had visited to get what he claimed was an injection to abort the baby. But he didn't know for certain if she took any of the medicine. Tom senior also told us a little more about the day she died. A man who shared a room with him when he was in the hospital was the same guy who called the police and helped him to try to administer CPR to Patricia.

"He was a young kid," Tom senior said. "I couldn't force air into your mom, but he knew how to give artificial respiration, and started getting air into her and stuff. It was too late; there had been three, four, five minutes—I really don't know. I was in a state of shock. I don't know how long I had been trying to get her to breathe and stuff. It may have been ten minutes. I mean, I was totally exhausted. I was wore out so much from pressing her chest. I think she was dead before I even started because what we was doing we had been playing a game. And you know how you play dead or you're wrestling and one of you is moving you around—all of a sudden, you jump up and you holler and go to wrestling?"

I nodded my head in agreement, but knew of no such game. I thought his account, based on what I knew of her condition at the time, was incredible.

"And we were setting there, and she had some Pepsi—and you're gonna hear something bad, now," he warned Tom. "I had some blackberry brandy. I had a glass of brandy on my nightstand and we had some potato chips and stuff, and we was watching television, and she just slumped over. And I thought she was joking."

He got up to adjust the TV because the picture "was rolling." He lit a cigarette and then turned, saw his wife and told her he didn't want to play anymore.

"And I guess I messed around with that thing another thirty seconds and then I heard her gasp, and she raised up and it was slobbers running down her chin; like, you know, and she was blue, just as blue as anything. I rushed over there and jerked her down into bed as fast as I could, you know, and I started trying to work on her. I found she wasn't kidding. It was really something awful. I blamed myself for years over that, you know, 'cause I stood there screwing around with the TV and smoking a cigarette. There was something seriously wrong. Really, I didn't know. How was you gonna know?"

The room became so quiet, I thought I was actually witnessing remorse instead of guilt. I asked him when he felt he started getting his life together.

"When I was in the penitentiary," he said, and for the next ten minutes we discussed his life in the state prison where he was incarcerated for five years. Tom and I did not ask probing questions and the mood was more upbeat. Tom senior told us he lived on a farm of about eight thousand acres and slept in a dormitory, not a prison cell. He started reading the Bible and found Jesus. He went through a period of self-discovery. And, after a long period on the wagon, he said, he "started having dreams, dreams, dreams, and things started coming back to me exactly how your mom died. What I told you is exactly how she died. What I told them [the authorities] was another story, but it was irrelevant, it's the same thing. There was no great lying, but my mind had put that out, out of my mind so fast that what I was telling them [the authorities] what happened didn't happen that way at all. No, not really."

*   *   *

I had a faded copy of a police report dated May 18, 1970. Joyce Schwab, who had kept it for twenty years, had given it to me and Tom when we interviewed her. According to the report, signed by police officer Timothy H., Cleveland Patrol Car 205 was dispatched by radio to 1920 Holmden Avenue at 8:44 P.M. to investigate a report of a sudden illness. The officer who signed the report said he observed Tom senior applying artificial respiration to his wife, who was lying on the bed.

"We checked the body and found victim apparently expired," the copy of the typed report read.

Upon questioning the husband, he stated that they had an argument during which he struck her in the face with an open hand. She then folded up and got the shakes and started gasping for breath. He further states he thought she was faking and realizing that she wasn't he started giving her mouth to mouth and other artificial respiration. About 15 minutes later, a friend Michael H., came to the house and victim's husband told him to call the police. Investigation revealed no signs of recent violence on body. Victim's husband stated that he had numerous quarrels with his wife for the past year and has struck her on other occasions and he also bound her hand and foot in the past. Neighbor William C. of 1912 Holmden confirms the fact that the WATERS family has had numerous domestic quarrels. Death apparently due to natural causes. Coroner to rule on cause of death. Body to Metro [Hospital] by Car 205. D.O.A. by Dr. L. at 10:10 P.M. Body to the Morgue by Car 203.

At the time, I didn't know what to make of the discrepancies between what Tom senior had told us and the information contained in one faded copy of a police report, though

I was expecting a second opinion on the autopsy when I returned to New York. Whether she died during a fight, after having sex, or while playing a game, as Tom senior told Tom and me, or she died writhing and gasping for breath after she was slapped in the face, as the police information related, her death appeared to be of significance only to Tom, his sisters, and me. The coroner's office certainly hadn't given it much thought.

15 • "The nastiest sore in God's eyes"

*T*om senior served five years in prison because of his "bad" attitude, of which he was still proud. He believed he didn't belong in jail because he hadn't committed a crime. But there he began to regain his senses after being so crazy after Patricia died, he explained, and "as far as I knew, I should have been given like a slap on the wrist, probation or something like that 'cause I didn't think I was that bad to the kids, I really didn't. I thought I was good.

"But I really wasn't good," he said, as he began to explain how he raised his kids, and Tom and I listened to him make a major admission. "Hate the damn world. That's the attitude I was teaching 'em. Hate like I hate. I hated the damn world because everything that I cared about in the world was dead."

He blamed his sister Joan "and all the rest of 'em" for giving Patricia medicine, which, he said without possibly knowing, "caused her to have a heart attack." I doubted all his hatred stemmed from the death of Patricia O'Reilly, though I knew her kids suffered more after she died, but I wanted Tom senior to talk more about his "bad" attitude, and I was being coy when I told him that his serving five years of a one-to-ten-year sentence was unusual (I didn't want to say harsh).

"Yeah," he agreed, "but I actually got that myself. When I went before the parole board, I was not humble or anything. I was under the impression that I was gonna get the parole. I felt good about myself, that I had went a year without drinking."

He had achieved sobriety, he said, without attending AA meetings or counseling but by the sheer force of his will and with the help of God. At his hearing, he appeared before a black woman who, he said, wore a bleached blond wig and who told him he was "in the penitentiary primarily because of alcohol." She criticized him for not attending AA meetings to get help for his drinking problem. He did attend a few but did not get credit for them, but he eventually stopped because he hated AA.

"That goes back to childhood," he told us. "You know, they used to tell my daddy what a wonderful man he was while I'd be laying in the other room, beat so goddamn bad I couldn't show my face or come out of the bedroom. That was AA trying to get him to come to the meetings. So, I grew up with the impression that AA people wasn't nothing but women beaters and child beaters. That's what I thought they were. And I hated it."

He also despised the parole board member.

"Here this son of a bitch, she is black and she wants to be white so fucking bad, you know, that she's got this bleach-blond wig on and she's setting there holding judgment on me. I listened to her for a little more. I said, 'Wait a minute.' I said, 'I don't go to AA because all they do is a bunch of bullshit over there.' I said, 'You've got convicts over there. You've got convicts over there running this stuff, handing down these little assignments. Convicts is running this here place.' I didn't really think of myself as a convict."

That attitude, he said, cost him four more years. Eventually, he was released to a halfway house in Columbus where he found a job working at a small plating shop. And then he started visiting his father, who had moved to Fairborn, which was about fifty miles from Dayton. His father was dying of black lung disease.

"He actually got me to taking my first drink again after five years," Tom senior said.

The night his father drew his last breath, Tom senior was too drunk to help him. His father, he said, had "bought me a fifth of liquor and I proceeded to get drunk with his old lady, and I remember waking up. He was hollering to me. And I was just drunker than hell. I just laid there. And then she called an ambulance, and when the ambulance come to get him, he was in a coma already. He had a spot about the size of a quarter that his lung would accept oxygen through. He had to take pure oxygen. I really truly learned to love my dad after he had been dead because I could understand that human side of him, of him and my mother too. They were just human."

Tom senior tried to explain how he had struggled to come to grips with his arrogance and gave his son some advice. "Just never do the things you can't forgive yourself for. That'll come home. Make all kinds of mistakes, don't make the ones you can't forgive yourself for," he said in a soft voice.

His tenderness and sincerity surprised me. I wondered if he was alluding to his treatment of his family. I asked him how he thought his daughters felt about him. I already knew the answer, but I wanted to know his impressions.

At first he said he had no idea; then he said, "I don't think they have any affection for me." Then he added that he believed Patty might have felt some sympathy for him because she had visited him in Florida.

"She's been the only one that's ever talked to me about any of her problems or expressed any of her feelings, truly," he said, his voice again etched in tenderness and sincerity. "And I can remember my own childhood, and I can see that in their eyes. I really can. I know how they feel, and some day they will understand that life is not a bed of roses, everybody has their human faults. It was a tragedy that your mom died, it was a tragedy and everything that happened that way, but it happened. A deep shock can put you in a state of mind that, believe me, you can lose all reasoning. You just give up."

The conversation shifted during the next fifteen minutes. I'm not certain why; perhaps it was because of Tom senior's plantive comments that he and his son talked about other subjects. They speculated about serial killer Ted Bundy's early childhood, pontificated about capital punishment, reflected on the arrest of the recently deposed Panamanian dictator, Manuel Noriega, denounced the evils of capitalism and materialism, and bemoaned the stiffing of the poor by an uncaring society.

When I saw an opening in the conversation, I asked Tom senior why he settled in Florida. I believed it was an innocuous question, but I had hit a sensitive spot. After his father died, he said, he had moved to Elyria to take care of Iva when she was dying. No one else in the family was up to it. I recalled Pam telling Tom and me how she had moved out of Iva's home because she was unable to deal with her grandmother's slow death by cancer. Pam said she regularly visited Iva during that period, but, in the interview, Pam never told us about Tom senior taking care of his mother.

After Iva died in Elyria, Tom senior remained for a while. But by then he had fallen off the wagon. He was eventually hospitalized. Tom senior was virtually whispering at this point, and I thought he was trying to answer the question honestly without revealing too much detail about that period. He ended up in Florida, where he and his brother, Brent, started their business, T. J. Electric, which closed, he said, because the two feuded.

Tom asked him how old he was, and when his father replied fifty, Tom told him, "You don't look fifty."

"I feel it," he said.

We all laughed.

"He comes home pretty tired, sometimes," said Fern, who had spoken very little most of the evening.

"A lot of these young kids don't believe it, too, 'cause they can't keep up with me working," Tom senior said. "Then they try harder when they find out how old I am. They're gonna beat that old man if it kills 'em."

We all laughed again.

"But they never do," Fern said.

When Tom senior discovered they were working better or faster, he bought another tool "that makes me quicker," he said.

We laughed harder.

Tom and I had decided before we arrived at his father's home that we would achieve better results if we could made it appear that Tom was the primary interviewer even though we both assumed I would ask most of the questions. But once Tom started asking questions, and Tom senior responded, Tom conducted the interview and I acted as his backup, trying to make sure we didn't neglect to ask pertinent questions.

Tom's participation in the interviews had improved with each one we did, and his interviewing style had evolved with little coaching on my part. In the Pam Haynes session, Tom had only asked a few questions before retreating to the couch to avoid her. With Laura and Candy he had asked a few more questions and he talked more. And with Joyce he had asked questions from beginning to end.

Of course, our motives were different. I asked the kind of questions one would expect from a researcher, a social scientist, a journalist. Tom wore several hats: researcher, social scientist, journalist, and son trying to learn the truth about his family. He was learning firsthand about Tom senior as Arlene and Patty had done before him, but he was much better prepared. However, just like them, he was also in a precarious position. It was easier for me to remain emotionally detached from the people we were interviewing than for him. For example, after three hours of conversation, we had done an excellent job of making it easier for Tom senior to talk and reveal himself to us. But I had the impression that by the end of that same period Tom was exploring the possibility of establishing lines of communication with his father. I thought Tom senior was being offered a chance to come home and for most of the night he had flubbed the opportunity. Maybe he didn't care. Maybe he couldn't imagine it. Perhaps I was expecting too much too fast from him.

Because I thought we had covered the most significant matters, and because Tom had been asking most of the questions and also because the tape recorder was running, I felt I could go to the bathroom without missing anything significant. As soon as I left the room, Tom asked his father a question I had been planning to ask Tom senior for more than three hours. I had been waiting for the appropriate moment. I hadn't realized that Tom also was waiting for the same opportunity.

"I keep hearing you talk about the Ku Klux Klan," Tom said. "Are you a member?"

Early in the evening when we first arrived and were asking Tom senior preliminary questions to learn if he would consent to an interview, Tom senior had described the Ku Klux Klan as a positive force in Boone County, West Virginia, when he was growing up. The comments were directed at me. The sight of an African-American showing up at his front door with his son probably added to his fear—he might have even considered it an insult—but he was too timid in the beginning to express directly what he really felt. The comments about the KKK were, of course, double-talk. He reasoned that he could make a racial taunt while pretending to express an innocent comment, as if it was a matter of opinion whether the KKK was a vile hate group or a philanthropic organization like the Boy Scouts. Tom senior thought he was slick.

I wasn't about to let a racial taunt distract me from my task. As long as he didn't reach for a gun or a knife or other weapon, I was prepared to let him do whatever he wanted. After more than ten years as a journalist for mainstream news publications and three years in the Rutgers journalism department, I had encountered enough racist remarks to know how to deal with inflammatory situations without resorting to unnecessary violence. I was unconcerned with Tom senior's feelings about African-Americans. Tom and I were interested in matters far more serious than one man's racial prejudices, though I was interested in anything that revealed Tom senior's true nature. I was not planning to allow the night to end until I confronted him, but I had not expected Tom to challenge him; he surprised both of us.

"Oh, I don't know," Tom senior responded at first; then, like someone caught in an embarrassing situation, he said, "No. I don't know what they are now today. I'm just saying that as a reference that most likely they saved our lives because of the simple reason is men feared them back then."

He had described the Klan as a great protector of Boone County's women and children.

"Then, there was no black people around there or anything like that," Tom senior said. "They [the Klan] burned a few barns down, whipped a lot of rednecks. And far as I know as a child they did good. I don't know what they're into today; I don't know what they do; I don't follow 'em."

"People get into that stuff just so they can act bad," Tom said, as if he was sermonizing. "They use it as an excuse, just like the Hell's Angels."

"That's right," Tom senior responded.

"People aren't in the Hell's Angels unless they want to stomp someone's brains out," Tom said.

"Right," Tom senior responded promptly, "just a gang."

"Right, but that's not why it was started," Tom said. "All these guys bent on stomping brains out are in because that's a big cover-up. That's an excuse. And these people who don't like black people and who don't like Jews, they say I'm gonna get into the Ku Klux Klan because that's a white supremacist group."

Tom senior might have been momentarily put on the defensive, but he was not about to back down. Speaking with a mischievous smile on his face, he told Tom, as I returned to the room, how he had met a lot of minorities during his years of struggle with alcoholism.

"I have slept side by side with 'em: the minorities, with the black, with this and that," he said. "I've been in institutions with 'em, detox centers with 'em, everything else, you know, from drinking. And when you get asked at AA meetings to speak a lot about certain things and if you got a guy sitting there and not paying no attention and you want to get his head listening, you make this statement, and it'll get a lot of eyebrows raised. And my God they'll be paying attention to what you say. I'll start out: I like country people, I really do, I love 'em. And I like black people, but goddamn, I hate niggers and hillbillies—and boy you'll see them heads, they'll come up, you know. Because, I'll say, they're both the same. It don't matter if you're a Russian, Polack. Slovac, German, Jew, or what. Niggers, hillbillies, all them—you'll find those qualities run in all races. They care nothing about anybody but themselves. They care nothing about their children, they care nothing about anything just themselves. They like to party and have their women and so on and so forth, and they don't give a damn if their children are suffering or any damn thing. And if you're ever aspeaking at AA or anything, or any group ever ask you to speak or something, you start it out like that. They will listen to you then because they want to see just in what depth you're going to go with that subject;

where you going to lead with it because mostly niggers and hillbillies is into that shit, because all of 'em are poor—there's a lot of poor. A lot of 'em are caged."

Just as I had been waiting during the evening for particular moments to ask questions, Tom senior had been waiting for an opening to express his racist sentiments, which he no longer felt compelled to conceal under the guise of passing comments about the benefits of a neighborhood chapter of the KKK. For people like him, saying "nigger" can evoke strong feelings of satisfaction, as if the word was a talisman for warding off the soul-wrenching feelings of inferiority and alienation that gnaw at their very identities. The derogatory comments made Tom senior an obvious target for scorn, and yet he wasn't much different from most mainstream bigots. In some ways he had a lot in common with some of my colleagues at Rutgers University, though he lacked the subtlety and veneer of civility that come from being privileged. Some bigots should be pounded where they stand. Others should be exposed for what they are. This night was not meant for violence.

We moved on to other matters. Tom senior asked us where we were staying and when we told him we were at the Holiday Inn in Melbourne, he realized we were probably in contact with Joyce Schwab. His eyes flashed with merriment.

"Oh, Linda and Joyce, both of them was trying to bed me," he said. "Joyce was coming over trying to bed me when Pat was at work, and Linda was bringing girlfriends there, and I'd say about two weeks before that she had me in the bed with her."

"Who?" Tom asked.

"Linda," Tom senior said. "Two weeks before that, she was drunk trying to get me to bed her. And my brother Brent had another girl she brought there, on the couch in the living room.

"Your brother Brent did another girl there?" Tom asked incredulously.

"Yeah," Tom senior said. "And Linda wanted me to bed her. She was only about fourteen, and she was drunk. She went out and got drunk with some boys and then she came home. Runs in the family."

First, he said Linda had tried to bed him, and then he said she had wanted to bed him. So, I concluded he never had sex with her, but that part of the discussion gave him another opportunity to slander Patricia O'Reilly, her mother, and her sister. His contempt for women was obvious, and it had started with his mother. Females he met during his life were, according to his descriptions, either untrustworthy, unfaithful, promiscuous, retarded and, in the case of his daughters, only good for sex and taking care of his needs. Tom had told me when we met that women were considered second-class citizens in the Waters family. That night Tom senior was Tom's unintended corroborator. I had noticed, however, that Tom senior did not make any disparaging remarks about his first wife.

During the interview, Tom senior told us Linda lived with Joyce and occasionally visited him and Patricia and even had stayed one summer with them. He said Linda spited Joyce even though her mother "would buy her good clothes and do everything for her that she had never done with Pat to try to get the kid to cooperate with her." He also said that Linda cut classes, got bad grades in school, and lied to Joyce, and that she and her older sister "probably didn't care much about each other at all because Pat was probably extremely jealous in her mind of why Linda got raised by Joyce and she didn't. Linda stayed with us during the summer to get away from her mother. So, she'd get out and kick up her heels or this and that. She probably wanted to get pregnant and do everything evil and bad to bring her mother great hardship. That's what I derive from it."

Tom senior, after commenting on Linda, admitted how much he had hated Joyce. I understood why she despised him, but I wanted to hear his reasons for hating her. What had she done to him?

"The things she had done to Pat," he said. "Money they gave her to have that abortion, the things they done behind my back and everything else like that. She brought the girl to her own destruction, totally to her destruction. And didn't care nothing about her. Really did not care nothing about her. She may be getting that now in her old age. She may be getting that way, you know, remorseful for all her sinful ways."

Joyce did feel guilty about her oldest daughter but it had little to do with sin and more to do with their relationship as mother and daughter.

I asked him a leading question about Joyce. Was she wild?

"Oh, yeah," he said. "She's in the Marine Corps. And what I'm saying is, she would act like a fifteen-year-old and at that time she must've been in her forties when she was coming down to the lake running around with young guys like me."

Women and girls as young as Patricia O'Reilly went to the Ninth Street dock to ride on yachts and boats. "I swear I'm not bragging. They used to line up," Tom senior said. "There'd be eight, nine girls down there waiting when I came down there. And I was the youngest guy down there on Lake Erie and after I would take one of 'em on the boat, the other guys—they were a lot older and stuff and had these yachts and so on and so forth, cabin cruisers—then they would take their pick of the girls then 'cause the girls wouldn't go with them until after I came there and took one of 'em out."

I didn't think he was bragging. Judging from his pictures, he was handsome and probably charming.

"The only sexual relationship I ever had was with Pat, and before it was always just taking a bunch of girls around for show," he said. "I never did have a sexual what you call drive. I never ever had that. Maybe I got turned off in childhood from seeing my mom's ass up in the air all the time, immorality and stuff that I did see. I didn't have a sexual drive. I really did after I met Pat. I really did; a tremendous sexual drive. Joyce even tried to throw herself on me down there on the lake. And then Pat after she seen I wouldn't go for it, her mother, you know, Pat was always around with me. She dated several guys on the lake, though, before she met me. And Joyce dated 'em and I knew all the guys quite personally. I know all the stories. Everything went around."

Tom asked him if he had heard the term "wharf rat" and Tom senior said no, but he also said, in essence, that the girls and women who went to the pier to hitch rides on the boats were sexually promiscuous. He said that one day, after he and Patricia had been living together, he discovered personal letters that she had concealed behind an old fireplace. According to the letters, he said, Joyce and Pat dated servicemen, and the letters "gave descriptions of all kind of sexual behavior."

According to him, the letters, which he no longer had, revealed Patricia's and Joyce's lascivious ways. And then he said, "But, see, I was raised on this thing of fighting and battles—bloody battles. I mean bloody. Big cuts. And, I mean, knock-down, drag-out over sex, and, You do this, you goddamn whore, and you did that, so on and so forth."

He told us he was no longer like that, and that he certainly didn't treat Fern that way.

"I'm a pretty forgiving person or I'm not just this dog-type thing. Hey, if you sneak around out there and get some on the side, as long as you don't rub my nose in it, what the hell, you know, I'm not gonna miss it," he said, as I recalled how Tom and I were told that he regularly accused Patricia O'Reilly of having affairs. His comment about "knock-down, drag-out" sex battles paralleled what Arlene and Darlene recalled, that he knocked their mother down in front of them and raped her on the floor.

I asked him how he felt seeing his son for the first time

in five years. He didn't answer, so I asked if Tom was un-
friendly or cold toward him the last time they met at Aunt
Pearl's family reunion.

"Shy," Fern said. "I'd say shy. To me he was shy."

"Like a stranger," Tom senior said. "He was cold more or
less."

Tom told them, "I didn't know how to react. I had just
gotten taken out of my home. I was real fucked up. See, you
know, you talk about being crazy and stuff..."

Fern, Tom senior, and I laughed; then we stopped suddenly because Tom was speaking so earnestly. It became still
in the room, as if Tom's voice brought everything in the world
to a stop.

"You talk about crazy and stuff, and I know what you're
saying," Tom said. "You may not think I know what you're
saying, but I know what you're saying. I was ready to kill Carl.
I think that's the reason why I can sit here and talk to you,
because I know what you're saying. I'd get my head put into
a wall, knocked out. And then two seconds later he would
be hugging me and him telling me how sorry he was. I'd have
him forcing me to do things to him."

He tried to describe the sexual acts but faltered. At one
point he spoke so softly we couldn't hear him. At another
point he spoke in bits and pieces of incomplete sentences.
Sometimes his voice just trailed off in the middle of an explanation. All Tom senior, Fern, and I could do was commis-
erate silently. It was obvious that he had endured more than
he had ever admitted. And he had never told me about Carl
slamming his head into a wall and knocking him unconscious.
Tom's and Patty's comparisons of their treatment by Tom
senior and Carl always made me uneasy. They said Carl never
beat them as Tom senior had, but in subsequent rap sessions
one or the other of them would recall Carl's acts of savagery,
and those revelatory moments reminded me I would never
know the extent of what really happened to them in the

Rimmer household, even if I interviewed them for the rest of my life.

When Tom repeated his intention to kill Carl, Tom senior revealed an incident from his past.

"See, I started to kill my mother and father, and Joan and Pearl wrestled me down and took the shotgun away from me," he said. "I went into the closet and got the shotgun and I had loaded it. I was gonna kill both of 'em [his parents], even though he had been beating her [Iva]. I hated her just as much because all she ever did was run away. And I was coming through there with the shotgun, and I had already been taught how to use this sucker ever since I was, God, I think eight, nine years old. And what I meant to say is, Pearl and Joan wrestled me down, and we got in a scuffle in the hallway with a shotgun. Then my dad rushed in to see what was going on. Well, naturally, he took the gun. From then on, boy, he walked a wide path around me, and there was no more fighting and this and that going on for about ninety days. And then it started again because I guess he figured that he could do it and there would be no shotgun or anything coming out."

After their mutual recollections of thwarted parricides, Tom and Tom senior swapped war stories, describing occasions when their fathers' rages resulted in absurdly funny situations. Tom senior described a day when his father and mother were "in a big fight in the bedroom." His half sister Jane "goes in the bedroom and gets in the middle of this fight. And my dad just slapped the hell right out of her, bloodied her nose. Well, she hauled off and she kicked the hell out of him. And, boy, she tore out of that bedroom, tearing through the house. The rest of us were sitting there at the table. She goes and cuts through the kitchen and she's going out this screen door. And he's chasing right after her, and she slammed it. He ran right square through that screen door. When he came back in after giving her hell, he had all these little checks all over him from the dust—but he's not aware that he's been [covered] with rows of checks that look like a string. You had to put your fist in your mouth to keep from laughing."

We all shook with laughter, swept up in a hilariously insane moment, and I realized that on one level the evening had been surrendered to a convicted child molester and KKK sympathizer who could depict the perversity of a horrifying childhood as episodes of slapstick comedy. Tom senior was a magician, who pulled from his magic hat snippets of a terrifying past, infused them with his personal brand of black humor, and, with the wave of a wand, enthralled with maniacal glee the son he used to beat unmercifully and the son's companion whom he taunted with racial insults.

After we calmed down, Tom described a similar incident with Carl. I could feel the room brace for another round of heavy laughing.

"It was a nice summer day, and we're all sitting around eating dinner and cooking out on the grill. And he'd sat down at the table, but the steaks were still on the grill, and we were just starting dinner. Well, he had shut the screen door and he didn't know it or he had forgotten. Well, he stood up real quick and wham. Right into the screen door and popped it right out. And all three of us just busted out laughing. But he got insulted by us laughing at him and just freaked out. And he's screaming at us, pounding on the table. And the more he did that, the more we laughed at him."

And the more Carl acted frenetically, Tom continued, the more he, Patty, and Jeanne howled with laughter. And there in Tom senior's home we all rocked again with laughter. When we sobered enough to talk, Tom senior asked us if "you think you'd get any truth out of Joyce."

We told him we expected her to give us her version. We didn't tell him we had already talked to her. Tom told him, honestly, that we wanted everyone's version and that he participated in the interviews because he wanted to learn the truth firsthand. But Tom senior, in a touch of sarcasm, told his son he thought his presence "was a bribe" to get him to agree to an interview. Tom and I both jumped on the defensive. I believed Tom's presence inspired Tom senior to talk more than he would have if I had shown up alone on his front porch. Tom senior might have consented to an interview, but he would not have been as open if his son hadn't been present. But we told him the truth: Tom was present because he wanted the information firsthand.

Eventually the discussion covered an area I hadn't expected. Tom senior told us about his attempts to get counseling when he was in prison. He despised all his counselors except one therapist, who had helped him. His recollection prompted Tom to talk about his psychologist and how he misled him for five years.

"I just started being honest with him because I realize that there's no other way that I'm gonna be helped out at all, 'cause I had that guy so twisted around my finger. He honestly thought that I was just amazing. I had him twisted, so much, that he thought my only problems were that I couldn't deal with myself, and that I thought I wasn't very good, that I had bad, low self-esteem. And all of a sudden I just started telling him things about me, truth. And he just sat there. He didn't want to let me see that he couldn't believe it."

I knew a few of the "things," but I assumed there was more that I didn't know. Tom senior's reaction surprised me.

"That still doesn't mean he can't help you, though," he said.

"Right," Tom said. "I know it doesn't because it's me helping myself by being honest with him, but if I don't want to be honest with him he can't help me."

Tom seemed impressed that he had deceived the therapist even though he admitted that the deception wasn't helping him to get better.

"So, for years, I would go in there and I'd sit down and

I'd get him to start talking about something. And before you know it, the whole session would be over and all we talked about was wrestling. Or all we talked about was work. And he'd say, well, next time you come in I want to talk about this. And I would come in the next time, and we didn't talk about it."

"If he's a real good psychologist, though, you tell him a lot more than you think," Tom senior told his son.

"Yeah, but, see, I'm like a lot of different people," Tom said. "I mean not so much anymore, and that's what we've been talking about, how I'm in this transition."

Tom was referring to his struggle to stop pretending to be someone he wasn't. But the transition, which he had perceived as giving up one kind of power to gain real personal power, was making him very anxious.

"Hand me another beer, honey," Tom senior told Fern, who complied though she was not happy about him drinking his fifth brew. "I get the urge, and I'm getting kind of nervous that you guys are taking off. I've been spending all my time talking about this bullcrap, and I'd really like to visit with you some."

It was about 9:00 P.M. and his comments made me notice how the mood inside the trailer had gradually changed. Perhaps that was because it appeared we had covered the most difficult topics, and also because he had been allowed to talk at length about his stay in prison, which he had described on and off throughout the four hours we were in his home as the cause of his redemption. He had even mellowed on his racist epithets. In his last several references about minorities he had met in and out of prison, Tom senior had not uttered one pejorative. His venom had not been spent, but he no longer felt threatened. He was relaxed and less defensive, more sympathetic to his son. And Tom was beginning to talk more about himself. When Tom senior expressed his concern about us getting ready to leave we assured him that we were in no hurry to go.

Tom senior asked Tom why he had not filed charges against Carl. Tom usually faltered when he tried to explain his decision to someone for the first time because he had yet to find a succinct way of explaining his ambivalence about Carl. As Tom stumbled through an explanation, Tom senior told him, "He was behind what happened to me."

"I knew he was," Tom responded. But Tom missed the point. Tom senior was about to conclude his version of his arrest in 1973. Two hours earlier he had given us part of the story. Now we were to get the essence of what he believed.

"You're saying you were set up," I said, when I realized that he believed he was the victim of a conspiracy.

"Oh, definitely," he said. "You didn't know that end of it? They were all setting it up then; huddling around in the bedrooms and talking and this and that. I was wondering why. And I kept telling that Cathy, come on, let's go, you know, we got to go. And they kept stalling me and stalling me, and all of a sudden she come out, she's crying, tears: I can't go with you."

Tom tried futilely to tell his father about that winter night in 1974, but he was talking to a man whose version of events had been hardened by eight months in the Lorain County jail, five years in prison, and another ten years of life on and off the wagon. Tom senior would not have liked my version of the events if I had chosen to tell him. My version was based on copies of court and police records and interviews: Arlene and Darlene told Iva Waters about a year before Tom senior was arrested that he was sexually abusing them, and Iva hadn't believed them. They told Pam, who told her mother's boyfriend, who supposedly made an anonymous call to the Oberlin police but nothing came of it. Adults who knew of the kids' neglect and squalor—if not, explicitly, the sexual abuse of Arlene and Darlene—did nothing to help. So, the twins, despite the obstacles created by bungling and insensitive adults, saved themselves and their brother and sister. Tom and Patty, however, did not share in the full benefits of that rescue because Children Services took them out of one dangerous situation and put them in another. If Tom senior had been a decent father—not perfect, just decent—his kids would not have been placed in foster care and Carl never would have gotten his hands on Patty and Tom.

"He set me up at that party," Tom senior said about Carl. "They had it all arranged even before I came over there, even with the police they called. They had to."

"If that happened today, I wouldn't want you to go to jail. I don't know if I feel if jail is right," Tom said.

At first, I was surprised to hear Tom express that opinion, but I recalled how Arlene and Patty had given Tom senior a chance to atone and be a real father to them when they visited him in Florida. I understood the turmoil Tom was experiencing. We came to Florida expecting to confront a great ogre and found instead a man who wanted pity.

When Tom senior said, ironically, that Carl was "screwed up in the head," Tom decided to give him a better picture.

"See, you don't know why I'm suing Lorain County, do you?" Tom commented. " 'Cause he did that before. He did it before I ever came into the picture. He did it way before you ever even came into the picture. And Lorain County knew about it. Lorain County knew about him molesting a little boy—way before any of us, any of the Waters, ever came into the picture. He molested Jeanne's friend's little boy."

"Well, I'm not saying that I would want him to stay in the electric chair," Tom senior said. "That man needs some counseling or something."

"Right," Tom said. "See, I'm torn, though. See, it should not be my responsibility to throw him in jail. Half of me hates him. Half of me wants to kill him. And half of me loves him.

And I don't know why. Okay? But everyone is always saying, Well, why don't you throw him in jail? Why don't you throw him in jail? Because I'm too close to the situation."

"Well, whatever took so long for them to prosecute him?" Tom senior asked.

"They were never gonna prosecute him," Tom insisted. "It happened five years ago when I was taken out of that home. Five years ago they knew about it. Five years ago, they knew goddamn well that I was being abused because they helped get me out of the house."

"Why in hell didn't they decide to prosecute him?" Tom senior wanted to know.

"Because I'm suing 'em! Because I am suing them," he said.

"They're gonna try and make it look good," Tom senior responded.

"It's been over three years, since I filed the suit," he said. "And they're all going to get what they deserve. 'Cause if you think I'm gonna shut up about it, I'm gonna go all over this country and I'm gonna tell what those fucking people did. If they think they can hide from it, they can't."

"You got to look at things at this point," Tom senior said. "So, you'll shout it on every stop, you'll holler it on every mountain, and you'll talk and talk and talk and talk about it, but then what if some old redneck stands up some day and tells you, Who gives a fuck?"

"I don't care," Tom said.

"But, see, that's what I'm getting at it. Most of the whole country could care less," Tom senior said.

"It's gonna scare the hell out of a lot of other children's services," Tom insisted. "If they see some kid sue another agency just like them, it's gonna scare them because all of a sudden all these other kids around the country are gonna start suing too. So, you know what it's gonna do? It's gonna change things."

"Even if it'll help one human being it will all be worth it," Fern added.

"Right," Tom said. "They're not all going to be saying, Baa, we don't care if we get sued, we don't care. They're not gonna be saying, We don't care if people drag our name through the paper—they're not gonna say that 'cause they do care. They care about their asses, and that's why I'm going after them. They're going to cover their own asses, and by covering their own asses they're going to start doing a better job. They're not going to screw up like that anymore. Well, maybe they will, but they're gonna pay for it."

It was about 9:30 P.M. when Tom and Tom senior's discussion tapered off and I started hinting that it was time to leave. I was tired. I preferred long interviews because I believed I could eventually wear down the defenses of the people I was interviewing and get them to talk more honestly. I also preferred long interviews because I could repeatedly ask the same questions in a different manner until I got satisfactory answers. But this interview with Tom senior was one of those rare ones in which I was becoming more weary than the person being interviewed. Tom senior was still going strong. I felt comfortable about ending the conversation because I believed we could resume over the weekend. Tom told him that we would return the next day, Saturday. And Tom senior dangled a prize before us. If we came back, he said, "I can give you a complete—what is it?—autobiography of all the skeletons in our family."

"That would be great if you could do it," Tom told his father, "but even if you just want me to come back and do something, you know, or get something to eat or do something, I will."

Tom senior was not ready for us to leave. "There was everything from murder and burying people up in those hills and everything that you could think of went on up there," he said, referring to Boone County.

I pepped up.

"I remember the old man and my mom dragging some guy out, who was dead. They took him up in the hills and buried him. They got into a fight about something," Tom senior said.

It was difficult to determine if he was just passing on rumors to keep us from leaving or if he was serious.

"Did they shoot him, or beat him to death?" Tom asked.

"Nah, beat him in the head with a club or something," Tom senior responded. "And I don't know whether the guy was dead or just had the hell beat out of him. They didn't know we was hearing this 'cause I was in the bedroom, but I heard 'em saying this. They were gonna take him up on the hill and bury him."

He resumed talking about living in fear of the violence in his home when he was growing up in Boone County and then told us that he, his ex-wife, as well as Iva, Joan, and Pearl and some other people lived on Twenty-fourth Street in Cleveland in an eleven-room house that his mother owned. His father lived with them at one point, he said. Tom senior was married then. I thought that this would be one of the areas that Tom and I would explore on our second interview because I felt too tired to ask questions. We knew very little about Tom senior's life as a teenager and when he actually left West Virginia for Ohio.

Tom senior also started talking again about his agony after Patricia O'Reilly died. He recalled periods when he had been drinking and did not know where he had been or what he had done. And that prompted Tom to talk about an experience when he had drunk too much rum at a volunteer firefighters' dance and went into a bathroom and later couldn't account for the twenty minutes he was in there. Tom senior described how his half sister Jane died.

"She was off of it for years, and Joan took a bottle of liquor up there [he didn't say where or when] and got her drunk.

Then it was just like with me, she couldn't get off of it. You know, she had to have it. She drank like I did. She'd pour a water glass full and drink it straight down. And then one night, Jane got up and was throwing up. And while she was throwing up, though, evidently she probably ate something 'cause, generally, you won't throw up if you're drinking like that, and she busted blood veins, either in her stomach or neck, and she drank that water glass of liquor and it sedated her, and she went back to sleep and she bled to death: Her ears, eyes, everything—hemorrhaged to death.

"She was abused terribly," he added.

Again, I thought, we would need to know more about how his father had abused her, but at the moment I wanted to leave.

"As far as a binge drinker or drinking booze, I dare not touch the stuff," Tom senior said. "A shot of liquor, believe me, I would love to have a shot of liquor."

"A rough time for him," Fern said, "was during the holidays when he was off from work. But he made it through it. And I'm proud of him."

"That is something to be proud of," Tom said.

"Drinking beer like that wouldn't faze me," Tom senior said.

"He really has about three or four beers a night before he goes to bed," Fern said. "But he works hard all day, and he deserves it. I guess."

Tom told him about his problems with drugs.

"I mean, like, I've told Greg a couple of times, that since we've been down here, I'll just be sitting there and I'll want it," he admitted about cocaine. Tom senior resumed talking about the dangers of alcohol and told Tom about a friend who drank herself to death and that her friends and family did not help her. I asked him how it was possible that no one helped.

"There was no love in the family," Tom senior said, and

then directed his next comment at Tom: "That's the same thing he really has right now. Is there really love and affection between you and your sisters? Probably not."

"Yeah, there is," Tom said softly.

"I doubt it," Tom senior continued. "See, psychologically, you, from childhood, you were raised: I have to love this person because they're my brother, they're my sister, they're my mother, they're my father."

Tom insisted that his love for his sisters was genuine but that his love for Patty was greater because they were raised together and survived by depending on each other. But Tom senior was relentless, and I wondered if he was talking as much about his relationship with his sisters as he was about Tom's relationship with his sisters. I also wondered if Tom senior wasn't trying to denigrate Tom's love for those closest to him.

"You may not love anybody, really," Tom senior said. "How do you know love?"

"I've struggled with that thought a lot, but I know love when I would be willing to die for someone," Tom said. "I know love when I'd be willing to kill for someone."

"If you're like me, when I met your mother, and I really found out what love was, you might throw everything you got out the window," Tom senior said. "Everything that you think that you're good and solid now, you might throw totally right out the window. And say, man, this is really love."

Tom senior was not talking about love. He was talking about obsession and madness. He wanted us to believe that love had driven him to all his excesses, for which, of course, he was not responsible because he was an alcoholic. He had spent almost the whole night talking about his sufferings. He expressed little, if any, sympathy, for the misery of Patricia O'Reilly or his children. Tom senior couldn't empathize. I hadn't heard him say one word about a sacrifice he had made for another person. Though I didn't believe a willingness to

306 Morris and Waters

die or kill were accurate measures of love, Tom, who had been denied real love in two households, understood that one measure of loving was the willingness to sacrifice for someone else.

"I think for a long time my relationship with my girlfriend was a dependency because of insecurities," Tom said. "So, now, I don't know. Now, I'm going through such weird feelings about her and about me and everything, and how things are gonna go. I know I love the girl, I love her. Okay? But I don't know what kind of love, all right? Now, Patty, is a totally different story. I mean, if anything ever happened to Patty, I don't know what I would do. I mean I really don't. Even though I live in Vermont, and she lives in Ohio, she is my only identification with this world. See, I have nightmares about it. I wake up bawling my head off. Sometimes I have nightmares where I'll wake up because I just had a nightmare that someone hurt my sister. And I'll wake up, no covers on the bed, thrashing, you know. I'll wake up because I'm crying, fists clenched, and thrashing around."

"Change that situation," Tom senior said. "What I'm saying is you should do something about it now. You shouldn't wait 'til a tragedy happens. You should start developing some close relationships with other people, people that you can lean on. People that'll care about you."

"But I do," Tom said. "It's hard for me to, it's hard. It's hard because I don't know anybody. I mean, I know people— oh, I know tons of people, but I don't care about 'em. I don't feel for 'em. I really think, wow, this person's really a good friend of mine and I'd hate to see if anything ever happened to him. And they'll leave, and I won't care. I won't lose a minute's sleep over it 'cause that's the way I've been brought up."

Tom senior reiterated that Tom's inability or unwillingness to form real friendships was "destructive."

"I know it is," Tom replied. "That's why I'm trying to

change it. I've had close personal friends that I really do care for. And I end up getting fucked over. Or they just end up splitting."

But, on the other hand, he conceded, when people had tried to get close to him, he pushed them away. He cited Tracie as an example: "We fight because she starts doing things, to try and get close and I'll push her away. I mean, I'll get all mean, you know. I won't ever strike her; I'd never attempt to strike her."

"See, that's like with me, you can't con an old con," Tom senior said. "I've been there. You're liable to make the same mistakes I made in life. Look where you're going to end up at. An old trailer out in the woods somewhere."

We all laughed.

"Okay, I just turned twenty-one," Tom said, after everyone stopped laughing. "And I'm already scared to death. Okay? 'Cause since we've been here in Florida I've had a beer every night. Ever since I was little that was always on my mind, what you were telling me earlier: Stay away from alcohol. I got into college and I know people who get drunk every night. So, me, I stay away from alcohol; I don't drink that much. I could go to a party and have one or two beers just because it was cool to do, and because it's a way to fit in with the people. But I didn't enjoy one second of it, and I didn't like the taste of it. Okay? So, all this time I'm fighting alcohol, and making sure that it doesn't get anywhere into my little circle. I don't keep my eye on other things and drugs come in 'cause those, I think, ah, those are a totally different story that's not programmed into my genes. I can't become addicted to marijuana. I can't become addicted to cocaine because that's not in me. It's only alcohol that's in me and cocaine will not grab ahold of me, and it almost did."

"I tell you what you want to do, really, and it's a good thing, too," Tom senior said. "You should get you a diary and put down all the things that bother you. And when you got all those things down on a piece of paper, all of 'em, you start within yourself just like it's a war: You kill every goddamn one of those emotions and life cannot touch you. I mean, it's like you're in a prison—you start working yourself out of that prison. And once you're out here socially sound, this and that, and you've killed all that shit within yourself, there's no fear in loving anybody or trusting 'em or this, that. The only fear of loving and trusting anybody is the inadequacies in yourself. You let people down before they let you down."

"Seriously?" Tom asked.

"Life done it to you," Tom senior replied, "but you have to overcome that yourself. If you can't tell the truth to other people, tell it to yourself. And then get rid of it, get rid of the fear. It's the way to do it. If you're bound by religions or anything else, get rid of it. Whatever you want to do, go do it. 'Cause the simple reason is, you're not gonna straighten your head out as long as you keep yourself locked up. Can't do it. And I won't lie to you, and if there's anybody that can help your head I can. I can tell you what put you there. I'm one of the persons responsible that put you there. You can't keep distrusting people because a few people let you down."

Tom senior's comments surprised me. His manner and his words were so out of context with so much else he had expressed that night that I was reluctant at first to recognize his sincerity. He told us another story from his past. I imagined it was a warning to Tom of what lay ahead for him if he succumbed to alcohol or cocaine. It was a bittersweet allegory—bitter because it revealed the depths of a person's despair; sweet because it had happened so long ago that Tom senior could recall it with a laugh.

"I was on my way from Texas; had three thousand dollars in my pocket," he said. "This is after I got out of the penitentiary. I started drinking. I had three thousand dollars in my pocket, I think it took me thirty days to get from Houston to Cleveland. I ended up at a Red Roof Inn, and, God, I don't know how much I had been drinking, but I had me about three fifths of whiskey before I went and got that room. And this little thing kept growing and growing and growing. It started out as a little ol' teeny thing under the sheet next to me. You know, it said to me, it said it was from outer space and it was sent here to seed with humans."

Everyone started laughing.

"And then that sucker started to growing wings, you know, and getting bigger and bigger as a gigantic grasshopper, that's what it was," Tom senior continued. "I went down there to the main desk and I told 'em about it, just as calm as hell."

The police were summoned, and a police officer accompanied Tom senior to his room. "So, I opened the door, I thought I'd seen it behind the door. I said, 'It's behind the door.' The cop said, 'Close the door, close the door.' "

Tom senior's voice, which had been getting louder as he spun his tale, was momentarily drowned out by the din of raucous laughter.

"I said, 'I'm leaving this son-of-a-bitchin' place. You guys take care of it.' I got in my car and drove away."

We were laughing out of control. Eventually, Fern, who had been participating more with each passing hour, recalled other spectral encounters. Once, when they were staying in Cleveland, Tom senior told her to feed popcorn to the little people who he said were living in the baseboard of the bedroom where they slept. There were other incidents she was describing as Tom senior started talking.

"Elephants," Fern recalled as Tom senior said, "You know you'll get used to those hallucinations. That's the hell of the bad side about it."

"Snakes," Fern added.

There was an additional bad side, Tom senior said. Sometimes it can be difficult to distinguish between reality and fantasy.

That prompted him to add, "I wouldn't be drinking this

beer if I didn't think I couldn't handle it. 'Cause it's too dangerous."

"Well, just in the last few weeks since I turned twenty-one, I've been noticing how beer's starting to taste better," Tom admitted. "And I like the taste of beer and last night I was sitting at the bar by myself in Melbourne—and I like whiskey, I don't know why. It runs in the family, I guess.

"But remember that night we each got a shot of whiskey," Tom said to me. "Well, I got a couple of shots of whiskey, actually; and then had some beer and last night I'm sitting there, and I drank a beer; took me about two minutes. And I said I want another one. And I sat there, I was about halfway through it, and I said I'd like a shot of whiskey. And I drank the shot; I was expecting it to burn but it gave me a buzz. I drank about half of it. And I thought, man, this is kind of weird 'cause it didn't work. The next drink I took was the rest of that whiskey. And I scared myself so bad that I finished my beer and left. Because I said if I don't pull myself away from here, now I'm gonna end up sitting here getting drunk, and then I'm thinking when I'm in bed: Should you ever drink again in your life. 'Cause I know what's in me, I know what's in me, I found out through cocaine, already."

"Well, yeah, but you can't never say never," Fern said.

"I'm saying should I stay away from it?" Tom asked.

It was about 10:30 P.M. and we had been talking for more than five hours. Because I was tired, I was only vaguely aware that something else had been evolving and that the evening was not winding down to a close. Tom was opening up about a crisis that he believed was threatening him, and it wasn't a laughing matter. He and I had talked about him being cautious about his drinking because of the history of alcoholism in his family, and I had assumed, from those occasional discussions, that he was smart enough to navigate the temptations. And from other similar discussions, I had concluded that his use of cocaine was a brief but dangerous flirtation that he had resolved in his counseling sessions with his psychologist. But he was saying that night that the temptations were still there, and he wasn't sure how he should handle them. He was seeking advice from two people who had been expounding so authoritatively about what they had learned through their firsthand experiences. Tom senior had talked about falling on and off the wagon and attending AA meetings and talking to psychologists and counselors and finally reaching into himself to rely on his inner strength and also finding God to help him. Fern had described how she had been there to support him.

"Should I walk around thinking, well, I've got the potential but as long as it's in my mind I can still drink and just keep a good control on it?" Tom asked.

"If you think you can," Fern said.

"But, no, that's how I got away from the cocaine," he said.

He escaped that addiction when he realized that he couldn't control it. He was just starting to tell them how hard it was for him to resist cocaine when Tom Sr. offered some words of wisdom.

"Isn't it a lot easier to say I'm not gonna drink today than to say that I'm not gonna drink for the rest of my life?" Tom senior asked, speaking rhetorically. "One day at a time, like life, one day at a time. Don't let pressures drive you because if you let the pressures drive you, you're gonna get drunk. 'Cause pretty soon all the pressures build up. Forget about what people say. You do what you want to do. If you don't want to drink, don't drink. But it's safe to say I don't have to drink today. And tomorrow, you might say the same thing again and again."

Tom senior told his son not to allow people to lean on him and to "be your own self. If people don't like it, tell 'em to kiss your ass. That's the way to do. You'll always continue to let people use you until you make a stand and you say no.

"It's like that cocksucker," Tom senior said, referring to

Carl Rimmer, "and then I hear you say, 'He's my father, I feel sorry for him.' I don't feel sorry for him 'cause you know why? I've never been involved with him except one night for a little while. I don't care if they put him before a firing squad tomorrow. You do because you was attached."

"But, you know what?" Tom said. "I wouldn't lose sleep if he was executed."

Tom senior started talking about his sister, Aunt Pearl.

"She's gonna come down here to cry," he said. "All I'm gonna be is an ear. That's all."

He said he loved his sister but he wouldn't allow her to use him or make demands that would result in him falling off the wagon again.

"She'll bring a fifth here so she's got to have her cocktails, and then Joan'll follow, and Joan adds her bit, and pretty soon I'll walk over to the table and take me a damn drink, too," he said.

"Noooo," he continued, "I won't let that happen. I might have to say to her, Now, look, who you should be discussing this with is a good psychologist and your husband."

He then lapsed into a profane description of his sister. Tom senior said, in essence, that Aunt Pearl, because she wanted her kids to have a better life than the one she had experienced, had made sacrifices that led to "nervous breakdowns" and alcoholism. I didn't meet Aunt Pearl when Tom and I were in Elyria over the Thanksgiving holiday because she did not want to talk to me, but I knew Arlene and Darlene were skeptical of her because she kept insisting they were never sexually abused. But if she had sacrificed herself for her kids, as Tom senior explained, then she deserved more respect than he was giving her.

The conversation shifted and Tom senior told us what he would do if he didn't have to be concerned about the laws of man and God. He would be "Jesse James," acting without fear of punishment if he decided to kill, especially if he murdered elderly people who drove forty-five miles per hour in a sixty-five zone. Tom sympathized. And for the next five minutes we all laughed at Tom's and Tom senior's varying accounts of the mayhem they would commit against elderly drivers if there were no laws. The interview had turned into a bullshit session, and I hoped that indicated we were nearing the end. Then Tom senior started talking about his quick draw with a gun.

"I used to be so good, man. I was really into it, you know, Jesse James stuff and Billy the Kid and everything," he said with glee. "I used to practice my fast draw all the time."

One day, he continued, he and his first wife visited her family in southern Ohio, and one of his in-laws, whom he did not like, was sitting at a table cleaning his nails while Tom senior was practicing his fast draw. At one moment when he was drawing the gun from his holster he accidentally fired the gun and destroyed the handle of a door. The in-law, he said, collapsed "like a wet noodle" on the floor.

"He thought he had been shot," Tom senior said. "I'm staring and my mouth dropped open, you know. I couldn't believe what I just did."

We were all rocking with laughter.

"Every time I went to southern Ohio," he continued, "I'd load up all these automatics and everything else, man, all them guns. Take me three or four hours just to set the cans and bottles and all this stuff on the hillside. People said it sounded like a small war. I bet I'd shoot up seventy, eighty dollars' worth of ammo in just a couple of days when it was really cheap. I mean, just rapid fire, man, just boom, boom, boom. As soon as one was empty, I'd throw it down, grab another one."

He had shotguns and large-caliber rifles, and he spent a few minutes describing his .50-caliber Swiss-made elephant gun and the technical distinctions between .410 and .44-40 shells. I understood some of what he said, but I believed Tom, who owned a few hunting rifles, understood him better. Tom senior said he had occasionally visited a boss who owned some land that was used as a firing range. Tom senior described with pride his shooting prowess, and then began talking about his violent temper.

"I have thanked God before for alcohol," Tom senior said. "The simple reason is, if it had not been for alcohol, especially in the early stages after your mother died, I would have killed every one of them. Every one. 'Cause you probably don't remember it, you know, but I had access to chemicals. I used to sit around and make these bombs. Boy, I was going to invite all of 'em."

"Who?" I asked. I wasn't certain if he was serious.

"A great big party—my family, her family, all of 'em," Tom senior responded. "Just take you kids and walk out and detonate that son of a bitch inside the house while I had 'em all there having a big-eyed time, thinking all is forgiven. I was just gonna' take you kids and get you aside and go on outside and detonate that son of a bitch."

But he could never detonate the bomb.

"And the next morning I'd be sitting there sobering up, disarming those suckers, taking 'em apart and washing them down the drain," he said.

As he described the ingredients of the bomb, the name of the first ingredient was garbled. I heard the words "chloric acid and sawdust." He also talked about putting "ball bearings and stuff in it. And strap it to a can of gasoline, and blowing those sons of bitches sky-high because I had reason to hate 'em. I had good reason."

I believed he was serious. But I did not believe he had planned to spare Tom and his daughters. That sounded like an afterthought, or that he was sugarcoating mass murder with a sentimental appeal to his son. I couldn't imagine him admitting to Tom, who was sitting next to him, that he wanted to kill him twenty years ago. He hadn't even admitted that he used to beat and terrorize Tom, though he did concede that he was one of the people responsible for his emotional and mental torture. I believed that Tom senior, if he had gone through with his plan, would have killed his kids as well as himself.

Tom senior also talked about flaying his relatives and family, adding that after he went to prison and found redemption "and got my head screwed on right," he no longer wanted revenge.

He started talking again about the perils of alcohol and I knew he was just remonstrating to keep us there longer. He talked about Aunt Joan and her attempts to stop drinking and described how they faltered along the way. Aunt Joan, he said, refused to get help.

"Yeah," Tom said, "we've got to take off. We've got a long way to go."

"I really hate to see you leave, driving at this time," Tom senior said. He was referring to the lateness of the hour and the thick fog outside. Because we had already made plans to have dinner at Joyce's home on Saturday and then interview Linda, Patricia O'Reilly's half sister, later in the evening, we could not stay overnight in a hotel and resume talking to Tom senior the next day. But we made plans to return Sunday. Tom senior wanted to take us out to dinner and then resume the interview. When I shook hands with him to leave, his grip was stronger and he seemed buoyant and almost grateful. He was smiling like a fox when he told us, as we walked out the door, to drive carefully because he knew we had a lot to talk about. After we got in the car, and started driving through the dense fog to return to Melbourne, Tom said his father was the first person who understood what was going on in his head.

16 • "This ugly monster lurking"

We drove through thick fog for an hour and then light fog for another sixty minutes before we could see a safe distance in front of us, but we were so busy rapping and laughing that we paid scant attention to the hazardous conditions. Tom senior was correct about us having a lot to discuss on the trip back. First we speculated about how much he might have fabricated or deliberately tried to deceive us or put his particular spin on events and circumstances that had happened twenty years ago. Tom didn't believe his father had planned to spare him and his sisters when he was considering blowing up the Holmden Avenue house. But we also didn't believe he had lied. Instead, we suspected he had rationalized what he felt in 1970. I did not believe him when he said that he couldn't recall what he had done to his daughters because he was drunk at the time. His daughters remembered him threatening to harm them if they exposed what he was doing. There also was a significant contrast between his description of the day Patricia O'Reilly died and that of the police report. But that hadn't stopped Tom and me from spending much of the night at his home, and on our return ride to the hotel, doubled up in laughter. The impressions of the interview and what we were discussing were so vivid that I thought I could postpone tape-recording them until after we returned to our room and I got some sleep. We arrived back at our hotel about daybreak, and when we got up late that afternoon, both of us felt as if we had hangovers and could only vaguely remember what we had discussed during the night ride. Our minds were blank, as if the fog had seeped into our brains and wiped out our memories. But I recalled the numerous times I had laughed at Tom senior's profane and irreverent comments, and I wondered if what he had said was really as funny as I had felt when I was sitting in his home. It was eerie. But Tom and I didn't talk much. Instead we watched the Cleveland Browns play the Buffalo Bills, and Tom was ready to bounce off the walls of our room every time the Browns scored. And when they won on a last-minute interception, he was ecstatic, jumping up for joy. When we left at about 5:00 P.M. to go to Joyce's for dinner, our mood was upbeat.

Fred, Linda, Joyce, and Brittany were there, and so were several others. We told Joyce that we had talked to Tom senior for several hours and that we had just returned that morning, and that we were planning to see him the next day, Sunday. During dinner, Joyce casually mentioned that her daughter's best friend, who had grown up with Patricia in Cleveland, had visited her sometime during the previous year, and that they were occasionally in touch. It was important, I thought, that Tom and I contact the friend. Tom senior's descriptions and comments about Patricia and Linda and Joyce needed to be checked against other sources of information. I had talked to Patricia O'Reilly's worst enemy Friday night, so it was perfectly reasonable to talk to her best friend. Her first name was "Vicki," but I didn't even know if that was the correct spelling. Her maiden name sounded like "Polles" or "Pollus." Joyce said she was Greek. So, when I asked Joyce in my best casual manner for the address or telephone number of the friend, she replied that she had misplaced them. I sensed, for reasons unclear to me, that maybe she didn't want us to talk to her. (I felt certain that she had the information I wanted.) I planned to ask Linda, and if that didn't produce results, to ask Joyce again.

After dinner Tom and I met Linda at her home.

Linda Semen lived in a comfortable ranch-style home with her daughter Brittany, about fifteen minutes from Joyce's home. Linda worked full time at the Harris Corporation. Her husband, Bernie, had died in 1988 in a car accident, and Joyce, who was helping her daughter to raise Brittany, told us that Linda had still not recovered from his death. Linda, who hid her sorrow well, was about two inches taller than five feet, had soft brown eyes and brown hair.

When Tom and I arrived at her home later that same evening and she told me that she was thirty-five, I was surprised. It also was easy to understand why Tom and Patty recalled their visits with her with so much joy. Linda was refreshingly candid and uninhibited.

Linda knew we wanted to talk to her about her sister but, because of Tom senior's interview, our focus had expanded. Not only were we trying to determine what hand he had played in her sister's death, we also had to know if his character assassination of her, her sister, and their mother was rooted in fact. After several minutes of general chitchat, the formal part of the interview started, with Linda recalling what neighbors had told her about the day that her sister died. Her account matched information Tom and I already had, and, because she didn't provide any significant new details, I decided not to pursue that line of questioning. Instead, for the next several minutes, I inquired about the neighborhood where she grew up and the schools she attended, and then asked what I considered were easy questions about her family. I eventually asked her how her sister felt about living with her grandmother instead of staying with her and Joyce. I was laying the groundwork for what I considered the sensitive but important questions that had to be asked. For example, Tom senior had told us that Joyce abandoned Patricia O'Reilly by having her live with her elderly grandmother, and that such a living situation allowed Patricia to run "wild" in the streets.

"Now that I am older I don't think too much of my mom for doing that," Linda also said. "It was like she got out of raising my sister."

I asked her if she knew how her sister, who was five or six years older than she, felt about that living arrangement.

"She never complained," Linda responded. "I think she was happy because she kind of got to run wild. She didn't have strict supervision."

What did she mean by wild? I asked, explaining that when I was growing up in Chicago some of my neighbors considered me wild. I did not tell her about Tom senior's comments. She understood my point.

"We all are in a way, I think because I was, I was a very wild and unruly child," she said.

When I asked her for more description of her "wild" ways, she said that when she was twelve or thirteen she was rebellious, that she cut classes, hung out with "the wrong crowd," and stayed in "the streets all hours of the night." For the two summers when she lived with her sister and Tom senior, she sneaked out of their Holmden Avenue house when everyone was asleep and joined her friends. She also sneaked out of her home when she lived with Joyce in Cleveland. Her friends hung out at a local playground or at a neighborhood swimming pool. The "wrong crowd," Tom and I learned, were kids her age who smoked cigarettes, drank beer, and occasionally tried to get high. She occasionally sipped beer. Her crowd was not involved in shootings, knifings, or gang fights. After about five minutes of talking with Linda, I realized that questioning her would be unlike interviewing all the other people whom Tom and I had questioned together, and that included the interviews I had done alone. Linda had nothing to hide. She was guilt-free. She wasn't ashamed of anything or anyone. She was not out for revenge. Still mourning her husband's death, she nevertheless wanted to help us. I realized we were in for an easy time. Tom apparently picked up on this revelation just about the same time I did, because he started asking pointed questions.

"And what was Joyce doing while you were doing all of that stuff?" Tom asked Linda. "Did she really care? She was pretty wild herself, wasn't she?"

It was about 8:00 P.M. Linda was sitting on a couch next to me. Tom was sitting in a chair facing the both of us. Brittany was asleep. Linda said she believed Joyce didn't care and agreed that Joyce had been "wild" but then clarified her comments.

"I came along late in my mom's life. She was thirty-nine, going on forty," Linda said. "I think I was very unexpected. I love my mom to death but she does have her faults. Okay? Nobody's perfect. And she was set in her ways when I came along. She had to work. She and my dad were divorced almost even before I was born. And on Friday, Saturday nights, she loved to dance, so she would drop me off at either her mother's house or my dad's mother's house. And it was like I was raised mainly by my dad's mom. My grandparents."

When her parents separated, her father, Frank Kurtz, was only required to pay fifteen dollars a week in child support, Linda said. He might have been able to pay more, but she believed he lost most of his money betting on horses. He was not, she insisted, an alcoholic, despite what Joyce told us. Linda grew up resenting the fact that Joyce worked so much that she didn't spend much time with her. And Linda occasionally did things to spite her mother, such as demanding to live with her father, because she knew that would hurt Joyce.

After listening for several more minutes, I told Linda that

her description of her wild ways was relatively mild by my standards.

"Back then it was considered wild," she said, "because it wasn't proper for girls to be out running the streets. You see, for boys it was different."

I commented that if a girl was identified as one who ran the streets, then that also implied that she was sexually promiscuous.

"Even if you weren't," Linda said.

"You said that you and your sister and your mother had a wild streak. Is that right?" I asked Linda.

"I believe we did. Yes," Linda replied.

"Your sister was like that," I said.

"I believe that from what I know, yes, that she had a wild streak in her too," Linda said.

"It was the same wildness that you were talking about," I said, referring to her self-description. I was trying to make a point for Tom's benefit.

"She was with my grandmother," Linda explained. "My grandmother was old, senile. Patty was out running the streets, or how else would she have met Tom senior and gotten in trouble? I mean nice girls at that time, they just got out of it."

"What's 'trouble' mean?" I asked.

"Pregnant," Linda responded.

Nice girls were the ones who were discreet about their sexual adventures or were lucky or wise enough to avoid getting pregnant.

"My dad says that my mom was doing things like that at fourteen," Tom said, referring to allegations that Patricia O'Reilly was sexually promiscuous.

"She could have been," Linda replied.

"They said that she was out running around with guys down at Pier Nine," he said, referring to the allegations of Tom senior and Pam Haynes.

"That could have been true," Linda said. "I don't know."

"Yeah," I interrupted, "that could have been true. But the thing is, that if you were out on the streets at night when you were a young girl then you were—"

"Doing it anyway," Tom said, finishing my statement. "Even if—"

"Even if you weren't," Linda said, completing Tom's thought.

Because I had been worrying that Tom senior's sanctimonious descriptions of Patricia O'Reilly might poison Tom's budding impression of her, I was hoping that Linda would help me expose the double standards that might taint his mother's image and provide him more insight. Patricia O'Reilly, who had little parental guidance, was a child of the streets. That made her an easy target for the stigmas attached to kids who turn to the streets for what they can't get in their homes. If she was having affairs when she was a young girl, I didn't want her memoirs tainted by sanctimonious double standards that pass for good American values. I also knew Tom needed more life experience himself to envision his mother's life. I hoped I could make the process less painful. I hoped Tom would keep in mind that his own first sexual experience with a female peer happened when he was thirteen, and that his subsequent assignations with girls his age enabled him to keep a grip on his sexual identity. He could not condone his own behavior and look askance on his teenybopping paramours unless he was planning to be as narrowminded as his two fathers.

I was pleased when Linda, who didn't need any prompting, described her sister as beautiful.

"You have your mother's color hair, and she was just a little taller than me," Linda said. "She was about five feet, three inches and bigger-boned, but she was—I just worshiped her. I always wanted to be like my sister. I worshiped her and I wanted to base my life basically on what she did. I can remember begging her to take me with her and Vicki wherever they went. I would just grab onto her leg and say, 'Take me with you.' "

Linda also confided that she briefly followed in her sister's footsteps. When she was in her early teens she got involved with a reprobate as ornery as Tom senior but she managed to escape because of her family's intervention.

I asked about her early impression of Tom senior.

"At first I thought he was a very nice person," she said. "He was nice to my mom. When he wasn't drinking he was as nice as he could be. But it was like as soon as he had that first drink it was like Mr. Hyde and Dr. Jekyll."

Linda became aware of his malevolent nature as she spent more time with him and her sister. She noticed that Tom senior got drunk several days a week, and, without Tom and me asking, she told us about the time she got drunk drinking Southern Comfort. She was taking care of Arlene and Darlene for her sister who was working an evening job as a waitress. Linda was about twelve.

"All I remember is the first time that I got drunk was on Southern Comfort and that is what him [Tom senior] and his brother Brent were drinking," she said. "They offered some to me and my girlfriend. He was very nice to me. I mean, I even got sick, throwed up, hugging the porcelain god there. That's how sick I was and he was nice, the nicest guy. He took care of me that night. He put a washcloth on my forehead. He told me not to tell my sister."

Of course, Tom senior had said that she and her friend came to the house drunk and that while she was having sex with Tom senior, her friend was having sex with Brent. For some reason, at that moment I could not tell her about Tom senior's version and ask for her comment, even though I knew Tom senior had contradicted himself about what had happened. I worried that my dislike of Tom senior and my affection for Linda would interfere with my interviewing her. I decided to make my inquiry later. Linda continued, telling us that she didn't know that Tom senior was married and already had a family until after her sister died. She believed they were married until Tom, sitting across from her that night, told her that they hadn't been.

I asked Linda when she noticed a change in Tom senior's behavior.

"I mean, did he feel that Patricia by getting pregnant made things more difficult for him or anything like that?" I asked.

"He kept her pregnant," Linda said, correcting me. "He drank heavy but he didn't really get real schizo that I can remember until after the twins were born. And I think that is when the violence started."

I asked her to describe the violence. I told her I only wanted to know what she herself had witnessed. I didn't want more secondhand accounts. Linda recalled the day Tom senior was angry that her sister borrowed Joyce's car. He grabbed an ax and destroyed a TV. He took a knife and butchered a sofa. He busted up other furniture and threw it out a window. "Probably the thing that sticks out most in my mind was the time that he pulled a gun on my sister and told her to beg for her life. I was sitting there on the couch next to her."

I asked what had instigated the incident. Linda didn't know. I asked what prompted him to put the gun away.

"My sister begging. Me begging. I begged for my sister's life," she said.

"Do you really think he was going to do it?" I asked.

"Yeah, he was drunk. I really believe he would have done it," she said.

She recalled other violent episodes. Sometimes she stumbled into confrontations when she entered their home and discovered her sister begging him to stop beating her or not to kill her. He frequently threw her on the floor and beat her with his fists but he backhanded Patricia more than he punched her, Linda said. Patricia did not fight back. When she got the chance, she fled with her children. Linda wasn't sure what precipitated the incidents, but she believed most started with Tom senior accusing Patricia of being unfaithful.

"She worked at little fast-food restaurants like Royal Castle and stuff like that, and he accused her of flirting with the customers and going to bed with the manager and that kind of thing. He was just paranoid. Something was going on in his mind."

"Was she seeing other people? Did she have a boyfriend on the side?" I asked.

"No," she said. "I really don't believe that."

A woman who married Tom senior in June 1972, and divorced him in 1973, told the Oberlin police, investigating him after his arrest, that he beat her regularly when he was drunk. "The reason he beat me was because he thought I was having sex with every man that came around," she said, according to the statement taken in December 1973. "He accused me of having sex with my stepdad, my brother and his brother. He was very possessive and insanely jealous of any attention I would show to anyone. Often when he was drinking he would tell me he killed Patricia [O'Reilly]; that it was all his fault and then he would cry."

Linda told us about Patricia's missing upper teeth and recalled that she had said they had been knocked out in a car accident. Linda didn't believe her.

I told Linda that Tom senior said that he had tied Patricia to a chair, and I asked her if she knew if he "tortured" her sister with lighted cigarettes. Linda replied that her sister told her that Tom senior burned her "breasts and her vagina and places like that. That's why I can't believe when you said he tied her to a chair. I mean I believe it was the bed and not the chair."

Linda said she learned of the burns the last time she saw her sister alive, which was the weekend she died. Patricia spent the weekend with Linda and Joyce and Fred, who were living in Brunswick. Tom senior had told us that he and Pat had spent the weekend together. Linda also told us what her mother had said earlier: that Joyce and Fred were planning to move to Florida because of Fred's health, and they wanted to take Patricia and the kids with them.

"I think she was seriously considering it. Why she went back that Sunday, I don't know," Linda said. "I know that whole weekend we had the Brunswick police at our house a number of times because Tom was harassing us." He was at the door or standing in the yard "calling my sister, wanting her to come out and wanting to talk to her and stuff like that. And why she left that Sunday and went back with him, I have no idea."

Linda never saw him beat or molest Arlene, Darlene, Patty, or Tom.

"Did he ever try anything with you?" Tom asked, finally.

"Nope," she said.

"Never?" Tom asked.

"Never," she said. "His brother did—tried—but Tom senior was always there and stopped the advances that Brent was making."

"Were these flirtatious advances?" I asked. "Or were these serious advances?"

"Serious advances," Linda said.

"So, it was not safe for you there when Brent was there?" I asked.

"No, it wasn't. It wouldn't have been safe for me with Brent in the same house alone. I wouldn't have felt safe at all."

She said Tom senior and Pat were regularly strapped for money and that Joyce frequently gave her daughter money to pay bills. She also said that the house was usually in a mess because her sister worked hard and was too tired to clean, and that Tom senior didn't help. Her sister lived off Pepsi-Cola and potato chips and "smoked like a fiend."

Because Tom senior had told us Patricia O'Reilly earned big bucks as a waitress, I asked Linda if her sister made a good living.

"Tips, minimum wage, working at a fast-food restaurant," Linda said. "Every time she would try to better herself, because she didn't finish school, Tom senior would always come up with some excuse where she couldn't finish night school or get her GED."

Linda believed that her sister finished her sophomore year in high school. "He would just make her feel like she wasn't worth doing that stuff," Linda said. "The best way that I can describe what her life was like was if you have seen Farrah Fawcett in *The Burning Bed* on TV."

The made-for-TV film was based on the book, *The Burning Bed,* about Francine Hughes, a Michigan woman, who killed her abusive husband by setting his bed on fire in 1977.

Tom eventually told Linda that Tom senior believed that his family had been in bad financial shape because her sister gave their money to Joyce.

"No, I don't believe that," Linda told Tom. "I really don't. My mom and Fred paid for that house that your dad and your mom lived in. They bought that house with inheritance money that my mom had gotten."

Linda continued, talking about her sister: "She never went to a doctor either. Whenever she was pregnant, she never went to the doctor. My God, when I was pregnant with Brittany, I went once a month. She, never. I don't know where all the money went. I have a feeling that a lot of it disappeared into alcohol and she always had to rob Peter to pay Paul, as the expression goes. She never went to the doctor the whole time, so I was really glad that all the kids turned out okay, that there was nothing physically wrong with any of them."

I asked again about Patricia's health.

"She looked bad, real bad. I mean, she was, I keep saying, she was a very beautiful person and it was like after Tom came into her life she wasn't beautiful anymore."

Tom started going over some previous points.

"You said that Grandma had this wild streak in her," he said.

"By wild I mean my mom going out dancing," Linda responded.

"I am going to say some things and I don't want you to think that I think it is true or that I believe it to be true," Tom told her. "But I am just going to say what I have heard. But what Tom senior said yesterday was that you guys were real wild. He said that what you guys, meaning my mom and your mom, Grandma, used to go down to the pier and hunt down guys, and Grandma used to go with my mom, and she would do something like use my mom in order to pick up guys for herself. Or she would use my mom as the bait. Then they would take these guys and bed them."

"I can't believe my mom doing that," Linda said.

"You know," he continued, telling her what Tom senior had said, "Grandma would be bedding this guy, quote un-quote—that's the way he puts it—in one room while my mom would be bedding another guy in the other room, you know at twelve, fourteen years old."

"If your dad believed all this stuff, why did he ever get involved?" Linda asked.

Tom didn't respond, but persisted with his questioning. "What are your feelings? I mean, you say you can't believe that."

"My mom thinks that sex is dirty, and it's nasty," Linda told him. "I mean, my God, that's why I find it very hard to believe that would be going on."

Linda's response was so direct that neither Tom nor I wanted to reply.

"Have you ever heard the term 'wharf rat'?" Tom asked.

I had assumed, wrongly, that he knew that the expression was nothing more than his cousin Pam trying to paraphrase what she had been told or overheard from her family.

"No," Linda said.

"You see," Tom said, "a wharf rat is a whore on the pier. Someone used that term to describe my mother, which wasn't very pleasing."

As the three of us continued talking, I told Tom that I thought he was more revealing "when we are talking to people." I made the comment to see how he would respond.

"You're right, I am more revealing because when I hear people, I am more revealing to you because you don't know me well enough yet" for him to open up as much as I wanted, he said, explaining that listening to other people talk helped him to recall memories and to express himself. "There's still a lot of stuff that has happened to me that I don't remember but it's there inside me."

"Also, it's a matter of comfort," he added. "You know, if I am comfortable enough to tell you, then I will only reveal certain things."

Tom was not telling me something that I didn't know, but I wanted to know how he felt and I also wanted to know how accurate my observations were.

I asked Linda how she felt about Tom senior and she replied, "I feel that he made my sister's life pure hell while she was here and that she is in a better place, but I don't hate him. I really don't have any feelings for him at all."

Linda believed that alcohol fueled Tom senior's madness. She recalled how he locked himself in his Holmden Avenue house and tried to kill himself after her sister's body was removed the day she died.

"And I remember him trying to lift her up out of the casket, saying he was sorry," Linda said.

As I was thinking that we were about to begin winding down the interview, Tom was just beginning to open up.

"I always think to myself that if something happened to me, I will find out," he said. "Just like in life, you know, you do something to me and you try to hide it, I will find out. Okay? That is my attitude. But I don't know if this will ever come out. Such a mixed-up thing. So many people have so much guilt and other things to hide. And it is so long ago."

I empathized with him. We were trying to discover the truth, and there were no definitive clues or facts. We were relying on interviews with people whose recollections were not always accurate or fair. Even the records were flawed. His mother's death certificate was an example. It was as if the official document was part of the conspiracy to mock her life. She died an O'Reilly, not a Waters, as it was listed on the record. She was not married. She worked for a living but her occupation was listed as "housewife." She was tied to a chair or a bed, punched, menaced with guns, her twenty-two-year-old body bore scars and bruises, and, yet, someone ruled that she died a natural death. And the records from Children Services weren't much better. Some information was possibly fabricated, according to Tom's attorney, Robert Vecchio. And the written documentation of the Rimmers family appeared even more grotesque when juxtaposed with Tom's and Patty's accounts. Under the right circumstances, it seemed that Children Services might describe an abattoir as a house of love.

I told Tom that as soon as I returned to New York I would contact the medical examiner's office that was to help me understand his mother's autopsy. Besides just getting a second opinion, I wanted to develop a working knowledge of the medical procedures for an autopsy, to try to discover if there were any improprieties or mistakes involved with the determination of her death. If everything appeared kosher, then we had no choice but to assume that the autopsy had been done properly, despite the fact that Patricia had lived in pain and in fear of being murdered on those occasions when she had a gun stuck to her head.

When Tom asked Linda if she knew if his mother was trying to have an abortion and she said no, he told her what Aunt Pearl had told him about Aunt Joan's efforts to help his mother abort the baby. He also told Linda what Tom senior had told us: that he found a large sum of money in Patricia O'Reilly's pocketbook and that he believed Joyce had given her the money to get an abortion.

"Yes, if your mother had any money on her person," Linda

told him, "it was to pay the bills. I believe my mom gave her money to pay the bills."

"Not to have an abortion," Tom said.

"Not to have an abortion," Linda replied.

Linda's opinion wasn't enough to convince Tom; he sounded flustered as he told Linda that his knowledge of what really happened to his mother was limited by what people told him and he despaired of ever learning the truth. I reiterated my point, that we would check with the medical examiner's office and then with the coroner's office in Cleveland, but I was beginning to believe that what I said wasn't making much of an impression on him.

We told Linda that Tom senior had said her sister had a slight cold the day she died and that Aunt Pearl told Tom that his mother was so sick, she offered to take care of her and the kids in her home in Lorain County. Tom asked Linda if she recalled her mother's condition that Sunday.

Was she "staggering around, looking like a ghost and puking her head off and just on her last leg?" he asked.

"She was fine Sunday night when she left, she was fine," Linda said.

I sensed Tom's despair at another piece of conflicting information, and I reiterated that when we checked with the medical examiner's office and the coroner's office, we could probably establish the circumstances of his mother's death with a greater "degree of certainty than what people have had to live with in the past twenty years.

"I was surprised that there wasn't some kind of grand jury investigation," I continued, "but I guess that was based on the autopsy report," which said Patricia died of natural causes.

Linda asked what Tom senior said about his treatment of his daughters, and Tom recalled our interview with him. Tom also told her that Tom senior "feels that he is sorry. He knows that he has hurt us all. He came right out and said that."

Tom was right, but I thought he was giving his father more credit than he was due.

"I am not trying to make excuses for him and I am not trying to say that that is the full case," Tom said, as if reading my mind.

But he said it was possible that Tom senior didn't recall what he had done. I thought of a better description: Tom senior did not want to accept responsibility for what he had done. But I knew this was a sensitive point with Tom, and I wanted to be careful about arguing with him. I believed he needed more time to put things together.

But we did argue.

I eventually told him that Tom senior's comments were typical of those of incestuous fathers.

"I am not by any means defending him," Tom reiterated. "I am not by any means saying that it didn't happen, I am not saying that it did happen. I don't know. I am not the one that had it happen to. So, I have no clue. I don't know what to believe, really."

I told him what I thought: "He molested them. Whether it was rape, oral sex, fondling, they were molested."

I was about to recall what he and his sisters had told me about the days and nights of bloodshed.

"But I also believe that it is possible that he does not remember," Tom said.

There in Linda's home, I was impressed with her accounts and recollections, and I wanted to convince Tom I was right, so we continued debating the fine points of Tom senior's culpability: Was he lying? How much was he lying? Was he simply indulging in denial? Had his memory been dulled by blackouts caused by his drinking?

Linda eventually asked Tom, "Do you feel like you want to stay in touch with him?"

"I don't know," Tom said. "Last night I certainly did. Last night I was like, Wow, I really would like to stay in touch with this guy because he knows a lot about me. He really does know a lot about me, about what is going on inside of me now. He knows stuff about me that absolutely nobody else could know because it is something that is going on inside of me and I don't necessarily tell people what is going on inside me. But he just knows stuff about me because he and I are a lot alike, which I didn't ever know. I never knew, but he and I, in terms of the way things have happened to us and the way things have unfolded throughout life for us, we have both had the same things and struggles. I mean yesterday he was giving me advice about stuff. He was like, Take all those things you have inside of you, and you write them down on paper. I won't go into the long discussion, but he was just telling me stuff. I mean, there is no way he could say something like that to me unless he had experienced stuff like that. And I have that explosive nature in me, which is exactly the way he is. It is something that has calmed down in me a lot, and what's really hard is right now is that I am just going through this transition. This part of me is going away. But he knows about that. He just knows why because he went through it. And so I think that he in some ways might be able to help me. But I don't want a father. I am too old to have someone trying to be my father now because I would only reject them. But I really don't know. It is something that I have to go to Vermont and sit in the corner somewhere and think about it, sit for a while.

"You know," he continued, "I thought the same way about Joyce, too. When I left Grandmom's house the other day, I was like, Wow, I've really gotten close to her, I felt comfortable with her. And I just felt that she is my blood and I should be more in touch with her than I really am. You know it is hard to have feelings for people in my family because I have not known them. I mean, I just, oh yeah, that is my Aunt Linda, but I don't know you from Moses. And I am not saying that to be a jerk or anything like that. But it is hard to have feelings for anyone in this world even if I do know them.

"So, that is another point that he knew about because he

was the same way. My mom, according to him, was the first person that he had any feelings for at all. And that is why he freaked out the way he did. He beat on her and abused her because he had all these wild things going through his head that he could not deal with or cope with. He didn't understand them. He was like she was the first person that he loved and lusted for. And he just did not know how to deal with it.

"This is not funny by any means but see, maybe that will happen to me someday. Who knows? I certainly don't think I am going to go pounding on them because I love them so much. I mean, I love Tracie, I don't deal with her that way. With her I run, I just run away because I don't want to deal with her.

"I mean, with him it was just weird because it was like hearing myself. Do you know what it's like for me, Linda? It was like hearing myself thirty years from now. That is what it was like. It was really scary because he is the only thing I have to go by right now. That is really me. That I am a product of this, okay. This is what I am a product of. Now if you were my mother and I was sitting here talking to you, then I could say, I am also a product of you. But all I have to work with now is what I know of him, what I have heard about him my whole life, what I saw of him yesterday. And I sit there and look at this man and he tells me these little stories about stuff he used to do. And I'm thinking, when am I going to start drinking and pounding on people? I don't think I am going to, but there certainly were other things less than that that went on in his life that I certainly want to avoid. Being a drunk isn't something that I am aspiring to at all. I have already had problems, not with alcohol, but other substances, and you know that really freaked me out for a while, but I know that it is there. It's like this ugly monster is lurking for me. And you know, even just like my sisters, too, they have the same problem, and it is unfortunate. I am doing this all mainly for us because we don't know about all this stuff. You know a lot of people, they grow up, they have the knowledge of how the family is."

For him and his sisters, he said, "it is all guesswork. And that is not a good thing to be doing now, especially since the girls have families now and I am headed that way. It is not a good scene."

I wanted to summarize my feelings about everything he said and express them in a carefully crafted message that Tom needed to hear. I felt it had to be done that moment. He needed to know: that Tom senior didn't understand him or know a lot about him even though he imagined they shared what appeared to be similar experiences, that Tom senior's advice probably was based on what he had learned in his repeated attempts at counseling to beat his alcohol problem, that Tom senior wasn't so much explosive as cruel in his treatment of Patricia O'Reilly and their kids, that Tom's self-awareness was much stronger than Tom senior's and that he wanted to accept responsibility for his actions, while his father blamed everyone else for what happened years ago. I wanted to tell Tom that it was not going to be easy, that he was carrying an onerous burden and that people had succumbed to lighter loads, that I knew he was strong and I had no doubt he would find the solutions but he would have to find them within himself. But I didn't have the presence of mind at the time to come up with a succinct statement. I didn't want the moment to pass without me conveying some kind of support, so I told him I believed he had a much better sense of himself and was in much better control than his father.

"I don't like what is going on inside of me at all," he said. "I don't like it at all. The way I think scares me. You know what I was thinking when Tom senior told us that story about someone driving in front of you really slow and you just want to waste him, I think like that—I mean, I don't want to waste them—I want to waste their cars so they can't drive anymore. Man, that's bad. If that wasn't exactly how I think I don't know what it is. I mean, someone is driving very slow in front of me, I told you, I wish I had the balls and the carefreeness and the car to whip out and get them off the road and destroy their car with them in it. And I have never done that and I never will, but that is the way I think and he thinks the same way, and it is scary to me because that is a mild thought for me.

"So what do you think?" he asked Linda.

"I am just taking this all in," Linda said.

"Yeah," he replied, "she should keep her distance from me."

"I haven't," I said quickly. I wanted him to know I trusted him, that I wasn't afraid of his monster.

"Yeah," he replied, "but you're six feet, two hundred pounds."

And then he continued talking, explaining that it was important for him to learn as much as he could about his family so he could make life better for him and his sisters and their kids. And then he was swamped with pessimism that the specters of alcoholism and violence might overcome him. Then, just as quickly, he reversed himself: He would not give in to the demons that defeated his father.

Tom had given us a glimpse of his seesaw struggle. The interview ended slowly, and when I thought I should be the one to have the last word, I told Linda, "I don't believe your sister was a whore. I don't think Pam knew what she was talking about. I think Tom senior was one paranoid, fucked-up macho man, one of those freaked-out people who create hell for everyone."

Tom and I left at about 10:00 P.M. Linda had to get up early the next day, and we also had to prepare for our return trip to Williston Heights to meet Tom senior for dinner. On Sunday afternoon, though, when it was time to leave, I was only slightly surprised that Tom refused to go.

17 • "I just wanted to tear somebody's ass up."

*T*om needed time to resolve his feelings about Carl and Jeanne; Tom senior and Patricia O'Reilly; Arlene, Darlene, and Patty; Joyce; Aunt Joan and Aunt Pearl; Linda; all the others whom he also knew as aunts and uncles; Pam; Tracie and her parents; his lawyers; and me. Except for his dead mother, each of us had an opinion concerning some aspect of his life, and many of us were making demands he felt obligated to fulfill. So, in our room the next morning when he announced he was planning to spend the day at the beach, I realized he needed time to reflect. I also knew there wasn't enough time for me to leave him alone. Money was low, and our return tickets were good only until Tuesday. I also feared we would jeopardize an important moment. Tom senior, who was primed to talk, could regard our failure to meet him for dinner as an insult, and he might refuse to meet with us again, I told Tom, who chuckled as if I was talking nonsensically. His father would talk another time, said Tom, who moved slowly about the room as he gathered up some personal items.

I snapped that we hadn't come to Florida for a vacation, that we were here to work. Tom chuckled. He wasn't angry and he didn't raise his voice and he wouldn't look at me. He was edgy. He put on his swimming trunks and picked up a

towel. I felt guilty for trying to compel him to do something
he obviously didn't want to do. But my guilt didn't stop me
from trying. He, however, was not about to be dissuaded. I
realized that the only way to salvage what Tom and I were
trying to do was to join Tom at the beach and try to get him
to reconsider.

Thus, about the time we were supposed to be driving
north to Williston, we were basking in the sun. Later, when
we should have been dining with Tom senior and Fern, we
were eating dinner in a Melbourne restaurant. But from the
moment I had stepped onto the sand, I had been working on
Tom. For the first hour or so, I was almost silent except for
occasionally bantering with him, and he seemed to relax more
as time passed. By the evening, he had become willing to
listen to me explain all the reasons I thought we should
return. Besides repeating what I had told him earlier in our
room, I added two additional reasons, which I knew would
be persuasive if my other ones were unconvincing. I told
him he had started something that had to be finished, and
that he owed it not only to himself but to his sisters to
complete it.

Late that evening he reluctantly phoned Tom senior, who
was upset that we hadn't even called him to cancel the dinner
with him and Fern. Tom, without lying to him or revealing
why he hadn't contacted him, apologized, and made arrangements for us to meet him the next day after he got off
work.

On Monday we drove north in silence. There was no
joking or wisecracking on this trip.

Everyone in the trailer felt awkward in the early part of the
evening. We made small talk but it was clear that there would
be no belly laughs this night. Tom was subdued and distant,
and, unlike the previous night, said little. I acted more friendly
than I felt, and wondered if it showed. Fern said hardly any-

thing, and Tom senior talked but not with the fervor of the previous evening. As soon as I saw an opening, I tried to get us to resume where we had left off in the previous interview when Tom senior was telling us about the murders he had witnessed in Boone County. This time, he spoke cautiously, recalling how Iva and his father carried a man, limp, from their home, but he said he didn't know if the man was unconscious or dead. He also couldn't recall any murders being committed in the hills of Boone County. And that was about all I could get him to say. I couldn't determine if he had just been exaggerating or if he now felt threatened.

After a few minutes and in a lighter mood, he told us he would take us to talk to Brent, his brother. He spoke harshly of him. As he talked, Tom suddenly announced it was time for us to return to Melbourne. Tom senior and I ignored him, and then Tom senior started telling Tom that his sons from his first marriage, David and Michael, had rebuked him for neglecting them when he started his second family with Patricia O'Reilly. He told us how Arlene, Darlene, Patty, and Tom "spited" him because he was "sent to prison. So, how could you win?"

He wanted sympathy. He chuckled. Fern chuckled.

"It's been rough," Tom said. "It's been rough for everybody."

Tom senior started talking again about his cruel childhood and I noticed that he was repeating what he had already said and that prompted me to ask him what caused the "arguments" between him and Pat.

"It was mostly over money or her running around, disappearing and stuff like that," he said. "Didn't account for her time.

"I'd come home," he continued. "The kids would have what-you-call-it, diaper rashes where they laid there with their diapers on all pissed-up all day. And she had slept all day, and they maybe got into the groceries, like in flour, and this and that and destroyed it all over the house. Maybe I'd walk in with one of my bosses or something. We'd be just checking to see that maybe she wanted to go to dinner 'cause we were, like, white-collar workers, executives. And for them to see my house like that, it was kind of disgraceful. Though, what I didn't realize, she was really a child herself. She had never grown up, never had a chance to, never had a chance to really mature to an adult. She was pushed into adult life quick as a child. There was a child trying to raise a bunch of children."

I didn't see any point in asking him why he hadn't pitched in and helped clean the house or why she was the only one raising their kids. After we talked for several more minutes, Tom senior decided to drive us to Brent's home in Ocala. Tom came along, as if he were being dragged by invisible chains. Tom senior and Fern must have noticed how subdued he was, but the three of us acted as if everything was normal. On the ride to Brent's house in Ocala, Tom senior told us that they weren't getting along well but he did not explain why. When we arrived, Tom senior drove into a large lot next to the house where he once lived and where Patty and Arlene had come to visit him. Brent, his wife, and her son from a previous marriage, were inside the simply furnished one-story building. Tom senior introduced me and announced that I was a writer working with Tom on a book about the family. Brent paid little attention to Tom. When I asked Brent if we could interview him, he responded with a rambling comment about the Korean War. I then offered what I considered a better description of what his nephew and I were doing, and he responded with another rambling comment, this one about Korean War veterans. I tried another description, and he responded with non sequiturs about the war fought several decades ago. I began to notice how creepy his voice sounded, and that the expressions forming on his face ranged from absurd to funny. After a few moments, I announced aloud that he apparently did not want to be interviewed, and Tom senior, Tom, Fern, and I prepared to leave. Tom senior invited him to go with us to eat but he declined. We left and on the short trip to a restaurant we said virtually nothing about Brent. At a buffet-style restaurant in Ocala, we had just started eating when a hostess told us that Brent had telephoned. He asked her to tell us not to leave because he was joining us. We ate in silence. Several minutes later as we were eating dessert, Brent appeared, walked quickly up to Tom, and embraced him.

"My favorite nephew," he exclaimed.

Tom was trussed up in his arms like a teddy bear. The creepiness was gone from Brent's voice, and he spoke articulately. He seemed more formidable and acutely aware. And he explained his behavior at his home. He had worried that Tom senior was "setting him up" but he didn't give any specifics about the purported setup. Tom senior remained quiet. After we left the house, Brent told us, his wife asked him why he had ignored his nephew. Brent hadn't recognized Tom, whom he hadn't seen in many years. When he realized his brother, Tom senior, was being honest with him, he rushed to the restaurant. Sure, he said, he was willing to be interviewed at his home.

Back at Brent's house, Tom senior stretched out on a couch, while Brent and I sat at a table. Tom sat away from us. Fern and Brent's wife were seated in another part of the room and the son of Brent's wife by another marriage, a boy of about twelve, shuffled about the room.

I had not planned to interview Brent, but when Tom senior said he would introduce us, I didn't want to pass up the opportunity. Brent was eleven years older than he, Tom senior told us, and he might be able to tell us more about Iva and James Thomas Waters. Tom senior also had told us before we entered the house that Brent cared for Iva more than he did, and that piqued my curiosity.

Brent was sixty-four, but he looked many years younger. He was about six feet, with broad shoulders and a solid build. There was an obvious resemblance between him and Tom senior. Brent's wife was slim and considerably younger than he was. I didn't pay much attention to her, though she chattered throughout much of the interview. In the early part of the discussion, Brent said he would be more comfortable sending us a cassette tape of him talking about his life, but he agreed to answer some questions.

His grandparents, Florence and Charles Workman, were Dutch, he said. He was born in Blair County, West Virginia, and moved to Boone County with his family when he was three years old. His father was a federal revenue agent during the Great Depression, and he "broke up" stills. When the agency was disbanded, he worked in the coal mines. Sometime in the early 1960s, long after he separated from Iva, he moved to Florida and opened a service station. Brent said he didn't know why his parents divorced. He was about eight when Iva married James Thomas Waters, and just as it appeared he was about to reminisce about his early years in Boone County, he announced that he wanted to show a videotape that he'd made during a trip there around Christmas. It was his first time home in thirty-two years.

The first five or ten minutes of film were unclear because the camera lens had fogged up as he was trying to film some outside scenes in the cold. We eventually saw jiggly scenes of people, including Brent and his wife, as well as shots of a restaurant and hills and of the house, he said, where he lived with Iva and his stepfather. Brent and his wife provided a running commentary, and Tom senior and Fern occasionally offered a comment. Tom sat quietly and said nothing. After the home video ended, Brent resumed talking about his early years. He and a younger brother ran away from home when he was thirteen because of his stepfather's violence. They worked for a local man in exchange for room and board.

When he was seventeen, Iva signed papers to allow him to work in Maryland for a defense factory, building airplanes. When the war ended, he returned to Boone County and "made up" with his stepfather. After a while he moved to Charleston, where he worked as an electrician until he was drafted in the Korean War.

During the interview, Tom senior, who was still stretched out on a couch, added an additional recollection.

"I remember Joan and Pearl and them putting strychnine in their food," he said. "They had the plates all dished out. And they poured this stychnine out. Damn shit was blue. Any fool could see that. And then they were trying to get rid of their food."

"Who were they going to get?" Brent asked.

"Mom and dad," Tom senior said, without explaining what happened after the plot failed.

Brent, without commenting, resumed talking about his life after he left the military. He was not in touch with anyone from his family for almost twenty years as he roamed the western part of the country, traveling and working in Alaska, Washington, California, and Arizona. For a while he lived in Texas. He had a severe drinking problem then. He also had a vicious temper, and he vented his spleen in the countless bars and taverns of the cities and towns he visited. He wasn't a bully, he said. He preferred to pick fights with men "twice" his size.

"I came home from the service still thinking about all this crap," he said, referring to his stepfather's violence. "I just wanted to tear somebody's ass up. And I'd just pick any big guy."

He lost as many fights as he won. After a while, he said, he worried that someone would "decapitate me or something," and he eventually stopped drinking and fighting. He made references to his stepfather's sexual abuse of his sisters, and he and Tom senior both agreed that Jane bore the brunt of the violence.

After about ninety minutes, I decided I didn't want to spend the rest of the night trying to pull details from Brent, who had been speaking circumspectly most of the evening. During the interview, Tom hadn't asked a question. I had realized after we had entered the house, when he didn't sit at the table with Brent and me, that he was distancing himself from everyone in the room. He spent much of his time flipping through a genealogical book that Brent had commissioned from the University of Utah. Brent was very proud of that book.

After we left, Tom senior complained that some of Brent's descriptions and accounts were inaccurate. For example, Tom senior said, the house in Brent's video was not the one where they had been raised. Tom senior also chastised me for asking Brent easy questions, and for not questioning him about Iva. He was right. I didn't ask Brent as many questions as I had Tom senior because Tom and I were primarily interested in Tom senior himself.

Back at his home, Tom senior seemed willing to talk more, so I went over some matters we had previously discussed. We talked again about him taking care of his parents when they died. He didn't do it for love, he said, clarifying what he had said earlier. He did it because he wanted to know why.

"Why what?" I asked.

"The childhood was the way it was. Why always I was there. Why I was shifted out. The other kids got to go on some of those year-long splurges or however long she [Iva] was gone. Or some of them always had a home. Me, I always got left, always the one that was out."

He repeated that Brent "told a lot of lies" during his interview. For example, he said, when Brent and his brother fled their home, Brent "went straight up to his grandpa's" to live. They were only gone a few months.

He talked again about the Ku Klux Klan, and I interrupted him before he could complete his sentence describing their benefits.

"Did the KKK ever rescue you? Did they rescue the kids in your family?"

"They didn't rescue for that," he said. "They come up and burn crosses on the hill. And then they called the old man out. The first warning was a cross burned on the hill by your house or something. Or a barn. They would always warn you. They burn a couple of crosses."

He said that the Klan terrorized whores and their johns and men who were cruel to their wives and kids.

"Did this ever happen to your father?"

Not that he knew of, he said. "But I know they burned crosses and things up there on the hill and stuff."

"So they went after blacks or Latins?"

"There were no blacks, no Latins, no minorities."

"Jews?"

"Just redneck peckerheads."

For the first time that evening, and the last time of that trip, we all laughed, but I didn't believe him. The Klan did not thrive because it beat up poor white men for being cruel to their wives and kids unless the Boone County chapter of the KKK had been unlike any other in the country. (However, I would learn much later that there were instances of white women asking chapters of the white supremacist group to confront errant husbands.)

After a while, the four of us exchanged farewells. Tom, who had said very little that evening, told his father that he planned to stay in touch. We rode back to our hotel in virtual silence. The next day we dashed to Joyce Schwab's home to say good-bye and raced to the airport to catch our flight.

*   *   *

Brent never sent his tape. But I got permission to interview Sammie, the former HRS caseworker for Arlene and Darlene. She said that after Arlene and Darlene were returned to Ohio, she had filed a complaint with her agency about the young boy living with Brent and his wife. The caseworker investigating the complaint botched the investigation and the case was closed.

Part V

●

Return to Ohio

18 • "The whites of her eyes"

On January 16, a week after we returned from Florida,
I called the medical examiner's office that had offered to help
me understand Patricia O'Reilly's autopsy report. My contact
at the office told me that forensic medicine, despite the popular perception of its precision as a medical science, wasn't
an exact science, and that twenty years ago some coroners
were not much better than medieval alchemists. That wasn't
true, however, of the Cuyahoga County Coroner's Office,
which "always did have a decent reputation," she said. The
physical examination of Patricia's body, based on the written
report, seemed to have been a good job, the source said. It
wasn't unusual for a twenty-two-year-old person to die of an
interstitial myocarditis, which is the sudden inflammation of
the muscles of the heart, but it also wasn't unusual for someone to recover from one. A number of factors, ranging from
rheumatic fever to a viral infection, can cause the ailment.
Some of the contusions on Patricia's body could have been
caused by cigarette burns, she said, but she added that none
of the injuries identified in the autopsy could have caused
her death. The contusions and bruises all appeared to be
superficial. However, several things missing from the written
autopsy report were causes for concern.

There was no indication that Patricia's neck or "the whites of her eyes" had been checked, my source said. "The autopsy doesn't describe her neck. There's no specific description of the neck muscles." Because of the history of violence and the marks on her body, Patricia's neck and the area under her eyelids should have been checked, and the findings should have been included in the report. If she had been smothered with a pillow, for example, pinpoint hemorrhages would have formed under the eyelids. Competent forensic specialists routinely checked under the eyelids in the cases of sudden deaths of people who were victims of domestic violence.

If Patricia was strangled, my source continued, "you would expect some injury in a strangulation, but in suffocation it is hard to determine," adding that bruises would not be apparent if someone had smothered her with a pillow. Patricia's chin had "a little abrasion" on it "that wasn't adequately explained" in the written report, she said. As for the quinine that Aunt Joan allegedly gave her, a significant amount would be detected in modern toxicology tests, but my source wasn't certain what kind of tests the Cuyahoga County Coroner's Office had been capable of performing twenty years ago.

"If anything," she said, "she would have been suffering gastrointestinal disorders, abdominal pains or stomach problems" if she had taken a sufficient amount of quinine. None of the people whom I had interviewed had recalled Patricia suffering from abdominal or stomach pains, I said. I tried to explain that I had new information that indicated that Patricia might have taken substances other than quinine to abort her six-and-a-half-month-old fetus, but my source was uninterested. She wanted to end the conversation. She told me that her office no longer wanted to help me because of the indications that Patricia hadn't died of natural causes. The case was "too sensitive," because it involved a possible homicide that happened in someone else's bailiwick, she said. She suggested that I go to a medical library to research forensic medicine or consult someone else. She reminded me that her office wasn't to be identified. She was anxious to hang up, but because she had described the death as a "possible" homicide, I pressed for a better understanding of the significance of her information.

Is there a significant chance that Patricia was killed or just a possibility? I asked.

Significant, I was told.

Could we go over this information one more time? I asked.

She refused but promised to send me some information. "Good luck,'" she said and hung up before I could reply.

As I hung up the phone, I mused about the weekend in April 1988, when Tom and I had met and planned on a happy ending for his story. I wondered how he would feel about the latest disclosure. Just as he was trying to resolve his conflicting emotions about Tom senior, a medical examiner's office suggested the possibility that his father might have killed his mother twenty years ago. But the project had become a string of unpleasant and unexpected disclosures, which Tom had faced, and I knew of no reason why he couldn't deal with the latest surprise. So, I called him, but when he answered the phone, I changed my mind and decided to tell him later, when I had a better idea of what we should do next. He, however, surprised me. He told me that he had telephoned directory assistance for Cleveland to try to locate Patricia's childhood friend Vicki, but that he was unable to get her number. I was impressed that he hadn't waited for me to try to get the information.

We weren't even sure we had the correct spelling of Vicki's name. And we also knew it was possible that she could be living in an area with a different area code or that her last name had changed when she married or that she didn't have a phone. Because his classes had started at Johnson State College, I told Tom I would call all the Polaces, Poles, Polises, and other similar names listed in the Cleveland phone directory. If I didn't locate her, I planned to check surrounding areas. I told him if that method didn't work we would have to go to Cleveland and canvass Patricia's old neighborhood. I thought it was important to contact Vicki because I was suspicious that Joyce was unable to locate Vicki's phone number or address and that Tom senior had grown visibly uncomfortable when I told him that we wanted to talk to her.

Tom surprised me again. Because the project had been compelling him to confront people and issues he might have ordinarily avoided, he reasoned that he should also confront the people whom he believed were responsible for all that he endured in the Rimmer household. He wanted to visit Elyria during one of his trimester breaks at Johnson State College, go directly to the office of Lorain County Children Services, and confront his former caseworkers and their supervisor, all of whom were concerned for his care when he was living with the Rimmers. Tom said they probably wouldn't talk to us, but he wanted the satisfaction of confronting people whose decisions resulted in the years of misery for him and Patty. I told him Vecchio would probably object, but he didn't want his lawyer to know.

I marveled at his idea and suggested that, in the spirit of confrontation, we should also visit Keystone Middle School in Grafton. We could confront the two teachers who paddled him when he was a student and ask them if they would have beaten him if they had known he was being abused at home. We also should ask the school officials if they had reconsidered their policy of paddling kids in light of what had happened to Tom and Patty and their friends when they were enrolled there. We also discussed flying to Arizona to interview the caseworker who dismissed as a lie Patty's account of how Carl sexually abused her. I was less certain about the Arizona trip because Tom was swamped with responsibilities. He was attending school full time, as well as working at odd jobs and on his lawsuit and on the book project.

We also planned to contact David and Michael Waters, Tom senior's sons by his first marriage, to learn more about Tom senior's life before he met Patricia. I doubted Tom senior's statements that his drinking problems had begun with her death, and it was hard for me to imagine that he was violent only with her and her kids and not with his previous family. However, Arlene and Darlene, who were in touch with their half brothers, were told he hadn't been violent with them. But I wanted the information firsthand. Tom and I also planned to talk to Tammy Mayle, Pam Haynes's sister, and Aunt Joan, Tammy's mother. I also told Tom I wanted him to make arrangements for me to interview his therapist, Dr. Paul Foxman.

During those first two weeks after our return from Florida we were in frequent touch, revising and rescheduling plans for all the interviews that he wanted to do. He was still being rocked by heavy emotional swells, but he said he was convinced that he could ride the highs and the lows. When I told him one time that I thought he sounded depressed, he replied that he wasn't certain how he felt. In the midst of his confusion, however, some moments were better than others. One evening I called to find him ecstatic because he had made the dean's list. On another day he was subdued because of an argument with Tracie. They had had a long productive talk, and he had told her that he had strong feelings for her, but his emotions confused him. She insisted that they belonged together, that their life could be better together, that they should marry after he graduated in May 1991. If he was confused about how he felt, she said, he should consult another therapist. He told her that her suggestion sounded as if she was avoiding the issues he was trying to explain to her. The problem with their relationship would not be resolved by him seeing a new therapist, he told her.

On Super Bowl Sunday, he was in good spirits. He had expected the San Francisco 49ers to beat the Denver Broncos, but he hadn't expected the 49ers to bomb them into submission. He also wanted me to know that he had stopped referring to Carl as his father. It wasn't a sudden change, he said, but something he had been mulling over for some time. His decision, however, didn't mean he planned to embrace Tom senior as his father, but he said Tom senior "at least put a new perspective on things." One of the reasons for the change, he explained, was that he had tired of Carl's guilt trips and his insistence that his childhood had been worse than Tom's.

When I asked him why he refused to talk about Carl's childhood, he told me he didn't understand why I accused him of not talking. At times, Tom was a paradox. After more than twenty months, our best discussions about the project and my best insight into how he felt occurred when we were interviewing other people. He and I were always tottering, I worried, on the brink of an adversarial relationship. I wanted to know what Tom felt and thought. And there were other times, such as in Florida, when I didn't want to wait for him to make a decision because I thought an important moment was about to pass. I constantly worried that in my eagerness to know everything there was to know about the Waters and the Rimmer families, I might take over the project—push it into areas where he might not want to go—or precipitate acts whose consequences he wasn't prepared to handle. I didn't want to force him to do something against his will; I also knew he wouldn't let me.

On the night in February when Buster Douglas knocked the mouthpiece out of Mike Tyson's mouth and pounded the heavyweight champion into ignominious defeat, I called Tom to tell him finally what I had learned from the medical examiner's office. But for no other reason than a gut feeling, I changed my mind about telling him and we talked about the fight. He was upset that Tyson lost. He identified with the man who was once quoted as saying he was "the baddest dude on the planet." Tom admired him. Tyson had had a rough childhood, Tom pointed out, and so had he. Up until the fight with Douglas, Tyson had vanquished foes inside and outside the ring in unrestrained fury. In contrast, Tom pointed out, he had to worry how his actions might affect people, many of whom often seemed more concerned with themselves. Tyson also appeared as if he wasn't saddled with ambivalence; he was decisive and powerful.

I sympathized with Tom, who was saddened by the humiliating defeat, but I was less sympathetic toward his idol. He had gotten his comeuppance.

Later that month, when I called Tom to finalize plans for our trip to Elyria, he told me that an assistant prosecutor from Lorain County had called him. The prosecutor asked if he was planning to appear for Carl's trial, which was scheduled for April 4. Tom told the man he hadn't discussed the matter with his lawyer, but Tom told him he was too busy with college and personal matters to appear.

"Don't you want to see him prosecuted?" Tom quoted the man as saying. The assistant prosecutor had said something about Carl being charged with rape.

"That's your interpretation," Tom said he told the man. He eventually told the prosecutor to talk to his attorney, but he should have done that as soon as the investigator identified himself. I thought Tom had said too much. He was supposed to refer all such contacts to Vecchio. He and Vecchio were already angry at Patty for providing information to Henry Marsico, the former Oberlin police officer who was involved with the arrest of Tom senior in 1974. Marsico had dropped by Patty's home in August 1989 and learned that Tom was working on a book. Vecchio didn't want the defense to know about the book because that knowledge could play a factor in any court settlement.

No one had told me when Tom and I first started working together that the project was to be concealed from the county and its attorneys. I too wanted to be discreet about what we were doing, but I had planned all along to contact the defense counsel as well as employees at Lorain County Children Services even before Tom suggested that he confront them. I had been delaying contact at Vecchio's request.

Tom and I talked for a few more minutes and finalized plans to rendezvous in Elyria in the first week in March, but I was unable to go. During the week that I had planned to be in Ohio, Jack Bradley, the attorney representing Carl, telephoned me. The Lorain County Prosecutor's Office was planning to subpoena Tom for Carl's trial and petition the Vermont courts to make sure that he appeared. Bradley explained that Tom would not be able to ignore the new subpoena as he had ignored the one issued by the grand jury that eventually indicted Carl. If he refused to show up, the Vermont authorities would be required to take him into custody. Bradley didn't want him to testify.

"My client has made an admission," he said. "If Tom testifies, Carl's going to jail." I suggested that he talk to Vecchio, and when he said he didn't know how to contact him—even though Vecchio's office and home were listed in the Cleveland telephone directory—I told him I would call him back once I located the number. I didn't know why he feigned ignorance about being able to contact Vecchio, but because I believed I might want to interview Bradley later, I told him I would call back with Vecchio's number. I immediately called Tom, who was staying in Elyria with Arlene. Tom didn't want to testify because he still felt obligated to protect Carl, but he would if he was required to appear. I knew how extremely difficult it would be for him if he had to take the stand. He still had not resolved his ambivalent feelings for Carl. After he returned to Vermont, Tom called me on March 15 and told me he and Tracie had broken up.

"Can you believe it? It's serious. We're just pretty much done," he lamented.

They had been arguing heatedly ever since he returned from Florida.

"If we quit now I'd feel like I didn't try my best to keep us together," he said.

About ten days later Tom called again and told me Vecchio was planning to fly to Vermont to meet with him and Dr. Foxman, his psychologist. Tom also said Vecchio worried that if he had to take the stand that he might damage his case by "telling them things that I didn't tell them in my deposition."

The Lorain County Prosecutor's Office was involved not only in prosecuting Carl but in defending the county and Children Services in Tom's lawsuit. Thus, a prosecutor in Carl's trial might ask Tom questions that hadn't been asked when he was deposed to test Tom to see how good of a witness he might be on the stand if his civil suit went to trial. I wondered if Tom's comments were additional signs of his withholding information from me as well, but I wasn't about to press him.

"They don't care if they win the case against Carl," he said about the Lorain County prosecutors. "They want to get at me. They want to damage my case. They could care less about Carl. He could stay in New York for the rest of his life for all they care. It's only for helping them to defend my case. There's no justice being done for the right reason."

If he took the stand and testified about everything that Carl forced him to do, Carl's jaw would end up on his chest, he said. For me, his comment was another hint that the abuse he suffered in the Rimmer home was greater than he had described. And I was confused because I knew he had told me more than he had told his lawyers and his psychologist. I wondered how he kept straight what he had told specific people about what had happened to him.

"I was super tore up a couple of days last week," he continued, "but then I go into denial and forget things."

Denial made it easier for him to study and work. Denial,

I wanted to say, may work for short-term purposes, but it posed potentially unpleasant consequences in the long run if the problems weren't addressed. But I didn't want to upset him, and I didn't want to sound like the psychologist I wasn't.

Vecchio had another reason for wanting to meet with Tom and Foxman. He was worried about Tom. When I talked to Vecchio two days after speaking with Tom, he said Carl's attorney wrote him and asked him to try to keep Tom from testifying. Vecchio wasn't about to help him. It would be illegal, he said, for Tom not to testify if he was subpoenaed.

"I'm not sure how he knew Tom was reluctant to testify," Vecchio said with a hint of annoyance.

I had inadvertently told Bradley that Tom wasn't anxious to take the stand against Carl. I didn't consider my comment to be too much of a goof since Tom had already implied the same sentiment to an assistant prosecutor.

"I'm scared out of my mind," Tom told me two days later. The pressure was beginning to take a toll, and he was considering running away so that he would not have to testify.

He was scheduled to appear at a hearing in a Vermont court because of the subpoena. For him to convince the Vermont authorities not to require him to go, he would have to prove that forcing him to testify would have a "detrimental" effect on him, he said. Vecchio told him if he didn't go voluntarily, the Vermont authorities would incarcerate him until they could put him on a plane to Ohio. Lorain County authorities had already forwarded tickets for him.

"I can't get anything done. I can't think about schoolwork," he said. "All I can think about is nothing—a blank nothing. I've had a terrible week, a terrible, terrible week."

We considered hopping into his truck and fleeing to Maine, but the next day, March 30, he called and told me he was taking Vecchio's advice to go to Ohio. Tracie was going with him. Even though they had broken up, she was planning to be by his side. And on Sunday, when we talked again he said he wasn't as afraid as he had been, that he had to start thinking more about himself and less about protecting Carl.

"Do you think that he was thinking about me?" he asked rhetorically.

We both knew the answer.

"I spoke with my father, even though he abused me too," he said, referring to Tom senior, whom he had telephoned for moral support, and got it.

If the judge at the Vermont hearing that Tom was to attend Monday told him that he didn't have to go, Tom said he planned to say, "Whoa! I want to go." He wouldn't need Valium, and he said Vecchio would be surprised when he learned about Tom's new attitude. "Carl is going to be a basket case. I'm going in John Wayne-ish. I know he's going to be freaked out in a major way."

I felt relieved.

I should have been more cautious.

19 • "It's just a game."

Shortly after 8:30 A.M., Tom, Tracie, and I left the hotel where we were staying, got in my rented car, and sped to the courthouse in downtown Elyria. They were both tense. The subpoena required Tom to be at the courthouse at 9:00 A.M., and though I knew there would be no problem if he was a few minutes late, he insisted that we arrive on time. He and Tracie, usually fashion-conscious, were dressed in nondescript casual clothes. That day, they both looked so young and vulnerable, they could have passed for high school sweethearts.

Tracie was an enigma. She and Tom were estranged, but she flew to Ohio with him because she knew the pressure he was under. He hadn't asked her to join him; she had volunteered. Considering the circumstances and the turmoil in their relationship, I thought that kind of support was rare.

When we parked near the courthouse, Tom appeared more apprehensive. As he entered the building, with Tracie and me following, he spotted Vecchio at the far end of a row of seats in the building's narrow hallway, which was crowded with people sitting in chairs or standing and moving about the corridor. With his attention focused intently on his attorney, Tom didn't notice the couple sitting in the seats closest to him.

"Tom," a bespectacled and impeccably dressed man said in a loud voice as Tom was about to walk past him and his female companion. The man rose quickly from his seat and hugged Tom, who, with his arms strapped to his sides by the man's embrace, looked distressed. The woman, slightly plump and with dark hair, also got up and and hugged Tom. She smiled warmly.

Tracie and I froze.

"That's Carl and Jeanne," Tracie whispered.

"It'll be all right, son," Carl said in a voice loud enough for all the people in the hallway to hear.

Tom said nothing. His arms stayed at his side. Carl and Jeanne probably looked like phonies to those in the courthouse who recognized them. I would have considered them a grotesque parody of Ozzie and Harriet if it hadn't been for Tom, who had given me some insight into the complexities of the Rimmers' family dynamics. After the Vermont authorities had removed him from their home, he and his adoptive parents tried to resume a relationship. But whenever they came together all of them resorted to their previous superficial roles: Carl the father, Jeanne the mother, and Tom the dutiful son. Those contacts caused Tom considerable stress because he was beginning the arduous task of developing his own identity, of establishing a personality separate from his adoptive parents. Carl and Jeanne, though they were in therapy as Tom was, did not want changes, Tom had said. At the courthouse that day it was obvious who had made the most progress. Tom didn't return Carl's hug, and he didn't resort to the role of dutiful son. He was a young man trapped in a bewildering situation.

When Carl released him, Tom walked away from his adoptive parents without saying a word, and made his way to Vecchio. Tom looked like he was in a daze until he reached his lawyer, who told us what to expect in the courtroom. A hearing had been scheduled before the trial because Jack Bradley, Carl's attorney, had filed a motion to have Carl's case

362 Morris and Waters

dismissed on the basis that the prosecution had waited too long to file charges. Bradley also had alleged in his motion that Carl's right to a speedy trial had been prejudiced by the prosecution's delay. If the judge ruled against the motion, the trial would start after a short recess. It wasn't clear if Tom would have to testify.

In the narrow, crowded hallway where the three of us waited for the pretrial hearing to begin, nattily dressed men, laughing and jabbering like members of a social club, shuffled about as if they were attending a cocktail party. They preened, they strutted, they exchanged confidences. Their gaiety gave the hallway the air of a carnival sideshow. Some were attorneys from the prosecutor's office and the law firms defending the county in Tom's civil suit. At times, a wispy blonde in heels made her way through the gaggle of standing males, as she shuffled from the courtroom to an office off the hallway. She moved as though she was with them though not in spirit. At one point, a voice over the loudspeaker told Henry Marsico, the ex-Oberlin cop turned investigator, to "come to the prosecutor's office."

In contrast, Carl, witnesses subpoenaed by the prosecutor, and their supporters sitting on the chairs looked as solemn as visitors at a wake. Tom and Tracie huddled briefly with Patty and her boyfriend, Buck, who sat at the far end of the row of seats, away from Carl and Jeanne. Patty was as tense as Tom because she had been subpoenaed too. Buck said little. Jeanne also had been subpoenaed, and so had Debra Durrell, the caseworker who had notified the Vermont authorities to get Tom out of the Rimmers' home. Durrell sat near Patty. Because of the TV, radio, and newspaper coverage in Elyria and Cleveland after the suit was first announced, I expected news coverage of the trial, but there were no reporters present. The hallway belonged to the lawyers.

About 9:30 A.M. almost everyone in the hallway, except the subpoenaed witnesses and their supporters, poured into the Common Pleas Courtroom of Judge Lynett McGough. I assumed that most of those in the courtroom gallery were there to see how the criminal court proceedings might impinge on Tom's civil suit against the county. After the hearing started, Bradley, as Vecchio had explained, said he planned to argue that the statute of limitations had elapsed before the state had acted against Carl. If the court disagreed, Bradley said, he planned to argue that his client's "constitutional right to a speedy trial" had also been denied. He told the court that Carl cooperated with the Vermont authorities and admitted his abuse of Tom because he "relied on the fact that he was not going to be prosecuted." For Carl to stand trial in Ohio, Bradley said, "certainly prejudices" his client's chance for a fair hearing.

Judge McGough asked if there was "any statement from any law enforcement or prosecutor's office that says that he will not be prosecuted?"

"No," Bradley said.

"Any statement during the juvenile proceedings in Vermont?" the judge asked.

"Not that I can prove," said Bradley, who proceeded to describe how Marsico had contacted Carl and told him he was investigating Tom's lawsuit for the civil division of the prosecutor's office. Carl asked if he might be criminally prosecuted, and Marsico, according to Bradley, told him he didn't know. During the course of the interview Carl admitted sexually abusing Tom. Bradley also said his client was denied his right to a speedy trial because Lorain County Children Services was aware of the abuse in 1983 but the prosecutor's office did not act until 1989. Bradley also said Carl had "advanced in position at IBM" in New York, where he was a computer programmer and that, under the auspices of the Vermont family court, he entered counseling in Vermont. Carl also had undergone counseling in New York.

When Bradley finished with his opening remarks, Jonathan Rosenbaum, the chief trial attorney for the criminal division of the county prosecutor's office, told the judge, "I don't even know why we are having this discussion. The state of Ohio has said we get six years to bring this case from the date the corpus delicti is discovered.

"If I'm a day late, I'm out," he said. "If I'm a day early, I'm in. That's all there is to it."

He said he knew of no promises of immunity to Carl because he sought treatment. After Rosenbaum completed his opening remarks, all witnesses in the courtroom were required to leave. Bradley asked that Assistant County Prosecutor Bob Flanagan, who was working on Tom's civil suit, be required to leave the courtroom because he might be called as a witness. Bradley said he was considering questioning Flanagan because he suspected that the criminal division and not the civil division had told Marsico to contact Carl.

Judge McGough asked Flanagan to leave. Rosenbaum asked the court to order Vecchio out of the courtroom. Vecchio looked surprised. Rosenbaum—short, solidly built, with a bald spot at the top of his head—argued strenuously against Vecchio's presence. Vecchio told Judge McGough that he was present only on the "behalf" of his client. Bradley told McGough he wasn't planning to call him as a witness.

"I don't anticipate Mr. Bradley calling Mr. Flanagan," Rosenbaum replied, "but if he does, I may call him [Vecchio] to dispute that. At this time, he is a potential witness, if this court is going to permit Mr. Bradley to get into these extraneous matters."

"I don't know what extraneous matters we have," the judge said. "We are not going to get very extraneous."

She smiled slyly, and told Vecchio he could stay. I thought Rosenbaum's complaint about Vecchio was a ruse to ruffle him, that it was Rosenbaum's way of saying, You, outsider, are on our turf. Tom was fortunate that his civil suit had been filed in federal court in Cleveland.

At one point, after I had been shuffling in and out of the courtroom like others attending the hearing, a bailiff approached me in the hallway and demanded to know who I was. He said he had become suspicious watching me entering and leaving the courtroom and talking to the witnesses sitting in the hallway. When I told him I was a journalist, he quickly excused himself and left me wondering who sent him over to confront me.

Durrell was the first witness. She was in her mid-forties, slightly stout, with light brown hair, had an easygoing manner that, for me, explained why Patty, who previously had been betrayed by Children Services caseworkers, had been willing to confide in her about her brother. Under direct questioning by Rosenbaum, Durrell testified she did not alert Lorain County authorities about the abuse because she believed it was the responsibility of the child care authorities in Vermont to decide what to do. She told the court that she expected them to let her know if further action was needed in Ohio. The Vermont authorities never contacted her. And she stuck with that response under several minutes of questioning by Bradley who was probing for information that the prosecutor's office knew of the sexual abuse before Tom's suit was filed in 1987.

Durrell testified that it was now policy to notify the prosecutor's office about allegations of child abuse, but that that wasn't the policy in 1984. She said she couldn't recall the previous policy, but Vecchio had told me earlier that Lorain County Children Services was supposed to report allegations of child abuse to the sheriff's office. That hadn't happened when Patty told a Children Services caseworker what Carl had done to her one day on the couch. After Durrell completed her testimony, Rosenbaum called Tom to the stand and questioned him about whom he had told of the sexual abuse. Tom testified he had confided in Patty, who told Durrell. While Tom was on the stand, Carl crossed his arms, and, sitting ramrod straight in his chair, looked straight ahead. When

Rosenbaum finished, Bradley, asking questions along similar lines, questioned Tom about the sexual abuse. Tom told him Carl had started molesting him when he was about four.

"When did you realize that these acts were wrong or criminal in nature?" Bradley asked.

"Then," Tom replied. "I always knew that."

"Why didn't you report them to anyone?"

"I was too afraid to say anything to anyone."

Bradley asked him when he overcame his fear, and Tom replied, "When I was sixteen and told my sister."

"Now, how did you feel when you found out that your dad was arrested and was being prosecuted for these crimes?" Bradley asked.

"I can't really quantify how I felt. I didn't feel good," Tom responded.

"Why not?"

"I'm not sure why not. There's a lot of different reasons."

"Did you want this to happen?"

"No, not really."

"Do you have any idea why this happened?"

"Because I filed the lawsuit."

Bradley asked Tom if he believed "that is why your dad has been criminally prosecuted?"

"Yes, I do," Tom said, and Rosenbaum immediately objected. His objection was sustained. Tom was dismissed. He had been on the stand for about six minutes. His answers were firm and terse. He was nervous, but it wasn't obvious. To me, he looked as if he was bristling with secrets to tell, waiting for the moment to unleash a torrent of information on the attorney foolish enough to ask him the wrong questions.

Bradley called Patty to testify. She was nervous, and it was more than stage fright. For someone who suffered severe panic attacks as she did, the whole affair was cause for extreme panic. Yet, on the stand, Patty appeared calm. She wore light blue jeans and a white jacket and glasses, and she too could have passed for a teenager. She leaned on her right hand—she was so nervous she had to prop up her head to keep it from shaking. Patty didn't look at Carl. On the stand, she recalled the day she and Tom were waiting for the school bus and he told her Carl was sexually abusing him. She expressed disbelief, Patty testified, and Tom told her he was joking. Rosenbaum asked no questions. Patty was only on the stand a few minutes.

Bradley next called Marsico, who carried a red file to the stand. Because I believed he had wormed his way into Carl's and Patty's confidences in order to help the county's investigation, I was looking for details so I could describe him as a snake. Marsico, with gray hair and a salt-and-pepper mustache, testified that he called Carl the second day of his job with the prosecutor's office because he was working with Flanagan on the civil suit brought by Tom. The criminal investigation began that day, August 22, 1989, after Carl corroborated the "allegations that were made in the civil lawsuit," Marsico testified.

Bradley asked him, "To your knowledge, had any criminal investigation been instituted regarding Carl Rimmer prior to that date?"

Marsico said no.

It was hard for me to believe that the prosecutor's office wasn't planning a criminal investigation the day Marsico contacted Carl, but it was easy to believe Bradley would never be able to prove it. Rosenbaum asked no questions, and Marsico left the stand. Nothing he had said on the stand could be used to portray him in any manner other than that of a law enforcement officer who had done his job. Moreover, Marsico and his partner had arrested Tom senior, and they had brought the Waters kids a puppy and their first Christmas tree.

Bradley called Carl Francis Rimmer to the stand. Carl was

much thinner than in the photographs Tom and Patty had shown me. He had an athletic build and a confident air as he walked to the stand. He·was clean-shaven and his hair was well-groomed. He looked more like an IBM executive than an IBM programmer. But he momentarily smudged that image when he exhaled harshly into the microphone. He could have been nervous. Or he could have been expressing his contempt for the proceedings.

Bradley asked him why Tom was removed from his home in Vermont.

"His disclosure of alleged sexual abuse," Carl said, referring to the abuse he had admitted to Marsico and which had also been described in documents.

Under direct questioning by Bradley, Carl said he was required to "get help and seek therapy" and that he started "almost immediately" seeing Dr. Paul Foxman, the Vermont therapist who also was treating Tom. After he moved to New York from Vermont, Carl said, he also enrolled in IBM's employee assistance program and "asked them to find me someone that could help me with my particular problem."

I wondered if Carl was referring to pedophilia, but he left the stand without being asked about his "particular problem."

Bradley, trying to put the best face on a feeble defense, told the court that his client had "followed all of the guidelines of the court in Vermont" and had sought counseling.

"I'm not unappreciative of that," McGough replied.

However, she said, she considered those actions possible mitigating factors, but not facts addressing Bradley's motion concerning the right to a speedy trial and the statute of limitations. She asked how the events in the Vermont court and Carl's actions could influence what should happen in her court. Bradley argued that the state brought charges against his client because of Tom's civil suit and that the delay was "unreasonable" and unfair for his client. McGough disagreed and told him she planned to rule that the state acted within the statute of limitations and that it was now his "burden to show actual prejudice" against his client.

Bradley did not offer much of an argument. In summary, he said, "I just think that it's detrimental to him to be in a system that encourages a person to admit their guilt, to admit what they did so they can get help and then tell them in the fifth year after they've done these things, Now, we are going to prosecute you. I think that's detrimental to his having a fair trial."

"That has nothing to do with having a fair trial," Rosenbaum argued. "A fair trial is the ability to bring in witnesses and defend yourself accurately against the allegations. There has been no evidence offered today that says he can't do that."

Judge McGough agreed. "I will find this case was brought within the six years statute of limitations, and that this is not a case where there is actual prejudice to the defendant's ability to have a fair trial.

"We have a jury waiting downstairs," she stated. "We will be ready to go to trial in about fifteen minutes."

After the recess, Bradley announced that Carl wanted to plead no contest to rape, a first-degree aggravated felony; gross sexual imposition, a third-degree felony; and corruption of a minor, also a third-degree felony. This meant that though Carl pled guilty in criminal court, his admission of guilt could not be used against him in a civil suit if Tom decided to sue him. But anyone who understood Tom's feelings knew he wouldn't sue Carl. His attorneys had suggested that to him years ago and he had refused.

The sentence for rape ranged from a minimum of four, five, six, or seven years to a maximum of twenty-five years. It was not a probationable offense, and it carried a possible $10,000 fine. The laws were revised in 1983. The old laws provided for indeterminate sentencing for the lesser felonies, ranging from one to ten years. The new laws provided definite sentences of either one year and one and a half or two years.

The choice was Carl's. His bond was continued. Bradley said he planned to file an appeal.

When the hearing ended, I introduced myself to Carl before he left the courtroom, and we shook hands. He eyed me warily. I told him I hoped that at some time he might agree to talk to me. I also talked to Bradley, who told me to meet him at his office later.

The drama continued outside the courtroom. While I was scampering about trying to collect information, I learned that Tom, accompanied by Vecchio, briefly met with Carl in a room. By the time I located Tom, the meeting had ended. He was near tears, and I knew how bad he felt, but I had to question him. He reacted as if each question was a punch in the stomach. He quoted Carl as telling him, "I never thought what I did devastated you this bad. Now, I've got to pay for my sins." Carl also said, according to Tom, that he would be fired from IBM even though he was out on bail, pending his sentencing.

"I understand that you thought that you had this all under control," Tom quoted Carl as saying about the civil suit that prompted the criminal investigation. "It's okay, I'll survive. Don't let it get you down." But Carl, according to Tom, also said, in an apparent reference to the criminal court proceedings, "It's just a game."

Tom said Carl began to bawl. As we were talking, Marsico walked up to us and extended his hand to Tom. Tom refused to shake hands with him. He believed Marsico was trying to ingratiate himself in order to get information to help the county fight the lawsuit.

"I've known you a long time," Marsico said, grinning.

Tom, grim-faced, refused to talk. He stared at Marsico.

"I'm just doing my job," Marsico said contritely.

I told Marsico I wanted to interview him. He winced, but gave me his card and asked for mine. As I gave him my office address and telephone number at Rutgers University, I wondered if he was the one who sicced the bailiff on me. Marsico was walking away from us when Vecchio rushed up to Tom and ordered him not "to talk to that son of a bitch under any circumstances." Minutes later, Tom, Tracie, Patty, Buck, and I had regrouped and were listening to Vecchio explain that the appeal process for Carl would take about five months and that he expected Carl would probably serve less than three years. As if on cue, Carl's attorney approached us and asked Tom and Patty to write letters to the judge or the probation department in support of Carl. Tom remained silent. He knew Vecchio would oppose him writing a letter because it could be used against him in his civil suit. Patty agreed, however. She would have felt uncomfortable telling Bradley no to his face, but her actions infuriated Tom and Vecchio, both of whom were already angry at her because of an earlier incident in the hallway. At some point during the morning, she was spotted talking to Durrell, her former caseworker, who was waiting to be called to the stand. Tom told Buck to interrupt the conversation. Tom was angry that Patty would talk to someone associated with Children Services. He felt she should have realized how Carl hurt himself by talking to Marsico, and that her talking to Marsico had tipped off the county's lawyers that he was working on a book.

Outside the building, Vecchio warned Tom to remind Patty about talking about the case, and later, back at the Holiday Inn, I could hear Tom berating her in his room, which was next to mine. I could not understand what he had said, but I knew it had to do with her talking to Durrell and promising to write a letter of support to Carl. At one point, he slammed a door so hard it sounded like a cannon report. Patty stormed out of the room but returned.

After I left the courthouse, I went to Jack Bradley's office in Lorain, Elyria's sister city. He said he was too busy to talk about Carl's case. He said he would be willing to talk to me at some other date, but I didn't believe him. I knew if I wanted information I would have to try to get it from Carl. Later that evening, I rendezvoused with Tom, Tracie, Patty, Buck, and Arlene at the Warehouse, a nightclub in downtown Elyria. We crammed into two small booths and waited for Dee to arrive. It was about 8:00 P.M. and a live DJ was playing rap, disco and rock music. Only two people ventured out on the dance floor, where, Arlene said, people rarely danced. When Dee arrived, we moved to a table in a corner.

Patty and Tom had made up. The healing process between them continued during the hours we were at the Warehouse. Most of us were throwing down shots of tequila. Some drank beer. In the beginning, Patty, Arlene, Darlene, and Tom were snarling playfully at each other. Then the conversation turned to what they considered were their personality flaws and why they had them. Arlene, her sisters said, snapped at people. Tom, his sisters agreed, was stubborn. Tom and Dee and Arlene accused Patty of berating Buck unmercifully. She complained that he made her angry because he wouldn't argue toe-to-toe with her. She described how she would follow him around the house, up and down the stairs, arguing and screaming at him, and yet he still refused to argue. As Tom and his sisters became more animated in their discussion, Tracie and Buck left the table and went to the bar. I followed them later to order more tequila.

At the bar, Tracie complained that she felt excluded and uncomfortable whenever Tom and his sisters got together and rehashed their cruel childhoods with Tom senior. That was the reason Buck also left our table and went to the bar. On some occasions when Tom and his sisters were together, they formed an impenetrable bond, becoming so wrapped up in themselves that they virtually ignored everyone around them. Those moments were exhilarating, and the one this night was particularly infectious. I sympathized with Tracie because she had no friends in the nightclub as Buck did, but I picked up the tequila and quickly returned to the table. I wanted to be where the fun was—and not just because Tom and I were working on a book.

He and his sisters were arguing and laughing and switching alliances as they quarreled gaily. Patty said she liked Dee's husband, Mike, because he argued with her, unlike Buck. Dee said she and Mike argued fiercely because neither one liked to admit being wrong; there were times when she wouldn't get off his back. But Dee insisted Arlene was more argumentative. Arlene quipped that Patty fought everyone except Tommy, "who can get over on her."

Everyone laughed.

"It's because you guys grew up together," Arlene added.

Tom, Patty, and Arlene agreed that Dee was the meanest when they were young and living together, and as the oldest she beat up everyone.

Dee smiled.

Arlene recalled the day Dee hit her in the head with a pipe and then the two of them scurried to rinse off the blood because they were afraid of what their father would do when he came home. In virtual unison, they all blamed Tom senior for their problems.

Arlene described how he raped their mother right in front of them. She added that her mother couldn't have been too smart if she stayed with Tom senior as long as she did, but she sympathized with her because she believed Patricia had been young and probably confused. Because of my interview with Arlene, and from what her sisters and Tom had told me, I knew it was unusual for her to talk about the past so openly. Arlene also confirmed what I had surmised from talking to all of them: that she and Patty went to Florida to confront Tom senior about what he had done to them as kids. She said he told them he couldn't remember molesting them, but because they insisted he did, he conceded maybe he had.

And while they were there, he continually propositioned her and Patty. He literally begged them to have sex with him. He wanted to do it one more time to remember their mother, she recalled him saying. Arlene described how his persistent begging reduced her to tears. She had described his incestuous longings in her interview with me, but Patty hadn't in her interview. Patty looked chagrined as Arlene recalled how Tom senior treated them, but I understood her reasons for not telling me. It was one of those matters that was too personally embarrassing for her to discuss.

Later in the evening, Tom talked positively about Tom senior and his sisters rebuked him.

"He's so full of shit," Dee growled, "that you better roll your pants legs up to your knees."

Tom retreated, but he reminded them that at one of Aunt Pearl's family reunions they were the ones who tried to persuade him to talk to Tom senior.

Marsico's name came up. Patty pointedly reminded Tom that Marsico had rescued them and brought them a puppy.

"Fine," Tom said, "but he's now working with the county."

Patty reminded Tom that Durrell saved him.

He winced. He hadn't forgotten what Marsico and Durrell had done for him, but he also knew both worked for the county, and weren't about to risk their jobs for him.

The next day, Tom, Tracie, and I ate breakfast in the Bob Evans restaurant at the Midway Mall. It was a farewell meal because they were returning to Vermont on an afternoon flight from the Cleveland airport. I was still under the spell of the previous night when everyone, except Tracie and Buck, was buoyant and happy. I started making wisecracks until I noticed how subdued Tracie and Tom were. I thought they had had a spat, when Tom said he was miserable about what was happening to Carl. Because he had been too worried about what he would have to say on the stand, he hadn't fully considered Carl's situation. But now, with the court hearing over, he couldn't get Carl's predicament out of his mind. Tracie and I couldn't convince him that he had done nothing wrong, that he shouldn't be worrying about Carl. By the time we finished eating, the three of us were glum—Tom because of Carl, Tracie and I because of Tom. After they boarded their plane to Vermont, I moved in with Buck and Patty in the house where they lived with Buck's mother. I was staying over to finish some work. I phoned Jeanne but she wasn't home, so I left a message saying that she could reach me at Patty's if she changed her mind about being interviewed. I hadn't approached her at the courthouse because I didn't want to make it easy for the people who had sicced the bailiff on me to know whom I was interviewing.

That evening, I talked to Patty to learn if I had missed anything else at the courthouse. Patty, who was reluctant to discuss her meeting with Carl and Jeanne, was still smarting over Tom's tongue-lashing.

"Yesterday, when he chewed me out when we were in his hotel room, he acted like he was a lawyer or a judge or something. He kept telling me things over and over six or seven times. He was treating me like I didn't have a brain. He thinks I'm an airhead."

Tom's harshness stemmed from the pressures and conflicts caused by Carl's trial and his lawsuit, but that didn't ease her anger. I told her that he and Vecchio worried about someone else deceiving her as Marsico had, and that in high-stakes lawsuits involving millions of dollars, mistakes can be costly. If Tom spotted her talking to Durrell, it was easy to assume that someone from the county also saw them talking. She had to be more careful because she could inadvertently say or reveal something that could hurt Tom's case.

"I never realized how important I was to this case, to this suit. Neither one of them have let me know how important I am in this case, and Tommy told me I didn't need to know how important I was. The only thing I need to know is that I should not talk to anybody about anything. You know, they didn't give me any guidelines. I hadn't talked to Vecchio in a year and a half. He told me not to talk to anybody until I called him. But I didn't see any harm in talking to Debbie Durrell. I was just going to say hi. She's the one I bared my soul to [about Tom being abused]. So, I thought it was okay if I talk to her. Tommy yelled at me for me just acknowledging that Marsico bought me an ice-cream cone [after Tom senior was arrested]. What is the harm in acknowledging that? If I were to talk to the garbage man that day I would've got bitched out. I'm sitting here in my house, living my life. I'm like totally out of the whole picture until I get a call and all this stuff happens and then they expect me to know everything."

I sympathized, but I reminded her what happened to Carl who was older and supposedly wiser. I told her he should have known better than to confide in someone from the prosecutor's office. Those comments got us talking about the day Marsico came to the house. She was lying on the couch and watching *General Hospital,* the soap opera, when the doorbell rang. Standing in the doorway was Marsico and another man. He asked if Tom planned to spend the money on expensive things and if the suit was for the money or if he was planning to share it.

"Tommy said, if he wins, the whole family wins," she recalled telling Marsico.

If she had been the least bit impish she could have asked Marsico if he had joined the prosecutor's office because it offered him more money to snoop for information to hurt the people she loved. But after talking to Buck, she called Vecchio and told him of her mistake. And he, of course, was upset that she not only had given them information but had tipped them off about Tom's book.

I told Patty I had been planning to contact Marsico after

Darlene talked about him in her interview. I also told her that Tom, in my opinion, talked too much to the assistant prosecutor who had contacted him in Vermont. And I revealed that I had angered Vecchio when I told Bradley of Tom's reluctance to take the stand against Carl. I told her she wasn't the only one making mistakes, and if Vecchio made any errors we probably wouldn't know about them. But I warned her again that she had to be careful.

The court hearing was a watershed for her and her brother. Tom had told her she now had to choose between him and Carl, that if she chose him she could no longer contact Carl.

Though the trial was over, she now had something else worrying her. She was scheduled to be deposed by the county's lawyers in two weeks.

"I'm really nervous about that. I'm more nervous about that than I was at the trial. I think it's because it's like a big, huge, spotlight and it's just centered on me. Yesterday it was centered on Tommy, my mom, all these other people. And now in two weeks it's on me, and I don't like it. I'm nervous that it's going to be in this small room and all these lawyers are going to be breathing down my neck around this big table and that I'm going to have to answer all these questions. I'm not worried about screwing up the answers. I'm worried about when I talk, if the words will come out of my mouth. And I'll look at the door [of the room where she is being deposed] and it's closed. Then I start freaking out. I mean, if they were to come over my house, sit here and talk with me like you are, that's fine; I'd be fine. But it's just the fact their suits and ties and stuff intimidate me, big-time. You know what I'm saying? If they were all dressed in jeans and sweaters like you, and came over that'd be no problem. I could answer any question.

"With everyday living I'm not nervous, I'm not so afraid, but I have all these little tiny phobias that build and build until they're so overwhelming that I can't even live right. I was really bad for a whole winter, having these feelings that I felt like I'm not here. I had them twenty-four hours a day, every minute of the day."

She added that Vecchio made her nervous and that she believed he disliked her. I told her to tell Vecchio everything she told me, especially about her panic attacks. When Tom was trying to decide whether to show up for Carl's trial, Vecchio, his psychologist, and I were checking on him constantly, I told her. I also told her to remind Vecchio and Tom that she needed support too, and to remind Vecchio that she didn't run away from the Rimmers. Tell him, I said, that she was driven out.

She agreed, finally, that she, too, suffered in the Rimmer household, and she told me something I hadn't known.

"Tommy says that when he wouldn't have sex with Carl, Carl would take it out on me," she said and then mimicked Tom's account of what Carl said: " 'Well, if you don't do this, I'm gonna treat Patty like shit; you just watch.' And Tommy would watch him treat me like shit and then he'd give in."

That she still wanted a relationship with a man who treated her and Tom like slaves was something we had already discussed, and though I knew he was undeserving of her affection, I didn't say any more than I already had. Patty also said her brother still wanted a relationship with Jeanne, whom she believed was still upset with her about defaulting on a car loan. Jeanne had co-signed the loan for Patty, who fell behind in her monthly payments after she and Buck broke up for a while. When the bank repossessed the car, Jeanne stopped talking to her, Patty said. They resumed contact after Jeanne was subpoenaed for Carl's trial. However, that didn't bring them as close as Patty would have liked. Jeanne, she said, seemed to be leaning on her for support, but people had been telling her that Jeanne no longer considered her a daughter.

"And he's been telling me lately," she said, referring to Tom, " 'Patty, we don't even have a mom and dad. It's just me and you against the world.' And it just hit me that we really don't. I still want to have a relationship with Jeanne. I still want to have someone to visit at Christmas."

She also was having problems talking with Tom.

"He takes things that I say certain ways 'cause I tell him about how I feel. I'm not interpreting how he feels by telling him how I feel, and he thinks I am when I tell him I still care about Dad, and I want to talk to him. With Tommy you've got to watch what you say. If he knows he's hurting me really bad, he'll start feeling guilty. But like yesterday, he surprised me 'cause I started crying 'cause he was hurting my feelings. And he said, 'Patty, I'm sorry that you feel like you have to cry.' A couple of years ago, he would've been like, Oh, I feel bad, I'm sorry you're crying—and come over and give me a hug. But yesterday he was like, I'm sorry that you feel like you have to cry."

There was no hug.

I left Ohio and called Patty when I arrived in New York City just to check up on her and Tom. Something major had happened in the short while I had been gone from Elyria. Tom told her he was thinking about killing himself. I told Patty not to worry, and then quickly phoned Vecchio, and left a message at his office because he was out to lunch. I phoned Patty back to reassure her everything would be okay, that Vecchio would be on top of the situation and would probably contact Tom and his psychologist. I wondered aloud if this was the first time Tom had ever talked about killing himself.

"Tommy," Patty said, "always talks about killing himself."

20 • "Two"

*T*om called me on April 9 at my office at Rutgers University to tell me not to worry about him. Vecchio and his psychologist, Dr. Paul Foxman, had been in touch with him, and he was feeling better. I felt some relief, but I was still concerned. Patty's comments had been a reminder that, even after two years of interviews and countless rap sessions and discussions, I shouldn't assume I knew the extent of how much they had endured and how it had affected them. I had told Tom that I didn't need to know everything about him, that a portrayal of him could be accurate without revealing his innermost secrets. Suicide, however, wasn't something I had anticipated. I wasn't an expert, but I was familiar with various studies, and I knew that people who talked of killing themselves were to be taken seriously. I decided to wait until I talked to Foxman before trying to discuss this matter with Tom.

That same day Tom also said that IBM had dismissed Carl because of his felony conviction. And because Carl was unemployed and couldn't continue paying for Tom's therapy sessions, Tom was negotiating fees with Foxman.

Tom had other concerns. He was trying to catch up on his courses and make up the exams he'd missed while he was in Ohio. But it was difficult for him to concentrate on his studies. When we talked the next week, we again discussed plans to interview all the people we had decided to see in March. Tom still wanted to visit Children Services and confront his former caseworkers and their supervisor. He told me he and Tracie had patched up their relationship, and I finally told him what I had learned from the medical examiner's office about his mother's death. I thought that information would cause him conflict because he was trying to establish a relationship with Tom senior, but if he was upset I certainly didn't detect it. I told him I planned to contact the forensic department at the University of Medicine and Dentistry of New Jersey, Robert Wood Johnson Medical School, which was affiliated with Rutgers. Tom was noncommittal. We continued to phone each other during April, and he seemed to be okay each time we talked. After a while I stopped worrying about him and concentrated on finishing up as much work as I could before the next trip to Elyria.

Robert Catz, who by April no longer was directly involved in Tom's litigation, had described Tom's suit as a landmark case, according to news reports. And Vecchio, in a radio broadcast, said he didn't know of a similar one. I wanted an impartial assessment and late in April I contacted the American Bar Association's National Center on Children and the Law, located in Washington, D.C. I briefly described the lawsuit to an official at the center. Similar suits had been filed but the official with whom I talked provided some insight on another area I hadn't fully considered. There weren't "a lot of lawyers" who were willing to litigate for "poor and destitute children," he told me. "Very few, if any, mainstream lawyers represent abused children. It's unusual. Most would want a retainer of at least five thousand dollars."

Attorneys who represent kids like Tom, he said, are "public-interest-minded lawyers. You're talking about dedicated lawyers." If a plane crashed, there would be no shortage of lawyers who would want a piece of the action, he said in comparison. The statutes are clear, and the plaintiffs and defendants are many.

The official's comments made me reconsider some of my negative opinions about Vecchio. After I had first met him in November 1989, and he told Tom that his working on the book could damage his lawsuit, I was angry and ready to regard him with the contempt I held for other attorneys I had met working on my various projects. But months later, after Tom and I had conducted several interviews, I decided no serious harm had been done to our working relationship. Tom was more reticent than I would have preferred but that had more to do with him and less to do with Vecchio. Tom talked in the interviews we conducted, so I thought I had no reason to be upset or particularly concerned. That was, until the day he and I visited Vecchio the day before Carl's trial. An incident made me question my assumption. Tom, Vecchio, Tracie, and I were sitting in Vecchio's office when the question was raised, what if a particular matter posed a conflict between the book and the lawsuit. Vecchio had just said it wasn't a serious matter when Tom snapped that he didn't care about the book, that he was more concerned about his suit. Minutes later Tom told Tracie and me he wanted to be alone with Vecchio. Later, after the three of us left Vecchio's office, Tom told me he had made the negative comment about the book to appease Vecchio and that they hadn't discussed anything of substance after Tracie and I left.

I was annoyed. I knew Tom was under considerable stress, but if he was telling me he made his comments merely to appease Vecchio, I wondered what he was telling Vecchio about me. Even though Vecchio had been cooperative about providing me with copies of the depositions he had been doing, I believed I wasn't getting everything I would have liked. I would have been willing to go off the record on the really sensitive issues, just as long as I knew what was happening in the case. But I believed I was being spoon-fed information, and, eventually I decided it was time to interview someone else with knowledge about the suit.

I went to Washington, D.C., to interview Catz, who was teaching at the District of Columbia School of Law. I had decided to narrow my focus onto the legal aspects of the case because of Vecchio's reluctance to share information, but I wanted to know how much information I could get out of Catz.

I was interested in two matters. First, in how Catz and Vecchio had become Tom's attorneys, which Tom had never clearly explained. And, because of my discussion with the ABA official, I wanted to know if there was anything else special about the case. In his office in the legal clinic of the school, Catz explained how he and Vecchio became Tom's attorneys. A colleague was contacted by a "public interest" lawyer in Vermont about a teenager who wanted to sue Lorain County Children Services because it had placed him in the home of a man who sexually abused him for twelve years. Some records indicated that the agency knew of allegations that the man had sexually abused another young boy. The agency apparently acted negligently in its placement. The Vermont lawyer decided that the case had to be handled in an Ohio court, and contacted Catz's colleague, who in turn contacted Catz, then a law professor at Cleveland State University.

Catz, who described himself as part of "a small network of public interest lawyers around the country, a group of people in their forties," became interested. Tom flew to Cleveland with Tracie and her parents. Tom described in specific detail what had happened to him, yet, for all he had suffered, Catz said, Tom "seemed to be incredibly centered and stable." Tom's demeanor persuaded him that Tom could give persuasive testimony on the stand. Catz said he explained to Tom that a suit would generate publicity and that as a public interest attorney he was more concerned with the issue of child abuse than the money. Catz said he told Tom that a lawsuit offered an opportunity not only for justice and vindication but also a forum for him to expose what Children Services had done to him and possibly to make a difference in the lives of other children in foster care. As Catz talked, I could imagine Tom's eyes lighting up at the possibility of doing what he had been told never to do: speak out about what happened to him. It was also Catz's suggestion that Tom consider writing a book about what happened to him, and after the rift developed with the original agent, Catz, who was starting a literary agency, became the agent for the project. As a law professor, Catz said, he was only allowed to do "good pro bono work," but for big-money cases he had to work as an adjunct to another lawyer because of law school regulations. He contacted Vecchio because they had worked together before. Vecchio was to be the principal lawyer. Catz said he wasn't seriously involved in Tom's case because he had been representing Alcee Hastings in the impeachment proceedings before Congress. That resulted in Vecchio doing almost all of the work for Tom's case.

Catz explained some important elements about the suit. It was filed in federal court in Cleveland because Tom was a resident of Vermont and Children Services was in Ohio. There was an extra benefit from filing the suit in federal court. "The judiciaries in state courts are not independent. They're political appointments," Catz said. "Can you imagine suing Lorain County in Lorain County Common Pleas Court and getting an unbiased judge?"

I couldn't.

One central feature of the lawsuit was Tom's adoption in June 1983. Three years later, the Ohio Supreme Court recognized a new cause of action, which Catz called negligent adoption. It was based on a suit filed by an Ohio couple who had adopted a baby from an agency that had concealed that the child had chronic diseases. The parents became "saddled with hundreds of thousands of dollars in medical expenses" and sued, Catz said. The lower courts ruled against them, but the Ohio Supreme Court eventually held that it "would recognize a cause of action for negligence in the context of adoption, that the adoption agency owes a duty of reasonable care and had an obligation to inform the parents, and give them an informed choice as to what the medical condition of this infant was when they placed the baby in their home," Catz explained. The top court's recognition of "a cause of action for negligence in the context of adoption" allowed Tom to sue Children Services. Tom's suit alleged that the adoption was negligent because Children Services had information indicating that Carl was unfit to be a parent.

"I brought a garden variety negligence claim because what you do is, in effect, the federal court in diversity cases sits as a state court," Catz said. "It looks at state law, it's guided by state law, and the Ohio Supreme Court ruling about negligent adoption is the basis of my legal theory."

Almost in the same breath Catz expressed surprise that Lorain County prosecuted Carl, because "his admission of guilt doesn't help Lorain County's civil suit. They didn't gain any benefit from it, prosecuting him. I don't know why they did it, maybe because of some political embarrassment from the suit."

The plea may have actually strengthened Tom's case, he said.

On April 26, a lawyer dedicated to another cause contacted me at my office at Rutgers. More than I would ever want to admit, his phone call justified Vecchio's worst fears about Tom's working on a book. His name was Ernie Auciello, and he was with the Cleveland law firm of Gallagher, Sharp, Fulton, and Norman, which was representing Lorain County. Auciello wanted to know if I had talked to Carl's attorney, and he also wanted to know of any "admissions made to" me. I didn't respond. He told me I could be deposed in New Jersey or that I could come to Cleveland. He sounded a bit nervous, as if he was waiting for me to slam the phone down. I was noncommittal. Auciello said that if I didn't agree to being deposed I would be subpoenaed. He was so vague about what he wanted that I suspected he was on a fishing expedition. I wondered if he was one of the prima donnas strutting and preening around the hallway of the courthouse the day of Carl's trial. I had been considering contacting the defense counsels just to get a response from them, though I assumed they wouldn't consent to an interview. I told Auciello I wanted to consult with my attorney and hung up. Even though I didn't have an attorney, I was not too worried because I believed I was protected. Shield laws—some states have them, some don't—provide a measure of protection for journalists who don't want to be compelled to reveal their sources. The degree of protection varies from state to state. Because I lived in New York and worked in New Jersey, I believed the shield laws of the two states protected me from Auciello and his cronies.

But to be certain, I contacted Rob Levy of the New York Civil Liberties Union, Jane Kirtley of the Reporters' Committee for Freedom of the Press, Debra Ellis of the Civil Liberties Union of New Jersey, and an attorney for the New Jersey Press Association. And from them I learned I was facing serious problems regarding shield-law protection. I had been in Illinois, Ohio, Vermont, New York, New Jersey, and Florida when I talked to Tom. It wasn't clear which shield laws were applicable. And there were times when he was interviewing people as I was interviewing him. We were co-authors, and the federal laws for discovery in civil cases made it easier for attorneys to subpoena information. I was told not to contact the county's attorneys for interviews because it could make it easier for them to argue that I had indicated a willingness to be subpoenaed.

One estimate of legal expenses I got from another source was twenty thousand dollars.

The legal opinions confirmed that the situation was more serious than I had anticipated. I alerted Tom and Vecchio, and while I waited to see how the latest development shaped up, I resumed preparations for the next round of interviews. In the third week of April, Patty called to tell me she had been deposed and that she was chagrined to admit that it hadn't been as bad as she had expected. There were only four lawyers and two court reporters present, and she wasn't nervous about the questioning, which covered the period of time from when she lived with Carl and Jeanne to the present. She also said she learned for the first time from some Children Services records that Carl and Jeanne weren't as concerned about adopting her as they were about Tom. That discovery hurt her feelings.

Early in the second week in May, Tom called. He had passed a difficult accounting class in which most of the students received failing grades, and he was shooting for dean's list again. Also, with the help of the mother of Patty's boyfriend, he received an internship at the Cleveland Psychiatric Institute where she worked. However, he wouldn't be paid for the first month, and he had to find a second job. That meant that he might be working two full-time jobs in another grueling summer schedule. But he was excited. Classes had ended, and he had only one more year of college to complete. After graduation, he wanted to study business or law. Despite all his optimism, however, he also expressed concern about "burning out."

"I'm totally strung out to the max," he said.

He was confronted by major issues that required major decisions with consequences he wasn't sure he could anticipate, and he felt he couldn't put enough distance between himself and the issues to reflect on his options. He wished aloud he could find a haven where he could relax. Instead, as soon as he arrived in Ohio, he had to look for a second job to make enough money to return to school. I sympathized. And then I told him we should discuss plans for the summer because he would have to make decisions about the interviews. There was no surcease for him. And a few days later, I called him again about another matter. I had located Patricia O'Reilly's friend Vicki.

Late in April I sent Joyce Schwab a note thanking her for her kindness when Tom and I visited her in Florida. She wrote back. Her letter included Vicki's telephone number and address. I had originally suspected that she knew the phone number and address, but didn't want to give it to me. I didn't know why she changed her mind, but I was elated she did.

On May 13, a Sunday afternoon, I called Vicki Caspar, who was living in Parma, a suburb of Cleveland. She was aware of Tom's lawsuit because of the news publicity. She told me in the course of the conversation that she had contacted Childrens Services shortly after she learned of Tom senior's arrest and that his kids were in foster care. Three times she told a caseworker she wanted to give the kids a home movie and pictures of their mother when she was in the sixth grade. She also wanted to visit them, but a caseworker never put her in touch with the kids, she said.

I asked her if I could interview her. Patricia O'Reilly's kids, I said, knew little about their mother, and the bits of information they had were spurious. I also said Tom and I needed information for his book. We had interviewed Joyce and Linda, I said, but I wanted to corroborate what we had learned.

Vicki consented to an interview on the condition that I bring Tom and his sisters to Parma so she could meet them. I was hesitant. Tom was seasoned enough to confront what she might reveal during an interview, but I wasn't sure about his sisters. And I also wasn't sure what he had told his sisters about what we had learned. I wanted to talk to Vicki alone in the event she would reveal harsh truths. Vicki was polite but firm. She wanted to see her friend's children, especially Arlene and Darlene. Those were her terms. I agreed, reluctantly.

Patty, Arlene, Darlene, Tom, and I met Vicki in her home in mid-June. Tom's sisters brought their kids. Vicki had planned a warm reception, and she had turned her huge, sunken living room into an amphitheater. Her mother, Ione, and two teenage kids, Michael, sixteen, and Jaime, thirteen, were there. The nine of us sat on plush sofas to watch the film of Patricia O'Reilly. Vicki also had a collection of snapshots, and she had invited her mother as a second source of information for Tom and his sisters. Vicki told them they could ask any question they wanted. She also told them that she was not planning to pull any punches.

Vicki lost touch with Joyce Schwab after Patricia O'Reilly's funeral, but she had remained in contact with some of her relatives. She and Joyce met again in 1989 when Joyce came to Ohio for her brother's funeral. She told us how she had contacted Children Services three times because she wanted to visit Patricia's children, or at least give them the memorabilia she was holding for them. Each time, she said, the agency failed to follow up on her contacts.

Ione told Tom and his sisters their mother was buried in Lutheran Cemetery on Pearl Road in Cleveland, but she wasn't sure of the location of the grave. Arlene learned that Vicki was her godmother and that Darlene's godmother was Joyce Schwab's sister, Clara, who was dead. After a little more general discussion, we watched the brief home movie of Vicki's and Patricia's sixth-grade graduation party. Ione had filmed the party in 1960.

"Patty was like a member of the family," Ione said.

Tom and his sisters watched the film intently but said little. When it ended, Vicki showed them snapshots of her and Patricia at the amusement park of a Cleveland zoo. She and Ione described Patricia as a beautiful, chunky, brown-haired little girl who had a "pretty voice" and liked to sing and was a good dancer. Vicki and Patricia, who met when they were in fourth grade, performed regularly in the school gymnasium and were members of a singing group that was featured on a Cleveland TV show. They were also written up in the *Cleveland Plain Dealer*'s Friday magazine.

During the discussion, Tom told his sisters that their father and mother had never been married, and his sisters disputed him. When he identified Tom senior as the source of his information, and they continued to disagree, Vicki interrupted and explained that though they weren't formally married, they "were married common-law." Vicki's diplomacy ended the dispute, but I didn't know if that satisfied Tom's sisters, especially Arlene and Dee, who didn't recognize their disadvantage. For almost two years, Tom had been interviewing sources and accumulating information that had been unavailable to them. Tom's oldest sisters were relying on information from sources that Tom knew were undependable.

Patty asked Vicki and Ione how Tom senior and her mother met.

She and Joyce, Vicki said, were at Cleveland's East Side pier when Tom senior offered them a ride in his boat. Patricia was fifteen or sixteen then.

"Your grandmother was quite a swinger," Vicki added about Joyce. "She was more like our buddy."

"And my mom was not too thrilled over that," she said as an aside.

"I was square," Ione said, and laughed. "I just didn't go for that too much: Go down by the docks and stuff."

Did her mother hang out at the pier to meet men? asked Patty, who was aware of some of the nasty allegations about her mother.

"Yeah," Vicki replied. "To meet men, not to find men to sleep with. Just to meet different people."

"It was a social thing," Ione said. "But that'll lead to things anyway. That's the way it goes."

"How else do you meet men?" Arlene said rhetorically.

There was a quick discussion among the three sisters and then agreement that there was less harm in meeting men on a pier to go sailing and boating than meeting them in a bar.

Tom questioned Vicki about Tom senior's allegations that Joyce used Patricia to pick up men. Vicki replied that they went out "to have a good time. A couple of times I'd be with them—no big deal. We mooched a ride."

"Patty was not promiscuous. They were not boy-crazy. They did not chase the boys. And I know," said Ione. "They had fun doing things. She was a nice clean-cut girl. She just met the wrong person. He had money, he was an older person, he was very clever."

Vicki said Patricia was living with her grandmother when they met in fourth grade and, because she had to take care of her grandmother who was blind, her friend didn't have much time to play or visit with friends. Patricia's girlfriends frequently sneaked into the house and stayed in her room. When Patricia was thirteen, she learned that her father, whom she had been led to believe was dead, was alive and living with his second family. Vicki said she never understood why Joyce had concealed the information from her daughter. The revelation hurt Patricia, and when she met him she was very angry and refused to see him again. Her father died a few months later. Vicki said he had served time in prison for manslaughter. Tom senior had told us he had served time for an armed robbery.

When she was almost sixteen, Patricia dropped out of school and worked as a waitress in a neighborhood diner.

"I was mad at her" for quitting school, Vicki said, explaining that was about the time they began to drift apart. Patricia was dating an older boy when she met Tom senior, the same year that she left school. Tom senior had told Tom and me that Patricia's boyfriend was named Dennis Leaper, but Vicki said his last name was Liebert.

Tom senior was very nice to Patricia in the beginning of their relationship. She was impressed with him because he was an older man who seemed sophisticated and who spent a lot of money on her when they dated.

"It was more than she ever had," Vicki explained. "He was like an escape for her, and it turned sour."

"Did Joyce voice any concern?" I asked.

"Joyce was busy with her life," Vicki said. "But she objected to it. She didn't like it that she quit school but she didn't stop her."

Patricia became pregnant a few months after meeting Tom senior, Vicki said, and after Arlene and Darlene were born she started "aging" and looking "haggard and like someone under a lot of pressure." When Tom senior started mistreating Patricia, she responded by trying to "understand his paranoia" and trying to soothe his feelings, Vicki said. After a while, Patricia was too afraid to leave. The violence was one reason Vicki stopped visiting Patricia.

"Every time I came over, there was a scene," she said.

One day Vicki visited the Holmden Avenue house, and discovered Patricia, who was then pregnant with Patty, with a black eye and her mouth "busted open."

Arlene, Darlene, and Patty gasped. Tom tensed and, shaking his head, said, "This isn't bothering me."

I didn't believe him. Even though he had weathered a virtual maelstrom of vicious comments and harsh descriptions of his mother during earlier interviews, Vicki's comments hurt him. Neither of us mentioned Linda's account of his mother begging for her life. Vicki must have sensed the tension increasing in the room because she told Tom and his sisters "don't be nervous" and "make this house your house and anyone who wants to cook can."

That provided a moment of relief, and everyone laughed.

Tom and I described Tom senior's claims that Patricia was having sex with other guys and that she was constantly cheating on him.

"Two," Vicki said, explaining that Dennis Liebert was Pat's first lover and that Tom senior was the second. She said Tom senior was paranoid, and to buttress her description of his twisted imagination, she described the day she and Patricia brought Arlene and Darlene from the hospital. Tom senior insisted that one child was his and that the other was Liebert's. Vicki said Tom senior, even though he was living full time with Patricia, "was running back and forth" between two households. Patricia and his first wife, she said, knew each other and talked regularly on the phone, especially when one was trying to contact him.

"Why did she have four kids in a row?" Arlene asked. "Why would she have four kids like this?"

Patricia was young and immature, Vicki explained.

At another point, Tom described, in a derisive tone, how relatives whom he had interviewed insisted that they had tried to keep him and his sisters from being placed in foster homes; he didn't believe them.

Joyce tried, but "got tired of trying to deal with your father," Vicki replied.

Tom wasn't persuaded by her comment. Even if Joyce had wanted them, he couldn't imagine how she could raise four young children if she wouldn't raise one of her daughters.

"I don't think she would have minded," Vicki told him.

Tom and his sisters believed that no one seriously tried to keep them out of Children Services. But my impression, based on Children Services records and interviews, was that no one wanted the kids in foster care. Joyce lied to the child care officials to get the kids away from Tom senior. When the kids were returned to him, she tried to get custody through the courts, and when that failed she tried to negotiate with Tom senior. According to Children Services records, Aunt

Pearl, Aunt Joan, and Iva Waters all wanted custody. But the history of those efforts was obscured by the lies and deceits of people concealing their shame and guilt about the life and death of Patricia O'Reilly. Because of so much recrimination and conflicting information it was difficult for Tom and his sisters to trust anyone's account about anything concerning their lives.

At another point, Patty mentioned that Tom senior believed Joyce wanted him. Vicki and Ione laughed derisively. "No," they insisted.

Tom and I, indicating the problems with his father's credibility, said that Tom senior had made a similar comment about Linda. After about an hour of discussion, Arlene announced she had to leave; Patty and Darlene said they had to leave as well. The three thanked Vicki and Ione, and promised to stay in touch. Everyone was smiling, but it was a bittersweet farewell. Tom and I stayed because Vicki offered to take us on a tour of Patricia O'Reilly's old neighborhood; Vicki surprised us when she said it was a mere ten minutes away.

With her as the guide, the three of us later cruised through the neighborhood on the West Side of Cleveland where she and Patricia had grown up. The tour seemed to soothe Tom, who appeared more relaxed than when he and his sisters were in Vicki's home. Vicki described the scenes—what was new, what was old, what had changed—as we drove around Meys and West Thirtieth streets and passed Lincoln West, a new school. Tom realized the neighborhood was not far from the Cleveland Psychiatric Institute where he was working for the summer. We visited 1920 Holmden Avenue and saw the vacant lot where his home once stood. It was only a few blocks from where he worked. Tom was subdued, staring intently at the lot as if he was comparing what he saw before him with what he recalled from the past. The three of us then visited Lutheran Cemetery on Pearl Road where we hunted for Patricia's grave, but couldn't find it. After we left there, we were cruising past a police precinct when Tom told me to stop. He wanted to go inside and inquire about his mother's death; Vicki was ready to join him. Tom believed no request was unreasonable because there was still so much that we didn't know. We talked for a few minutes, and I eventually convinced him to postpone his plan until we got a second opinion about his mother's death. I doubted we could get much information about the death of a woman who reportedly died of a cardiac problem twenty years ago. But I came up with another suggestion. After we drove Vicki home, we returned to Holmden Avenue, got out of the car, and knocked on doors. We wanted to know if any residents recalled his family living there twenty years ago. The residents were not helpful. One man closed a door in Tom's face. Another, who said he had only lived in the neighborhood about eighteen years, referred us to an elderly guy sitting on a porch nearby. He reportedly had lived in the neighborhood more than twenty years, and his home was located across from the vacant lot. When we approached him and asked if he could help us, that we were trying to get information about the family that once lived across the street from him, he declared he didn't know anything. As we walked away, we overheard a younger woman ask him why he refused to talk to us. We couldn't hear his response, but we understood his gestures, and couldn't understand his disdain.

I had hoped that Vicki's and Ione's recollections of Patricia O'Reilly would be a refreshing antidote for Tom and his sisters, and I hoped to witness the salubrious effects of the visit. Later, when I talked to Patty, I learned I was expecting too much too soon. After she and her sisters left Vicki's home, Arlene, who was driving, cried all the way home. Patty and Darlene also grieved, though they did not cry. They were still haunted by questions: How could their mother love a reprobate? Why did she tolerate the abuse? Why didn't she run away? Why four kids so fast? A few hours in the company of strangers who fondly recalled Patricia would not easily resolve those questions. I thought the answers were obvious, but they would have to discover them in their own way and in their own time.

When I returned to New York City, I called Lutheran Cemetery in Cleveland and asked for the location of Patricia O'Reilly's grave. When I was told that there was no listing for her, I asked for the location of Patricia J. Waters. Section Q, Lot 93, I was told. I notified Darlene, and within a few days, she and her sisters, for the first time in as long as they could remember, visited the cemetery and placed fresh flowers on their mother's grave.

21 • "After a thousand stitches they stopped counting."

On the morning of July 19, about the time I normally would have been picking up mail in my department office at Rutgers, a man who looked like a messenger approached the department's secretary, Marsha Bergman, and asked for me. She told him I wasn't there and that she wasn't sure when or if I would show up. He told her he wanted to serve me with a subpoena and that he would be back later. When he left she called me, and I alerted Vecchio and Tom.

About two weeks later I learned that Tom was involved in a new crisis. Even though he and Tracie had talked about marriage, he had resumed a romance with an old girlfriend soon after he arrived in Elyria for the summer. One day in July the girlfriend, Amanda,* told him she was pregnant and that she believed he was the father. It was possible he was the father, but it was also possible he wasn't. Tom eventually told Tracie about the affair but not about the pregnancy. Tracie, who suspected more, told him she was coming to Ohio. She wanted the whole story finished. There was more bad news. He could not live with the Nadeaus when he returned to Vermont to finish his senior year in college. Tracie's parents were angry at him for betraying their daughter, and they didn't want him in their house. Their decision meant

that Tom faced a serious financial problem because he was
not making enough money to cover the costs of room and
board while he finished college.

His sisters were another source of pressure. When they
learned Amanda was pregnant, and that she was saying that
Tom was responsible, they insisted he live up to his responsibilities even though it wasn't clear what that entailed.
Though it was possible he hadn't fathered the child, they
didn't want to hear him making the kind of denials that reminded them of Tom senior, who after twenty years still
insisted that one of his twin daughters wasn't his.

Two weeks after learning of Tom's dilemma, I called Patty
to make plans for me to stay with her and Buck when I
returned to Elyria. Patty was extremely upset. One evening
she and Tom had gone drinking with some friends, and later
they stopped at an all-night diner. After waiting twenty minutes to be served, Patty announced she wanted to confront
the waitress. Tom suggested they leave, and told Patty not to
complain. Everyone got up to leave, but Patty confronted the
waitress anyway. Tom accused her of embarrassing him in
front of his friends, and they started arguing. Patty said he
was insulting her so much that she screamed at him, and they
continued arguing outside the diner.

"All of a sudden this big ugly monster came out," she
told me.

She described how Tom suddenly grabbed her in a head-
lock. He screamed he wanted to kill her, that he wanted to
die, that he hated himself and everyone in the world. Patty
screamed for him to let her go. He did, and told her he wanted
to drive her home, but she was reluctant to get into his van.
He apologized and insisted he wouldn't hurt her. When they
got inside his truck, he started screaming and driving errat-
ically. He wailed that no one understood what he was experiencing, that he was being overwhelmed by violent
thoughts.

Patty was terrified. Until that night, she had never been

afraid of Tom despite all their fights as kids and all their disagreements and arguments as adults. And she told me that she had never seen him so angry and hurt. But she was wrong. They both had been down that road before. Years earlier when he believed his only choice in life was to kill Carl or himself, he made a desperate plea to Patty, and she helped him to escape. Patty, he had said several times, was his link to life. His threat to sever that link revealed the depths of his anguish. But though he was talking about death, he also had to have been thinking about life, and his terrorizing Patty— as scary as it was—was another cry for help. This time Patty didn't know what to do, and neither did I. I believed his psychologist needed to be informed, but I didn't want to breach my trust with Tom by contacting his therapist without his permission. All I could think of doing was to tell Patty to keep me informed. About a week later I talked to Tom on the phone. I didn't tell him about my conversation with Patty. He said he was trying to persuade Amanda to get an abortion. In the early days of their affair, he told me, she had said several times she didn't want to raise kids and that she would get an abortion if she ever became pregnant. But now she was hesitating. He was angry. He believed she deliberately allowed herself to get pregnant.

"I was so dumb," he said. "This is a nightmare. Put it in the book. This is a classic for sexually abused people: They are promiscuous."

The pregnancy was unfortunate and would cause some problems but it didn't have to be a nightmare. That Tracie was coming to Ohio to confront him indicated that he still might salvage that relationship if it was important to him. Perhaps what he suffered in the Rimmer household led to his self-described sexual promiscuity, but his behavior wasn't much different than that of many other young people his age. But I didn't lecture him. He wanted me to listen to him, not preach. It was possible that the girlfriend wanted to get pregnant, and it also was possible she became pregnant because she was as irresponsible as he was. And it was also possible that he wasn't the father. I didn't know the whole story. She refused to talk to me, and I was only getting his side. But my sympathy was with him. I knew him. She was a stranger.

For most of the summer, Tom worked sixty to seventy hours a week because he needed the money to pay his college expenses. During the day, he worked at the Cleveland Psychiatric Institute, which had started paying him an intern's salary about the fourth week he was there. When his shift ended at the institute, he returned to Elyria where he worked nights and weekends for his brother-in-law, Kurt Tabar, who managed a service station. I didn't know that his grueling schedule would interfere with our doing interviews until one evening in mid-August I arrived in Elyria, picked up Patty at her home and the two of us drove to Kurt's service station. We arrived just as Tom was ending his shift. He acted upbeat when we met and went out of his way to entertain us. His clowning caused me, Patty, and Arlene, who had joined us, to laugh. I knew him well enough to recognize his playfulness as his way of concealing his misery and trying to keep us from worrying about him. He and I met later to talk, but we weren't together long. He couldn't stay up late because he had to go to bed early in order to get up early the next day to go to work at CPI. He doubted he would be able to participate in the interviews we planned because of his work schedule. We agreed that he would join whenever he had the chance.

Two days later I met him at CPI and we drove to a McDonald's for lunch. I wanted to talk to him about the interviews, but he didn't want to discuss the project. He wanted someone to listen to him. He was in agony. He told me he was seriously troubled by violent thoughts, which he was reluctant to describe. He spoke as if he was in physical pain. He had described some of his violent thoughts when we first met in Vermont, and he had talked fancifully about torturing and killing any man who might harm him or his sisters. He described how he would tie them to a pole and ignite the gasoline that he would pour on them. He also had railed against Jeanne and Carl, but at that time in his room it was obvious that he was only indulging in harmless speculation and what-if scenarios. But now, in the McDonald's restaurant, I sensed his desperation. He was worried that he might be overpowered by his violent imagery and lose control. Except for the initial moments when he talked of his misery, we sat in virtual silence for most of the fifteen minutes we were in there. Of all the times I had been with him I had never seen him so miserable. All I could think of at the time was that he should see Foxman as soon as he returned to Vermont. On the trip back to CPI we said very little. Later, when I talked to Patty, she said he had told her what he really wanted in life: to wake up one day and "not think what he is thinking."

I worried about him, but I also worried about the interviews that still needed to be done. So, I asked Patty for help, and she agreed because she wanted to help her brother. She and I contacted Pam Haynes who helped us contact her sister, Tammy Mayle, who lived in Cleveland. I wanted to talk to Pam's sister because I was certain that Aunt Joan would not consent to an interview, and I wanted more information. I also wanted to meet Tammy because her cousins were constantly urging me to talk to her. She was an enigma to them. After her name had been mentioned in countless discussions and rap sessions over a period of two years, I came under that same spell, and any mention of her piqued my interest as well. Pam had once described the night Aunt Joan was thwarted at the last moment from throwing Tammy off the Harvard-Denison Bridge. Dee had recalled how Tom senior and Aunt Joan forced her and Tammy to box when they were young. Patty related rumors about the time Aunt Joan set the house on fire and told the authorities Tammy was responsible. Grandma Waters rescued Pam from Aunt Joan, but Tammy, according to the best information I had then, continued to live with her mother. I had often wondered what her life was like with Aunt Joan.

So, at about 5:00 P.M. when Patty and I drove up the driveway of the three-story frame house on Cleveland's West Side where Tammy lived, I was hoping to learn about the woman who had survived two close brushes with death. Tammy had been married once and was now a single parent raising two sons. Their apartment was simply furnished but meticulously clean. They had moved there from a homeless shelter. Before living in the shelter they had lived on the streets. Tammy was twenty-five. She had short, wavy brown hair and brown eyes shaped like perfect ovals. She was casually dressed. She told us she had slimmed down from 170 pounds to 130. She was as short as Patty, not nearly as slim, but just as attractive. Patty brought along her son, who played in the kitchen with Tammy's two sons, while Patty, Tammy, and I sat in the living room and talked. By now I was not so uncomfortable having someone with me while I conducted interviews. Although I was interested in talking to Tammy, I didn't expect her to tell me much more than I had learned from Tom senior, Brent, or Pam.

I was in for a surprise.

I expected Patty to proceed cautiously, as Tom had done in his first interviewing session.

That was another surprise. The interview began with few pretensions and little small talk. We were there to ask questions. Tammy wanted to talk. But we didn't engage in a standard question-and-answer format. It started with her and Patty engaging in repartee, as if they were two friends who, after inadvertently bumping into each other for the first time in several years, paused to rehash old times. I felt as if I was someone who just happened to be nearby and was allowed to overhear what they had to say. I asked occasional questions to clarify some details, but I was not conducting the show.

They were.

After several minutes, I believed Tammy would have talked if I had shown up alone but I'm not sure she would have expressed herself in the same spirit as she did with Patty present. Tammy was about to provide details that Pam had neglected to discuss, either because she didn't know or because she didn't want to discuss them with Tom and me. In a stream of consciousness covering two hours, Tammy was about to provide an incisive look at *the family*.

Early in the meeting Patty asking Tammy if it was true that Aunt Joan and her husband had beaten up Tammy's father so severely one night in a bar that he needed one thousand stitches to close up a wound.

"My dad said that the doctor said that after a thousand stitches they stopped counting," Tammy replied, adding that the stitches were inside and outside the wound.

"After a thousand?" Patty responded. "That's what Pam said. I thought she might be exaggerating."

"A thousand," Tammy said. "That was true."

Continuing, Tammy told us about an older sister who committed suicide and about another sister who died of complications from surgery when she was eighteen and that Pam was a stepsister who was about seven years older. That information about Tammy's sisters was new not only for me but for Patty. I quickly became aware of a new dynamic in this interview. Tammy candidly responded to questions, but she also interjected information that she wanted revealed or wanted to discuss. Though neither she nor Patty tried to dominate the conversation, I believed they both were responding to each other according to agendas I didn't understand.

In the course of the conversation Tammy nonchalantly told Patty she had lived in seven foster homes and a child care facility similar to Lorain County's Green Acres.

"I used to envy you guys because you got to stay in one home," Tammy said, referring to Patty, her sisters, and Tom. "I was always switched around."

That comment surprised Patty, and she, without elaborating, told her cousin that foster care was no picnic for her and Tom. Tammy's life as a foster child started in grade school after a teacher, who had noticed that Tammy had worn the same clothes for three consecutive days, took her to the principal. Worried that Joan would beat her for talking, Tammy told them her mother was working so hard that she was too busy to change her clothes. The principal wasn't convinced. A social worker and police officers accompanied Tammy home, where they found Joan in bed with a man whom Tammy didn't recognize. It was her mother's first time home in three days. The police arrested Joan because she refused to stop cursing them for being in her home and threatening to take her child away. Tammy was placed in a foster care facility. She was ten years old. In the facility, she celebrated her first birthday party ever and remained in the Cuyahoga County foster care system until she was eighteen. During those years, when her home placements were unsuccessful, she was returned to Joan's custody until new arrangements could be made.

"I couldn't understand why they took me away from my mom because even though my mom beat me and did things to me, I still loved her," Tammy said.

"Exactly," Patty said. "Still loved her, that's what we say."

Joan worked two jobs in order to give her daughters a taste of the finer things in life. She came home from the first job to change clothes, cook dinner for her kids, smoke a cigarette, and go to her second job, which was across the street from their home near Eighty-first and Detroit Avenue.

"We had the best Christmases," Tammy said, reminding me of what Patty had said about her Christmases at the Rimmers'. "It wasn't nothing for my mom spending three hundred fifty dollars each on us for gifts. My mom was off on Sunday all day, and then Monday night was our night to go out with our mom. She always took us out for dinner, always did something to give us that quality time. On Sundays my mom would make soups and dinners and stuff all day long and put them in the freezer and then lay 'em out when she would go to work in the morning. And then, when she would come home for that hour between jobs, she'd cook 'em for us. Our clothes were clean, they were pressed. I mean we had the best of everything. We had stereos, TVs, the best clothes. We just didn't have the mom, the love that we needed."

Joan, like Tom senior, kept her kids isolated as much as she could.

"We were not allowed to go outside and play," Tammy said. "Her reason was that she didn't want us to get molested or kidnapped or something like that. We weren't allowed to have friends come over, so we would always sneak them in and then we would get beat up because my mother would find out that we were letting kids come in the house. I just had a slumber party for my son and there was about ten kids here and I was going, Ahhhh! But it was fun for me because I could never do that. I wasn't allowed to do that. We weren't even allowed to talk on the phone."

Tammy said she was six when Pam, who was about thirteen, went to live with Iva Waters. And that recollection caused Tammy to recall the night she was in a jeep with Iva, Tom senior, and all his kids. Tom senior, drunk, was making a late-night visit to the grave of Patricia O'Reilly.

"He must have done it several times," Tammy said, "because I remember one time we were in this giant, huge bomb of a car and he always drove with all five of us [Tom, Patty, Arlene, Darlene, and Tammy] in the backseat."

Tammy continued talking, telling us that she recently had been experiencing flashbacks. She might be cleaning or going about her business when she would suddenly experience a vision or vivid impression of some brutal experience from her past. She worried that she might harm her kids during one of those episodes.

"Exactly," Patty said. "And you don't want to do the same thing your mom did to you."

Tammy, who agreed with Patty, said the "real beatings" started after Pam moved in with Iva.

"What do you mean," I asked Tammy as I had asked Tom and Patty, "by beat? Are we talking about a slap or ..."

"No, I'm talking about boards. Whatever was in her hands," Tammy said.

"Beat!" Patty emphasized.

"Beat!" Tammy agreed.

"Fists!" Patty added.

"Kicked!" Tammy responded.

"Ass-kicked!" Patty insisted.

"My mother would bloody my nose for no reason, black my eyes," Tammy added.

"Rip your hair," Patty reminded her.

"And I was so stupid then that if someone would ask me what happened I would say I had fallen or something," Tammy continued.

She wasn't stupid. Terrified would have been a better description. Tammy minimized the severity of her beatings just as Tom and Patty had when they told me that Carl, who punched, beat, and slammed heads into walls, was not nearly as brutal as Tom senior. Because of Tammy's comments, I finally understood that Tom and Patty gauged the severity of the abuse according to the terror they experienced: With Tom senior, they constantly feared for their lives; with Carl, they worried mostly about being maimed and occasionally about dying.

"My mom never hit me or beat me when she was sober," Tammy explained. "Only when she was drunk. And then if she was sober and I did something wrong she would just overlook it."

"Sure," I said.

"But, mind you, when she got drunk and she remembered what I did, I got my ass kicked," she said.

I told her I understood.

"Boom, boom, boom, boom," she replied matter-of-factly in case I didn't understand.

Tammy recalled the evening nine years earlier when she was in her bedroom talking to a friend on the phone, and her mother suddenly banged on the door. Joan was carrying a knife and screaming that Tammy was about to die. Fortunately, Tammy's door was locked but that didn't deter Joan, who poured kerosene on a blanket and started a fire outside Tammy's room. Tammy climbed out a second-floor bedroom window and when the authorities arrived, Joan told them that Tammy started the fire. Tammy was taken into custody, but the friend who had been talking to her on the phone when Joan started the fire gave a statement to the authorities who released Tammy. Tammy was unable to explain to us if Joan was arrested or charged.

Patty's questioning and my occasional inquiries eventually got Tammy talking about her mother's bleak childhood. Tammy's descriptions of home life in Wharton, West Virginia, paralleled Tom senior's. Joan and her siblings, Tammy said her mother told her, frequently went to school either barefoot or with holes in their shoes, and their parents, Iva and James Thomas Waters, "disciplined" them by whipping them with a switch.

There was a twist, however.

"When my grandma was alive, and I'd tell her what Joan had said, my grandma said my mommy was a whore," Tammy explained, recalling her talks with Iva. "That's what she told me. She goes, my mother was nine years old and instead of going to school, she'd be in a dugout somewhere messing around with boys. She said that's why they beat her."

I was about to tell Tammy what Tom senior and Brent told Tom and me about James Thomas Waters's so-called "discipline" when Tammy said, "Nobody knows about this but Grandpa tried to molest me when he was drunk."

"He molested Darlene," I replied.

"He molested your mom," Patty said.

"You know who else was like that?" Tammy said.

I didn't, but Patty did.

The cousins described how one of their relatives constantly reached for their breasts whenever they were in his presence. Tammy recalled how he tried to put his hands down her pants and that Iva told her that he had tried to molest one of her younger cousins. Pam also had problems with him, Tammy said.

"And I told him—he's got a wooden leg—I told him, I said, you touch me you're gonna have two wooden legs," Tammy said, recalling an incident that happened when she was fifteen.

She was fourteen when another relative tried to molest her in a hotel.

"And I never told my mom until about two years ago," Tammy said.

"Because you're always afraid they won't believe you," Patty told her.

And then Tammy described how her mother one night came home with a man who molested her while Joan, drunk, was passed out on the couch.

"I had to be about seven or eight years old," Tammy said. "I was too afraid to say something. I was scared, like, maybe he'd kill us."

"You're so afraid that people aren't gonna believe you that you just say forget it," Patty repeated.

Tammy told us about the time she was molested by a baby-sitter who was eighteen years old. She never told Joan. After her fourth casual description of being molested, I asked her how the sexual assaults affected her. I thought her casual manner of describing the attacks served as a cover for deep pain, but I was not so much interested in what she was concealing from me as what she concealed from herself.

"You know, for a long time it never did bother me. I never thought about it," she said. "I don't know if it just comes with the age, but after I had [my oldest son] it seemed like things started bothering me more. That's why I told Pam, I think it's about time that I do something about it. Because nothing ever bothered me. I never thought about it. It was just something that happened. I took it for an experience and just went on. But recently, it's been bothering me."

She told us that Pam had turned to religion and that she was considering getting help from a therapist. But it wasn't clear how close Tammy was to acting on her decision.

I asked her how she felt about her mother, and she replied that she hated her because Joan always thwarted her attempts to meet or learn about her father. She hated Joan more for that than the beatings. "She knew where my father was and knew things about him and didn't tell me. She said she never knew where he was and come to find out on weekends she would go stay at his house. My dad said she never mentioned me. When she came back she'd never mention him."

Tammy learned about her mother's deceit when she was reunited with her father for the first time in twenty-three years. "I found his brother's phone number in the book and I was talking to his brother's daughter and I lied and told her I was dying of cancer because I figured if he's around he'll get in touch with me because I'm dying. And she got hold of him and he called my mom and my mom gave him my address."

Because she had a copy of her birth certificate, which listed his occupation as a real estate dealer, she expected her father "to be this wealthy guy, somebody that I'm gonna be so proud to see him and introduce him to all my friends," she said. But when they met at her apartment, he was working as a roofer and was toothless.

"He looks like he crawled out of a gutter," Tammy said. "I told Pam, I said, 'He went from real estate to Gutter City.' He's my dad but I'm not proud to say he is my dad."

But Tammy didn't seem particularly impressed with her stepfather. He and Joan, she said, had lived together for about twenty-four years and had been married about fifteen.

"He used to beat the shit out of her," she said. "I can remember me and Pam having to run out of the house. And this is no small man. He's about six feet five, about two hundred fifty pounds. He's broken my mom's nose. He beat my mom with a chain right in front of us, broke her ribs so many times."

Tammy said her mother had been married several times. Some of her husbands were wealthy and some treated Joan with respect, but her mother appeared to prefer abusive men.

"My father even told me that she would beat him up. One morning he woke up to go to work and she had ripped all of his business suits, threw 'em out in the middle of the street, trying to start a fight to get him to hit her."

"She's a good lady," Tammy said about Joan a half hour after telling us how much she hated her. Tammy's ambivalence about her mother was apparent throughout the time we were in her home. "I think my mom should have gone to counseling before she had kids. Because whatever happened to her when she was a kid or whatever happened in her marriages, she took out on us when she got drunk. Like I said, when she was sober I could bust her best dish and she would just go over there and clean it up and not say a word about it. But mind you when she got drunk, she remembered that, and we would have to leave.

"Like when that baby-sitter was molesting us," Tammy went on, segueing again to another brutal episode from her childhood. "He would bring guys over and like we'd be on the couch and there was about four. And he laid me across them naked. And I had bruises all over from where he'd hit me. That's what I remember him doing. They may have done something else but I can't remember it. That's why I said maybe I should go to counseling and get hypnotized and it might come out."

Tammy talked with envy about how she believed Pam

escaped most of the real torment, and Patty asked why she too wasn't allowed to live with Iva.

"Because my mom knew if she took me that they would cut welfare off," Tammy said as she revealed, in a stream of consciousness, additional descriptions of how she was sexually assaulted as a child. One incident involved a clerk at a local store. Another involved another man Joan brought home with her.

I asked her again about the effects on her self-esteem of the sexual assaults, her life in foster care, and the beatings by her mother. She talked about periods of severe depression and described how she became obese because she dealt with her pain by gorging on food. She had few friends. Acquaintances told her she was obnoxious and mean. She recalled how she and Pam fought over the years whenever they lived together, but she also said that Pam helped her a great deal.

"Pam was here for me when my dad came," Tammy said. "She knew I was down in the dumps since I've seen him. Pam started crying, she knew how I felt because we've always looked for our parents. I really felt sorry for her because she's still got that missing link. I told her that even though she couldn't find her dad, we still had each other and I would stick with her no matter what happened." In the same breath she recalled how Tom senior and Aunt Joan made her and Dee fight when they were young.

"I think that's why that girl don't like me to this day," Tammy said. "At the last get-together, she wasn't friendly at all and it hurt my feelings."

"Dee's never said she doesn't like you," Patty replied. "I think maybe she just doesn't know you."

I told Tammy that the cousins and siblings of her generation frequently misunderstood each other, that they regarded each other with mistrust and envy, that all of them misunderstood the full extent of the violence and how it had affected their lives.

Tammy described her life with the father of her oldest son. She had lived with the man four years before discovering he was married and had another family living in another country. He eventually brought his overseas family to Cleveland, moved them into the home he shared with Tammy and their son, and expected all of them to live together. After a while he started punching Tammy, giving her black eyes and bruising her body. He didn't harm his wife.

"And he had me convinced that I had two kids and no other man would want me," Tammy explained. "He had me brainwashed. He did. I thought I was going to have to live like this for the rest of my life 'cause who was gonna want me. I weighed one hundred seventy pounds, so nobody was gonna date me or ask me out."

But with the help of a friend she moved out one day.

"He tried to get me to come back and the way I was living for the past year [on the streets then in a homeless shelter], I wanted to go back badly because I knew what I had lost and how good it was," she said.

But he had mistreated her too much and, in spite of her poverty, she had found the strength to refuse.

Tammy also described her Aunt Gail as kind and gentle, and she said Aunt May also was nice too and that she was living in Georgia. They, she said, seemed to have escaped the consequences that had made life so miserable for Tom senior, Aunt Pearl, and Aunt Joan.

Aunt Gail and Aunt May rarely associated with *the family*, Tammy said. "They don't want nothing to do with them. I mean they come at the reunions but that's as far as it goes."

Tammy also recalled with affection her Aunt Jane, who occasionally took care of Tammy before she was placed in foster care. Jane, she recalled, suffered from asthma and diabetes. She had three kids.

Tammy learned about James Thomas Waters's cruelties by overhearing conversations. "A lot of times at sister get-togethers, I was the only one kid there 'cause my mom couldn't find a baby-sitter. I would overhear things and re-member them. Jane was a very good woman. I really loved her. When she died it really hurt me because I used to tell people at school she was my mom. And she used to take me to school. I lived with her when my mom worked her two jobs. I really loved her. When she died I was devastated. It took a long time to get over that. And then that's when my mom started really beating me up. And I can remember one time she was gonna hit me with this two-by-four. I was crying so hard and I said, 'Please, Aunt Jane, help me.' And Aunt Jane had already been dead a couple of years. And my mom said, 'Why did you say that?' Then my mom threw me in a cold shower, and said I was crazy because I said that but that was, I think, the only thing that saved me that day. Aunt Jane would never let my mom hit me. She never let her touch me."

Tammy provided more anecdotes and inside information about the Waters and Workman families than anyone Tom and I had interviewed. But it was her information surrounding the death of Patricia O'Reilly that interested me.

"He thought he'd killed her," Tammy said. "And he didn't. You know why she died?"

Patty and I knew the official cause of death. And I was in touch with the forensic department at the medical school affiliated with Rutgers. So, I didn't believe that Tammy had much to offer.

"Why?" Patty asked.

"Well, I know she had a heart attack or whatever, but did you know my mom had taken her that day to have an abor-tion?" Tammy asked.

"Well, I know that Joan took her to get an abortion, but I didn't know that was the day she died," Patty replied.

"Yeah, same day. It was the same day," Tammy insisted.

I wasn't sure if Tammy was correct, but I didn't challenge her account. Patty and Tammy were specific about what Aunt Joan supposedly did. My best information up until then had come from two sources: Tom, who had gotten his information from Aunt Pearl, who said Joan had given Patricia some quinine pills; and Tom senior, who told Tom and me how Joan had tried to help Patricia abort her baby.

"Where did Joan take her?" I asked.

"I know it was a lady doctor, 'cause my mom's had eight abortions and that's when before abortions were legal," Tammy said.

Tammy, speaking to Patty, said the woman gave Patricia "some pills or something to calm her nerves or something so your dad wouldn't find out 'cause your dad didn't want your mom to do that."

I told Tammy about the autopsy and that Patricia hadn't aborted the baby and no one knew if she took the pills.

The pills "must have come from that place that gave the illegal abortions 'cause my mom went there all the time," Tammy said. "But they had been to see these ladies. I know that because I heard my mom talking to people about it. And my mom always blamed herself."

The eight illegal abortions must have affected Joan's physical and emotional health. I twice asked Tammy why Joan didn't use prophylactics—I was not about to make moral judgments—and her responses were vague. But she said the effects of numerous illegal abortions were exacting revenge. "She bleeds twenty-four hours a day. All the time. My mother's stomach looks like she's nine months pregnant. She was supposed to have a hysterectomy three years ago."

Tammy reminded us that her mother was married several times, and she rattled off the names of former husbands as well as former lovers and provided information about all of them. "She married a guy one time and her in-laws bought her a double house, brand-new, for a wedding present. The guy was from Germany, his parents were from Germany. They had money. She had it made."

I thought not. Joan lived as if she had been programmed from childhood with an irresistible urge to self-immolate, not in one fell swoop, but a piece at a time. Like her brother, there was no joy she couldn't subvert, no peace she couldn't destroy.

Tammy was a treasure trove of information, but after about two hours of listening to her talk, I started wrapping up the interview. By 7:00 P.M. I had noticed how self-conscious I had become about asking her questions. I felt I was losing focus and being drained, that the cumulative effect of listening to people's immeasurable pain had finally caught up with me in Tammy's apartment. Though Patty was with me, I had started this quest with Tom, who was not there to let me know just how far he wanted to probe and how much he wanted to expose about the Waters family. I was beginning to think it was time to end what we had started.

Patty and I knew Dee was throwing a get-together that evening, and we convinced Tammy to come to Elyria with us. Dee would be happy to see her, Patty and I told Tammy. That night at the LeMaire home in Elyria, Arlene, Darlene, Patty, Tom, and Tammy partied into the night and, like soldiers who had survived awesome battles, they swapped war tales about *the family*. I didn't stay very long, returning to Patty's house alone. I wanted to reflect on all I had learned.

The next day, Saturday, August 18, Patty called Aunt Joan to ask if she would talk to me. Joan was upset about the book—it wasn't clear where she got her information—but insisted that Arlene and Darlene were not sexually assaulted by her brother. Joan, fifty-four, also complained that no one loved her. Her nieces and nephews, she said, had stopped visiting her. Patty listened patiently. Joan told her that if she decided to talk to me she would say Tom senior had been a loving father and he had never abused his kids, whom she knew loved him very much. After Joan hung up Patty was furious. I later sent Joan a letter telling her I had interviewed Tom senior and Brent and that I wanted to talk to her to. She never answered my letter. And because I had interviewed her two daughters and brother, and because Tom had talked to her sister, I decided it wasn't important.

22 • "And everybody down there, they really liked him."

When Tom returned to Vermont for his last year of college, he was undergoing another period that he could have called his worst ever. He was haunted by visions of mayhem and violence, and he considered himself a failure whose touch could sully the brightest moment. He imagined that his relationship with Tracie was over even though she had visited him in Elyria, and he felt he had lost face with her parents, who had treated him like a son and now regarded him as a philanderer. By late August, I had eventually stopped telling him things would get better with time. It was as if he were afire, and I was telling him to be patient, that his burns would heal after he discovered how to extinguish the flames. By the late summer we had stopped talking about the project, and it was obvious that we would never confront his former caseworkers and their supervisor at Children Services or his former disciplinarians at Keystone Middle School. His seventy-hour work week was one factor. It kept him either busy until the late evening or too fatigued to do much of anything when he was free. But even if he had found spare time, I doubted he would have participated because of the upheaval in his life. I wasn't surprised when, shortly before he left Elyria, he said he wanted to wrap up the project as soon as possible.

One Monday night late in August, Patty and I drove to Oberlin to interview Cathy Ives, Tom senior's former wife. She was just about to watch the San Francisco 49ers–Minnesota Vikings football game when she invited us into her home. During the thirty minutes the three of us talked, Cathy corroborated Tom senior's accounts of how he tormented her and what Tom and Patty had told me about her. It also was obvious that the past was still very much a part of Cathy's life. Pictures of Tom and Patty were on one wall of her smartly furnished house, and she also showed us a picture album of them and their sisters. Cathy, who had brown eyes, dark hair, and plain features, wore glasses and was slightly stout. Except for Tom senior, she still longed for the family she once had for about two weeks.

A few days later, I drove to the Cleveland suburb of Brook Park to interview David Waters. I wanted to know more about Tom senior's life before he met Patricia O'Reilly. Patty accompanied me. So did Arlene and Darlene. The twins decided to join us after they learned that Patty was participating in the interviews, but Tom's half brother was to be my last delve into Waters lore.

David, thirty-one, lived on a quiet residential street with spacious modern homes and neatly trimmed lawns. It was early evening when he opened his door and invited the four of us in. Almost immediately I recognized his close resemblance to his father. He was slightly taller with blond hair and blue eyes. David was mild-mannered, almost humble. He told us that his wife Annette was pregnant and that they had a daughter, four.

We sat at his kitchen table. His wife remained out of sight but within earshot. I sat across from David. Darlene sat next to him. Arlene and Patty flanked them. David did not seem the least bit concerned that he was surrounded. His mother and older brother, he told us, did not want to be interviewed.

Tom senior and his mother met at a carnival in Oak Hill,

Ohio, which is about twenty miles from the Ohio River. His mother was raised there, but David was uncertain why Tom senior, who was nineteen when they met, was there. Tom senior and his wife later moved to Cleveland. Pam, Tom's cousin, had told us that they lived for a spell with Iva in a big house with a number of other people. Eventually, Tom senior and his wife left and started raising a family. They were married about six years and divorced after David's mother learned about Tom senior's involvement with Patricia O'Reilly.

Vicki had said David's mother and Patricia talked frequently with each other, but David disputed that information. According to him, his mother confronted Patricia at the Holmden Avenue house and they argued, and that was the extent of their contact. When Tom senior left his sons and wife to live with Patricia, David didn't see him for almost three years. Then his father reestablished contact, and his two sons served frequently as baby-sitters for him and Patricia. Sometimes, the two were gone for the weekend while David and his brother took care of the kids. Because Tom senior had visitation rights, David's mother did not challenge the arrangement, and David and his brother regarded baby-sitting as the best means to stay in contact with their father.

David's paternal grandfather, James Thomas Waters, occasionally stayed with Tom senior and his first family and, later, with Tom senior and Patricia and their kids. David did not like being in the Holmden Avenue house when the adults were drinking. "I've seen them consume half a gallon of whiskey, and starting drinking another," he said, as he reenacted someone reaching under a table to grab another jug. There were times when he and his brother rounded up the kids to flee the violence that erupted.

I asked David to describe Patricia O'Reilly. I wanted her daughters to hear from someone whom I considered a reliable source what I already knew.

"She was a nice person. She was never mean toward me or my brother," he said.

When asked if she drank alcohol, David said "a lot," especially on the weekends when she and Tom senior went out to party.

"Do you remember," I asked, "how she treated the kids—sober and not sober?"

"There was a difference between when she was sober and when she wasn't," he said as he carefully chose his words. "When she was sober she was a good mother. When she was drunk she didn't have the patience."

"Did she smack 'em?" I asked, hoping he would say no.

"I've seen her smack the kids, yeah, but what I mean by patience is when your kids are kids, they're gonna get into stuff," he said, carefully choosing his words again. "If you don't want 'em to get into it, you should put it out of the way. A kid doesn't deserve to be smacked because it got into something you put down there. That's patience. She didn't have the patience."

His father, of course, had less.

"As long as things went his way there was no fighting," David said. "When things weren't going his way he could be a real mean person. My dad was an alcoholic. He used to beat my mother."

How often? I asked.

"It happened more than once, but I wouldn't say it was frequent, no. It was just he'd be real drunk or something, or things didn't go his way, or mostly it was at the end when Mom found out that he was cheating on her and that's what caused the divorce," David said. "That's when it got bad because she didn't want him coming around anymore."

"The Waters family seems to think that he didn't start acting like that and drinking the way he did until he met my mom," Dee said.

David disagreed.

"My dad owned a boat and he used to belong to the Edgewater Yacht Club, and I believe that's where his drinking started," David said. "I think that led to his whole problem. I think his whole life would be different than what it is right now, to be honest with you. I think he just got in with the wrong crowd, started hanging around with the wrong crowd of people."

The yacht club, he said, "wasn't for the average person." Most of its members had more money than Tom senior.

"My dad had a smaller boat compared to what they had. Their boats were twice the size compared to what he had. Big fancy jobs," David told us.

He recalled accompanying Tom senior to the pier, where his father would "hang out with them guys and drink and go out and play cards and gamble and come home with no paycheck." There were late-night card games where the booze flowed. After Patricia O'Reilly died, "that's when he just drank and drank and drank," David said. "At least before then he did go to work. He had a very well-paying job for a time. He took me and my brother for a tour of the plant. He told us he could have been a vice-president of that corporation had he had a high school education. He was a chemist. He used to strip metals and stuff."

David told us he had virtually no contact with his father's relatives after Tom senior "abandoned" his family. David, however, did stay in touch with Aunt Joan.

"I realize she wasn't a good mother to Pam and Tammy, and I know that, but she was good to me, so I'm basing this on how she treated me," he said. "She was always good to me. She still cared about my mother even. She was the only one out of the family that cared about my mother. Rest of the family didn't even care about her."

"Well, everybody hated our mom," Dee told him.

"Well, they didn't like mine that much either," David replied.

"I thought they did," Dee said. "I thought they all liked your mom and they hated mine, said all his problems would've never started if he would have never met my mom."

It would have been difficult for anyone in the Waters family to disrespect David's mother. She hadn't allowed Tom senior's drinking to destroy her family or cripple her sons. She was alive. She knew the truth. And David didn't appear to be someone who would tolerate anyone insulting her. But it was easy to understand *the family's* open contempt for Patricia O'Reilly. She was dead. Her kids could barely recall her, and no one in *the family* was about to stand up for her. What was especially cruel about the sordid slandering of her memory was that her kids were made to suffer. Without a mother or a father or the truth to oppose them, it had been easy for a generation of alcoholics to heap their shame and guilt on four defenseless kids.

After Tom senior started living with Patricia O'Reilly, David's mother and her sons had a difficult struggle.

"He was supposed to pay child support and never did," David said. "He had that good job too. He'd be three, four, five months behind in child support and he wouldn't even call or care if me or my brother had anything to eat. I can remember my mom working at American Greetings making sixty-five bucks a week, raising me and my brother. We were on welfare for three years because my mother couldn't find work and dad wouldn't pay any child support. She had him in and out of court and at that time, of course, it didn't do anything."

Aunt Pearl had told Tom that Tom senior had financial problems because he was supporting two families. Even Vicki Caspar, who scorned Tom senior, believed the financial problems stemmed from his supporting two families. But that wasn't the case, according to David. Two families were struggling, and their problem was Tom senior.

Except for Joan, David had vowed never to associate with
the rest of the family because of their deceit about his father's
imprisonment. Whenever he inquired about Tom senior, Iva
or Aunt Pearl or Aunt Joan told him his father was traveling
around the country. That went on for a few years, until one
day David learned from his cousin Pam that his father was
incarcerated.

"The first time my brother and I went down there he was
real apologetic, you know, for all the things he did wrong to
us all our life," David said. "It was the first time he actually
broke down and told us he was sorry for what he did to us."

Tom senior told them he was in jail because he seriously
injured someone during a fight in a bar.

The last visit, David said, was the best. "He was telling us
he was going to be getting out soon and he was going to
come and see us more often on a regular basis. Things were
gonna be better. It was pretty nice. I mean at that time I was
still young, about sixteen, and I cared about him. It was, finally,
the first time I sat down and had a conversation with my
father about what I'd done the last five years of my life instead
of talking about his problems. I still loved the man at that
time."

After his father was freed, they met briefly, but there was
no regular contact. The last time David saw Tom senior was
in 1985; Tom senior was drunk. David got a call from him a
year later, drunk and begging for money to buy food. David
told him he would send him food or drive to West Virginia
and rescue him but he wasn't sending him money for booze.
That was the last time he talked to his father.

"Me and my brother have set down and talked about this,"
David said. "If my dad was to die I don't even know if I'd go
to the funeral. I really don't think I would. If I did, I think I
would go for maybe Joan's behalf because she may have been
a drinker and that, but she was still good to me. She was the
only one on that side of the family that was good to me or

cared whether or not I was eating. Like I said, he was a selfish man and I know that he cares for nothing but himself. I've seen what he did to my mother, what he did to their mother, how he treated us, how he treated them."

After about ninety minutes, Dee started asking questions.

"Did you guys have a lot of resentment towards us four?" she asked.

"No," David replied, explaining that neither he nor his brother blamed them for their father's infidelity.

For the next few minutes they swapped stories. Arlene and Darlene told them how Joyce Schwab tried to convince them that they didn't have older half brothers, and about their surprise at seeing him at Arlene's wedding. David described his attempts to try to meet them.

I asked him if he drank. Except for an occasional beer with friends, he didn't drink, he said. He conceded, however, that in high school he had a chip on his shoulder and got into a lot of scuffles. But, he said, he had since settled down.

"I wonder why he turned to beating people," Dee said with resignation about her father.

"Out of frustration," David told her. "He figured he was miserable, he wanted to make you miserable right with him."

But David also said there were people who still respected his father. His uncle in Oak Hill was one.

"If my dad was to pull up in front of his house right now, my uncle said he would have to welcome him in," David said, describing a recent discussion with his uncle. "He said my father was always a nice young man when he came down there, when him and my mom were going out. Because when he first started taking my mom out down there and they left and got married and came to Cleveland, he got a good job. I don't know how much he was making but in the sixties he was making excellent money. And everybody down there, they really liked him."

*   *   *

Shortly before I left Elyria to return to New Jersey for the start of classes at Rutgers, Patty and I argued in the kitchen of the house where she and Buck lived with his mother and two brothers. She was upset that the book was taking so long to complete. She was indignant. She paced. She postured like a lawyer giving a closing statement to a jury. Her eyes flared slightly and she stared unflinchingly at me. She was blunt. TV talk shows featured people like her, her brother, and her sisters all the time. What's so special about us? she wondered. She rattled off other complaints. I responded with a simple explanation: It was time-consuming trying to corroborate information and piece together various accounts in order to tell an accurate story. I agreed, the project was taking longer than I had expected, but its scope had broadened. After a few moments, her indignation subsided and we started laughing. Patty and I were buddies. She had gone out of her way to make my stay in Elyria comfortable, and I wasn't bothered that she didn't understand the complexities of what I was trying to do. I also wondered if she was repeating what Tom had said to her. I regarded Patty as Tom's soul mate. If something was bothering him, she would know. I couldn't determine if that was because they were in constant touch or if they were one of those special cases of sisters and brothers who magically knew how the other felt even though they were separated by great distances. Patty didn't have to tell me when she and Tom talked because I would pick up on it in the course of a conversation with her. I suspected that all the factors that had been eating away at Tom during the summer were weighing in on him. The pressure was enough to make anyone miserable, but Tom was carrying an extraordinary burden that made everything in his life appear perilous.

23 • "I'm a child molester."

*B*efore the trip to Elyria, I had moved from New York to New Jersey to be closer to Rutgers. I fantasized that the move would make it difficult for a process server to track me and that idea made it easier for me to concentrate on what I thought were the remaining tasks.

I phoned Carl Wednesday afternoon, August 29, at his home in Saugerties, New York. His attorney, Jack Bradley, had said he would consider arranging a meeting for me with Carl after the appeals court ruling, but I didn't believe he would. I had phoned Bradley several times for information about the appeal, and when he hadn't returned the calls, I decided to contact Carl.

When I asked him if I could interview him, he refused and told me to talk to Bradley. I agreed but asked if it might be possible for me to talk to him in the future. I wanted to keep him talking.

"I doubt it," he said, and then complained that his life had been ruined and that he was about to lose "everything"—his car, his house, his freedom. He accused me of wanting to make money off his woes. Five years ago, he said, he had done everything the Vermont court had required of him, and it hadn't mattered.

"Suicide," he said, was his next "fucking choice," and "that'll be the last chapter in your book, and you'll be happy."

I thought he was being melodramatic, though I know that people who talk about suicide are to be taken seriously. I wouldn't have been happy if he had killed himself because his death would have devastated Tom and Patty. But I couldn't help noticing that Carl's outburst was similar to Patty's descriptions of Tom's despairing remarks about killing himself. I knew, from talking to Patty and Tom, that Carl had said in their presence more than once how much he wanted to kill himself but lacked the courage.

I told Carl I didn't want him to kill himself, and he snapped that I wanted him dead or in prison. I insisted that wasn't true, and he insisted "that's what you and Tom want." I told him I believed he was prosecuted not out of any sense of justice but so that Lorain County could appear to be doing its job and, perhaps, mitigate the damages from Tom's five-million-dollar lawsuit. I knew Carl was a casualty of realpolitik, but he wouldn't have been in trouble if he had put his son's best interests before his. I told Carl the truth: Tom did not want him imprisoned.

Carl sighed. He complained that Tom's lawyers were "going to make two million bucks" because of the suit and that his life "was devastated." He said he couldn't find work because "I'm a child molester; nobody will hire me. And it's all because of some money, and it just doesn't make sense."

He complained again that he believed he had lived up to his responsibilities five years ago when he did what the Vermont court required of him: get therapy. "I don't understand why this happened," he moaned.

I could have told him that the Vermont authorities did not punish him more because Tom had told them that the sexual abuse ended in Ohio. If Tom had not been so concerned about protecting his adoptive father, Carl might have faced felony charges in Vermont. At that point in the conversation, I asked him if I could talk to him at length, and he responded that his lawyer told him not to talk to anybody. "As a matter of fact," he said, "a phone call is what got me in this position 'cause I confessed on the phone."

Something else was bothering him. The Lorain County Prosecutor's Office was challenging his release on bail while he waited for a decision on his appeal. That upset him, and he commented, "I'm telling you too much on the phone right now. I'll never learn to keep my mouth shut."

His therapy, he said, required him to be honest about what he did, but I knew, from talking to Tom and Patty, that he hadn't been completely honest. I told him I wanted to stay in touch with him and his lawyer, and he told me that he was "thinking about writing a book." He said he had been "approached" to write "my life story," but his lawyer advised him to wait until after a decision on his appeal.

In September, shortly after classes began, I phoned Dr. Robert Trelstad, chairperson of the department of pathology at the University of Medicine and Dentistry of New Jersey, which is affiliated with Rutgers. I told him I needed an expert's second opinion about the death of Patricia O'Reilly. He sounded amused at my description of the reaction by my source at the medical examiner's office. According to him, some medical examiners get overly suspicious about the prospects of death by homicide. He wasn't too concerned. He told me that he had trial experience and that he would be willing to give a second opinion after he read the copy of the autopsy report. With Trelstad handling the forensics part of my investigation, I had one more interview to conduct.

I phoned the residence of Denis Liebert, Patricia O'Reilly's former boyfriend (he spelled his first name with one *n*). He confirmed everything that Vicki Caspar had told me about him and Pat: He was Pat's first lover, and they broke up when she met Tom senior. He recalled that he bumped into her one day on the street after they hadn't seen each other for a long time, and they barely exchanged hellos. He said he would always remember her as a really nice person. After I talked to Liebert, I was convinced that he, Vicki, Linda, Joyce Schwab, and David Waters were the best sources of information for Tom and his sisters about their mother. Tom senior and members of his family had done an effective job of besmirching Patricia O'Reilly's name but I firmly believed their damage was no longer irreversible. All that was missing, I thought after that phone call to Liebert, was an opinion from Trelstad and a trip to Vermont to deal with some nagging concerns.

Part VI

●

Tracie

24 • "Somebody who truly loved him"

*T*he Wednesday before Thanksgiving, I drove to Vermont and at about 9:00 P.M. I arrived at Tom's apartment in Mor- risville, a small town ten miles from Stowe. Tom and Tracie were waiting for me when I arrived. Tom had cooked the turkey and Tracie had helped with the meal. We feasted for about two hours. Tracie was looking trim and fit, but Tom was carrying extra weight. His studies and his job at a local service station left him little time for exercise and sports. When I first met him he had the physique of a nimble, strong running back, but on this night he looked like the kind of running back who smashed through defenses and trampled on anyone blocking his way to the goal line.

After we finished our meal and the three of us talked for a while, Tracie left. During dinner, she and Tom had done a superb job of concealing their misery. When Tom first told her about his affair with Amanda, he and I had expected her to break up with him. When he eventually told her about Amanda's pregnancy and that he might be the father, we had expected her to sever their relationship. She probably con- sidered that too but, again, she didn't. Instead, because her parents insisted he move out of their home, she helped him find an apartment and checked on him regularly to make su' he was okay. In his apartment, Tom repeated what he had been saying for a long time: He loved her and needed her, but he also was confused about how he felt. She wanted to marry, he was ambivalent. Her pastor, her two sisters, her parents, her psychologist, and his psychologist believed they weren't good for each other, he told me. But Tracie was as stubborn as he was. She had decided that their lives would be better together, and no one was about to change her mind. He felt guilty. He didn't want to hurt Tracie, yet he knew his indecision was making her unhappy. He was miserable and my concern for his suicidal impulses were the reasons why I was in Morrisville.

When Patty told me shortly after Carl was convicted that Tom thought about killing himself, I reacted with surprise and alerted Vecchio, who contacted Foxman. And when she told me he "always" thought about killing himself I fretted over that revelation but hoped Tom would work out his problem with his psychologist. One fall day during a telephone call, Patty told me that Tom had been musing aloud the past summer about what it would be like to kill someone, and the shock of these comments forced me to take stock of what I had been hearing for several months. I had been rationalizing each disclosure so that I would feel comfortable encouraging him to continue working on the project. But Patty's comment and the tone of her voice finally forced me to recognize that whatever was eating away at him appeared to be getting worse. I had researched enough cases and interviewed enough people to know that for some of us a thin line separates violent thoughts from violent actions. Tom was in serious trouble. I wanted desperately to talk to his therapist. If Foxman did know, I wanted an explanation of Tom's problems because he obviously wasn't as well off as I had been led to believe. If Foxman didn't know about the severity of Tom's problems, I wanted him to know what I knew. And I wanted to accomplish this task without betraying Tom's confidence.

He and I had agreed early on that I could interview his

psychologist. But when I eventually did contact Foxman he had told me that he would not talk to me until he received a notarized letter from Tom consenting to the meeting. But Tom would not send the letter. During one phone conversation weeks before I drove to Vermont, I accused him of procrastinating. He insisted he would send the letter. But when I became convinced he would not send the notarized consent, I decided to meet face-to-face with him. I also wanted to interview Tracie. I assumed she and Patty knew him better than anyone else, and I wanted to know if Patty and I were the only ones worried about what he was feeling.

That night at Tom's Morrisville apartment I told him what I wanted to do, but didn't explain my motives. He was not sure if Tracie would agree to talk to me. She was angry that I had waited almost four years before proposing formally to interview her. He also wanted to talk about the book—something we hadn't done in almost three months—but he wanted to wait. He had planned to take me deer hunting. Tom's plans called for us to get up at 4:00 A.M. but, because I was worn out from the trip and he was fatigued from his work schedule and nights of insomnia, we overslept and didn't get to the hunting ground until 11:00 A.M. It was not unpleasantly cold, and I enjoyed trekking along with Tom as he pointed out what he described as "sightings"—deer feces, tracks, scars on trees possibly caused by deer antlers. He was intense and methodical. For an hour we sat motionless on the property owned by Tracie's parents and then we had to dash to their home in Underhill for the traditional Thanksgiving feast. I couldn't detect any resentment or tension. The Nadeaus still treated Tom like a son. They treated me again like a visiting dignitary. It was a pleasant meal.

After we ate, Tom and I returned to the hunt. He was waiting for deer to come out of the woods to bed down or start feeding on the plains, but it got dark and started raining, and we left and returned to the Nadeaus' home where we watched TV with Tracie for a while. Tom and I eventually returned to his apartment in Morrisville. The next day we went to Hilary's, a local restaurant, to eat breakfast. We laughed and joked as we ate. After we finished eating, we got down to business. As if on cue, we began arguing. It lasted more than three hours.

He told me he believed I was working with him on his book because I had been abused by my parents; otherwise, why would I be so interested in people who had been as severely abused as he and his sisters?

There were several reasons for my working on his life story. He and his sisters were victims of colossal injustices; I was awed by his willingness to confront situations that most people would avoid; helping him tell his story was a way for me to make up for the story I didn't do when I lived in Rochester, New York; I hoped we might generate something of value that could benefit others; finally, I had become his friend and I wanted to help. I hadn't planned on becoming personally involved in his quest. But every time we encountered an obstacle to learn the truth, I felt I had to help him find a solution, and each step along that path to truth brought him face-to-face with a painful situation that he had to overcome in order for us to proceed. I drew close to him during that inexorable process. I didn't think that only someone who also had been abused as a child could sympathize with him and his sisters. Anyone who wouldn't tolerate the mistreatment of another human, or who had ever been politically oppressed or systematically mistreated as if he or she was a second-class citizen—and who understood the reasons for the mistreatment—could empathize with him and his sisters.

But his question, and the emotion behind it, caught me unprepared, and as I faltered, trying to make conscious my subconscious reasoning—I always thought he knew my cards were faceup on the table—Tom changed the subject. He complained about the book taking too long, that in April 1988, I had told him we would finish it in two years.

I argued that the scope of the book had changed when I

realized he couldn't provide the kind of details we needed to tell his story in the first-person narrative form we had originally planned. We'd had to do interviews I hadn't antic- ipated, I told him, and that required more time, but it had been well worth the effort. He didn't agree. It had sounded easy in 1988, but the reality was a series of brutal revelations. He complained it was taking too long to get an opinion about his mother's death. The forensic expert I had contacted at Rutgers was very busy, and we were trying to work out some logistical problems, I told him. The Cuyahoga County Cor- oner's Office had agreed to allow him to review the slides used to determine the cause of Patricia O'Reilly's death, but he had to review the slides in the coroner's office in Cleveland.

Tom was not satisfied with my answer.

Good businesspeople know that once they commit them- selves to a schedule, they are required to complete a project, he said. I became angry, and my voice rose as it does in heated arguments. And several times Tom, wincing, reminded me to lower my voice, that we were discussing sensitive issues about his life and he did not want me blabbing them all over the restaurant. I snapped that there weren't many people in the restaurant, and the few patrons there were not paying any attention to us. I told him I would try to speak softly but that it was difficult for me to maintain a moderate voice during an argument. I added that he shouldn't worry so much about what other people think, especially strangers. He retorted that it was easy for me to feel that way because I hadn't lived his life.

That interchange infuriated both of us.

He was again scolding me for the schedule delays when I said angrily that "certain people" had withheld information from me and that had resulted in my having to do a lot more work than I had anticipated. He knew what I meant. I was referring to him and his lawyers.

I demanded to know why Tom hadn't sent Foxman the

notarized okay so that I could interview him. Tom responded that he didn't know how to locate a notary public. I didn't believe him. We had spent the last two years locating people who were supposedly difficult to find. I insisted he was deliberately stalling and that we should talk about why he didn't want me to talk to Foxman. He denied he was trying to keep me from talking to Foxman and changed the topic again.

Tom was upset that I planned to describe how he had considered killing Carl just before he was removed from the home in Underhill. Only someone weird would consider killing his father, he said. Was I trying to portray him as weird?

I argued that a desperate kid who feared for his safety had the right to protect himself by any means possible and that he should know I didn't think he was strange and that I wasn't about to portray him as weird. But we were in agreement on one point: Lots of people would be less sympathetic.

He was also upset about other details that I had planned to include, details that we had agreed upon two years earlier. And we continued arguing until I finally told him I planned to finish the book with or without him. In a calm, deliberate tone he asked me if I realized that the book could expose him to ridicule. I agreed that it was possible some people might be cruel to him, but I told him his bravery and willingness to go public was one of the reasons I originally decided to work with him. He didn't believe he was brave. He also expressed concern that the book might make it difficult for him to get a decent job when he graduated from college. I told him I hadn't considered that possibility, but, yes, it was possible. And again I told him that his bravery was one of the reasons I wanted to work with him and that he would "have to tough it out." He again said he didn't think he was so brave, and then, somehow, the conversation got around to him explaining how he could have been a better wrestler at Mt. Mansfield High School if he had only worked harder. He could have been a state champion if he had pushed himself; he hadn't trained as hard as he could have, he said, and he then went on to explain how he should have been a better athlete at Elyria Catholic High School. I told him that he had done extremely well in light of the extraordinarily painful life he was forced to endure and that I was awed that he had accomplished as much as he had.

He disagreed.

He said he could have accomplished more and described himself as a failure in wrestling as well as in life. His self-reproach saddened me. Eventually, he agreed that I should continue with the project but he said he could no longer participate in any interviews. Contacting Foxman would be his last contribution, he said. We both grew quiet and pensive and then we left the restaurant. A few steps from Hilary's we broke out in laughter. I'm not sure why we were laughing, but both of us felt better. As we got in his van, he also told me that Tracie wanted to be interviewed.

Hours later, when I was driving from Morrisville to Underhill to talk to Tracie, I realized that Tom and I had been arguing so heatedly that I had misunderstood a major point of the argument. Though I'm sure he wouldn't have been upset if the project miraculously disappeared, the argument wasn't as much about him changing his mind as I had suspected when we were in Hilary's. He was concerned that he was relinquishing control over something that could have a major effect on his life. He was feeling extremely vulnerable. Someone else was calling the shots, and he would have to live with the consequences.

Tracie was a senior at Mt. Mansfield High School when she first became aware of Tom, a sophomore, in the hallway of the school. A friend pointed him out and told her he looked like Michael J. Fox, the actor. She disagreed, but she thought he was handsome.

"And he looked over at me at the same time that I was looking at him and we both had a stare-off because both of us are pretty cocky people and we just stared at each other," she recalled.

They stared at each other whenever their paths crossed at school. Sometimes he was with his girlfriend and she was with her latest flame. Her account of how they finally started dating regularly was not much different from the account Tom gave me when I first met him. But from her I learned why she wanted to go out with him.

"He was cute and he was just different. He didn't smoke, he didn't drink. He was a jock. I had always gone out with older guys who like to take you out to dinner. From my freshman year all the way through high school, we," she said about her, her sisters, and her friends, "always went out with older guys. They would take us to different places and we would get all dressed up, and then they'd go buy a case of beer and everybody would sit in the backseat and drink. I had gone through that being drunk every weekend for three and a half years. Tom was different. Tom was really into sports. I had never gone out with a jock in my life. So, this was a neat change."

When did he start confiding in her?

On their second date when she invited him to her parents' home to cook him dinner.

"Tom said, 'Before this goes any further, I think there's something you need to know.' And he told me that he was sexually molested by his father for so many years."

Tracie recalled responding with a nonchalant "So?" to let him know that "it didn't matter to me."

We were sitting in her room at her parents' home in Underhill. She was relaxed and talking in a casual manner, but I knew she was choosing her words carefully. She listened intently to my questions and measured their meaning. I tried not to give up any information about what Tom had told me during the years that he and I had worked on the book, yet I wanted her to reveal what Tom might have told her but not me. In the early moments of their relationship, Tom was living with a friend and his family under the auspices of Vermont's Department of Social and Rehabilitation Services. About two months after she and Tom started dating, Tracie met Carl and Jeanne, whom Tom was still occasionally seeing. It was during that period that he was trying to resolve just how much of a relationship he wanted with them.

"Every time we would go and see them, after we left, he would either freak out all over me or just be a total dick," Tracie said and giggled.

"Describe 'dick' and 'freaked out,' " I said.

"He would just holler and scream for no reason," she replied. "You'd say, do you want Pepsi or milk, and he'd say I don't care and then you'd bring him a glass of milk and he'd bitch to you because you didn't bring him a Pepsi."

One extended outburst erupted at a wedding. The groom, who married Tracie's cousin, kissed Tracie after they finished dancing.

Tom "flipped out" and accused her of embarrassing him in front of everyone at the party, she said. "He was being a jerk all day. He didn't want to dance; he didn't want to talk to anybody. He just sat there and moped. And then, finally, when he started freaking out, I said let's go. And then we got into an argument all the way home. He started hollering and screaming about me letting my cousin's husband kiss me. And then we went back to my house, and we talked and talked and talked and then finally—he was still furious—he said, 'I want you to take me home now.' "

He stormed out of the house and got into her car and punched a big hole in her dashboard. He cried as he drove home, and made her stop the car before they arrived at the house where he was staying. He got out and stormed away and then stormed back and started "swearing and screaming and calling me every name in the book."

Then, he suddenly punched the window, but she let him back in the car nevertheless, and in his anger he accidentally ripped out her gearshift.

Then he suddenly became apologetic.

She managed to drive the car to her home and "we sat in my parents' driveway and he started crying and sobbing and telling me that he wanted to die, he wanted to commit suicide, he didn't want to be here anymore, that the only way he was ever going to be happy is if he died—and he really wanted to commit suicide—and we both cried and we talked for a long time."

What prompted that outburst, she said, was an angry letter from Jeanne accusing Tom of being insensitive and selfish. But after Carl moved to New York, Tom stopped throwing tantrums. He and Tracie still quarreled but he did not erupt in rage.

How had she tolerated him during their early years together?

"I understand why he was doing it, and I knew that it was going to take him a while to get help and to get through it," she said. "And I felt that I loved him and that I wanted to be by his side. If there was going to be anything that I could do to help him I was going to do it. Everybody else had abandoned him and I didn't want to and I wasn't going to. That was just something that I was brought up with, from my growing up in a strong Catholic family where my parents were always taking people in and helping 'em. And I felt that Tom just needed some guidance and some love, somebody who truly loved him for who he was, to help him become a responsible adult. I felt that I could help him do that and that my family could help him do that. We could give him the things that he needed—not material things—but the love that he needed."

Even though they had talked about marrying after he graduated, she had worried about him being faithful to her after he started Johnson State.

"I always had this hard time trusting Tom," she said, "because all through his college years he would get letters from girls and he would call up and say he didn't want to come home for the weekend 'cause there was this party, and these girls would always be in his room when I visited him at Johnson. So, then I became a wicked snoop."

Tom constantly complained that she snooped, and she admitted that she was constantly checking for telltale signs of infidelity.

"For all these years, it was four more years 'til we get married, three more years 'til we get married, two more years to get married and then this spring we were both like, You're graduating next year. Are we ready?" Tracie said, recalling a discussion with him last spring. "I mean, we always told everybody that once you graduated, we were going to get married, so, maybe we should go our own ways for the summer just to make sure, so we can really see who we want. Because we've been going out for a long time, and you're really young and you never really dated a lot of other people where you had a car and money to take people out, and maybe we should separate. Maybe we should just separate for the summer."

They agreed that they would date other people, and she told him that while he was living in Ohio for the summer she would learn to trust him. But they spatted during phone calls.

"Whenever I would tell him that I went out with somebody, he would always give me the third degree, like, Well, did you kiss them? And all this stuff. You know, going the whole nine yards," Tracie said. "And one time I went out with a guy and he gave me a kiss good-bye, after like four times going out, he gave me a kiss good-bye. And that was it." But she eventually stopped dating, she said, because "Tom was in the back of my mind every single time I went out."

She assumed he was dating but not involved in a serious relationship with anyone. When he finally told her in a phone call about Amanda, she told him she was coming to Ohio. After she arrived, he told her that Amanda was pregnant, and he confessed to other affairs he had had during the four years they were dating.

"And I flipped. And I just started hitting him and punching him and screaming and crying and calling him every name in the book and then I asked him to stand up. And I asked him, 'Do you know what I'm going to do?' And he said, 'Yes.' And I said, 'Do you think you deserve it?' And he said, 'Yes.' And I smacked him right upside the head. And then he just stood there for a second, turned around, and walked into his bedroom and I walked into his bedroom a couple of seconds later and he was bawling his head off."

We had been talking about an hour in her room at her parents' home. In the early stages of the interview, she was upbeat and girlish, concealing her unhappiness. Although she was candid in her remarks about her relationship with Tom, I felt she also was very guarded about not revealing their confidences. There were moments when she tried to solicit information from me. Eventually, our conversation got around to one of my main reasons for talking to her. Tom, she said, used to tell her more about himself than he told Foxman, but he had lately stopped talking to her.

"That's why I'm so angry. It's like, Why don't you talk to me, why don't you let me know what you're thinking and what you're feeling because when you did it helped us both," she said. "It helped me to understand the things that you were going through and why these certain things were happening. Now he doesn't want to talk about it."

He had stopped seeing Foxman because he was embarrassed that he had deceived him for so long, that "he had held back so many things that he was thinking and things that he was doing, like the fact that he smoked cigarettes," Tracie said. "He was so embarrassed to tell Dr. Foxman that he smoked cigarettes because he thought Dr. Foxman would look down upon him. And he held a lot of things back."

I said several times that I didn't believe that Tom deliberately misled people, but he withheld information, and each time Tracie agreed.

"I mean there's stuff that he's talked about that when I remind him that we talked about it, it makes him very uncomfortable," I told Tracie.

"He's like, oh, God, I told you about that," she responded.

I was hoping to bait Tracie into telling me about the "stuff" Tom withheld from Foxman, but she balked at supplying specific details. She was angry but she was not about to betray certain confidences to someone who might print them in a book. She did talk about Tom being "at the end of his rope," saying that his chameleonic performances and efforts to appease people had caught up with him and "he just can't play anymore." Tracie was angry that he had cheated on her, that he had betrayed her, and, being a strict Catholic, she talked of him paying for his sins. I also thought that she was so personally involved with him that she did not realize just how much he suffered and was suffering, and that she did not understand, because of her own concerns, the struggle he was undergoing.

I inquired about what was happening with them now. Until I had arrived Wednesday evening, I had been under the impression that they were estranged.

"I don't know because at this point when I ask Tom what he wants: 'Do you want me? Do you want to keep trying? Do you want to work this out?' And all I get is 'I don't know.' So, at this point I told him I'm feeling like I'm just someone to hang out with 'til you graduate from school because you don't have anybody else here, and you don't want to be alone."

"Are you?" I asked.

"Yeah, I guess so," she replied solemnly and then, slipping into a stream of consciousness, described some of his complaints about her.

"Some of the things that he says, for example, that I'll call him every night or call him two or three times a night or go up and visit him every Monday without fail, but it's not because I'm dependent on him," she insisted. "It's just he's my best friend, and he's my boyfriend and I'll think of something that I forgot to tell him when I talked to him the time before. And then I'll hang up and a couple of minutes later I call because I forgot to tell him something, like, we got invited to do this and this and this. And he's like, will she just leave me alone. But I don't know how he feels until he just blows up: 'You call me all the time; I'm just so sick of it.'

"So, the week before, I said, 'Fine. I'm not going to call you.' I didn't call him once last week and he called me every single day. But he doesn't remember that. One minute we talk, and he's on the verge of saying, I don't want this anymore. And then the next day he'll call up and he'll act like we never even had that heart-to-heart conversation about us not knowing if we're right for each other and everything is peachy keen."

"Is he still seeing Dr. Foxman?" I asked.

"No."

He wasn't in therapy. He wasn't talking to anyone. She admitted she was aware of his thoughts about killing people, but she resisted my questions about them. Her main fear was that he was backing out of his commitment, not that he might hurt someone.

Tracie did say that in the past year she had learned to become more concerned about what she wanted out of life, and at one point I thought she covertly was talking to me so that I might deliver a message.

"You know, every time I went to go see him I would make sure that my makeup was on and my hair was done and that I was dressed really nice and wearing things that made me look my best," she said. "And I'd buy him things and do the thoughtful things to let him know I was thinking about him. I'd stop and pick him up a soda and some cigarettes. And he'd say, 'Well, what'd you buy yourself?' And I'd say, 'I didn't buy myself anything. I wanted to get something for you because I love you.' I was doing everything I could to show him that I loved him. I mean, from buying him a pack of cigarettes to, You need some money? You need some money? Oh, I know you don't have any money, here's some money—and to try to remind him, Don't forget you love me. But, now, it's like, I don't care, Tom. I love you with all my heart, but you know what? I love me too. When I look in the mirror, and I feel like it was a rough day, I'm no longer spending a lot of time doing my hair and my makeup. I'm not putting on a show anymore. I finally realized that if Tom and I break up there are other people out in the world."

Why hadn't her parents ostracized Tom?

"Because they know that the more they run Tom down or try to convince me to stop seeing him the more it's going to hurt me, and they respect me enough to respect my judgment, and my parents love Tom a lot," she replied. "My parents do love Tom. And they care about him, and they'll always care about him and they've told me this all the time: Tracie, we don't want you to feel trapped. If you and Tom break up we will always love Tom. We want to see Tom equally as happy as we want to see you happy.

"And they were very hurt about what he did to me. They felt equally as slapped in the face as I did, which I got angry about and kind of gotten in arguments with my parents when they first found out. I told them, 'You have no right to feel that way. He didn't do anything to you, he did it to me. And I felt like this is my anchor, you can't be mad too.' "

She reiterated her complaint about his mimicry.

"All his life he portrayed a role of what Carl wanted him to be. So, when he is with his teachers he acted the way his teachers wanted him to act; when he was around kids his own age, he didn't know what he was supposed to be doing, but he acted the way they wanted him to act. And in a lot of ways I think that the reason Tom feels so comfortable when he's screwed up on alcohol, drugs, whatever, is because he feels a little bit like that's him. He feels at peace. Because Tom has a hard time having a good time without being drunk or using these other things that he was using."

I asked her what he was really like.

"The Tom that I know, that I know that is hidden somewhere inside of him is very shy and is very sweet and not from things he does, just from feeling the warmth. He's very nice," she said. " 'Cause sometimes you can feel how sincere he really is. And it's a wonderful feeling to be with him when he's at those times. And other times, it's just really confusing because you don't know whether he's being him or if he's being who you want him to be. I think Tom feels that he is a really rotten person and that every time he might start feeling good about himself, he has to prove to himself that he's still that rotten person because that gives him an excuse of why he's still feeling bad. And I don't want him to feel bad.

"Tom, before he came back to Vermont, he was saying that he really knew that he was screwed up and that he really wanted to get help. So, I bought all these books on self-healing, struggle for intimacy, the twelve steps, dysfunctional family, and I sat down and read them."

And she suggested that he try joining a support group because he might more easily work through his problems by drawing on the support of people who had similar experiences.

"He always said that he never felt comfortable telling Dr. Foxman exactly what he's thinking, exactly what he was feeling because he knew that Dr. Foxman never had those thoughts and feelings, so how could he understand," she explained. "So, I told him about these support groups: AA, Al-Anon, codependency groups, incest survivors, all these different groups. And I'd open up the *Burlington Free Press* and there was one every single night of the week at different places at different times in certain areas. And he's like, Oh, I want to go, I want to go, I definitely want to go."

But he never went.

25 • "It's not engraved on stone tablets."

I drove to Chicago to spend Christmas with my parents. On my way back to New Jersey a few days after the start of 1991, I stopped in Elyria to visit Patty. And to make a cursory check on the status of Tom's lawsuit, I visited Vecchio in Cleveland. Shortly after I entered his office, I abruptly confided my fears about Tom. I hadn't planned on it, but I realized after I started talking that I wanted someone who might be able to influence Tom to know what I had learned about him. I told Vecchio of Tom's homicidal and suicidal thoughts, that he feared he was losing control and might harm someone. I told him about the incident between him and Patty.

I told Vecchio that I believed Carl had continued to force Tom to have sex with him after they moved to Vermont, and that Tom probably had been forced to engage in more than just oral sex. If that was so, I told Vecchio, he and I were dealing with a young man who could be suffering from the catastrophic effects of extreme sexual abuse. The literature I had been reviewing indicated that the short-term and long-term harmful effects of sexual violence were directly related to the kind of sexual violence that kids suffered. All forms of sexual violence are harmful, but kids forced to endure anal intercourse and sexually sadistic acts and other perversions, and who also were physically and psychologically abused as well, can suffer grievous harm.

I told Vecchio that my opinion about Carl continuing his sexual abuse of Tom in Vermont was based on information from Tom and Patty. During our first meeting in April 1988, Tom recalled how George Karson, the Vermont SRS social worker who had first contacted him, had asked several times if Carl had sexually abused him in Vermont. Because he hadn't resolved his painful ambivalence about Carl, Tom still felt compelled to protect Carl, so he lied to Karson to keep Carl from being arrested. Tom had told me, without going into detail, that there had been one sexual incident between him and Carl after the Rimmer family moved to Vermont. He was unsure if he wanted to reveal that information because he still worried that Carl might be arrested by the Vermont authorities. At the time, both of us were under the impression that Carl would not be imprisoned because of Tom's lawsuit. Tom also was concerned that he personally could be arrested because he believed he had perjured himself by denying that any sexual abuse had occurred in Vermont. I told him then that he hadn't perjured himself, but because of his concerns, I said we could postpone deciding what to do with the information. One reason for that decision at the time was that I had been led to believe no one else knew. Later Patty told me that the abuse had continued in Vermont, and she wasn't talking about just one incident. She surmised that it was the continued sexual abuse that had driven her brother to consider killing Carl. Because of her disclosure, I had planned to tell Tom at the appropriate moment that he should no longer withhold that information, that it was too important to conceal. I wanted to wait until I was certain he would be comfortable discussing it. I believed time was on my side. After I witnessed his pain in the aftermath of Carl's conviction, I decided not to raise the issue with him until I thought it was appropriate.

There was always the chance that Tom had confided more in Vecchio, and that he was already aware of what I was telling him, but there was no way for me to know. Foxman was unavailable to me. Patty and Tracie had done all that they could; Vecchio was the only one left. Tracie had told me during her interview in November that Tom had a lot of respect for him.

Vecchio said he had always been aware that Tom concealed a lot of his pain and that there was information Tom probably withheld from him, but he also indicated that my descriptions were new to him, especially the descriptions about Tom's homicidal and suicidal thoughts and what Patty had described. He surprised me when he confided that Tom was hurting his case. Tom had not been in therapy for almost a year, and because he lived in Vermont and not Ohio, Vecchio could not exert much influence on him. The best he could do was to phone him more frequently.

That Tom was jeopardizing his case by not visiting Foxman only underscored how much Tom was suffering. I told Vecchio I was planning to visit Tom and would try to convince him to visit Foxman. Vecchio also said he was looking for another specialist who would be willing to testify at Tom's trial and possibly treat Tom if he continued to refuse to see Foxman. I promised to try to develop a list of potential specialists. Vecchio wanted someone whose practice was conveniently located for Tom.

We also shared one wry moment. He and I had been adversaries from the day we first met. I had always regarded him with suspicion because I felt he had threatened my working relationship with Tom. I also suspected he was withholding information that I could have used, though he never refused any of my requests for material. And he, of course, was angry that his client was making admissions that might hurt the lawsuit and that he had no say in how we proceeded and little knowledge of what we were planning to expose in the book. Though we had agreed to cooperate to help Tom, we were still adversaries. But when Vecchio told me the lawyers representing Children Services were demanding that he turn over copies of my notes and records of my interviews with Tom, we both laughed. They probably believed Tom was telling us everything we wanted to know, and that impression only added to the moment.

Vecchio also confided a piece of significant information. One night during the previous summer, he drove to Elyria and picked up Tom. The two of them then drove to the home of Gwenda Adams, the unidentified woman described in news accounts as the one who had allegedly phoned Children Services to complain that Carl shouldn't be allowed to take care of Tom and Patty because he had molested her six-year-old son. Because Children Services was required to make a report of phone calls, Vecchio had expected to find a copy of that report in the records the court had ordered the agency to turn over to him. But there was no such copy included in the records; Vecchio believed Children Services had destroyed the information because it would strongly support Tom's lawsuit. However, Gwenda told Vecchio and Tom that she had never phoned the agency—she had visited it to complain. There was no record of her visit included in the material provided Vecchio, as there should have been.

Gwenda, Vecchio told me, was hesitant about testifying at Tom's trial because she was concerned that the publicity would expose her son, who was about Tom's age, to shame. Despite that drawback, Vecchio was convinced he could persuade her to testify in what would be a significant trump for Tom's case.

When I left Vecchio's office, I drove back to New Jersey feeling a little more relieved.

That feeling didn't last long. A few days later Tracie phoned me with unsettling news. Tom had groused aloud one day about wanting to kill Carl and Jeanne and others he wouldn't name. She asked him if he wanted to hurt her, and he said no, but she told me she wasn't sure if he was being honest with her. She was no stranger to his anger, but this was the first time he terrified her. I told her to make sure she was never alone with him and that she shouldn't visit him in Morrisville. I told her I would phone her after I devised a plan to encourage Tom to see a therapist. After the conversation ended, I felt a twinge of guilt, as if I had betrayed Tom by telling his girlfriend to be wary of him. But the other choice was to stand by and do nothing until a crisis happened.

As I promised Vecchio, I began drawing up a list of potential specialists based on information from the National Committee for Prevention of Child Abuse, the National Clearinghouse on Child Abuse and Neglect Information, and the National Resource Center for Child Sexual Abuse. I also contacted the Family Violence Resource Center at the University of New Hampshire. And it was during that period of numerous phone calls that I also contacted Parents Anonymous in Montpelier, Vermont, and talked to a representative. After hearing background information about Tom, she gave me a clinical glimpse into his living hell.

He was experiencing "flashbacks," she said without hesitation, and I realized that during the years we had been working on the project, I had never thought to ask him if he experienced episodes similar to those described by his cousins, Pam Haynes, and Tammy Mayle, who suddenly reexperienced traumatic events from the past.

"It's a frightening experience," the PA representative said, adding that she believed Tom was "panicking" because of the flashbacks and that he probably was experiencing "feelings of alienation and isolation, that he is facing this situation alone." His behavior was not uncommon for someone who had suffered as much as he had, she said. She cautioned me to regard his flashbacks as "warning flags." He needed to be in therapy; he needed a support system, she said.

I groaned.

I told her he was avoiding his therapist. She suggested that the best alternative was for his "close good friends" to be available to help him during this period. As for his comments about killing Carl and Jeanne, she said, people undergoing the "healing process" can experience "fantasies of violence" and "that it is not unusual for such a person to disassociate and get in trouble with the law." Vermont, she explained, had strict laws that required people in her field to alert the authorities about people making violent threats. I wasn't about to identify him so that she could alert the authorities. When I told her that Jeanne lived in Ohio and Carl lived in New York and that there was "no way" Tom would leave Vermont to go hurt them, she said the authorities did not have to be alerted.

Through several phone calls, I eventually learned that Morrisville, where Tom lived, reportedly had one of the best outpatient clinics in the state for people experiencing severe emotional problems stemming from sexual abuse. I passed on that information to Tracie, who set up an appointment for Tom. He visited the clinic once and refused to return.

I later told Tom during one phone call that he had to talk to a therapist. He told me he was dealing with his problem his way, that he had his life under control, that he was perturbed that I might be implying he wasn't trying to help himself. He was trying to finish school. He was working long hours at his job. He was dealing with other pressing matters, and he wished that Vecchio, Tracie, and I would get off his back.

I told him I knew he was doing the best he could but he needed extra help. I told him I worried that he might lose control. He sighed, and we both became quiet. The phone call ended with us agreeing to stay in closer touch. But after he hung up, I felt as if I had been talking with a victim bleeding from a gaping wound, and I was trying to stop the hemorrhaging through touch-tone counseling. In later phone calls, I tried not to harangue him about seeing a therapist. Even though I stopped raising the issue, it was obvious he knew from the questions I asked that it was on my mind.

Late in February, Tracie phoned me. At her suggestion, Tom started visiting a psychic whom she often consulted. And during one meeting, the psychic told him that his mother was murdered when he was a young child and that he would be involved in seeing that justice was done. The psychic's comments, Tracie said, renewed Tom's interest in working on the book.

I wished the psychic had told him to see a therapist or to give me permission to talk to Foxman, but I told Tracie that I was winding down the project, that there wasn't much else to do, that all I needed was a response from the forensics specialist who had agreed to help us. But, if Tom wanted to resume working on the project, I told her, she should tell him to send Foxman the notarized consent.

Weeks later I learned why I had not heard from the forensics specialist. He was on sabbatical from Rutgers for the spring semester. I was told that I would have to be a little more patient if I wanted his help, but I was running out of patience waiting for the forensics specialist, waiting for Tom to send Foxman the notarized consent, waiting for the phone call telling me that Tom was in serious trouble, that he had hurt himself or someone else or both. Thus, when Tom phoned to tell me he and Tracie were going to Florida for spring vacation and that they wanted to know if I wanted to tag along, I was stunned. I was still feeling guilty about telling Tracie not to be alone with him. Thoughts raced through my mind: Had I overreacted? Had she merely described a bad moment?

I told him I wanted to go with them, but I wasn't certain if I could make it and I would call him back when I knew for sure. I eventually told him I couldn't go but I wanted him to stay in touch with me. We talked once on the phone while they were on vacation. He sounded relaxed and teased me for not joining them. And when they returned to Vermont, he phoned to let me know that they both had had a good time.

Shortly after they returned to Vermont, the *Chronicle-Telegram* newspaper in Elyria published a five-day series about Children Services. The news articles portrayed the agency as an evil empire. The stories reported: that Children Services had been sued for $85 million by a family alleging that it had been harassed by the agency after a hospital mistakenly concluded that an eighteen-month-old daughter had been sexually abused; that Tom's suit alleged how "Children Services put him in the home of a known pedophile"; that the attorney for a woman whose thirteen-month-old daughter died after being placed in a foster home by Children Services had "discussed the possibility of filing a civil suit"; that additional lawsuits "loom on the horizon"; that the director of Green Acres Children's Home, operated by Children Services, was under investigation for alleged felony theft of food; that a former Green Acres child care worker had been arrested on charges of rape and sexual battery involving teenage boys at the facility; that Children Services "sometimes" failed to protect kids; that for some families it created more problems than it resolved.

According to the paper, two judges who handled domestic and juveniles court cases and who served as alternate trustees for the board "were not familiar with all the cases." The paper reported that several other board members "complained that they have been kept in the dark. 'Why didn't they tell us about this,' " one member was quoted as complaining.

I hoped the news coverage bolstered Tom's lawsuit, but some of the news was unsettling. The paper reported not only that the county was inadequately insured for the $85 million lawsuit but that the county commissioners were "scrambling to obtain coverage from the state of Ohio in the Waters-Rimmer case because a company that insured Children Services for $11 million in coverage went bankrupt." The state was only good for a maximum of $500,000. Of all the problems facing Tom, the fact that he could win a big settlement and not get paid was not an issue he, Vecchio, or I had anticipated. Another sour note in the coverage was a story quoting Tom. He wasn't supposed to talk to reporters. Vecchio, I thought, would not be happy.

That same month an Ohio appellate court rejected Carl's appeal but Carl remained free on bail while he filed another appeal. And in April, Tom called and asked me if I wanted to accompany him to Carl's home in Saugerties, New York, where he planned to teach his adoptive father the full meaning of terror. The trip was to be less of a visit and more like a SWAT team operation. Tom wanted to tie Carl to a chair and stick a gun in his mouth. He wanted his adoptive father to know how it felt to be at the mercy of someone who could kill him. Tom didn't want to kill Carl. He wanted to terrorize him.

I was prepared to go to Saugerties just to keep Tom out of trouble, but it was obviously a dangerous plan. I explained how such situations can get out of hand and that someone could be seriously injured or killed. I also said that even if someone wasn't hurt, we could be arrested on serious charges. I told him he had come too far to risk losing everything he stood to achieve.

We talked for several minutes, and then he said the trip wasn't worth the risk. Sometime after that conversation, I realized he was using me to help him evaluate his judgments, that he wanted to know how someone else regarded some of his plans before he made a decision and acted on them. That he was out for revenge but obviously didn't want to get in trouble with the law made me feel better, but it didn't relieve my worries.

In May, Dr. Trelstad contacted me. He said it would be

easier if he made arrangements for someone else to review Patricia O'Reilly's death. I wasn't happy with the decision, but I didn't have much choice but to go along with the new plan. I had checked with other sources about consulting with other experts, but each prospect presented another set of logistical problems. Trelstad put me in touch with Dr. Michael Lamm at the Institute of Pathology at Case Western Reserve University in Cleveland. Lamm told me he would make arrangements with Dr. Robert Challener, chief deputy coroner of the Cuyahoga County Coroner's Office, to review the case. Challener, Lamm said, had worked at the institute. Challener would call me after reviewing the case. I phoned Tom and explained the new plan. He was pleased to hear that we were finally getting some action, but he questioned whether we should trust the coroner's office for an impartial decision. I agreed with him, but I told him that Trelstad assured me that we would get an evaluation as good as the one he would have provided.

During the second week of May, I drove to Elyria and picked up Michael LeMaire, Dee's husband, and then drove to Vermont to attend Tom's graduation. Dee and Patty and their kids rode in a second car driven by Patty. It was the first time she had been out of Ohio since the onslaught of her panic attacks several years earlier. She experienced one severe attack the morning she left—she thought she would die as soon as she walked out of the house—but she got into the car and drove to Vermont because she wanted to support her brother. She didn't experience any problems on the trip.

All of us rendezvoused with Arlene and Kurt in Morrisville. The trip was like a big picnic. Tom was miserable, but he concealed his agony and appeared upbeat. That helped everyone to have a good time. We made trips to local state parks, played two-hand touch football games, spent a couple of nights out on the small town to celebrate, and partied in his tiny Morrisville apartment. On May 11, beneath a huge canopy on the campus of Johnson State University, a commencement official asked for the parents of the graduates to stand.

No one stood up for Tom.

But when the official asked for friends and relatives to rise, Tracie and her parents and Arlene, Darlene, and Patty and their families, and I stood for him. After the ceremony, everyone celebrated at a big picnic organized by the Nadeaus. It was a pleasant time, but there was an underlying tension. Everyone except me wanted to know if Tom was returning to Ohio to live near his family or staying in Vermont to be with Tracie. (He and I had talked about hopping in his truck and cruising back and forth across the country.)

There also was concern about what I was planning to write. Some worried that they had confided more to me than they had intended. No one talked directly to me about their concerns, but I could sense the fears. I left a few days later and returned to New Jersey. Dee and Michael and their kids and Patty and her kids returned to Ohio a few days after I left. Patty drove all the way without any problems. I wasn't surprised. She had told me in Vermont that driving the car helped to ease her mind.

There was, however, one incident that revealed how much pain Tom was experiencing during an otherwise glorious few days. On the night of his graduation, he somersaulted over the railing of the second-floor landing of the hotel where I and his sisters and their families were staying. He sprained an ankle. He could have broken his neck.

Three weeks later Challener phoned me and said that, based on his reexamination of O'Reilly's case material, he didn't believe she died of an interstitial myocarditis. He couldn't determine the cause of death. In a small percentage of cases, it is impossible for pathologists to know what caused someone to die, he said.

Recalling what Patricia O'Reilly's kids and sister and

mother had told me, I asked why the coroner's office hadn't turned the case over to the police or the district attorney's office.

"The police who originally handled the case did what they were going to do," and he doubted if the prosecutor's office would have been interested after it was decided that the woman died of natural causes, Challener said.

"There wasn't anything to accuse anybody of," he added.

What about the marks on her body?

"There's no broken bones," and no injuries severe enough to cause death, he said. "There's absolutely nothing."

He did, however, cite one concern. He couldn't determine if or how well the neck was examined. There should have been some indication in the report. Other than that, he said, the person who said Patricia O'Reilly died of natural causes had made "a judgment call" and that was not unusual in his profession. Challener also said, in response to a question, that the cause of death and the coroner's ruling could be changed if new information indicated that the first ruling was inaccurate.

"It's not engraved on stone tablets," he said.

If her death had resulted from the myocarditis, he said, someone with knowledge of forensics might inquire if there was any injury "sufficient" in combination with the myocarditis to warrant a ruling of homicide.

There wasn't, he said.

He also said it would have been "nice" to know that there were no hemorrhages present in the membranes and linings of the eyes and eyelids. Because that clarification was missing from the report, it allowed "room to speculate that they weren't examined," he said. But that didn't necessarily mean she didn't die of natural causes. He also said that the person in the medical examiner's office who had first agreed to help me before declining had overreacted in implying that Patricia O'Reilly might have been murdered.

I listened to everything he had to say and then told him I wanted to come to Cleveland to do a formal interview. I needed sufficient information from him to explain to Patricia O'Reilly's children the latest wrinkle concerning their mother's death. I had wanted to put an end to the rumors and come up with answers to the questions surrounding the autopsy. But all Challener seemed to be offering was the possibility that important questions would never be answered.

26 • "Easily slipped past"

On the evening of July 10, I started the nine-hour journey from New Jersey to Elyria, where I was to stay with Patty and Buck. Patty was planning to join me for the meeting with Challener. I believed it was fitting for one of Patricia O'Reilly's children to be present at an official explanation about her death. But after six hours on Interstate 80, I stopped for the night in a small Pennsylvania town. I resumed the trip early the next day but at the point where I-80 west crossed I-77 in Ohio, I drove north to Cleveland instead of continuing west to Elyria. I had changed my mind about taking Patty with me. Challener had told me that Patricia O'Reilly couldn't have died in the manner listed as her official cause of death and that he couldn't determine what caused her to die. For me, that implied the possibility of more inexplicable questions or more gruesome revelations about her life and death. I hadn't forgotten how Patricia O'Reilly's kids had reacted when they heard Vicki Caspar describe how Tom senior abused their mom. I also hadn't forgotten how Tom confronted one painful episode after another in order to learn the truth about her. Patty was as intrepid as Tom, but she also was just as vulnerable. Patricia O'Reilly's children had the right, as Tom frequently reminded his relatives, to know everything there was to know about their family. But if there were to be more painful disclosures, I wanted the information disseminated in a more gentle fashion. I wanted to learn it first and then I would pass it on.

So I drove to Cleveland alone.

It was my second trip to the coroner's office, which is located in a nondescript building adjacent to a hospital on the campus of Case Western Reserve University. I made the first trip with Tom in November 1989, when we rushed to Cleveland to get a copy of his mother's autopsy.

Challener was busy when I arrived around 10:00 A.M. But several minutes later he invited me into his office and, without shaking hands, we got down to business.

"So, the cause of death was listed as acute interstitial myocarditis," I said, beginning the interview.

"Yes," he replied.

"But you took a look at the slides, and I assume other material, and said that based on what you had reviewed, you would find it difficult to conclude that killed her," I said, referring to our telephone conversation in May.

"That's a fair summary of what I said."

"So how'd you reach your decision?"

"Well, I reviewed the case really from scratch and sought out all the material that we still had in existence on it, including one single photograph that was taken of her," he said.

The coroner's office required photographs for identification purposes. Challener showed me the picture taken after her autopsy. I was pleased that Patty was not with me. What followed was a forensic tour of the findings made more than twenty years earlier. Challener began a systematic explanation of Patricia's autopsy. He started with the external findings and discussed the colors, lengths, and shapes of her injuries. All the marks were superficial wounds, he concluded, just as he had in May, though his comments then were less specific.

"And there's only one that's really dignified as a contusion and that's not a recent contusion," he said. "So that externally there was no significant injury."

Huge and well over six feet, Challener sat behind a large desk in a large, well-lit room. O'Reilly's autopsy report was in front of him. A folder with pages of written material was nearby.

Continuing with his remarks, he said O'Reilly's eyes were "inadequately described" and that notes referring to them were confusing.

"I have no idea what he means by that, except that it suggests that at least he may have looked at them," he said about the pathologist who performed the autopsy.

The report did not indicate if petechiae—pinpoint hemorrhages—were present under the eyelids or in the membranes of the eyes. The presence or absence of petechiae is not significant since they can occur in people who die of heart attacks or other causes. But because the tiny hemorrhages are known to form under the eyes of strangulation victims, their presence can be significant if there is suspicion of foul play.

"Just as an aside," Challener added. "The police, when they were at the scene, saw no evidence that she'd been hurt. That's just as an independent, not adequate, but an independent observation that the police at the scene of her death saw no evidence that she'd been injured."

The internal examination showed no evidence of broken bones or injuries to vital and nonvital organs or hemorrhaging that could have led to death. But Challener said he couldn't determine from the report if the neck was examined.

"The neck organ includes the larynx, the part of the trachea, and the upper part of the esophagus and you just can't tell from the description whether it was removed or not. When I do a case, I try to say the neck organ remains are examined in situ, the neck organ is removed en bloc, so as to not leave the reader in doubt as to what I've done. But you can't tell from this protocol."

Because of the history of violence in Patricia's life, her autopsy report should have contained the results of examinations of her neck and the conjunctiva, the area under her eyes, Challener said without elaborating. Continuing with his methodical descriptions, he explained that his review of the tissue samples of her heart revealed that an unusually high number of sections had been examined.

"I ordinarily have about three. But there must be ten sections of the heart that were taken in this case. And I think it reflects the fact that when he ended up with his autopsy done, he didn't have a cause of death. So he went back and put in more sections of the heart, searching for a cause of death. I'm speculating, but I think that's a reasonable speculation."

But there was nothing unusual about the cells, described by Challener as a "focal collection of lymphocytes." Such cells can be found in the heart tissue of people who died of causes other than an interstitial myocarditis. In an acute myocarditis, the telltale cells would be florid and numerous; tissue would be scarred and there would be additional signs of the disease. None of those conditions were evident in Patricia O'Reilly's tissue samples, however. The differences between her tissue samples and those of someone who suffered an acute interstitial myocarditis would be like "night and day," Challener explained.

"So in reviewing these, the case of materials that we have here, from the gross examination, from the microscopic examination, it doesn't really leave me with anything that I can be sure is the cause of death."

His office's chief toxicologist had told him that the toxicological screening tests the year that Patricia O'Reilly died would have been unable to detect quinine in her blood.

"So the allegation that perhaps some family member provided her with quinine to abort the infant can't be proven or disproven by the tests that were available to us then."

I thought he was about to wrap up his reexamination and

send me off to tell Patricia O'Reilly's kids the coroner's office had no idea how their mother died, that he was sorry but such things happen. Case closed. But he continued his tour, telling me that there was another area of concern.

"The police report says specifically that the husband said that they had an argument during which he struck her in the face with an open hand. She then folded up and got the shakes and started gasping for breath. He further states he thought she was faking and realizing that she wasn't, he started to give her mouth-to-mouth and artificial respiration. The coincidence of being struck in the face and sudden collapse and death raises the question of whether the death could have been due to cardiac inhibition.

"Cardiac inhibition is a reaction which occurs as a result of impulses, neural impulses, arriving at the heart through the vagus nerves that slow the heart down. It can arise in a variety of different ways. More commonly there are pressure-sensitive areas of the neck, the carotid sinus, and it's well known that if you massage the carotid sinus, it sends an impulse which goes through, down to the heart. It will slow the heart.

"There's other names for this," Challener continued. "It's called also nervous apoplexy, reflex cardiac death, instantaneous physiologic death, or by the reference that I'm using, cardiac inhibition. The reference, if you're interested, is Dr. Lester Adelson, *The Pathology of Homicide*, pages 526 to 527. Now certainly, it's possible that a slap on the face could initiate a fatal cardiac reflex, it would cause her to collapse and die. And under those circumstances, if that were in fact the case, then it would be homicide."

I had arrived at Challener's office hoping to get sufficient information to explain why a pathologist decided more than twenty years ago that Patricia had died of natural causes; and then why Challener in May had said that, based on the information in her case file, he couldn't determine what had killed her. Now, Challener was talking about homicide. Was he saying in a circumspect way that O'Reilly was murdered twenty years ago and that the pathologist botched her autopsy and allowed Tom senior to go free? I was comfortable with Challener's explanation unfolding piece by piece in the same manner as everything else I had learned in the four years Tom and I had been working on the project, so I didn't ask blunt questions at this point. I digressed, telling Challener Tom senior's version of how Patricia died—the one he told Tom and me in his home the day we interviewed him and the one he alluded to but didn't describe when he told us about talking to the police. I also described for Challener what Tom senior said about his conversations with the pathologist who performed the autopsy.

Challener said that there was no indication of any contact between the coroner's office and Tom senior.

"If I were doing the case and thought it was significant, I might well leave a note in the record, make it part of the permanent record. But there's no such note in our records," he said, responding to a question.

I told him Tom senior said he was told by the pathologist that the myocarditis amounted to an "infection of the heart" that interfered with the electrical current in Patricia O'Reilly's heart, causing it to skip a beat, leading to her death.

"It sounds like he really did have conversation with the pathologist," Challener said, because that description would have been the explanation given to a layman to describe an acute interstitial myocarditis (even though the conditions for the disease were not evident in Patricia).

"In the past when I've been in desperate straits I've used it," Challener remarked.

It sounded as if an interstitial myocarditis was a convenient peg on which baffled pathologists could hang inexplicable causes of death, but Challener, remarking about Patricia O'Reilly's demise, added, "But if you look up the criteria that people use for myocarditis, it's gotta be more than just a little focal collection of lymphocytes."

Challener indicated that the original pathologist would have been on firmer ground if he had listed Patricia O'Reilly's cause of death as "not determined," but that, too, would have been insufficient in light of "what the husband says: I struck her and she immediately collapsed and died. And it's hard to escape that there's some association between those two events.

"Now there's one other thing that can be considered along the lines that we are discussing this," Challener continued, "and that is that perhaps there was some underlying myocarditis of which I don't see much evidence, and it could have been the combination of this, of the slap plus the myocarditis. That's certainly a possibility, too. In other words, maybe she was more vulnerable because of this, the [myocarditis] in the heart, than a person would be otherwise. That doesn't alter what I told you before. That wouldn't make any difference. It would still be the same ruling. It would be homicide."

The first pathologist decided that Patricia died because of a disease, a viral infection, but Challener was suggesting that she died because of the slap across the face, as described by Tom senior in his police statement, or the slap plus a disease that hadn't been detected.

"In this case," Challener opined, "it could be that the impact on the face initiated a neural reflex which slowed the heart and slowing the heart was incompatible with life. If as little as one percent is due to violence then the death is no longer natural, it's violent."

What would happen if she died in 1991 under the same circumstances?

The coroner's office of the 1990s would hopefully provide a more "adequate description of the conjunctiva and her neck," as well as perform better toxicological testing. The police, prompted to do a more thorough investigation, might administer a polygraph or do a better interrogation, Challener responded.

I asked, again, what would happen if she died in 1991 under similar circumstances?

"I think it would be ruled a homicide," Challener said. "Might well have been ruled a homicide then too. A lot of these things can be lost in the shuffle. It's a busy place. And I had the opportunity to review this with Dr. Adelson who was here at that time."

"Oh, he was," I remarked, surprised that Adelson was the colleague of a pathologist who, faced with a baffling death, resorted to a hunch instead of consulting with the resident, nationally known homicide expert who had written a paper on the evanescent causes of an unusual form of homicide.

"Oh, yeah," Challener said, "he probably signed the case out."

So, it was more than just the irony of one colleague overlooking the expertise of another. Adelson was the supervisor responsible for reviewing Patricia's autopsy.

Challener said that after he first talked to me—and probably after he concluded that Patricia didn't die of an interstitial myocarditis—he contacted Adelson and they discussed the case, though Adelson did not recall it. And they were baffled by her death until Challener read Adelson the police report with Tom senior's statement about the slap, and the nationally recognized homicide expert realized he was hearing the ingredients of cardiac inhibition or nervous apoplexy or reflex cardiac death or instantaneous physiologic death.

"Now, maybe when it was reviewed back in 1970, he didn't have the opportunity to hear the police report," Challener said without elaborating.

Maybe it wasn't reviewed, I thought.

Because the coroner's office was such a "busy place," the real cause of Patricia O'Reilly's death could have "easily slipped past," Challener added.

How busy was it the year Patricia died? There were 1,624

autopsies in 1970. In May that same year, when Patricia died after being slapped in the face, 118 autopsies were performed. Adelson did 26 that month, and the other pathologist did 50.

"And I can tell you that's a hell of a lot of cases for one person to do," Challener said. "Fifty is very high to have to be done."

How many other cases did Adelson's subordinate have the day he performed Patricia's autopsy?

Zilch.

Challener said that even if the coroner's office had ruled her death a homicide, there was no way of knowing how a grand jury or a jury might have acted.

"The criminal justice system's very unpredictable," he said, citing anecdotes disclosing the eccentricities of an imperfect system. In one anecdote, Challener told me about a man who died of a cerebral hemorrhage after a violent argument. His death was ruled a homicide, and his foul-mouthed antagonist was indicted but a judge threw out the case. In another tale, Challener talked about a deputy sheriff who died about five minutes after scuffling with a prisoner in a county jail. Although the dead deputy had a "profound, underlying heart disease," his death was ruled a homicide because "it was thought that this struggle precipitated the heart attack and the struggle was in violation of the rules," Challener said. The prisoner was indicted, but Challener was uncertain about the outcome.

I understood Challener's comments to mean that there was no evidence that Tom senior intentionally planned to kill Patricia by slapping her in the face. His intent would have played a major factor in a grand jury investigation or trial if the coroner's office had not let the circumstances of Patricia's death slip so easily past. But I wondered how a grand jury or a trial court would have reacted after hearing Tom senior explain that he tied her to a chair or backhanded her when she made him angry or repeatedly threatened her with a gun. I wondered how jurors would have responded to Linda Semen's accounts of her begging for her sister's life or her descriptions of Patricia begging for her life or her recollections of them both begging Tom senior not to pull the trigger. Maybe, at some point, some jurors would have gotten it in their minds that it was only a matter of time before Patricia died a violent death.

I asked Challener what would happen if Patricia's family demanded that the case be reopened.

"The problem is we don't have the cause of death. The only thing we have really is his statement and the supposition that something that happened between the two of them is precipitated in sudden death and if he struck her then it would suggest [a homicide]."

Citing another problem, Challener said, regarding the allegations that Patricia was given quinine, that "there's some uncertainties about the toxicology" and that Patricia was buried so long ago that exhuming her remains to try to examine her neck, for example, would be fruitless.

After a few more minutes of discussion, we wrapped up the interview. We had been talking for about an hour.

"Well, my sympathies to the family, I'm sure it's been difficult," said Challener.

He paused.

"I guess the foster home wasn't very good either," he added.

27 • "Never"

*T*he next day I visited Vecchio to tell him about the meeting with Challener, and he surprised me with news that the trial was scheduled for the first week in September. Because of his opposition, I had lost interest in keeping up with the legal maneuvering of Tom's case, and was under the impression that a trial date could be as much as a year away. Vecchio, who had always been low-key and reserved in my presence, was upbeat, expressing relief that the suit was about to be resolved. He had been worried that the book would be published before a settlement or trial could be concluded, that he would be faced with the monumental task of resolving what the county's attorneys might insist were discrepancies between information in the book and things Tom was alleging in his lawsuit. When he first met me, Tom and I were working on a book about a youth who had overcome the effects of a brutal childhood, while he was arguing that his client had suffered grievous and permanent harm because of the negligence of Children Services. Despite my personal misgivings about Vecchio, I had often wondered what kind of frustrations he had faced during the years he worked on Tom's case. One time I detected what I thought was a yelp of consternation about one of the witnesses whom he wanted to testify for Tom, but when I tried to get Vecchio to open up about the problem, he quickly became noncommittal. That sense of relief he expressed in his office hinted at more than just satisfaction that the case would be resolved before the book came out.

We were still adversaries, but our mutual concern for Tom allowed us to find a small patch of common ground. However, I was alarmed about Tom testifying. I realized there was a chance for an out-of-court settlement and that Tom might not have to take the stand. Vecchio had said that the county probably wouldn't make any serious offers until the day of the trial, but there was no way of knowing for certain that would happen, and he was preparing as if the case would go to trial. I knew Tom also had to prepare, and that bothered me.

I had two conversations with Tom a few weeks before the meeting with Challener, and in each instance I was reminded of the first time I had spoken to Tom on the phone: He had talked hesitantly, with a mild stutter that suggested not a speech impediment but someone grieving, in agony. To hear that voice again—with its unmistakable tone of vulnerability—made me apprehensive. I told Vecchio I didn't believe Tom was ready. Vecchio was almost blasé as he insisted that the trial was going forward, that Tom would either rise to the occasion or fail. Vecchio made it sound like a crap shoot, but I knew he had invested too much time to be so nonchalant about even the slightest possibility that his client might falter. Vecchio was wearing a poker face; he was holding trump cards that I couldn't see. I also knew how unwise it was to underestimate what Tom was capable of doing. I hadn't forgotten how he had summoned up incredible reserves to take the stand at Carl's hearing and to go to Florida to see Tom senior. So, in Vecchio's office, I offered no argument, but I hadn't forgotten the aftershocks of Tom's last courtroom appearance, and I knew that Tom was in for another rough time.

Before I left his office, Vecchio also said he had located

another expert to testify at Tom's trial. The expert had done extensive work with people whose symptoms had mirrored everything I had been witnessing in Tom, he said. The expert lived in Ohio.

Before I returned to New Jersey, I phoned Jeanne Rimmer one more time. She refused to be interviewed, and complained about Tom and me doing the book. When I told her Tom believed she knew all along that Carl was forcing him to have sex, she insisted she hadn't known, but my statement was not enough to prompt her to say more than her brief denial. I did not tell her one of the points that the experts make in describing the dynamics of incestuous families: Mom knows. The experts report that children suffer in homes where mothers are either powerless or their roles are subordinate to their abusive spouses. The more undemocratic the home, the more likely kids will suffer. Patty had said that Jeanne had complained that she, too, was powerless, but I would have preferred hearing Jeanne's side from Jeanne, not from her former foster daughter whom she had failed to protect.

In late July, Tom phoned to let me know he had given Foxman a notarized consent to talk to me. I was surprised. I had actually lost interest in interviewing Foxman, but I was willing to talk to him just to inform him of what I had learned about Tom's torment, if he didn't already know. I also hoped for some reassurance that Tom's participation in the book did not significantly contribute to his misery.

Carl and Jeanne were patients of Foxman when he first started treating Tom in January 1985. Foxman, a licensed psychologist with a doctorate in psychology from Vanderbilt University, eventually decided that Tom would be in therapy for two to three years. In his evaluation, he diagnosed Tom as suffering from moderately severe anxiety and mild depression; and as experiencing a severe hostile-dependent relationship with Carl, what many people would mistakenly call a love-hate relationship. His early evaluation also concluded that Tom didn't trust people and didn't assert himself. He diagnosed Tom as suffering from an adjustment disorder. Four years later, when a lawyer representing Children Services deposed him in September 1989, Foxman admitted that Tom was not as well off as he had initially believed, that Tom had minimized the extent of the sexual abuse, that he had concealed a lot of problems during their counseling sessions.

Tom's anxiety, he concluded, was much more severe, and he said that Tom might need another two to three years of therapy. Their counseling sessions had been good in getting Tom to open up a bit to another human being, "but not so good in treating some of his problems," Foxman conceded. But he also believed that the sessions minimized Tom's chances of passing on the deadly legacy of abuse to his kids, if he decided to have a family. It was during that deposition in Foxman's office that Vecchio—who, like me, wanted to know everything he could about Tom—first learned that his client had been using marijuana and cocaine. Foxman, under questioning, said he saw a connection between Tom's use of drugs and what he had suffered at the hands of Carl. Foxman described it as a matter of Tom trying to self-medicate himself. Foxman also said he believed Tom no longer relied on the drugs because of the counseling he had received once the drug use was revealed. In later sessions, Tom started confiding that he was having "frightening thoughts and violent fantasies." After he had to testify at Carl's hearing, Tom stopped coming to the therapy sessions.

On July 31, I phoned Foxman at his office in Essex Junction, which is about ten minutes from Burlington. I told him I wasn't concerned about what he and Tom had discussed. I was more interested in making sense of what I had learned from talking to Tom, Patty, and Tracie. I wanted to relieve myself of a burden I felt I had been carrying too long; I wanted the person involved with his treatment to know what I knew.

I told Foxman I had consulted a suicide expert, Professor Harty Mokros, who was one of my colleagues at Rutgers School of Communication, Information and Library Studies, where the journalism department was located. When I told him how Tom, the day after he graduated, somersaulted over the railing of a second-floor landing, he told me that it was not unusual for people like Tom to be hospitalized. I told Foxman of Tom's comments about killing Jeanne and Carl, and I described the occasion when he phoned me about accompanying him to New York to confront Carl. I also told him about Tom's confrontation with Patty.

Foxman said that Tom had "never" talked to him about suicide, though he knew from their counseling sessions that Tom had been depressed at times. In those sessions, he said, he had never noticed any symptoms associated with suicidal thoughts or feelings. He was aware of Tom's violent thoughts about Jeanne and Carl, but he had "assessed that and talked with Tom about that and it is my opinion that the likelihood of him acting on those thoughts is low. I think that he was dealing with anger about what had happened to him in that family, anger, which he had repressed and suppressed for many years and really wasn't in a position to really even acknowledge to himself or to anyone else that he had until recently. It wasn't until he was at Johnson State College in a more stabilized situation, and I think older and more mature, and I would say that in fairly regular counseling during that period, that he was really able to deal with these feelings to acknowledge his anger."

Foxman repeated that it "was unlikely" that Tom would ever harm Carl, but he also added, "Now, psychologists, mental health professionals, really ought not try to predict human behavior. If he ran into Carl Rimmer and under certain circumstances, I suppose, it's possible that he would get physically violent."

His last contact with Tom was in March 1991. "When he came in, he was very angry. I mean he had a lot of things going on," Foxman said.

Those things included Amanda's pregnancy and his relationship with Tracie, his sisters, Carl, and Jeanne. There were also the lawsuit, school, and the project, though he was letting me handle most of the remaining details. But the sum and substance of my discussion with Foxman was this: Everything I had told him was all new to him. Because the onslaught of Tom's torment coincided with his testifying at Carl's trial, Foxman said he believed that the appearance in Lorain County Common Pleas Court triggered everything that I had described.

There was only one bad moment during the interview. When I tried to tell him that, based on my conversations with Tom and Patty, I believed Carl continued his sexual abuse of Tom after the Rimmers moved to Vermont, Foxman bristled and became indignant. I was trying to learn what his former patient, Carl, had told him; but I also thought it was important for him to know that Tom suffered far more than the people close to him knew. Foxman did give me one bit of pleasant news: Tom's working on the book had probably benefited him.

"It sounded, from some of his remarks, that you two had an unusual adventure," he said.

In one conversation with Tom early in August, I told him what I had learned from the coroner's office about his mother's death. He was interested, but he also said he had to focus on his suit and the preparation for that did not allow him the energy to reflect on what I had told him. The pressure, he said, was building on him as his court date neared. He later called to tell me he and Tracie were engaged and planned to marry in June of 1992.

A few weeks before he was to leave for Cleveland, I inadvertently added to his pressure when I casually mentioned to Patty during a phone conversation that I was concerned that he would not be able to testify. Patty, who also was worried about Tom, called him and relayed my concerns, which I hadn't meant for him. That prompted hurried phone calls from Vecchio and Patty and Tracie, assuring me that Tom was ready for court and that he wished I would stop doubting him.

28 • "Outside the range of usual human experience"

Tom and I had been together since April 1988, but a few days before he was scheduled to appear in federal court in Cleveland, I drove to the Adirondacks in upstate New York, not to Ohio. Vecchio did not want me at the courthouse. He was concerned that I might be subpoenaed, and probably had other reasons, such as his concern that my appearance might rattle the county's attorneys, making it difficult for him to negotiate an out-of-court settlement if an opportunity arose for one. However, it had appeared to me that the county's attorneys were not serious about knowing what Tom and I had discussed for more than four years. There had been only one serious attempt to subpoena me even though they had known for a long time that I was working on our project. But because of Vecchio's concerns, I hid out in the mountains to write about the events leading up to Tom's courthouse confrontation.

On Friday morning, September 18, Vecchio filed additional papers for the trial, which was to begin Monday. And because the federal judge for Tom's lawsuit was already involved in a criminal trial, Vecchio checked on the status of Tom's case, and was assured that Tom's trial would begin as scheduled. Vecchio was confident that his preparation and strategy were firm. The court was to hear a concise account of Tom's life, from the time he was a baby living with Tom senior to the present. Vecchio also planned to explain how and why Tom and Patty were placed with the Rimmers; identify Carl as a "pedophile" who molested Tom psychologically, physically, and sexually for the next twelve years; point out that Children Services had ignored several warnings that Carl was a danger to children; cite several violations of agency regulations in the placement of Tom and Patty with the Rimmers; introduce as evidence a letter from the psychiatrist who informed the agency that Carl was unfit to be a foster parent; and include evidence that Children Services ignored that professional opinion and accepted the recommendation of a psychologist because his suggestion "was more positive" about Carl.

For the case, Vecchio had subpoenaed several witnesses. They included: Patty and Tracie; Jeanne Rimmer and Gwenda Adams, Jeanne's former friend whose son was sexually abused by Carl; Laura, the neighbor who had alerted the school authorities and Children Services about Carl sexually abusing Patty; and Debbie Durrell, the Children Services caseworker who tipped off the Vermont authorities about Tom's plight.

Vecchio also planned to introduce evidence that Carl had admitted to Children Services that he had molested Gwenda Adam's boy once, and she was to testify that she had complained to the agency that her child had been molested by him a number of times. There were other evidentiary matters that Vecchio planned to introduce, including testimony from Foxman and another psychologist, Walter R. Knake, about the deleterious effects of the twelve years of harm Tom had suffered in the Rimmers' home.

Vecchio was expecting the county attorneys to argue that most of Tom's emotional problems stemmed from his early years with Tom senior, that Tom's graduation from college, his ability to hold jobs, and his relationship with Tracie were all proof that he hadn't suffered severely during his years with the Rimmers. The county attorneys were also expected to argue that there was no way for Tom's caseworkers and supervisor to know what Carl was doing to Tom. After all, Vecchio expected them to say, Tom didn't tell anybody but his sister.

The case never went to trial, however. On the afternoon of that same Friday he was assured that the trial would proceed, Vecchio was notified that the judge wanted him and the county attorneys to try to reach a settlement because the judge's criminal trial was expected to take another five weeks. On Monday, both sides in Tom's case began negotiations, which were mediated by a federal magistrate. Once they reached an agreement, they also agreed to seal its terms. The *Plain Dealer* reported that Thomas Porter, executive director of Children Services, told a reporter that his agency didn't admit to any liability in Tom's case. In the same story, Vecchio was quoted as saying that the settlement "will provide for his [Tom's] financial security for the rest of his life," and Tom was quoted as saying, "I just hope that people will learn from what's happened to me and so many other people." The story also indirectly quoted Vecchio as saying that Tom would be in therapy for the rest of his life.

When Tom called me a few days later at Rutgers, he playfully introduced himself as Thomas J. Waters, his coy way of informing me that he had legally changed his name back to Waters. Though he still was gripped by strong ambivalent feelings for Carl and Jeanne, he had ended, forever, the bond that had made him their legal hostage. We did not discuss the financial terms of his settlement because we both knew it wasn't important for me to know.

Children Services' claim that it was not liable for Tom's harm sounded vaguely similar to the comments of the typical unrepentant pedophile who insists that he isn't responsible for harming his victims. The county, of course, needed that

legal claim in order to strengthen its defense for its next round
of lawsuits (especially the $85 million lawsuit filed by a family
alleging that it had been harassed by Children Services after
a hospital mistakenly concluded that an eighteen-month-old
girl had been sexually abused). Child molesters who refuse
to admit responsibility for their sexual violence against kids,
who refuse to speak the truth about what they did, are likely
to continue molesting kids even if they undergo therapy
(their recidivism rate, according to some studies, is around
90 percent). Carl, at least, was in jail, but Children Services
was unshackled, free to continue its brutal record of bureaucratic negligence. In May, four months before Tom's settlement, a Lorain County commissioner complained in a letter:
"In the last two years, Lorain County alone has had more
cases than I care to think about where Children Services has
been involved and the children have wound up dead." The
letter, signed by Lorain County Commissioner Mary Jo Vasi,
also read: "We are finding more and more cases . . . whereby
children are put through more abuse by the system than they
were in the home." The May 6 letter by Vasi, who regularly
criticized the operations of Children Services, was addressed
to Ohio state legislators. It was accompanied by a list of
specific recommendations for changes in the child protection
operations in Ohio.

The comments from a commissioner who was a co-
defendant in Tom's case were telling, even though the thrust
of Vasi's letter went beyond acknowledging the body count
of kids victimized because of Children Services' negligence.
She focused on the system of child protection in Ohio, stating
that the problems with Lorain County Children Services reflected the problems in "many, many" other counties in the
state (she could have said child protection agencies across
the country). In her criticisms, Vasi also wrote about child
care agencies harassing foster parents and lodging false allegations that caused decent people "to lose their jobs, homes,

marriages, families and savings . . . and fighting for years to prove their innocence. Due to coercion and threats, they [foster parents] cut deals with the Prosecutor or agencies." I wished the contents of Vasi's letter had been included in the *Plain Dealer* story to put into context Children Services' claim of no liability.

Tom, of course, was a casualty of negligence and cruelty, not a fatality, and a packet of information Vecchio sent me after the settlement provided clinical testimony of the harm he suffered. One part of the packet was a transcript of the videotaped testimony of Dr. Foxman, who would have been unable to appear in court if there had been a trial. Parts of his testimony were similar to the statements he had given me in our interview, but the deposition, which started at 11:30 A.M. and ended at 3:30 P.M., was longer and more thorough and more revealing. Based on new information and a reevaluation of Tom, Foxman concluded that he had underestimated the depth of Tom's suffering. "This is, in my personal experience, professionally, the most severe case of abuse that I've been involved with, personally," Foxman stated. Tom's trauma was "outside the range of usual human experience." If he were to rediagnose Tom, Foxman said, he would say he was suffering from posttraumatic stress disorder (PTSD), a term first used to explain the severe emotional problems of veterans of the Vietnam War. In World War II and the Korean War, combat veterans with similar symptoms were described as victims of "shell shock."

Because Foxman originally had said Tom had an adjustment disorder, which is usually less severe than PTSD, the following analogy might help to explain the significance of his comments. If the first diagnosis is compared to a toothache, then the new one could be compared to the pain Tom would experience if a dentist removed all his teeth with a pair of pliers and without anesthesia.

According to the bible of the psychiatric profession, the

revised *Diagnostic and Statistical Manual of Mental Disorders* (*DSM-III-R*): "The essential feature of this disorder is the development of characteristic symptoms following a psychologically distressing event that is outside the range of usual human experience (i.e., outside the range of such common experiences as simple bereavement, chronic illness, business losses and marital conflict)." The reference to a "psychologically stressing event" includes trauma occurring over a long period of time, such as the violence found in death camps or in the homes of families like the Rimmers.

Tom exhibited symptoms of PTSD, such as "intrusive" recollections of what he had suffered as well as nightmares and flashbacks, feelings of estrangement from others, a lack of intimacy, difficulty falling asleep, irritability, and outbursts of anger. When Foxman told the county lawyers that Tom was "reexperiencing" the trauma he had suffered in the Rimmer household, I assumed he was speaking about those experiences that Tom had described during their therapy sessions. Foxman, of course, didn't know that a lot more had happened to his patient because Tom had withheld information even in their privileged professional relationship.

Also in the packet Vecchio sent me was the deposition of Walter P. Knake, Jr., a psychologist who also had diagnosed the disorder in Tom. Knake had served in the U.S. Army and was involved in the pioneering studies of Vietnam vets with the disorder. Knake, who was deposed in his office in Beachwood, Ohio, also was involved in one of the first studies of PTSD in civilians. While Foxman believed that Tom faced a difficult road and would need substantial therapy, he didn't consider Tom's future "as being bleak." Knake, however, saw things differently.

"I think there's a real side to Tom that he's extremely scared of and frightened, and that is rage. He's scared to let any of his anger out . . . he is frightened by the intensity of his feelings." Tom was terrified that he might lose rational control over his impulses. Knake said those fears were realistic. Plagued by nightmares, cold sweats, and flashbacks, Tom drank beer to kill the pain and to help him sleep. But, at the same time, when he got drunk, he risked opening up a flood-gate of emotions and memories, of being swamped by the violent impulses that terrified him.

"This is permanent trauma; it's always going to be with him, that's bottom line. He's got a lot of work to do; a lot of qualitative work to do," Knake said, referring to the long-term therapy he and Foxman believed was necessary for Tom to lead a normal life. Knake said Tom needed to participate in group therapy with male victims of sexual abuse as well as involve himself in individual psychotherapy at least once a week.

"In my opinion, Tom needs to be able to relate in a ther-apeutic way with other victims and survivors of sexual abuse. I feel that he's very vulnerable, unless that [therapy] happens over a prolonged period of time. And vulnerable, meaning, vulnerable to a loss of impulse control, acting out suicidal or homicidal impulses."

Despite Knake's "very guarded prognosis," I was fasci-nated by his clinician's description of Tom's efforts to cope, of Tom seizing upon socially acceptable ways for dealing with his anger. Tom's participation in football, track, basketball, and wrestling, according to Knake, helped him "to mute" his anger; it provided him with a means for expressing "the in-tensity of that anger." Tom, despite missing some therapy sessions, had made significant progress with Foxman. And his suit against Children Services, first and foremost, was a means to get "validation" of what had happened to him.

"The money won't change a thing regardless of how much he gets," Knake said. "The money won't bring back his self-esteem, it won't bring back his innocence, it won't bring back his security, it won't bring back anything." When an attorney

asked him to explain, Knake said that "there is a need for
traumatized individuals to be validated, to have someone else
believe that, and affirm them as individuals and affirm the fact
that they were a victim and not to blame."

The lawsuit also was Tom's way of making others aware
of the sexual trauma that kids can suffer; suing provided him
with a means to try to protect others from what he suffered;
and, again, it was a socially acceptable means for him to
express his anger at what happened to him. Despite the ambivalent feelings that eventually developed, Tom's working
on a book was another form of seeking validation. That his
sisters, cousins, and even Tom senior were being allowed to
"validate" their experiences was the unexpected conse-
quence of one young man's extraordinary valor in going
public.

Knake's deposition provided additional insight into Tom's
life. The horror of living with his father, Tom senior, and then
with the Rimmers had not blotted out Tom's memories of
the Greenlesses, in whose foster home he was placed temporarily after Tom senior was arrested. His stay with them,
as brief as it was, gave him a hint about the realities of love
and affection. The flashbacks Tom experienced were signs of
his "mind trying to heal itself," and Tom, under proper care,
could make more progress in moving that healing process
along, Knake said. He didn't believe Tom had an addictive
personality—a fear Tom had expressed openly in the years
that I knew him—though Tom had to be wary of drugs and
alcohol. And though he had serious problems with intimacy
and trusting people, there was a side of him that did feel
protective of others, Knake said. For me, the best example of
his sensitivity were those moments he consoled Patty when
they both lived with the Rimmers. She had described how
Tom held her hand after their brutal encounters with Carl,
how Tom cleaned up after her when she became sick from
drinking too much alcohol, how he tried to include her in

his playtime with his friends, how he sacrificed himself to Carl's sexual demands to keep him from hurting her. During his most acrimonious periods with Tracie, he still expressed concern in my presence about hurting her because of his hesitancy about making a commitment. I also recalled how Tom chastised Tom senior, who was trying to insult me by praising the Ku Klux Klan and referring to African-Americans as "niggers."

But reading Knake's testimony made it perfectly clear that all those qualities that I and others admired in Tom wouldn't be sufficient to sustain him without the therapeutic support the two psychologists were recommending. The settlement, allowing him to be financially secure for the rest of his life, eliminated one potential source of stress, and it would also allow him to afford the long-term therapy he needed. But because a real therapy program would require him to relive the pain, I knew he was facing a formidable task. The wish to avoid pain was one of the reasons Tom had skipped sessions with Foxman, but his best chance for ending, with certainty, the cruel legacy left him by his fathers was to get help.

We would have been ecstatic if Tom's lawsuit had forced Children Services to live up to its mandate to protect kids, or if we could have claimed that his litigation forced the agency to make changes, but we were too much the realists to believe that would happen. We had to settle for hoping that public exposure of what had happened to him would help fuel criticism of the agency and, perhaps, provide ammunition for community activists and the county's one elected official, County Commissioner Mary Jo Vasi, who had been lobbying for change. Although the *Plain Dealer*'s September 14, 1991, news story reported that the county's insurance companies were "likely" to pick up the tab for Tom's undisclosed settlement, I learned in early 1993 that Lorain

County might have to dip into its general funds to help pay the bill. If that happened, I wondered how the county planned to contend with the other lawsuits, which were carrying heftier demands than Tom's.

I hoped it was possible that the need to tap into general funds might arouse the interest or ire of the taxpaying public, perhaps giving it a taste of the consequences of Children Services' foul-ups, which normally only hurt the families the agency was supposed to serve. Perhaps that might be an incentive for people who normally would not be affected by the agency's shenanigans to demand some changes. I also was told that more kids had died and that there were three other multimillion-dollar lawsuits pending against the agency.

Because Tom and I didn't get to do the kind of research that would have allowed us to recommend specific changes, I am providing recommendations proposed by Commissioner Vasi in her letter to Ohio state legislators in May 1991. She called for changes in:

- The annual evaluation of county services, because the reporting system being used allowed the county agencies to evaluate themselves.
- The guidelines for handling anonymous allegations. Every person, Vasi wrote, should have the right "to face his or her accuser; clients cannot defend themselves against anonymous accusations."
- Allowing reasonable access to agency files for inspection by an involved party; agencies do not make files available to clients. "This only protects the agency and clients cannot refute errors or defend themselves," Vasi wrote.
- Improving the quality and performance of caseworkers.
- Improving accountability on the part of county commissioners. "It stands to reason," Vasi wrote, "that we would want to know of an abuse of power and the possible misuse

of funds. Yet, the only real authority we have is to appoint board members who meet once a month for two hours. Boards are not created to be directed by the staff, they are created to direct the staff. The county agencies should be under the total control of the county commissioners."

Vasi also recommended the establishing of a Citizens Review Board, with the board members' appointments made by the county commissioners.

About two weeks after Tom's settlement, Carl, who had exhausted his appeals, appeared in Lorain County Common Pleas Court before Judge Lynett McGough, who ordered him to begin serving his sentence. According to the *Plain Dealer,* he was to serve, concurrently, four to twenty-five years for rape as well as two additional sentences of three to ten years for lesser felonies. His attorney was indirectly quoted as saying that Carl had "successfully" completed sexual therapy.

Carl was remanded to a state facility in Grafton and then later transferred to the Marion Correctional Facility in Marion, Ohio. He agreed to an interview, but because of deadlines, I was unable to visit him, and he was unwilling to be interviewed over the phone. However, he eventually sent a letter providing me with some background information and commentary. A summary follows. He claimed he was "deeply remorseful for my compulsive and intrusive behavior and victimization of Tom. I hope you can understand that I did not realize the impact that I was having on Tom. I rationalized that I was showing him love and caring." Carl blamed his "abnormal and dysfunctional childhood" for his psychological, physical, and sexual abuse of Tom. Hinting but not providing details, he gave a brief description of that childhood. His parents separated before he was born, and he was told that his father was an alcoholic and a womanizer. His mother had two other boys before him. Eventually, he and his brothers were removed from their mother's custody. The older boys were placed in a Catholic home for children, while Carl, because of his age, was placed in a foster home in Langhorne, Pennsylvania, where he lived until he was six years old. He could not recall his years with his foster family. "I understand from what my mother told me recently that on one occasion she came to visit me and found both the parents drunk. I can only imagine what may have been happening in that home. I have my suspicions based on feelings and compulsions I have experienced since I was six or seven years old. In retrospect, I have been obsessed with sex all my life. Most of my early friendships were based on a sexual relationship."

He was eventually placed in Girard College for boys, in Philadelphia, where his sexual relationships were exclusively with males. He remained there for eleven years, and when he later entered the army, he remained "closeted."

"The only thing that I regret more than anything else is the time I spent ... trying to learn [in therapy] to be straight while I was married," he wrote. He also wrote that there were times when he was "a good husband and father in most respects but this is all eradicated by the horrible secret I was keeping." It wasn't clear if his "horrible secret" was an allusion to his sexual preference for men or a subtle admission to pedophilia. His past incidents of sexually abusing kids—Tom, Gwenda Adams's son, and Patty—point to the latter.

Carl also wrote that he believed Tom was coached by his lawyers to feign the effects of a severely abused kid. He believed Tom testified at his criminal hearing in Elyria to protect his lawsuit. "I was assured by Dr. Foxman before I moved to New York that Tom was fine and was adjusting well. In spite of my infringements, he had been having normal social experiences. He was supposedly well adjusted and stable."

In the letter, Carl insisted he was not a threat to society, that what he had done to Tom "will never happen again." He expected to spend a minimum of thirty-three months in prison before he was eligible for parole, which he would get on his first appearance before the parole board. In May 1992 he petitioned the governor for a commutation and was awaiting a response. He also wrote that he had finished several chapters of his book, which was tentatively titled *Reasons Not Excuses*.

29 • "Only a kid"

Shortly after the Fourth of July holiday in 1992, I took a scenic cruise, via train and bus, to Vermont to spend a few days with Tom. He and Tracie arrived at the bus depot in a mammoth pickup truck, which Tom had purchased specifically to tow his recently purchased eighteen-foot boat to Lake Ontario. It was the first time the three of us had been together since Thanksgiving, and we sat in the truck munching pizza, drinking Coke, and gabbing. I chided him about the extra twenty pounds he was carrying, and he pointed to my stomach and joked about the additional twenty I was carrying. Tracie, slim and tanned, was looking good. After we finished eating, we drove back to Underhill, where they were living in the house Tom had purchased from her parents. He and Tracie had remodeled the home, and were finalizing plans for their wedding in September. A few days later Tom took some time off from some of his chores so that we could go fishing in a stream located near a big cow pasture several miles from Underhill. We were there several hours, and despite innumerable nibbles, Tom caught the only fish, which was a minnow he tossed back into the water.

When we fish, we hardly talk, each of us is absorbed in his own thoughts or in what he is doing, and yet, we act as if our movements are synchronized. That for me accentuates the pleasure of fishing with him—we can feel both alone and together at the same time. Later that week, we drove to Burlington with his boat in tow, and I helped him launch it for the first time out on Lake Champlain despite storm warnings. While many boats were heading in to escape the approaching high wind and rains, we chose to head out. After an hour, our boat was virtually the only one in the water. When the waves, wind, and rain became too intense, we dashed for safety, but, unlike everyone else, we cruised slowly around the inlet until the storm blew over. It was an exhilarating experience.

During my five-day stay, we had one brief exchange about the project. "I can't believe you included all that stuff," he said, and then changed the subject before I could reply. Though I didn't know how much of the latest draft he had read, I was surprised that he had read any of it at all. From conversations over five years, I knew he had been concerned I would be including material that he both wanted and didn't want included in the book. He felt ambivalent for two reasons. He wanted what he considered sensitive material included because he wanted to tell the whole truth about his life. At the same time, he didn't want that same material included because he was concerned about how it would cause people to perceive him. After all, he had once told me, "I'm changing, and people will be forming opinions about me based on things I did in the past. They won't know the new me." We didn't discuss the other reason for his ambivalence, but I knew what it involved: He probably either hadn't come to terms with or hadn't developed insight into the material that I was including in the book. I reassured him as best I could, telling him I didn't believe I had written anything that would cause him shame or portray him in a negative manner, but at the same time, he was right to be concerned about how people would perceive him and his sisters. Some, I knew, would be unsympathetic or insensitive.

I stayed in Underhill for five of the most enjoyable days I had experienced since we started working on the book. Less than a month later, early on the morning of August 5, I sped to Underhill again to rendezvous with Tom, Kurt Tabar, and some of Tom's friends for an improvised bachelor's party. We all were supposed to meet at a Burlington bar that was to feature some conventional ingredients for a groom's pre-nuptial bash: inexpensive beer and a bikini contest. However, a bad storm kept the contestants from showing up at the bar, and stopped me from arriving on time. That minor disappointment was the only setback for a grand, two-day festival in preparation for Tom and Tracie's wedding.

On August 8, 1992, they exchanged vows in St. Thomas Church in Underhill Center, Vermont. About one hundred people attended, including, of course, Tom's sisters and their families, Tracie's parents and her sisters, various friends of Tom and Tracie, and the Nadeaus. I was an usher. After the ceremony, everyone drove to the Knights of Columbus Hall in Essex Junction. We partied for most of the afternoon. A live band thumped out rock and country music that kept most of us on our feet dancing. Tracie was resplendent in her white gown; Tom looked dashing in his black tux. Arlene, Darlene, and Patty, who again had overcome her panic feelings to drive to Vermont to be with her brother, were picture-pretty. Kurt and Michael LeMaire, Darlene's husband, looked like real studs. This time I did not take notes; the people I had come to know, after more than five years of asking questions and ferreting out information, wanted me there only as a friend. I detected only one sour note. While everyone was celebrating Tom and Tracie's wedding, a young boy who had just been severely disciplined by his father told me in a plaintive voice, as he rubbed his arm, "My father doesn't know how strong he is . . . he grabs me by the arm and it bruises. He keeps forgetting that I'm only a kid."

*   *   *

In May 1993, I was in touch with Tom and Tracie and Tom's sisters, but I had had no contact with the other people who were interviewed for this book. Thus, I decided there were only one development and two milestones to report.

The development: Patty had split up with her boyfriend, Buck, and moved into her own apartment in Elyria, where she was working and raising her two kids.

The milestones: Tom and Tracie were expecting their first child in June. And Tom had read the final manuscript four times and recommended corrections regarding some names and some events. We talked for several days.

He also wanted to clarify some matters. One involved my suspicions that he was anally raped by Carl.

He wasn't.

"I am telling you this as a friend, but you can put it in the book," he said.

He also said he could recall Carl sexually abusing him only once in Vermont and not repeatedly as I had suspected. However, Tom also said he couldn't be certain that other incidents of sexual abuse hadn't happened.

Finally, he added, he and Tracie were concerned about the constant references to his rage and violent thoughts. I had described him as someone even they would be afraid to meet on a dark street, and I virtually, though unintentionally, had given the impression that there was a mass murderer lurking inside him. Yes, he said, he was very, very angry for the way Carl had treated him, but the Rimmers were no longer part of his life, and he had been making significant improvements.

"I am not the same person I was two years ago," he said, adding that in another two years he would be even better. But people were going to form their impressions of him based on the descriptions of his anger.

I agreed with him that there were risks involved and suggested that he should wait a few years until he and Tracie had settled into their new roles as parents and then he could tackle his concerns and any other issues by doing another book.